Marketing Research

second edition

Marketing Research

second edition

George Kress

Reston Publishing Company, Inc.
A Prentice-Hall Company
Reston, Virginia

Library of Congress Cataloging in Publication Data

Kress, George
    Marketing research.

    Includes index.
    1. Marketing research. I. Title.
HF5415.2.K75   82   658.8'3
ISBN 0-8359-4269-4

©1982 by Reston Publishing Company, Inc.
          A Prentice-Hall Company
          Reston, Virginia 22090

10 9 8 7 6 5 4

Printed in the United States of America

Contents

11   Data Collection

12   Processing the Collected Data

15 Presentation of Findings   341

16 Industrial Marketing Research   365

Preface

"Something old, something new, something borrowed, and something blue." That describes the bride's supposed wedding attire. With the exception of the "something blue," it also describes this second edition of *Marketing Research*.

The "something old" is the book's basic objectives and general format. The original book's goals also apply to this second edition:

1. to introduce readers to the mechanics of sound marketing research;
2. to apprise the readers of the influence that such factors as time constraints, limited finances, interviewee bias, and sample size can have on research results; and
3. to enhance the reader's ability to evaluate the research of others.

This edition also follows the format of "how to conduct research," recognizing that if a manager is to effectively evaluate research data, he/she must first understand the basic ingredients of sound research.

The "something new" is the addition of two new chapters: *Industrial Marketing Research* and *Guidelines for Users of Research*. These two new chapters cover aspects of research that have been largely ignored in most marketing research and business books.

The "something borrowed" is the updating of a good deal of the material with more current secondary data. New secondary sources have been tapped to provide recent coverage and findings on such activities as test marketing, electronic observation equipment, and legislation potentially affecting researchers.

Chapter One defines research; explains why marketing is an art rather than a science; distinguishes between laws, theories, and hypotheses; and describes the place of each in marketing research. Chapter Two identifies the role of marketing research in business firms and the contribution it makes to various marketing decisions.

Chapter Three introduces the actual research procedural model used throughout the remainder of the book. Each of the steps involved in carrying out research is presented in chronological order, along with a brief description of what each entails.

The remaining chapters cover each research step in greater depth: selecting the project's direction; determining the types of information needed; selecting techniques for acquiring this information; choosing and using samples; gathering the data; processing, analyzing and interpreting the collected data; and finally, preparing the actual research report.

The final three chapters touch on aspects of the research not covered in many other research texts: unique requirements of research when applied to industrial markets, ethical aspects of research, and the role the research user can play in improving the quality of research received.

The book is intended to serve the following audiences:

1. Students in introductory courses in marketing research or general business research. Although aimed primarily at undergraduates, this material has also been used successfully for research courses in M.S. or M.B.A. programs.
2. People taking short courses for management/executive development programs or in-house training sessions, aimed at making decision makers more effective users of research.
3. Businesspersons, who may have been assigned some temporary research responsibilities but possess little or no experience in such activities, and who need to obtain a quick introduction to the "how to" of research.

This book is best suited to those teaching situations in which the instructor gives students quick coverage of the basic components of research and then follows up with actual research projects. Statistical procedures are presented in a manner that readers with only a limited background in statistics should be able to handle.

I am grateful to the Literary Executor of the late Sir Ronald A. Fisher, F.R.S., to Dr. Frank Yates, F.R.S., and to Longman Group Ltd., London, for permission to reprint Tables III and IV from their book *Statistical Tables for Biological, Agricultural and Medical Research* (6th edition, 1974).

Marketing Research

second edition

1

The concept of marketing research

The creator of Sherlock Holmes, Sir Arthur Conan Doyle, was exceedingly proud of his own observational and deductive skills. Once, while with friends at a restaurant, he boasted that he could usually tell someone's occupation from just a brief observation of that person. When challenged to demonstrate this skill, Doyle stopped the first man walking by his table and attempted to identify his occupation.

After a brief scanning of the person's attire and physical characteristics, Doyle said, "You play in an orchestra." When the man acknowledged that he did, Doyle's friends, in amazement, asked how he came to that conclusion.

"His protruding lips, his baggy cheeks and large chest indicated this man engaged in excessive intake and expulsion of air, leading me to conclude he played a musical instrument. By the way, young man, which instrument do you play?"

"The drums," was his response.

On the eve of the 1980 Presidential election the results of most polls indicated that the race between incumbent Jimmy Carter and his Republican challenger Ronald Reagan was "too close to call." Although they had been interviewing voters for many months, the majority of pollsters still did not feel their results identified a clear-cut winner.

When the votes were finally counted, Reagan had received over 43 million popular votes compared to only 35 million for Carter. Even more decisively, Reagan had received 489 electoral votes compared to only 49 for Carter. Reagan was a very one-sided victor. The inability of most pollsters to predict this outcome strengthened the position of many critics who have raised questions about the overall value of the entire survey process.

These critics were provided additional fuel for their argument on the basis of the adverse publicity received by the 1980 population study carried out by the Census Bureau. Two major cities, Detroit and New York, initiated lawsuits accusing the bureau of significantly undercounting their populations and requested the figures be revised upward. Such actions were financially motivated since an "undercount" would lead to a reduction in the dollars provided to cities by the federal government based on population size and makeup.

Both of these situations illustrate major research efforts that provided seemingly erroneous data and have led increasing numbers of people to question research activities.

Even decision makers in the business world question research. They cite the high proportion of "researched" products that have failed in the marketplace and question the cost-effectiveness of many marketing research activities especially test markets.

At the other extreme are decision makers who feel that some type of research should precede any decision that has a large dollar implication. They cite situations in which marketing research identified profitable new market segments or uncovered potential product problems, resulting in major financial turnarounds for companies.

In truth, the contribution of marketing research lies somewhere between the two extremes. It is not an infallible tool that will enable decision makers to always make the right choice. But neither is it the high cost activity its critics claim could be better done by simple seat-of-the-pants decision making.

Marketing research, if conducted properly, should significantly lessen the uncertainty that surrounds many of the decisions faced by managers. As one marketing research firm adver-

Research— useful or useless?

tises: "We don't replace decision makers, we just make their jobs easier."

Definition   Marketing research is the systematic investigation of marketing activities carried out in order to discover new information and relationships as well as to expand and verify existing knowledge. Simply put, its two major functions are to provide information for decision making and to develop new knowledge.

Although the specific problems dealt with in marketing research may differ from those of the physicial or natural sciences, there are certain basic steps common to all research regardless of the subject. The purpose of this book is to present these common procedures and to describe where and how each fits into the research process. The combination of these steps is labeled the "Systematic Model for Marketing Research" and the following chapters describe in depth the individual steps of this model.

Before presenting the components of this model, it is important that the reader be made aware of some of the issues that have arisen over the years pertaining to the quality of marketing research when compared with the research carried out in other disciplines.

Science vs. art issue   Some researchers feel that true research can only be performed in the physical or natural sciences. In fact, they view research and science as synonymous terms, the implication being that research is not in the baliwick of the arts.

Distinction between art and science

A few scholars feel that the distinction between science and art lies in the self-sufficiency of the discipline. If the discipline creates its own tools and basic principles completely from within itself, it is a *science*. If it depends on other disciplines for its tools, it is an *art*. If this reasoning is accepted, it would mean that mathematics and logic are the only sciences, since the theorems of mathematics and canons of logic are the building blocks for chemistry, physics, astronomy, etc.

Most authors dealing with the "art vs. science" controversy are less restrictive than the above case. They feel that science is a body of knowledge based on factual empirical data, whereas art is the application of this knowledge. Mathematicians develop potentially valuable formulas, and engineers prove the utility of these formulas by applying them in their work. Here science (the mathematician) supplies the basic knowledge, and art (the engineer) applies it. Similarly, the information developed by the physiologist (science) is applied by the physician (art).[1]

The weakness of this latter distinction is that it still doesn't enable each discipline to be neatly categorized as an art or a science. For instance, is psychology a unique and basic body of knowledge? How about economics?

Business – an art

No matter how the available definitions are interpreted, most authorities (business and nonbusiness alike) view business as an art. But being designated an art does not mean a discipline cannot conduct research. As previously stated, it is the procedures used in the investigation that determine what is research, not the subject matter being studied. Whether the study deals with a mathematical theorem (science) or consumer buying decisions (art), if appropriate investigative procedures are followed, legitimate research occurs.

Applied research vs. basic research issue

Another area of controversy among researchers concerns basic (pure) and applied research, since some feel that basic research is the only legitimate type of research. The distinction between basic and applied research hinges on the motive of the researcher.[2] Basic research is undertaken to satisfy the researcher's thirst for knowledge. Like George Mallory's oft-quoted reason for climbing Mount Everest – "because it's there" – pure research is conducted because of the researcher's innate curiosity about some phenomenon.

Applied research, on the other hand, is undertaken with the goal of uncovering data to solve an existing problem. The driving force behind most business investigations is to improve some aspect of the organization's operations. Very little research is undertaken in business solely for the sake of pure knowledge. Firms such as DuPont or Dow Chemical employ some researchers (generally chemists) who are given free rein as to the direction of

---

[1] Information on the "art vs. science" controversy is found in the following texts: C. J. Ducasse, *The Philosophy of Art* (New York: L. MacVeagh, The Dial Press, 1929), pp. 23–25. Margory Adams, *Science in the Changing World* (New York: Books for Libraries Press, 1968), p. 56. "Science versus Art," *Encyclopedia Britannica*, Vol. II, 1969, p. 485. T. S. Clements, *Science and Man* (Springfield, Ill.: Charles C. Thomas Company, 1968), p. 56. A. D. Ritchie, *Scientific Method* (New Jersey: Littlefield and Adams, 1960), p. 345.

[2] J.E. Walters, *Research Management: Principles and Practices* (Washington, D.C.: Spartan Books, 1965), p. 3.

their investigations. But even here it is hoped that their discoveries will have some eventual product possibilities for their employers.

Pure or basic research is largely limited to the academic world where educational, governmental, and foundation financing enables it to survive. Scientists such as Newton, Galileo, and Copernicus are generally cited as prime examples of pure researchers, but the ranks thin rather rapidly when we get beyond these few names. There is generally some motive other than "knowledge for the sake of knowledge" guiding most research. This is true whether the research is conducted in business, economics, sociology, or even the physical sciences.

If the investigator's motives were the only criterion for determining what is or is not true research, very few studies would qualify. But once again, it is the techniques used by the investigator that determine what should be classified as research, not the motives for undertaking the study.

Scientific method and the development of laws

Charles Pierce, the American philosopher, identified four ways in which humans acquire knowledge about a particular topic: (1) method of tenacity — accepting something as true because others have accepted it for a long time (old wives' tales); (2) method of authority — accepting the statement of a person because he/she is in an authoritative position (religious leader, college professor, etc.); (3) method of intuition — accepting an idea because it seems intuitively reasonable; (4) method of science — accepting an idea only after it has been vigorously tested.[3]

This latter method attempts to understand the occurrence of events by proposing certain explanations and then testing their validity. The explanations are accepted or modified on the basis of the test results. Logicians call this procedure "the inductive process of learning." Statisticians label it "statistical investigation." Other areas describe it as research methodology, but the most widely used description is the "scientific method."

The scientific method as described by various authors is comprised of anywhere from 5 to 12 steps. The following list contains the main points found in most definitions:

1. Awareness of problem situation
2. Development of alternative solutions to problem (hypotheses)

---

[3]Fred Kerlinger, *Foundations of Behavioral Research* (New York: Holt, Rinehart, and Winston, 1964), pp. 4–6.

3. Thorough investigation of alternatives
4. Analysis of all results
5. Revision of ideas to reflect findings

"The scientific method is a way of handling intellectual problems, not things, instruments or men; consequently, it can be employed in all fields of knowledge."[4] While this statement reflects the thinking of many authors in the fields of science and philosophy, there are also many who feel that the goal of scientific method is the eventual development of laws.

This emphasis on laws raises the question: Can the investigations carried out in marketing lead to "laws"? This question can be answered by looking more closely at the processes leading to the development of laws.

Laws emerge from the following chain of events: Concepts are developed; these concepts are then related to other concepts; hypotheses are made about the consistency of these relationships, and if invariability exists in some relationships, a law has been discovered.[5]

Concepts — These are tags or brief terms used to describe or think about specific phenomena and enable a more rapid and precise communication of ideas. As a discipline matures, concepts borrowed from conventional conversation and from other disciplines become inadequate. Thus, the discipline develops some terms more appropriate to its own area. For example, the concept "middleman," is used in all business areas, but it is usually not precise enough for marketers. More specific concepts such as "commission merchant," "manufacturer's agent," and "resident buyer" are used to distinguish between middlemen providing unique services.

Hypotheses — These are tentative statements describing relationships between concepts. The economic concept of "inelastic demand" can be tied to the marketing concept of "specialty goods" with the resulting statement being — "The demand for specialty goods is inelastic." This relationship is then tested under various conditions to see how well it holds up.

Law — When a relationship has been thoroughly tested and determined to be invariable, it is called a law. Laws are assertions of invariable associations. Under given conditions, the same type

---

[4]Marco Bunge, *Scientific Research I* (New York: Springer-Verlag, Inc., 1967), p. 15.

[5]Many of the ideas used in the following section were taken from one book: Norman Campbell, *What Is Science?* (Dover Publications, Inc., 1921).

of relationship will continually reoccur and in many cases these relationships can even be quantified. For example $S=16t^2$ is a law describing the distance traveled by freely falling bodies.

Theories — A theory explains why the relationship described in the law occurs. Boyle's law states that the pressure of gas on the walls of a container is inversely related to the volume of the container. This law and other laws involving gases and their pressures are explained by what scientists call the "kinetic theory." This theory proposes that gases consist of infinitely small particles called molecules. These particles or molecules move freely through the gases in all directions at about the speed of sound, impacting with the container's walls. The speed of their movement increases as the temperature of the gas rises. Thus, the theory that states that molecules exist explains Boyle's law and also explains some other laws involving gas, temperature, and pressure.

It is important to note that the most important feature of molecular theory is not that it states molecules are subject to the laws of dynamics. Rather, the key feature of the theory is that it states that there are such things as molecules existing in gases.

Theories are invented; they are the result of individual genius. Laws, on the other hand, are discovered. They have always existed, so it was merely a matter of someone uncovering or discovering the permanence of a relationship. In the hierarchy of knowledge, theories are the most powerful tool.

Laws and marketing

In describing concepts and hypotheses, examples from marketing were used. In the presentation on laws and theories, all the examples were from the physical sciences. Does this mean there are no laws in business? We talk about the "laws of supply and demand," and "Reilly's Law of Retail Gravitation," but are these really invariable associations between concepts? No!

The fact that humans play the central role in most marketing activities prevents the emergence of laws. It is impossible to isolate man from all the factors that influence him. Social scientists should not set up "ceteris paribus" restraints, because the influence of extraneous factors (environmental conditions, economic conditions, climatic conditions) on man and man's reaction to these influences are necessary parts of any study involving human activity. If we impose the condition that all things be held constant, we create an abnormal atmosphere and greatly dilute any study involving man.

Marketing principles

Although human activities do not follow invariable patterns, their actions are often predictable because the "law of averages" sets in when people are viewed as part of a group. Statements describing such relationships are called principles. A principle lies somewhere between a hypothesis and a law since it is a relationship that recurs and has been tested, but is not of an invariable nature.

Some marketing principles would be: the demand for specialty goods is inelastic; the longer a trade channel, the less control the manufacturer has over the product; the greatest responsibility for promotion of convenience goods rests with the manufacturer. While exceptions can be found for each of the above statements, they "tend" to be applicable for the majority of situations. Thus, these principles can guide marketing decisions.

Since there are no laws in marketing, does this mean that the scientific method does *not* apply to marketing? No! A desired goal of scientific method may be the eventual discovery of laws, but knowing at the outset that an investigation will not culminate in a law does not preclude its use. In fact, the vast majority of studies undertaken in the physical and natural sciences do not result in laws.

SUMMARY

Research involves the employment of systematic procedures to obtain information. It is not the subject being studied, the intent of the investigator, or the eventual discovery of laws that identifies what is or is not legitimate research. Rather it is the employment of the scientific process that legitimatizes research. Marketing researchers can and do use that process.

QUESTIONS AND EXERCISES

1. Laws are discovered, but theories are invented. Why the distinction?

2. In many colleges of business an MS degree (Master of Science) is awarded to graduate students. Is this a proper use of the term "Science"? Shouldn't all business degrees be BA's or MA's (Bachelor of Arts, Master of Arts)?

3. Prior to reading this chapter, what was your interpretation and use of the term "theory"? Why are theories (as defined in this chapter) the highest form of knowledge? What are some examples of other theories in the physical sciences?

4. Why are there no laws in marketing?

5. Some marketers explain consumer behavior through Freudian theory. Is this a legitimate use of the term "theory"?

6. Your company produces products of a very technical nature, and all the key executives are either engineers or chemists. They hire you, a recent marketing graduate, to provide them with a staff member possessing a business background. In one of the first staff meetings you state that your firm should become more involved with marketing research. One of the other members of the group (a chemist) laughs and says, "There's no such thing as marketing or business research. All business can do is count noses and carry out rather low-level investigations. Research is limited to the sciences." What is your response?

2

Marketing research— An overview

During the 1960s, Procter & Gamble's research staff found that the average number of household wash loads increased from 6.4 to 7.6 per week and cooler water temperatures were being used. The reason was the large number of clothes made from synthetics and synthetic blends. These clothes required different washing procedures and led Procter & Gamble to develop an all-purpose detergent capable of handling almost all types of laundry needs and at various temperatures. The product was named Cheer and became an immediate success on the market.

Procter & Gamble, the nation's 23rd largest business firm, says it has more frequent contact with consumers than any other business firm. In 1980, it had phone and personal contacts with over 1.5 million people through over 1,000 different research projects.

The firm constantly questions consumer likes and dislikes of its products. In addition, Procter & Gamble continually researches consumer clothes washing methods, meal preparation, dish washing, and other household tasks.

Generating the information is only half the job. The researchers distribute the data to every major segment of the company, where they are evaluated in terms of potential implications for Procter & Gamble's marketing, advertising and product development activities (condensed from Wall Street Journal, *[April 4, 1980].*

This chapter provides a broad look at the role of marketing research in business firms. Its coverage includes a brief look at the historical development of marketing research in the United States, a description of the general types of firms conducting marketing research, and methods firms can use in determining whether or not to conduct marketing research. Finally, it identifies the role of marketing research in marketing information systems.

Historical aspects

People have always wanted to be able to foresee the future in order to better plan their present activities. Thus, some rough form of marketing research probably has existed from the first time people began exchanging merchandise. But since little is known about the historical development of marketing research, its past cannot be separated into precise eras that depict distinct changes in its sophistication or usage.

The first evidence of formalized survey techniques being used in the United States was the attempts by newspapers to predict elections in the 1820s. These straw vote procedures were later adopted by some producers of agricultural machinery to estimate the potential demand for their products. These firms sent letters to state officials and newspapers throughout the country requesting information on expected crop production in their areas as well as information about weather, soil conditions, etc. They then used this information to estimate demand for their farm equipment.

1900s–1940s

There is some evidence that a few quasi-marketing research firms existed in the years from 1907–1912. Around that same time a bureau of business research was established by the Harvard Business School, and in 1918 the Northwestern School of Commerce instituted its own business research bureau. During this same period firms such as Kellogg Company in Battle Creek, Michigan, and the Curtis Publishing Company in New York had what might be described as business researchers on their staffs. Around 1918 some of the first books dealing with marketing research and its procedures were published.

Up until the mid-1920s there were little statistical data available to researchers except that which flowed from the Censuses of Population, Agriculture, and Manufacturers. Then, in 1929, the first Census of Distribution (the forerunner of today's Census of Business) was undertaken.

It is difficult to ascertain when the first courses in marketing research were offered in colleges. No doubt there is a link between these courses and the existence of the first textbooks (1918) touching on marketing research. In 1937 the American Marketing Association sponsored a publication, *The Technique of Marketing Research*. In the same year a textbook by Brown, entitled *Market Research and Analysis* and published by the Ronald Press Company, became the first widely used textbook on the subject.

It is important to recognize that until about the mid-1930s much of the introductory course work in any statistics courses seldom went further than developing averages, some secular trends, and simple correlation. Progress was made in sample design in the late 1930s and early 1940s, and this breakthrough added some sophistication to the marketing reserch used in business and taught in colleges.

Increased importance of marketing research

The rise in importance of marketing research within business firms is tied directly to the increased role played by marketing within business in general. In the early 1900s marketing was really synonymous with selling. The activities of most firms centered around production, and marketing activities were viewed merely as auxiliary to the production of the product. This attitude resulted from the demand – supply conditions that prevailed prior to 1930. While there were occasional business downturns, they tended to be of short duration, and upon their conclusion emphasis was back on increasing production since demand tended to consistently exceed supply.

However, the prolonged depression of the 1930s made many firms aware that movement of goods was critical to their total operation, and thus marketing as a functional area was given more emphasis. But, even then, the era from 1930–1950 (with the exception of the war years) would have to be viewed as sales oriented as opposed to marketing oriented. The thrust was toward trying to improve sales procedures rather than trying to develop a total marketing program. In the 1950s firms became aware of what is now called the "marketing concept." This concept states that a firm's activities should revolve around customers' wants and needs – the customer is the focal point of all business activities.

With increased acceptance of the marketing concept, it became evident that more information about customers and potential markets was needed. The desire for such information gave impetus to marketing research. Prior to 1940, most of the so-called *marketing* research should have been labeled *market* research since it usually was concerned with obtaining data about specific locales. In the 1950s research related to marketing activities was broadened to include all managerial aspects – price, product, place, and promotion.

This emphasis on marketing research was carried to an extreme in the late 1950s, especially as it related to motivational research. This led to some ridicule of marketing research, primarily through the accusations made in a best-selling book of that time, *The Hidden Persuaders* by Vance Packard (New York: David McKay, 1957). This book described some questionable methods used by firms in an attempt to manipulate customers. Although the book exaggerated what actually was going on in most firms, it did cause researchers to reevaluate some of their activities. Part of the reason for the original thrust toward motivational or psychological research was that business managers demanding more information about customers were often forced to use those researchers with the greatest experience in human behavior – psychologists. These criticisms shook up enough business executives that the pendulum hurriedly swung back to more pragmatic marketing research and away from a heavy emphasis on psychological aspects.

By the mid-1960s research courses had been in most business schools for over a decade. Publications such as the *Journal of Marketing Research*, the *Journal of Advertising Research*, and the *Journal of Consumer Research* were introduced, and an increasing number of textbooks on marketing research became available. Business students in colleges not only received training in computers, but many had two or three courses in statistics, giving them a much more quantitative background than their predecessors. All of these conditions resulted in business college grads – the future decision makers in business – becoming more knowledgeable about marketing research activities.

Most firms, regardless of their size, will have to occasionally use some type of marketing research (MR). The intensity and frequency of their use depend upon the general nature of the firm as well as the size of its operations.

1. *Consumer goods manufacturers.* Since they are usually quite remote from their customers, they rely heavily on MR to keep on top of situations. They use MR to test new

THE PRESENT ROLE OF MARKETING RESEARCH

The users of marketing research

product ideas, new package designs, measure effectiveness of their promotional efforts, and determine brand and company image.

2. *Industrial goods manufacturers.* These firms make less use of MR than group 1 since they have fewer products and customers. They also have shorter trade channels and thus are in closer contact with their customers. Their major use of MR is to determine market and sales potentials by territory, product, and customer. They also place great emphasis on sales forecasting since demand for their products is so sensitive to economic fluctuations.

3. *Wholesale intermediaries* (agents, brokers, merchant middlemen). This group does little MR since they are fairly close to their customers. Also, since these firms usually handle such a wide number of products, MR is often impractical for them.

4. *Consumer services* (banks, insurance firms, etc). Financial institutions are one of the few in this category using MR in any significant amount.

5. *Media and business services* (ad agencies, consultants, TV, newspapers, magazines). This whole category is a heavy user of MR, especially advertising agencies and consulting firms. Their research deals with a wide variety of subjects, and they attempt to use the most sophisticated qualitative and quantitative techniques available.

6. *Nonbusiness users* (government agencies, philanthropic and educational firms). Most government agencies (federal, state, and local) collect data to aid them in their decision making as well as being of use to the general public. Educational institutions also conduct a great deal of research, but much of it would not qualify as marketing research.

Marketing research is primarily used to provide information on markets as well as information needed to guide decisions involving the marketing mix—price, product, place, and promotion. Table 2-1 contains a description of some of the most common usages of marketing research.

WHO CONDUCTS THE RESEARCH?

Firm's own research staff—Most large firms use their own marketing research staffs unless a project requires special equipment or unique procedures that entail high overhead costs (i.e., a

Applications of Marketing Research   **Table 2-1**

1. Research on Markets
   a. Forecasting demand for existing products
   b. Identifying new markets for existing products
   c. Providing information on general trends
   d. Identifying new product needs, estimating potential
   e. Providing information for segmenting markets
   f. Developing market profiles
2. Research on Products
   a. Market testing new products
   b. Evaluating packaging, brand designs, etc.
   c. Comparison studies on competitors' products
   d. Obtaining consumer response to present products
3. Research on Pricing
   a. Identifying price elasticities
   b. Cost analysis
   c. Testing alternative pricing strategies
4. Research on Place (Distribution)
   a. Analysis of different storage/transportation methods
   b. Analysis of alternative sites
   c. Evaluating trade offs between different sized inventories
5. Research on Promotion
   a. Testing different ad messages
   b. Establishing sales territories
   c. Selecting advertising media
   d. Evaluating advertising effectiveness

national consumer panel). A significant number of smaller firms either have no formal research department or have just one person responsible for this activity. A 1978 survey sponsored by the American Marketing Association disclosed a direct relationship between the size of firms and the establishment of their own research staffs (see Table 2-2). Over 85 percent of firms with annual sales in excess of $100 million have formal research departments, whereas less than 46 percent of firms with sales of less than $25 million have such staffs.

Syndicated research services (Nielson, MRCA, Pulse, etc.)— These firms conduct continuous research for their clients using consumer panels, store audits, monitoring TV viewing in the home, etc. They try to use research programs that serve a large number of comparable clients enabling them to spread their high overhead costs among these customers.

Specialized research services (Burke Marketing Research)—These firms offer custom-tailored research programs and usually have special testing apparatus or procedures, which the average research user could not afford or maintain.

Table 2-2   Incidence of Marketing Research Departments
                                        Among Firms, Based on Annual Sales

Firm's Annual Sales (000,000)	Formal Research Dept.	One Person	No One Assigned
	%	%	%
Under $5	46	22	32
$5-$24	44	44	12
$25-$49	55	36	9
$50-99	72	24	4
$100-$199	87	10	3
$200-$500	85	11	4
Over $500	87	10	3
All firms in study	73	19	8
(n = 771)			

Source: D. K. Twedt, *1978 Survey of Marketing Research* (Chicago: American Marketing Association, 1978), p. 13.

General researchers—This is the most numerous and widespread group, usually serving the local areas in which they are located. They are hired to handle a specific project rather than being used continually by a firm.

Interviewing agencies—A few are national agencies, but the majority are of a regional or local nature. Their sole research activity is interviewing, and a lot of the interviewing done by national organizations is subcontracted to them.

Nonbusiness organizations—The U.S. Department of Commerce through the Bureau of the Census conducts the largest single marketing research undertaking in the world (Censuses of Housing, Population, Business, etc.). Foundations and some universities also maintain separate bureaus for conducting business research.

Amount spent on marketing research

Much data exist on private industry's research and development (R & D) costs because they are required on a firm's federal tax forms. This figure, however, *excludes* all expenditures on marketing-related research.

In an attempt to estimate marketing research expenditures, authorities have developed a model in which research costs are estimated from advertising expenditures on national media and R & D expenditures.[1] These experts presume that total market-

---

[1]John G. Myers, et al., *Marketing Research and Knowledge Development* (Englewood Cliffs: Prentice-Hall, 1980), pp. 119-121.

ing research outlays would be comparable to either 5 percent of advertising expenditures on national media or 5.5 percent of R & D expenditures.[2,3] If this is true, 1980 estimated expenditures on marketing research were between 1.4 and 1.5 billion dollars.

The previously cited 1978 study sponsored by the American Marketing Association identified the expenditures on marketing research among six different categories of business firms (see Table 2-3). A key finding among the firms surveyed was that manufacturers of consumer goods spend considerably more on

Amount Spent in 1978 on Marketing Research   **Table 2-3**
By Various Types of Firms

	# of Firms	Mean $000 spent	% Change from 1973
Manufacturers of Consumer Goods	176	$1,072	+60
Manufacturers of Industrial Goods	187	$257	+53
Advertising Agencies	51	$500	+29
Publishers and Broadcasters	47	$358	+84
Financial Services	101	$153	N.A.
Others	125	$242	N.A.
Total	687	$473	+65

Source: D. K. Twedt, *1978 Survey of Marketing Research* (Chicago: American Marketing Association, 1978), p. 28.

marketing research than do manufacturers of industrial goods. A second major disclosure was the significant increase (65 percent) in the amounts spent on marketing research between 1973 and 1978.

Allocation of research funds within firm — The distribution of research funds within a firm depends on the firm's organizational structure and spending philosophies. In some firms the entire research budget is assigned to the research department, and it covers the costs of research performed firm-wide. In other firms, each division or department has its own research budget, and it can be used to purchase internal or external research.

The amount of money a firm allocates for research is often tied to expected sales (i.e., 0.5 percent of expected sales for 1983

[2]Advertising expenditures on national media were estimated at $30.4 billion. Figure obtained from *Advertising Age,* January 5, 1981, pp. 10+.

[3]R & D expenditures for 1980 were estimated at $26.2 billion. Figure obtained from *Business Week,* July 7, 1980, p. 47.

will be allocated for marketing research for 1983). This allocation procedure may not seem logical (sales dictate research dollars), but it is frequently used because it is a simple way for management to establish a research budget.

Compensation of research staffs — As marketing research departments have grown in recent years, a series of new positions emerged, such as statisticians, analysts, and field work directors. Table 2-4 contains information on the compensation of these various research positions and the changes that have taken place since 1973. It appears that, at the professional staff level (first five positions), the percent change in compensation has kept pace with inflation. The compensation for lower echelon positions, however, has declined in terms of 1973 dollars. These figures also indicate that while marketing research is becoming increasingly more important in the typical firm's activities, the research directors' compensation is still considerably lower than the compensation for other key officials of the firm.

WHEN TO RESEARCH

Marketing research projects are often expensive undertakings. Therefore a lot of thought may precede the decision of whether to actually perform the research. The basic question that must be answered is: will the value of the information obtained from the research be greater than the cost of acquiring it? While this requirement is simple to understand, it is difficult to apply because of the problems involved in accurately assessing the value of information.

Table 2-4

Mean Compensation for Marketing Research Positions (1978 Figures)

Position	Mean Compensation	Compared to 1973 (%)
Directors	$35,800	+46
Assistant Directors	31,100	+56
Senior Analysts	24,200	+48
Analysts	18,200	+40
Statisticians	22,600	+37
Field Work Directors	15,800	+33
Librarians	13,900	+15
Full Time Interviewers	10,000	− 2
Clerical-Tabulators	10,000	−12

Source: D. K. Twedt, *1978 Survey of Marketing Research* (Chicago: American Marketing Association, 1978), p. 57.

Identifying the cost of a particular research undertaking is fairly straightforward. The actual research activities must be identified, and then the specific costs of carrying them out can be estimated. It may be necessary to add an overhead charge to cover the fixed cost of the firm's research organization. If the research is to be done by an outside firm, then the estimated costs will be provided in its research proposal.

Identifying costs

The difficult task is identifying the value of a particular research project. The net value of marketing research equals the expected value of the decision made with the aid of research, minus the expected value of the decision made without the aid of research, minus the cost of research.

Identifying value of research

$$V_{MR} = (VRMD - VMD) - CR$$
V_{MR} = real value of marketing research
$VRMD$ = value of researched decision
VMD = value of decision not researched
CR = cost of the research

Although the term "expected value" is used, it should be emphasized that research rarely can tell the firm precisely what the outcome of a given event will be. Research just narrows the range of error associated with the possible outcomes of decisions or the probabilities assigned to these possible outcomes. The true value of research is how well it reduces the costs associated with uncertainty.

Emphasis on loss

Methods for estimating value of information

This method is a fairly simple way to determine the value of research information. It concentrates on the potential *loss* associated with a wrong decision. The major assumption in its use is that management can actually determine the potential dollar loss. If it can obtain information that will minimize its chances of making a wrong decision, it then can determine the net value of such information.

Example: The X Company is in a dilemma. It doesn't know whether to introduce a new product. If it is introduced and fails, it will cost around $400,000. It presently feels its chances of success are 60 percent (40 percent possibility of failure). If a $20,000 proposed research project were undertaken, it would significantly improve its chances of making a correct decision. Should the research be undertaken, assuming the chances of making a correct decision could be improved to 75 percent?

$$\text{expected cost with no research} = \$400,000 \times 0.40 \text{ (chance of incorrect decision)}$$
$$= \$160,000$$
$$\text{expected cost with research} = \$400,000 \times 0.25 \text{ (chance of incorrect decision)}$$
$$= \$100,000$$
$$\text{value of research} = \$60,000 \ (\$160,000 - \$100,000)$$

Since the value of the research (improving chances of correct decision from 60 to 75 percent) is $60,000, the $20,000 research should be undertaken.

This method is fairly low level and emphasizes only the loss side. Note that no mention is made of the potential dollar gain associated with the product being a success. This method is probably of more value as a conceptual model than as a practical method for placing a value on information.

Return on investment

This method is primarily of use for estimating the overall value of marketing research on an annual basis as opposed to assessing the value of individual projects. Assume a firm spent $600,000 last year on marketing research. It estimates that the information obtained in this research contributed about $3,000,000. Without research, it feels management would still have made the correct decision 66 percent of the time. This reduces the worth of the research to 34 percent.

$$\frac{\text{value of findings (\$3,000,000)} \times 0.34}{\text{research expenditures (\$600,000)}} = \text{R.O.I. for research (170\%)}$$

Thus, an estimate can be made of research's contribution to the company. The key assumption in this procedure is that the "value of findings" to the company can be quantified.

Formal analysis

This procedure combines three different factors to determine whether a research project should be undertaken:

1. The possible outcomes of a marketing action
2. The payoff associated with each outcome
3. The probability of each outcome occurring

It uses both objective and subjective information. The objective information is the dollar figure (loss or gain) associated with the outcomes; the subjective information is the estimated chance of each outcome occurring. The need for the subjective estimates stems from the fact that although many marketing activities are fairly "unique," an experienced observer can establish reasonable estimates as to the probable outcomes associated with these activities.

Example: Acme Company is trying to decide whether to introduce a new fire alarm for use in homes. Comparable products are already on the market, but it would be a new addition to Acme's product mix. Various management and sales personnel with Acme have been asked to estimate the number of fire alarms they feel Acme could sell. Table 2-5 combines their estimates. As indicated, they feel Acme has a 100 percent probability of selling between 60,000 and 140,000 units. Specific probabilities are also assigned to five possible levels of sales.

Formal Analysis Procedure   Table 2-5

Unit Sales (1)	Estimated Probability of Occurring (2)	Profit or Loss (3)	Opportunity Loss		Expected Opportunity Loss	
			Introduce (4)	Not Introduce (5)	Introduce (6)	Not Introduce (7)
140,000	0.10	300,000	0	300,000	0	−30,000
120,000	0.25	180,000	0	180,000	0	−45,000
100,000	0.40	0	0	0	0	0
80,000	0.15	−200,000	−200,000	0	−30,000	0
60,000	0.10	−350,000	−350,000	0	−35,000	0
	1.00				−$65,000	−$75,000

The breakeven point is 100,000 units. The extreme outcomes would be that possible profits could reach $300,000 and possible losses might go to $350,000. In columns (4) and (5), the concept of "opportunity loss" is introduced. These losses could arise from two conditions: (1) the product is introduced and never even reaches the breakeven point; or (2) the product is not introduced when it could actually have reached a profitable sales level.

In column (4) the decision to "introduce" the product would result in a loss if sales don't reach 100,000 units. Above this amount, there would be no opportunity loss. Column (5) shows that if the product were not introduced, potential profits of $180,000 and $300,000 would be lost.

Management should take the course of action that will result in the lowest opportunity loss. This can be determined by multiplying the probability of each of the five sales levels occurring times those sales. Columns (6) and (7) show these results. In this example, the company would have the lowest expected loss ($65,000) if it introduced the new products.

This information can then be used to decide whether to spend money on research that will aid in the decision of whether or not to introduce the product. If perfect information existed (i.e., management knows which of the five sales levels would be reached), the opportunity losses could be reduced by only $65,000. Therefore, the maximum amount it would pay for research to improve its knowledge about sales would be $65,000. Since this assumes that perfect knowledge is obtained (an unrealistic assumption), it should pay something less than this amount.

An assessment of the models

This procedure provides a method for estimating the maximum value of research. Bayesian models similar to the one in Table 2-5 have been described in many academic journals and texts as the most effective method for identifying the expected value of information (EVI). However, recent surveys of business firms have shown that less than 20 percent actually use these methods in evaluating proposed research efforts.[4] And this percentage may even be overstated since the study was conducted among a sample of Fortune 500 firms—i.e., primarily large firms with full-time research staffs.

The likely explanations for the limited use of Bayesian analysis are: (1) many decision makers feel uncomfortable with having to quantify uncertainty and (2) the process can be costly if a variety of decision makers must be contacted to obtain probabilities on the various possible outcomes.

Advocates of the procedure feel that as more managers become familiar with the tools of formal decision analysis, it will be widely adopted. They have, however, been making this prediction over the last decade.

MARKETING INFORMATION SYSTEMS

Two general types of information are used by marketing managers: (1) information provided on a regular basis—weekly sales reports on products and sales territories, sales expense ratios on individual salesmen, weekly warehouse inventory reports, weekly

---

[4]Gerald Albaum, Donald Tull, and James Hanson, "The Expected Value of Information: How Widely Is It Used in Marketing Research?" 1977 Proceedings of Educators Conference, American Marketing Association, pp. 32-34.

store sales, etc.; (2) information coming from discrete or nonrecurring projects—projects undertaken to obtain some specific information.

This first type of information generally moves to the decision maker through some type of planned system. In most firms such a system usually had its beginnings with the distribution of routine accounting reports. Gradually, these reports became more sophisticated as marketers began requesting breakdowns of information by product, territory, or customer. In the 1960s some firms formalized their methods for collecting and distributing information and called them marketing information systems (M.I.S.).

M.I.S. defined

A marketing information system consists of people and/or equipment organized to provide an orderly intake and exchange of the information (internal and external) needed to guide a firm's decisions.

Two conditions arose that led to the increased interest in the development and use of marketing information systems. Marketing decision makers recognized that they needed more sophisticated information and at a faster rate if their firm was to compete in an increasingly volatile business environment. Second, the increased availability of computers enabled tremendous amounts of data to be generated, analyzed, and disseminated.

Elements of an M.I.S.

Figure 2-1 is a simplified model depicting the components of an M.I.S. It includes an information facilitator, a data bank with accompanying analytic equipment, and the capability to undertake special research projects.

The "information facilitator" is the equipment or person(s) through which the decision maker obtains the desired information. It can be a librarian, a major computer center, or perhaps cathode ray tube equipment (CRT) available in the decision maker's office.

The "data bank" is the equipment used to store and access the raw data the firm obtains on a regular basis. This includes the routine or internal data the firm obtains as well as the data it regularly receives from outside sources (external data). Both of these types of data are covered at length in Chapter 5, "Obtaining Secondary Data."

The "analytic bank" contains quantitative programs that can be used to give the raw data increased value. This might include such statistical models as regression and analysis of variance as well as software packages that break raw sales data into cate-

Figure 2-1   Simplified Model of M.I.S.

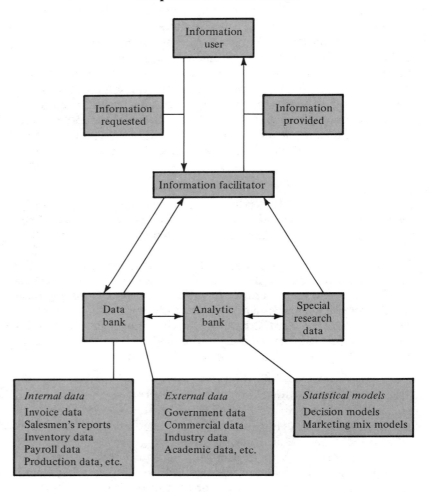

gories of unique interest to different decision makers—sales by territory, by type of customer, by profit category, etc. In some situations only raw data might be requested, so no analytic procedures need to be applied.

Finally, an M.I.S. also includes the opportunity for special information requests to be met. These are one-time-only requests and are generally carried out by marketing researchers.

An M.I.S. can be a full-scale operation, given a formal place in the firm's organizational structure and headed by an information officer or director with vice presidential status. General Foods, Pillsbury, and Schenley are examples of such firms. Or, the M.I.S. can be a less sophisticated operation with only limited computer involvement, but with an effective system for dispersing information in the desired form to decision makers when needed.

A firm does not need extensive computer capabilities with elaborate software packages to have an effective M.I.S. Rather, an effective M.I.S. is one that constantly provides its decision makers with the types of information they need to perform their jobs.

1. The system must be designed to provide information in a form that fits the present management decision processes. Management must not be deluged with paper printouts, only a small part of which is useful to them.

2. The people using the output must participate in creating the parameters of the system's capability (the control activity).

3. The information gathered should be placed in a disaggregated data file. In such a file new information is maintained with previously received input. This arrangement enables all previous inputs to be recreated by the system at any time.

4. The system must be designed so that it can be altered to fit the firm's changing needs.

5. The system must have the support of both users and upper-level management if it is to receive the funds needed for effective operation.

Conditions needed for a successful M.I.S.

Marketing research provides discrete information that can be incorporated into the M.I.S. The existence of a successful M.I.S. does not weaken the role of marketing research; rather, it makes it more efficient. It enables researchers to concentrate on major projects requiring specialized information and minimizes the time they spend seeking out data already available within the firm.

Marketing research and the M.I.S.

1. Too much emphasis is placed on the computer. Not every firm needs a computer-oriented marketing system, and even those with computers should not lose sight of the importance of human processors.

2. When a marketing information system is developed, some executives mistakenly feel there is no longer a need for basic marketing research. Marketing research is still required for discrete projects.

Some warnings about the M.I.S.

3. The regular computer outputs are too often accepted as "gospel." Not enough questions are raised about the quality of the data in these printouts. The old adage "garbage in – garbage out" always applies.

4. Some marketing information systems lack the flexibility necessary to serve all levels of management. The information needs of upper-level managers usually differ significantly from those of middle- and lower-level supervisors. The system should be able to adjust to the specific needs of its users.

5. There is a trend toward information overkill. The computer printouts are often so voluminous that they discourage use by decision makers.

6. When developing a marketing information system, some firms attempt to make it too sophisticated at the outset instead of improving it by stages.

7. Many managers are not properly trained in how to use the information, nor are they allowed to describe the types of output they want from the system.

SUMMARY   The material in this chapter provides the reader with a broad background on the role of marketing research in business firms.

Surprisingly little is known about the historical development of marketing research. Its greatest impetus came in the 1950s with the recognition of the marketing concept as the overall philosophy that should guide a firm's activities.

The role it plays within individual firms is directly related to the nature of the firm's operation (manufacturer, wholesaler, retailer), its size (dollarwise and geographically), and the nature of its products or services.

Most firms with annual sales in excess of $100 million have their own research departments. There are also a wide variety of private firms available to carry out research on an individual project basis.

In some situations the need for marketing research is so obvious that it is not necessary to spend the time, energy, or resources to analyze a project's potential value. In other situations, management may want to determine whether the value of information obtained from the proposed research will exceed the cost of acquiring this information. Three methods frequently used for such analyses are: (1) estimating the potential loss associated with a wrong decision, (2) determining the "return on investment" of the research, and (3) using formal analysis where probabilities of various outcomes are assigned. The major benefit of all three methods is that they force management to pay closer attention to the possible benefits of research prior to the actual approval of a project.

Marketing research is one form of input into a firm's marketing information system. Where these systems are effectively structured, they provide marketing managers with data on a continual basis. Marketing information systems will become more widely used and sophisticated as managers become better qualified in their use of the computer. Regardless of how effective these information systems become, marketing research will still be needed to provide input of a discrete nature.

AN ACTUAL M.I.S.—WHIRLPOOL COMPANY

This example is condensed from an article in the July 1976 issue of the *Journal of Marketing*. It was written by Jack Sparks, at that time a group vice president for the Whirlpool Corporation. He describes why and how Whirlpool revamped its M.I.S.

The appliance industry receives too much and too little marketing information. Too much in terms of sheer volume since the appliance industry is second only to the automotive industry in the amount of data that is available on all levels of its operations. Too little, in terms of the difficulty a firm encounters in sorting, absorbing, and using the data.

In the early 1970s, computer printouts were piled high in dozens of Whirlpool offices. More than 70 different analyses were spun out daily and weekly. But the information system was labeled a "paper tiger" by managers—all paper and no substance. A more astute label of the system would have been "paper elephant"—real substance, tenacious memory, but very bulky.

The many criticisms of the system forced the firm's marketing services department to set out to tame its "paper elephant."

Defining the problems

The first step was to identify the problems. Were 70 computerized reports too many or too few? Were they inadequately organized, inappropriately interpreted, indiscriminantly distributed? Questions to Whirlpool sales and marketing managers revealed:

1. There was an adequate industry information base.
2. There was adequate information being circulated about the firm's own activities (inventories, product sales, territorial sales, etc.).

3. Managers were receiving too many reports, and many overlapped.

In summary, sales and marketing managers were both pleased and disturbed by the services provided. On the plus side, they had been provided excellent material for marketing decisions. On the negative side, paper had been proliferating, reports had been building up on every desk, and personal "guilt" had been building up even faster due to human inability to absorb all these findings.

The strategic solutions

One key conclusion was that the system had been providing so much computerized data that the "right" numbers often were hidden. Thus a single objective was pursued: improved usage of data for all facets of decision making—for product planning, forecasting, pricing, promotion planning, field sales management, even financial planning or other corporate purposes. In light of this objective, the following four tactical moves were pursued:

- An "enclave"—a point of central referral—for marketing information would be developed with experts, reports, and files in one place. This "enclave" would be comfortable, attractive, and convenient for users.
- Report distribution would be cut down. The usual Monday morning "paper route" would be replaced with brief bulletins on information and analyses.
- Printouts would be replaced by readable communications.
- Technical talent would be used to provide true "exception" monitoring.

The new communications tactic was greatly appreciated. Although no marketing manager would admit that it was a chore to read previous reports, he/she welcomed a cover sheet on "how to evaluate" or "what it means."

The investment required

It took time and money to design and build the "REFROOM" (a deliberate tongue-in-cheek nickname for reference room). It also took time and money to write an "ANSWER-BOOK"—a volume that describes all the available data, as well as how to read and use those data. Finally, it took considerable effort to merchandise the new system and to orient all prospective users to its potential effectiveness.

The investment had immediate payoffs. Although costs climbed considerably in EDP, printing, and payroll, overall costs for the Whirlpool marketing information services leveled off. More important, there was a dramatic increase in the usage of sales and marketing information. Strong evidence on the success of the new M.I.S. is that at coffee break times, any number of marketing managers now head for the REFROOM rather than the cafeteria. Most managers (and distributors) greet marketing information with more hope than guilt, with grins, rather than groans. Whirlpool tamed the paper elephant.

---

1. What is the "marketing concept"?
2. Why is the growth of marketing research so closely entwined with the adoption of the marketing concept?
3. How do the marketing research needs of consumer goods manufacturers differ from those of industrial goods manufacturers?
4. Why are advertising agencies so heavily involved in marketing research, and what are the major types of research they perform?
5. What is the difference between *market* research and *marketing* research?
6. In the early 1960s it was predicted that all firms would have marketing information systems and that these systems would be widely used by the firm's marketing managers. By the late 1970s such systems were still not widely used. Why? What are the reasons for their slow adoption?
7. What impact will growth in the usage of marketing information systems have on a firm's marketing research department?

QUESTIONS AND EXERCISES

The Johnson Company is considering adding a new product to its offerings—a folding cart customers can take with them when shopping in a mall to carry their packages. If it is introduced and fails, it will cost it $200,000. It presently feels its chances of at least breaking even are 50 percent. The marketing research department has suggested a test market study that will cost around $30,000. The results of this study should cut down on the chances of making a wrong decision to 40 percent. Should the study be undertaken?

CASES

Case 1

Case 2 The Dowdy Company meat packing firm is interested in entering into the production of canned dog food. It presently sells their waste products to a broker who in turn sells it to dog food manufacturers. It has done a preliminary study on costs and has some ideas of the costs per can at various levels of production. It asks a number of "experts" in the field how many cases of dog food it could expect to sell in the seven-state area encompassing the Rocky Mountain region. These estimates are combined in the following table. The experts feel the company will be able to eventually sell between 10,000 and 60,000 cans annually.

Case Sales	Probability of Attaining	Profit or Loss Associated with Each Level of Sales
10,000	0.35	−$140,000
20,000	0.20	− 50,000
30,000	0.20	0
40,000	0.15	25,000
50,000	0.05	75,000
60,000	0.05	125,000

What would be the dollar value of having perfect information? What would be a reasonable amount to pay for marketing research that could improve the firm's knowledge about what actual sales might be?

Case 3 You are a division manager for Triple K, a firm that manufactures and distributes microwave ovens. The firm has recently developed a new position on the staff−information systems director. Her primary job is to develop an information system that will provide key managers with weekly and monthly reports that guide their decision making efforts. The new information officer meets with you and requests that you send her a list of both internal and external types of data that you would like to receive on a regular basis. Develop such a list and identify the format in which you would like the data.

3

A procedural model

The purpose of this chapter is to provide the reader with a brief overview of the various steps involved in systematically conducting research. The combination of all of these steps is called the "Procedural Model for Marketing Research." An extensive discussion of each step is presented in the remaining chapters of this book.

The diagram in Figure 3-1 depicts the step-by-step process researchers should follow in initiating and carrying out their investigations. The number of steps involved will vary from project to project since the activities to be performed depend upon the type of research being conducted.

Three types of investigations are carried out in business — basic research, applied research, and simple fact gathering.

Types of research

Basic research is exemplified by those studies whose sole purpose is the discovery of new information. The primary goal of basic research is knowledge for the sake of knowledge.

Applied research or solution-oriented research refers to the application of basic principles and other existing knowledge to the solution of operational problems. Common examples are finding causes of declining sales or poor morale of salespeople, evaluating various promotion alternatives, or making site selections. In applied research the investigator generally has a tentative problem condition identified for him, and his job is to gather data that will provide insight towards the solution of this problem.

Simple fact gathering differs from both basic and applied research in that the researcher's task is merely one of gathering some predetermined data. For instance, the sales manager of Acme Television may want to know how many households in Kansas have color television sets. The task here is merely one of collecting this desired information.

Thus, the nature of the research determines which activities must be performed by the researcher (see Figure 3-1). In designated fact gathering studies, the direction and nature of the study have already been chosen; thus the researcher can begin at the data collection stage. In applied or problem solving research, a general direction for the study has been designated for the researcher, but this direction is quite broad and must be narrowed. All steps of the research process must be performed when basic research is undertaken; the researcher must select the general area to be studied as well as the study's specific direction.

Figure 3-1   **Steps Involved in Marketing Research**

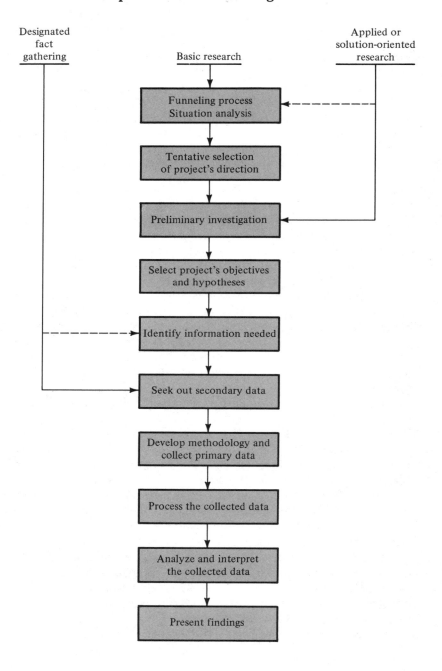

Funneling process – situation analysis

The funneling process involves narrowing a broad subject area down to one that lends itself better to research. This step is especially critical in basic research since the researcher has so many directions and possible topics to pursue. Funneling is also necessary in some applied research projects when the researcher feels uncomfortable with the breadth of the assignment or when it is felt the identified problem may not be the central issue. Thus, it is necessary to analyze the total situation before choosing the specific direction of the research.

For example, the marketing manager may state to the researcher: "Product X's sales have fallen drastically because its price is too high. We need data that will shed light on what is a more effective price." Actually, the decline in sales may have been caused by any number of factors – poor product quality, competitors' actions, poor salesmanship, etc. Research dealing solely with the product's price would not have provided the data needed to overcome the real problem. A situation analysis would have provided a broader perspective as to what type of research was needed.

Tentative selection of project's direction – Preliminary investigation

Out of this initial funneling and situation analysis, a tentative problem or disorder will emerge. The researcher identifies the general subject to be dealt with in the research and then makes a cursory review of the literature and talks to people knowledgeable about the subject to solidify this choice.

Choose objectives and hypotheses

The researcher is ready to select the specific objectives of the study. Will the study deal with the entire identified problem or just a portion of it? The distinction between "identifying the problem" and "stating the study's objective" can be confusing and is covered in depth in Chapter 4.

An effective tool for guiding a research project is the establishment of hypotheses. If appropriate hypotheses are chosen, their eventual acceptance or rejection ensures that the study's objective(s) will be accomplished.

Identify information needed

Once the project's objectives (and hypotheses) have been selected, it is necessary to identify the types of information needed to accomplish these objectives. In developing this list, the researcher will become increasingly aware of what sources (secondary and primary) will probably have to be used to provide such data. This will also provide better insight into the potential costs and time commitments associated with the project.

Search for secondary data

The first step in actual data gathering begins with a thorough search of secondary sources to uncover any information that can aid in accomplishing the project's objectives. Once this existing data have been uncovered and evaluated, the researcher can then determine whether additional data are needed from primary sources.

Select methodology and collect primary data

Research methods for collecting primary data can be grouped into three categories — survey methods, direct observation methods, and experimental techniques.

Survey methods — Data are collected by asking questions of people who are thought to have the desired information. These questions can be asked through personal interviews, telephone interviews, or mail interviews.

Direct observation — The researcher observes the objects or activites in which he is interested. These observations can be made either by individuals or with mechanical devices.

Experimental techniques — When this method is used, the researcher (1) introduces selected stimuli into a controlled environment, (2) systematically alters these stimuli, and (3) records the results of these changes. This alteration of conditions by the experimenter is what distinguishes this method from either the survey or observational methods, since in these two the information is obtained under normal conditions.

Data Processing

The primary and secondary data that have been gathered must be processed prior to their analysis. This processing includes editing, coding, and tabulating.

Editing involves (1) inspecting the data gathering forms for accuracy, completeness, and consistency, (2) making editorial additions or deletions where necessary, and (3) classifying the data into meaningful categories. *Coding* involves preparing individual answers for transference to punch cards or other types of recording systems. *Tabulating* the results may be done either mechanically or by hand, depending on the quantity of the data, dollar and time restraints, and the type of analysis to be performed.

Analysis and interpretation

Once the data have been processed, the critical task of analysis and interpretation begins. *Analysis* is concerned with dissecting the data. *Interpretation* involves the reassembly of the data into a form that is applicable to the study's objectives and is also meaningful to the people using the research findings. Various statistical treatments can be applied to the data to test the significance of the findings.

Based on the conclusions emerging from the analysis and interpretation, the researcher can recommend particular courses of action. Recommendations may not be part of the assigned research task, however, since the party requesting the investigation may assume all decisional responsibilities.

Presentation of findings

It is essential that the research findings be reported in an organized manner appropriate for the potential users. Since the audience is often comprised of executives as well as their technically oriented subordinates, the reports should be presented in a form and language useful to both groups. They should include a brief summary of the key findings plus a more detailed explanation of the procedures, findings, and conclusions for that part of the audience interested in more detailed explanations. Even when the findings are to be orally presented to an audience, it is usually necessary to have an accompanying written report.

4

Establishing the project's direction

THE IMPORTANCE OF DEFINING THE RIGHT PROBLEM

Firm A, a manufacturer of surgical sutures, hired a market research firm to undertake a study among the readers of a medical journal in which it advertised. The readers of this journal were primarily surgeons, and Firm A wanted to determine whether the surgeons remembered its ads and the extent to which this influenced their choice of sutures.

The research firm asked Firm A if it really knew who selected the brand of sutures used at hospitals. Firm A assumed it was the surgeons. The research firm did an informal investigation and found that the brand of sutures used was chosen by the hospital's operating room supervisor. Thus, instead of performing a readership study, the researcher investigated ways in which Firm A could improve its position with operating supervisors. The moral: Researchers should view themselves more as problem definers than problem solvers. If researchers act only as order takers and clients act only as order givers, research will often focus on the wrong problems.

"Defining marketing problems can be more important than finding solutions," *Marketing News,* June 6, 1975.

Unless the researcher knows specifically what he/she wants to do, the project will wander. Just as a ship with a faulty compass may eventually reach some form of land, so too a misdirected research project will ultimately come up with some findings. In most cases, though, such findings will be of limited value. Thus, this first step can be viewed as the most crucial activity in the research process because it sets the direction for the entire study.

Although researchers and authors of research texts agree on the necessity of establishing the study's specific direction, there is little agreement among these same people as to the best procedure for accomplishing this task. This lack of consensus stems from their different interpretations of such terms as "problems," "objectives," and "goals."

Difficulty in selecting the project's direction

The amount of difficulty encountered in selecting the study's specific direction depends upon the nature of the research involved. In the previous chapter it was pointed out that a research assignment falls into one of three categories: (1) The assignment may involve designated fact gathering activities where the researcher's task is to gather information that has been precisely identified. (2) The research assignment might be of an applied or solution seeking nature. Here an operational problem exists, and the investigator's job is to provide information that will aid in solving this disorder. (3) The third type of research is basic research. This is usually very unstructured at the outset since its purpose is not to solve a specific problem, but rather to accumulate new information which may or may not have some application to marketing.

Direction of fact gathering investigation

In this type of investigation, the specific direction is spelled out for the researcher. For example, Ordways, a supermarket chain, is thinking of changing its customer checkout procedures, and it needs to determine the number of people checked out per register during peak hours. The specific direction of the research has already been designated and the researcher merely has to select the technique to be used in making the desired head count. Another example of a fact gathering assignment would be to determine the number of nonwhite households in California with annual incomes in excess of $30,000. Once again, the specific information to be gathered has been stated and the researcher merely has to find the sources of such information and collect it.

Direction of applied or solution seeking research

Under solution seeking research, the general nature of the problem is presented to the researcher, who must define more precisely the direction the investigation will take. A researcher may be asked by a trade association such as the Colorado Flower Growers to investigate the most effective distribution network for mass-marketing roses and carnations. Although the association has determined the *general* direction of the study (mass-marketing of fresh flowers), it is the researcher's job to select its *specific* direction. Which particular method of mass-marketing—street vendors, supermarkets, discount stores, or a combination of these—should be evaluated?

Direction of basic research

This type of research generally causes investigators the most difficulty since they have complete freedom in the choice of the subject areas to be studied. Basic research is not very common in marketing since most research assignments stem from some existing disorder. An example of basic research would be the situations where firms such as DuPont or Shell allow chemists to conduct freelance experiments with some synthetics in the hope that some of these findings may eventually have some business application.

Procedures for establishing a project's direction

Depending upon the nature of the research itself, there may be anywhere from one to six steps performed prior to the formal investigation (see Figure 4-1). Most beginning researchers find that the subject they originally chose as their research topic turns out to be so broad they can't get a solid grip on it. For instance, a researcher might establish the subject as "An Evaluation of Cents-off Coupons as a Promotional Tool." Progressing into the study, he/she finds there are so many different aspects connected with such coupons that the topic is dropped as unmanageable, or it is considerably narrowed down, i.e., "The Effect of Cents-off Coupons on Sales of Liquid Detergents."

Following are guidelines that will aid researchers in selecting their study's ultimate direction. An example using basic research is presented since this is the most difficult type of research for which to provide a direction. When either applied research or fact gathering is conducted, fewer steps are needed.

Steps in Establishing the Direction of the Project   **Figure 4-1**

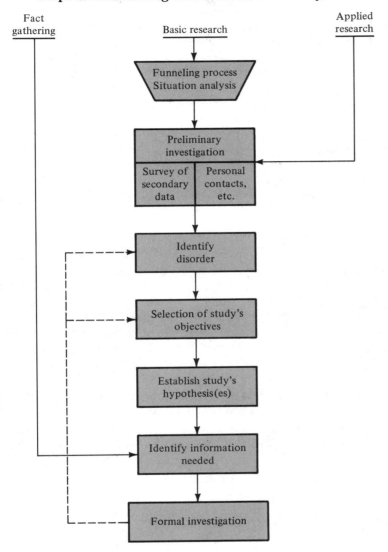

The funneling process

The starting point involves a funneling activity. In this process the researcher begins with a broad subject area and keeps narrowing it down to a more manageable level. This funneling is illustrated by the following example which assumes the researcher is starting completely from scratch in selecting the direction of a study. This is a common situation for graduate students searching for a topic for a thesis or major research paper.

First, a general area of study is chosen. In most cases, this general area is related to the researcher's own background — pricing, promotion, channels, or products. Then this area is further refined. If promotion were the area chosen, one type of promotion such as advertising might be selected. But even advertising is too broad, so it must be defined more narrowly. Some examples of more workable units might be creative aspects, media selection, ad construction, or the effectiveness of advertising. These in turn must be broken down into more manageable categories. The unit chosen for our study will be the effectiveness of advertising (see Figure 4-2).

Situation analysis

At this point the researcher is involved with a subject area in which he/she may have only limited knowledge. It started out with a broad area (promotion) in which the researcher had some background and moved to a sub-area (effectiveness of advertisements) in which he/she may have only sparse knowledge. Thus, a situation analysis must be performed. The researcher reads available information and talks informally with people knowledgeable

Figure 4-2   **The Funneling Process – A Method of Narrowing Down the Subject to be Studied**

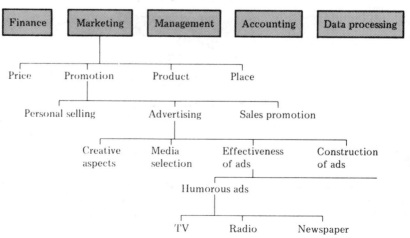

about the subject. During this informal investigation, conditions that might lend themselves to further in-depth investigations are uncovered, and the researcher can select one of these conditions as a possible research topic.

In our example the researcher feels the topic "The Effectiveness of Humorous Advertising" needs further research. Thus, in the situation analysis he/she gathers and reads secondary information related to this subject. People familiar with advertising such as advertising agency personnel, commercial artists, and media people are also contacted.

It is during this "situation analysis" that many basic research projects are dropped or drastically altered because much of the information on the subject is found to already exist. The situation analysis really serves two purposes. It provides the researcher with background information in a proposed area of study, and, second, it identifies what has already been done in this area and tells whether the study is really needed.

Preliminary investigation

Upon completing a situation analysis, the researcher must further define the direction of the study. Thus far he/she has chosen the specific sub-area with which the study will deal. It must now be pinned down more precisely. At this point the reader is probably wondering whether the funneling activities ever end. They do, in the preliminary investigation.

The preliminary investigation involves cursory studies of secondary data and making more contacts with people knowledgeable about the selected subject. Whereas in the situation analysis the researcher searched a rather broad subject area, in the preliminary investigation the efforts are concentrated on a specific subject. The situation analysis dealt with a fairly general topic, "Humorous Advertising." In the preliminary investigation the researcher concentrates on an evaluation of the effectiveness of this type of advertising. The researcher finds that the major area of controversy surrounding the effectiveness of humorous versus nonhumorous ads exists in television and decides to limit the study to this particular medium.

As shown in Figure 4-1, a preliminary investigation is even required in applied research. Although the general direction has been established in these studies, the researchers will usually have to pinpoint further the subject areas to make them more manageable.

Assume the researcher has been given the task of investigating "The Impact of Credit on Retail Prices in the Clothing Industry." In the preliminary investigation the researcher discovers that the large number and variety of stores handling clothes in the United States make it almost impossible to measure the total impact of credit on prices. The investigator then limits his study to single-line men's clothing stores.

At times, a researcher involved with an applied research project may even find it necessary to conduct a situation analysis. This occurs when the researcher is not familiar with the general subject area assigned. For example, the author was hired to investigate the feasibility of a meat packing firm's entry into the production of dog food. The first thing the researcher had to do was familiarize himself with the dog food industry, its terminology, operations, and types of products. This background information was obtained in a situation analysis.

The 'problem' with identifying the 'problem'

Most research texts list "identifying the problem" as the next step following the preliminary investigation. But in trying to describe what this step entails, writers differ greatly on what the term "problem" means.

Example: Sales in McDonald's Restaurant #962 have dropped 25 percent in the last year.

Many researchers would disagree with the above description as being the problem. They feel the decline in sales is merely a symptom. The "problem" is the unknown condition or factor causing this sales decline. Generally in research texts the problem is interpreted as being the condition that necessitates the research. But the examples provided oftentimes are more confusing than enlightening.

To avoid this semantic hangup, this writer does not use the term "problem identification," but instead uses "identifying the disorder." A disorder is *the condition causing the state of unrest.* In the previous McDonald's example, the disorder would be: "The McDonald Regional Office doesn't understand what factors caused sales in Restaurant #962 to decline 25 percent in the last year." The inability to explain the sales decline is the condition necessitating research.

Identifying the disorder

In most research projects the disorder is a lack of information or state of confusion about either (1) what specific factor(s) is causing a state of unrest or (2) which alternative action should be selected.

In the advertising example the disorder is that there is no solid information comparing the effectiveness of humorous TV ads with nonhumorous ads. In the example involving the impact of credit charges on retail prices, the disorder was the lack of data to accurately evaluate the impact of credit.

Objectives flow from the disorder

The distinction between identifying the disorder and selecting the study's objectives can be a confusing one. In fact, some researchers use the concepts interchangeably. This writer views them as separate and distinct activities. The disorder (problem) is the unsettled condition requiring a solution or decision. The existence of this condition is the reason the research is needed. The project's objectives are the specific purpose or goals of the research. Since the objectives flow from the disorder, the identification of the disorder must precede the selection of the objectives.

When choosing the research objective(s), it is essential that researchers ask themselves: "What is the purpose of this research, and what do I intend to accomplish with it?" (See Figure 4-3.)

Choosing study's objectives

If the research is merely a fact gathering assignment, then the objective of the research project is to collect the information requested. For example, if the research assignment is to determine the number of independent truckers in the state of Alabama, the gathering of such data then becomes the research objective. But, if the research assignment involves some condition causing a state of unrest—a disorder,—then the objective is not so evident. As shown in Figure 4-3, if the cause of the disorder is unknown *(a)*, then the research objective would usually be to identify that cause.

Using the McDonald's example again, the research objective would be: "Determine the reason sales are down 25 percent in Store #962."

If the cause of the disorder is known *(b)*, the research objective then becomes: "Determine alternative methods for handling

Figure 4-3   Identifying Research Objectives

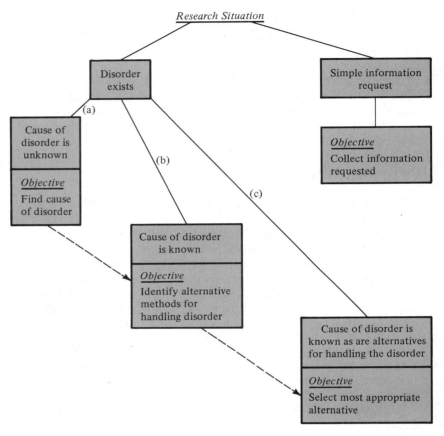

the disorder." Assume the decline in sales of the McDonald's out-
let was directly related to the opening of a Wendy's in the vicinity. The research task then seemingly would be to identify ways
of dealing with this new competitive situation.

Finally, if the cause of the disorder is known and alternative
ways of dealing with the cause are also known, then the objective
of the research is to determine the most appropriate alternative
(c).

Carrying the McDonald's example one step further, the manager has identified three possible ways of improving the store's
sales, but doesn't know which one should be implemented. The
objective of the research then becomes: "Identify the most effective promotion program for Store #962."

Figure 4-3 also indicates that in some research projects there
can be multiple objectives.

1. Identify the cause of the sales decline.
2. Identify alternative ways to overcome this sales decline.
3. Select the most appropriate alternative.

In some research projects the objective involves the investigation of the entire disorder or stated problem. In other projects the recognized disorder is so broad or complex that the researcher can only deal with a portion of it.

Objective must be manageable

Research where objective deals with entire disorder

Assume a researcher sees the poor sales performance of one of a firm's products (e.g., a fire alarm buzzer for homes) and identifies the disorder as "An unexplained decline in sales of our fire alarms over the last three months." In light of this designated disorder the researcher lists two objectives: (1) determine the causes for the unit sales decline and (2) identify alternative methods for rectifying the situation. Because this disorder was quite specific, the objective of the study was to deal with all aspects of it.

Research where objective deals with only a portion of disorder

In many actual research situations the recognized disorder is so broad that a single study can deal with only a portion of it due to limited time and resources. Assume that the major disorder facing Colorado carnation growers is that they don't really understand how to effectively reach mass markets with their products. They hire a researcher to evaluate various ways of mass-marketing their carnations. This task is of such a scope that it can't be handled realistically in one study. Realizing this, the researcher will only pursue certain facets of this total assignment.

The objective might be to "determine the impact of age and income on the flower-buying activities of consumers." The results from such a study certainly would not handle the disorder. What it would do, though, is provide some of the basic information needed to identify the consumer segments that comprise the market for cut flowers. With this information, another study might be undertaken with the objectives of finding the most effective method of reaching the different market segments identified in the previous study. Thus, this objective dealt with only a portion of the disorder originally posed to the researcher.

In summary, then, the specific direction or goal of any research undertaking is found in the statement of that study's objectives. The objectives, in turn, flow from the overall disorder identified by the researcher. In many research projects, the stated disorder is so broad that a single study can only deal with a portion of it.

Example: In the previous advertising example the disorder was a lack of information on the effectiveness of humorous television ads. In light of this stated condition, the objective of the study became: "Determine the Effectiveness of Humorous Television Ads in the Sales of Deodorants." Note that the researcher has further defined the scope of the study by limiting it to television ads involving just one type of product — deodorants. This is a manageable subject.

The researcher also must define the key words in the statement of objectives. The researcher intends "more effective" to mean increased sales and increased memorability or retention of the ad's message. The necessity of pinning down such terms will become evident in the next section on hypotheses.

Development of hypotheses

The final step in choosing the direction of the research is to develop working hypotheses. Their acceptance or rejection enables the researcher to accomplish the project's objectives. Hypotheses add greater specificity to the research. They can take two forms: (1) declarative statements that the researcher sets out to accept or reject on the basis of the data collected in the formal study; or (2) alternative courses of action that the researcher investigates, intending to select the most appropriate one in light of the data collected.

Hypotheses as declarative statements

Some examples of the first type of hypotheses as they apply to the TV advertising study are the following:

1. Humorous deodorant ads on television result in a significantly greater sales response than do nonhumorous deodorant ads.
2. Viewers retain the message in humorous deodorant ads for a significantly longer period than they do for nonhumorous deodorant ads.

Remember that the objective of the study was to determine the effectiveness of humorous ads. "Effective" was interpreted as increased sales and longer retention of the ad's message. The preceding hypotheses are tied directly to this interpretation.

The words "significantly greater," or stating the difference in actual figures (i.e., will increase by at least 15 percent), provide the researcher with a meaningful basis on which to accept or reject each hypothesis. A hypothesis such as "Humorous ads will increase sales" is useless since an increase of only one unit would necessitate its acceptance, a gesture that would be of little help in accomplishing the study's objective.

Statistical techniques such as Z tests, chi-square, and analysis of variance can be used to test whether "significant" differences do exist. These techniques are discussed in later chapters dealing with ways to analyze the collected data.

Hypotheses as alternatives courses of action

Hypotheses might also be stated as alternative solutions or courses of action. For example, assume the project involves a bank in Des Moines, Iowa. The objective of the study is to determine the most profitable way to use the excess capacity of the bank's computer. The listed hypotheses could be alternative courses of action.

- *Hypothesis One*: The excess capacity should be used by leasing time to smaller banks in surrounding communities.
- *Hypothesis Two*: The excess capacity should be used by leasing time to some of the smaller business firms in Des Moines.
- *Hypothesis Three*: The excess capacity should be used by leasing time to the Des Moines school system.

The researcher would investigate each alternative, eventually selecting the most appropriate one. Gathering information to accept or reject these various statements accomplishes the study's objectives—determining the most profitable way to use the computer's excess capacity.

Are hypotheses necessary?

Not all research projects require formal hypotheses. In deciding whether to include them, the researcher must decide whether their acceptance or rejection will aid in accomplishing the study's objective. For instance, the purpose of most fact gathering studies is spelled out in precise terms and is usually so narrow in scope that it is not necessary to develop hypotheses for them. Of what value are hypotheses for a study intended to determine the number of people listening to radio station WGN between 6 A.M. and 8 A.M.?

Some problem solving research may also be fairly precise, so establishing formal hypotheses would add little to the clarity of their findings. On the other hand, most basic research projects should include working hypothesis to give greater credence to their findings.

Identifying information needed

A list of the precise types of information needed to accomplish the study's objectives and test its hypotheses should now be developed. The placement of this step in this part of the procedural model, however, is somewhat misleading. The implication in Figure 4-1 is that identifying the actual information needed begins only after the objectives and hypotheses have been chosen. Actually, the activity of identifying the information needed begins in the funneling process and continues throughout all the early stages of the research project. But the identification of the specific information needed to accomplish the project's objectives can come only after these objectives and their accompanying hypotheses have been selected.

Selecting the study's direction using the advertising example

All of the suggested procedures of this chapter are now tied together via the advertising example. It was assumed the investigator was involved with a basic research project. A subject was chosen (advertising) in which the researcher had background and interest.

The subject of advertising was too broad so it was necessary to funnel it down to a more manageable level (humorous ads). A situation analysis was carried out in this newly defined area to strengthen the researcher's background on the subject and to aid in narrowing it down still further. It was then decided to concentrate on television commercials.

A preliminary investigation was conducted into this newly defined subject by gathering limited secondary data and talking informally with people knowledgeable in the field. This background enabled the researcher to recognize a problem worth pursuing—the lack of information on the effectiveness of humorous television ads. In light of this recognized disorder, the specific objective of the study was defined as "Determine the Effectiveness of Humorous TV Ads in Selling Deodorants." Hypotheses were then established, the acceptance or rejection of which would enable the stated objectives to be accomplished.

With the construction of working hypotheses and an identification of the information needed, the specific direction for the study has been set. The researcher is now ready to proceed with the formal investigation.

Certain conditions are essential in establishing the study's direction.

- The study must have specific direction or the researcher will waste a great deal of time, energy, and money.
- The difficulty in choosing the study's direction varies with the nature of the study. The direction of fact gathering projects is immediately evident, but selecting the specific direction of problem solving or basic research projects can be quite complicated.
- The identification of the disorder (problem) is the first step in setting the scope of the study. A disorder is an unsettled condition needing a solution. It may be necessary to go through a rather lengthy funneling process in order to uncover the central issue.
- The objective of the study describes its specific purpose. It is based on and flows from the identified disorder. The objective might deal with the entire disorder, or only with limited portions of it.
- Hypotheses can be either declarative statements or stated alternative courses of action. They are constructed around the study's objectives. Their eventual acceptance or rejection enable the study's objectives to be accomplished.

SUMMARY

---

1. Why does so little marketing research fall into the category of basic research? What would be an example of basic research in marketing?
2. Explain the funneling process.
3. Why must the disorder or problem condition be identified before the study's objectives are chosen?
4. What is the difference between a situation analysis and a preliminary investigation?
5. What contribution do hypotheses make to a study? Are they always needed?

QUESTIONS AND EXERCISES

6. What is the difference between a problem and a symptom? Give some examples.

7. Why don't we "prove" hypotheses in business?

CASES

Case 1

In the fall of 1979 the president of Prill Press decided to investigate the possibility of distributing its novels through supermarkets and super drugstores.

Although drugstores and supermarkets had long been a channel of distribution for magazines and paperbound books, to date hardcover novels had not been marketed through these outlets. In defending his selection of these channels for novels, the editor pointed out the following facts:

a. Fewer than 20,000 sales will put a book on the bestseller list.

b. There are only about 2,500 bookstores in the country catering to 17 percent of adult Americans who read full-length, hardcover books.

c. There are 40,000 supermarkets and drugstores catering to 100 percent of adult Americans who eat, drink and have headaches.

The president continued, "So you can see, if we sell only one copy in each store and not one in a bookstore, we have still got a bestseller guarantee. And if we pull it off, just wait and see—every publisher in the business will be trying to get into the supermarkets."

The books' prices were usually around $9.95. Other members of the publisher's management team were enthusiastic over the new channel, pointing out that the average bookstore demands 50 percent margin whereas the supermarket operates on an average of 19 percent of sales. They felt that this lower margin demand by the supermarkets would relieve some of their cost pressures. The cost of publishing books has constantly been rising, but the retail prices obtained for them have remained relatively stable.

It was decided to use an outside research firm to carry out a study. You are the project director of that outside firm and have to prepare a proposal.

a. Identify the disorder or problem condition.

b. Identify the general types of information needed.

[Handwritten margin notes:]

a) Problem: Whether or not hardcovers can be sold in a supermarket.

b) 1) store attitude
2) cust. attitude
3) distribution costs
4) bookstore reaction
5) distribution channels

c. Develop the study's objectives.

d. Develop some hypotheses associated with these objectives.

The higher prices for gasoline, maintenance of delivery equipment, and employee salaries have intensified a problem that has been with retail florists for years — how should they handle the expenses associated with delivering their merchandise? At present some florists charge a nominal fee ($0.50 to $1.50) for any deliveries they make, while other florists cover delivery costs by just providing fewer flowers in those purchases that must be delivered. Still other florists feel that since they describe themselves as "full service" retailers, they should include delivery as part of their services and absorb this expense in the markup they place on their merchandise. Since most florists belong to a wire agency — FTD, Teleflora, or Florafax — there has to be some agreement among them as a group, so that when flowers are sold by telephone there will be no confusion on whether or not a $10 wire order, for example, includes delivery expenses.

Case 2

Problem: Florists don't know how to handle expenses incurred in delivery.

The Society of American Florists comes to your research firm for help. They ask you to develop a research proposal on the subject. The first steps of such a proposal are to:

a. Identify the general disorder or problem condition.

b. Establish the general types of information needed to deal with the disorder.

c. Establish the specific objectives of your study.

You have been approached by the editor of *Gentlemen Today*, a fashion magazine, to carry out a research study. The magazine has been unsuccessful in attracting shoe manufacturers as advertisers. When it has tried to secure advertising from these manufacturers, it has been told that men's clothing stores are a small and dying segment of the men's shoe business. Since *Gentlemen Today* goes chiefly to men's clothing stores, the manufacturers reason that it is therefore not a good vehicle for their advertising.

Case 3

The editor believes that a survey (via mail questionnaire) of the men's clothing stores in the United States will show that these stores are actually important outlets for men's shoes and are not declining in importance as shoe outlets. He asks you to develop a proposal for the study and submit it to him.

a. Identify the general disorder.

b. Describe the general types of information needed.

c. Establish objectives for your study.

d. Develop some working hypotheses that will enable you to accomplish these objectives.

e. Following are some objectives and hypotheses other stuents have developed. Evaluate these. What are their weaknesses?

Possible Objectives

1. Determine that men's clothing stores are not a poor segment for men's shoes.

2. Determine that men's clothing stores have a reasonable share of the men's shoe market.

3. Determine if clothing stores like to carry men's shoes.

4. Poll clothing store salesmen and determine if they believe shoe sales are declining.

5. Establish that advertising in *Gentlemen Today* will benefit shoe manufacturers.

Possible Hypotheses

1. In over 70 percent of men's clothing stores the sale of men's shoes has remained steady or increased in the past five years and has accounted for 5 percent of the store's total assets.

2. The majority of men prefer to buy their shoes at men's clothing stores, but will buy shoes at regular stores for convenience.

3. Effective channels of distribution can (cannot) be established between shoe manufacturers and clothing stores.

4. The advertisement of men's shoes in *Gentlemen Today* will increase sales accordingly.

5

Obtaining secondary data

THE VALUE OF SECONDARY DATA

Rev. Kneeland Pew of the First Methodical Church of Condo Canyon, Colorado, recently discovered the value of obtaining and using secondary data. "My Sunday messages were being greeted with yawns and nodding-off by my congregants. Somehow I'd gained the impression that my flock was composed of young singles in the 18-to-35 age segment, so I would lecture them sternly on avoiding excess of the flesh.

"Be fruitful and multiply, I told them. But as I looked down from my pulpit, I saw not a single child. I was perplexed and sorely afflicted until I commissioned Theo-Graphics of Tulsa, Oklahoma, to analyze the census tracts from which I drew my parishioners. Theo-Graphics came back with the surprising information that there was not a living soul under the age of 75 in my market area. I dashed back to the rectory to change the theme of my next sermon from 'Go to Heaven and Not to Pot' to 'How to Find Peace of Mind in Your Golden Years.' "

This example demonstrates the value of good secondary data. If you are thinking of opening a chain of liquor stores in Saudi Arabia, go ahead and do it. Statistics show that less than 1 percent of Saudi households reported buying a bottle of liquor in 1979. There is obviously an unfulfilled consumer need.

But, if you are thinking about a cross-country ski center in Death Valley, erase that thought: the population density is just too low.

(Condensed from American Demographics, *June 1980, p. 48.)*

Once the specific objectives of the research project have been identified, the researcher must decide how and where to obtain the information needed to accomplish these objectives. Likewise, data must be acquired to accept or reject any hypotheses that might have been established. This will involve either primary or secondary data since these two encompass all the various types of information the researcher might actually use or desire to use.

PRIMARY AND SECONDARY DATA

Primary data originate with the specific research undertaking. Secondary data are data that have been gathered for some other purpose but are applicable to the study.

Too often people distinguish between these two types of data on the basis of the gathering party. If I gather the data, they are primary data. If someone else gathers the data, they are secondary data. This is an erroneous interpretation as the following example will show. In 1975 John Jones studied the effect of point-of-purchase advertising on the sale of grocery items in selected food stores. In 1980 he did a study on location of end-displays in supermarkets and included some of the findings from his 1975 study on point-of-purchase advertising. The 1975 data were secondary data since they were gathered for some other purpose and did not originate with the 1980 study.

Conversely, if a research firm was hired to obtain consumer attitude data on a new package design, these would be primary data since they originated with the particular study. Thus, origin of data, not who gathered them, is the factor that distinguishes secondary data from primary data.

Although no precise figures can be cited, it is this author's strong belief that the vast majority of business research projects can be at least partially satisfied with secondary data. For that reason, the search for information should begin among secondary sources and only when such sources have been exhausted should primary data be sought.

TWO TYPES OF SECONDARY DATA

The amount and variety of secondary data facing the business researcher tax the imagination. A person familiar with an average city or college library has been exposed to only a minute portion of the total information available. Certainly only a small portion of existing secondary data will be useful in any one project, but the researcher should know where to seek pertinent information and be familiar with procedures that will save time in such a search.

To enable a more lucid presentation of the material, secondary data will be categorized on the basis of either the gathering or distributing source. In terms of individual firms, the starting point would be separating secondary data into either *internal* or *external* data.

Internal data

Internal secondary data are compiled by a firm in its normal business operations. Information such as sales results, advertising expenditures, salesmen's reports, credit reports, inventory records, transportation costs, and raw material costs are just a few examples of the internal data available.

In most firms the internal data are gathered in such an unorganized manner that there is little knowledge among that firm's own departments as to the actual types of information being compiled. This confusion has led many researchers to go outside the firm for data already existing within the company. For example, Company X manufactures metal casters. Its production department wanted to know who its chief competitors were, so questionnaires were sent to a variety of potential customers asking them about the products they were now using. The production people weren't aware that their own salesmen were keeping files on customers and potential customers indicating the brand of caster each was presently using or had used for the past three years. This lack of communication between departments is the rule rather than the exception.

Almost as great a sin as not knowing what information exists in the firm is passing up opportunities to obtain additional potentially useful information. Many firms could structure their sales receipts so that more specific information about the buyer of the product could be obtained. Accounting records could be structured in such a way that expenses and revenues could be more accurately assigned to products, salesmen, and territories.

There is growing awareness among firms that greater interdepartmental cooperation is needed in order to get maximum benefits from internal data. This realization has led to the development in some firms of formal "information systems." Since these systems were already discussed in Chapter 2, only a brief reference will be made to them in this chapter.

Information systems

An information system was previously described as an organized system of people and equipment designed to provide the orderly collection and dispersion of information obtained from both internal and external sources. Ideally such a system would be similar to an intelligence center that accumulates and generates all data (secondary and primary) of potential use to the firm's decision makers (see Figure 5-1).

Ideal Relationship Between Information System and Data Sources

Figure 5-1

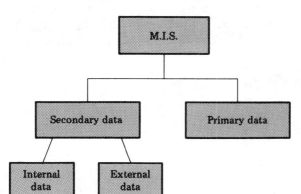

Most firms claiming they have an information system are really talking about a low-level system in which their managers regularly receive computer printouts of the firm's sales and production records. Figure 5-2 is a more realistic depiction of the typical usage of information systems within firms.

For many firms information systems are still in the idea stage. Many administrators view such systems as having potential value but feel their firms don't have the funds, facilities, or personnel to set one up. It is safe to assume, though, that the number of firms developing information systems will grow at a rapid pace in the future. This growth will be linked to the increased and more sophisticated usage of computers by firms.

Additional information pertaining to the future role of the M.I.S. is provided in Chapter 16.

External data

This type of data comes from myriad sources outside the firm. In fact, the number of external sources is almost mind boggling. In 1975 more than 40,000 books were published in the United States, 90 percent of which were nonfiction. There are over 55,000 periodicals presently published throughout the world. *The Monthly Catalog of U.S. Government Publications* has almost

32,000 listings annually, which are only a fraction of the total government output.[1]

Figure 5-2   **Typical Relationship Between Information System and Data Sources**

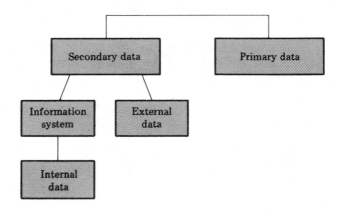

The various types of external data are so numerous that to effectively use them, a researcher must be a skilled user of indexes, abstracts, and directories. If such skill is lacking, much time will be wasted in information searches, and a great deal of secondary information will never be found. Figure 5-3 illustrates the role of the "aids" to the person seeking external data.

The various types of external business data can be divided into categories based on the agency or firm providing the data. These categories are: (1) government sources, (2) commercial sources, (3) inter- or intra-industry sources, and (4) a catch-all category covering sources not found under (1), (2), or (3). Before looking at each of these four categories some guidelines for searching for the desired data will be presented.

SEARCHING FOR EXTERNAL DATA

Search procedures depend upon the general nature of the data sought. In those situations where specific data are needed, the search may be rather narrow and short lived. For instance, you may just want information on the number of florists in the state

---

[1]Emory, C. Williams, *Business Research Methods* (Homewood, Ill.: Richard D. Irwin, Inc., 1976), p. 178.

of New York with annual sales in excess of $100,000. If you know the specific data source, you can go directly to it. In this case the Census of Retail Trade will give the desired information; thus the search ends.

In many cases the researcher will not be aware of a specific information source, so some type of organized search procedure must be initiated. A pet food manufacturer may want to know how many dogs there are in the Rocky Mountain region, or a producer of plastic wrap might desire an extensive study on packaging in the meat packing industry.

When gathering information, it is important to systematically use indices, abstracts, directories, and other available guides. The major difference between an abstract and an index is that abstracts present the basic contents of a publication in capsule form whereas indexes present only minimum data about the publication—author, publisher, date of publication, etc. Directories will be discussed separately in a later section.

Systematic use of 'aids'

Secondary Sources of Business Information

Figure 5-3

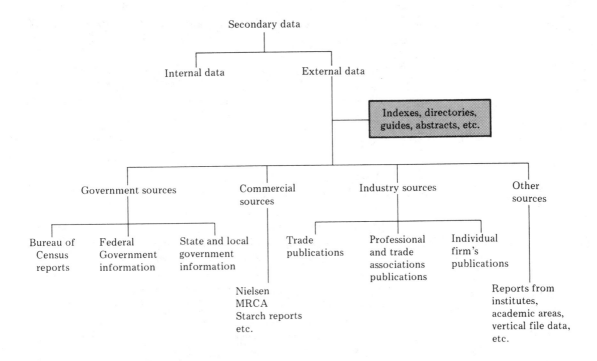

The starting point is to properly identify the topic about which you are seeking information. The researcher should list all the possible categories or headings under which the topic might be discussed by other researchers or authors. If the topic is defined too narrowly and information is perused only on a single subject, a lot of useful information may be forfeited. For example, a researcher seeking information on dog food should be aware that there will be data pertaining to that subject in articles under such topics as "pet food," "pets — feeding of," "meat by-products," or even "animal feeds."

The broader the vantage point taken by the researcher when seeking secondary data, the better the chances of covering all possible data sources. It is important to have a number of these possible subject headings in mind prior to the information search so that you won't have to be constantly returning to these references because a new subject heading has been identified.

Once these headings have been established, attention can be turned to "aids" that will direct the researcher toward the desired information. The first step is to determine whether a bibliography on the subject already exists. Thus, the publication, *Bibliographies Index: A Cumulative Bibliography of Bibliographies*, published by the H. W. Wilson Co., New York, should be consulted. This lists various books, periodicals, and other publications pertaining to identified subjects. If the desired subject heading is listed in that book, a large bibliography has been identified.

If the subject is somewhat unique, a bibliography probably will not already exist, so one must be developed. Different "aids" are available for constructing such a list from books, periodicals, newspapers, and government publications.

Aids for books

Researchers seeking secondary data from books can use these aids to find the ones most appropriate to their needs.

1. *Card Catalog.* This is a file kept by the library on its offerings and should be the starting point for most library research. Most card catalog systems present information on books in at least two ways: an *author-title* section for those seeking a particular book or the works of a particular author; a *subject* section for those researchers seeking information on a specific subject but possessing little or no information on the titles or authors of books on that subject. If the researcher is uncertain which is the proper

subject heading to use, a special reference exists that identifies the headings used in any catalog following the Library of Congress system. That reference is entitled "Subject Headings Used in the Dictionary Catalog of the Library of Congress," 8th edition, 1975 and should be available in each library or may be obtained from the Government Printing Office.

2. *Publishers Weekly*. A journal for the book trade that gives a complete record of American books published during given weeks and includes brief descriptions of the subject matter of each book.

3. *Book Review Index*. Published monthly by Gale Research Company in Detroit. It provides an index of book reviews that have appeared in hundreds of periodicals and annually covers over 8,000 books.

4. *Cumulative Book Index*. Monthly index by subject of books published throughout the world. Books are also listed by author and title.

5. *Economic Abstracts*. This is a semi-monthly review of abstracts of books and reports on economics, finance, management, real estate, etc.

6. Book review sections in journals, such as the *Journal of Marketing, Journal of Business, Journal of Marketing Research*, and *Journal of Consumer Research*, all provide lists of recent books that might contain useful information.

Aids for periodicals

The large number of existing periodicals and the wide variety of articles force researchers to rely heavily on indexes in the search for appropriate data. Most of these indexes are found in the reference areas of libraries.

1. *Business Periodicals Index*. Lists articles by subject headings from approximately 150 business-oriented periodicals. *Forbes, Business Week, Fortune, Harvard Business Review, Management Review, Industrial Marketing*, and the *Journal of Business* are just a few of the magazines indexed in this aid.

2. *Predicast F and S Index of Corporations and Industries*. Provides information about companies, industries, and products from over 750 financial publications, business-oriented newspapers, trade magazines, and special

reports. It is the most detailed index available on business-related subjects and is updated quarterly. The information is arranged by numerical industry and product codes and also by company name.

3. *Reader's Guide to Periodical Literature.* Indexes articles from magazines of a more general nature: *Newsweek, Time, Saturday Review, U.S. News and World Report.*

4. *Applied Science and Technology Index.* An index of approximately 200 periodicals from the fields of automation, chemistry, engineering, and physics, as well as other technical fields frequently researched for business purposes.

5. *Ulrich's Periodical Directory.* Covers over 20,000 current foreign and domestic periodicals. It is published by R. R. Bowker Company in New York.

6. *Public Affairs Information Services Bulletin* (PAIS). Another index of value to business researchers. It overlaps somewhat with the *Business Periodicals Index,* but it includes more foreign publications. It also indexes by subject many books, government publications, and even many nonperiodical publications.

Aids for newspapers and business news

Quite often there are articles appearing in newspapers or business publications that could pertain to the research project. Indexes for these publications are available in most libraries.

1. *Wall Street Journal Index.* A monthly index of articles that have appeared in this national business paper. Corporate news is listed alphabetically by firm name, and general news is listed by subject.

2. *New York Times Index.* A semi-monthly index which gives entries by subject and gives brief notes about the contents of these entries.

3. *Predicast F & S Index of Corporations and Industries.* Mentioned in the previous section, this also lists newspaper stories about products or companies.

Aids for government information

The Department of Commerce maintains excellent reference libraries in field offices located in 35 major U.S. cities. The Small Business Administration also maintains field offices in 54 cities. Following are some aids for use of government data.

1. *Monthly Catalog of U.S. Government Publications.* A monthly list of all federal publications published by the U.S. Superintendent of Documents. This aid is probably the most useful tool available for identifying government publications. Throughout the country are libraries designated as "depository libraries." These libraries hold a collection of the major government documents. A list of these depository libraries is given in the annual September issue of the catalog, but even these libraries will not have every publication earmarked for depositories. (A heavy black dot placed next to an entry in the *Catalog* identifies those items available at depository libraries.)

2. *Monthly Checklist of State Publications.* Records those state documents received by the Library of Congress.

3. *Government Statistics for Business Use.* Hansen and Leonard's book provides a great deal of information about the sources of federal information.

4. *Guide to U.S. Government Publications.* A book by John Andriot (McLean, Va.: Documents Index, 1970) that provides access to U.S. government periodicals by issuing agency, title, or document number.

Miscellaneous aids

1. *American Doctoral Dissertation Index and Dissertation Abstracts.* A service of the Microfilm Library Service, Ann Arbor, Michigan, it contains abstracts of many of the dissertations written by Ph.D. candidates. A lot of valuable information is found here; and much of it has never been disseminated to the general public.

2. *Index of University Publications of Bureaus of Business and Economic Research.* This publication from the Bureau of Business Research at the University of Oregon lists the articles and papers published by the various bureaus of business research found on the campuses of many universities.

Directories as aids

Directories serve a dual role. Some are guides to information on available services, associations, and specialists. Others operate as marketing tools in that they identify groups of prospective customers by giving company names and addresses, analyses of company operations, and detailed information about a firm's product.

1. *Standard and Poor's Register of Corporations, Directors and Executives.* An annual directory of manufacturers and suppliers in which firms are classified by products and arranged geographically. It also lists the firm's products, address, and capital ratings.

2. Two Dun and Bradstreet publications. (1) *Middle Market Directory*, an annual directory listing approximately 33,000 U.S. companies with indicated worth of $500,000 to $999,999. It lists key company personnel, Standard Industrial Classification System (SIC) data on company, sales and number of employees. (2) *Million Dollar Directory*, similar to the above directory except that it provides information on 31,000 U.S. companies with an indicated worth of over $1 million.

3. *Moody's Manual of Investments.* Published by Moody's Investors Service, Inc., in New York, this aid contains historical and operational data on selected firms as well as five years of their income accounts, balance sheets, and dividend records.

4. *Directory of University Research Bureaus and Institutes.* Some 1,300 organizations that are set up on a permanent basis and carry on continuing research programs are classified according to 16 broad functional areas.

5. *Ayer Directory of Publications.* List of American newspapers and periodicals arranged by state and city. It also has an alphabetical list of trade, technical, and professional journals. Useful to identify trade publications for product categories—pet foods, dry cleaners, etc.

6. *Encyclopedia of Associations.* Published by Gale Research, this publication provides information on the size of associations, their officers, and their publications.

Aids for obtaining statistics

Numerous firms and agencies publish statistics. The problem the researcher faces is identifying the types of statistics available and finding the publications containing them. Following are some sources that can help locate various sets of statistics.

1. *American Statistics Index.* Published by the Congressional Information Service, it is a comprehensive guide

and index to the statistical publications of the U.S. government.

2. *Statistics Sources*. This is a monthly publication of Gale Research that identifies sources of statistical data from government, business, and international sources.

3. *Guide to U.S. Government Statistics*. This book by John Andriot (Arlington, Va.: Documents Index, 1973) may be used to find a description of all statistical publications of the U.S. Government.

4. *Statistical Abstract of the United States*. Published annually by the Government Printing Office, this is the best single source of government statistics. It provides statistics on a wide variety of social, industrial, and political subjects. It should be in the personal library of every business researcher and is one of the first sources to consult when business-related statistics are needed. *The County and City Data Book* is a supplement of the *Abstract* and provides 196 statistical items for counties, cities, and standard metropolitan areas.

5. *Survey of Current Business*. Published monthly by the Department of Commerce, this publication provides a comprehensive summary on some 2,600 different statistical series covering such topics as general business indicators, real estate activity, and income and employment by industry.

6. *A Graphic Guide to Consumer Markets*. Published annually by the National Industrial Conference Board. Contains six categories of statistics: population, income, expenditures, market advertising, prices, and production.

7. *Sales Management Survey of Buying Power*. This annual publication of *Sales Management* magazine contains valuable data on markets broken down by state, county, and standard metropolitan area. Statistics are provided on population, retail sales of a variety of categories, and household incomes. This special publication also combines these data to develop a "Buying Power Index" for each geographic area.

Computerized search systems

The tremendous variety of secondary data poses a search problem for even the most highly trained information specialist.

Therefore, the recent availability of computerized searching systems has enabled information sources to be retrieved in a more efficient manner. Such computerized searches are available from several government agencies as well as from private commercial firms. The private firms generally lease or buy groups of data bases containing bibliographic references filed on magnetic tapes. Each data base stores thousands of citations, which contain the title, author, publisher, and in some cases even an abstract of the work.

Bibliographies are usually accessed through certain key words that identify the types of information desired. For example, assume the subject area to be researched is "Supervisory problems associated with flexible work schedules with the computer industry."

The *key words* that would be used in the search could be: supervisory, supervisor, supervision, flextime, staggered hours, flexible hours, computer industry.

The total cost for the above search would be $25 to $35 and would likely result in 30-35 printed citations. At present there are a number of commercial information retrieval firms in the United States and their names can be obtained from the Information Industry Association in Washington, D.C.

Human 'aids'

Key "aids" to anyone searching for secondary data are the reference librarians. They are knowledgeable about their libraries' resources, and if a specialist is available (business/economics), he/she can provide the researcher with a number of new sources. In fact, because of their potential contribution, these specialists should be sought out immediately after the list of potential subject headings has been developed.

TYPES AND SOURCES OF SECONDARY INFORMATION

The preceding section dealt with the aids to use in searching for data. This section describes the actual types of secondary information available to business. As indicated in Figure 5-3, these data can best be presented by separating them into four categories based on the source providing the data.

Government sources

In terms of pure volume, no one agency circulates as much data as the federal government. A wide variety of useful data also comes from state and local governments. Following are examples of some of the most widely used government publications.

Bureau of Census reports

The Bureau of the Census is a general purpose statistical agency whose primary function is to collect, process, compile, and disseminate statistical data for use by the general public and government agencies.

The bureau is a federal agency operating under the Department of Commerce. In addition to the eight major census studies, the bureau also carries out special censuses for local governments seeking more up-to-date population figures, prepares the *Statistical Abstract of the United States*, and publishes *County Business Patterns*, which is derived from employment and payroll information reported to the Social Security Administration.

The census data are maintained on punch cards and computer tapes, which can be processed for cross tabulations. Many of these tapes containing nonconfidential information can be purchased from the Census Bureau. The main job of the bureau, however, is to set up and carry out the eight major census studies. Table 5-1 shows the titles of these studies, the frequency with which they are carried out, and the year of the most recent study.

Description of Eight Census Studies　　　　**Table 5-1**

Census Title	Frequency of Study (years)	Last Census	Next Census
Population	10	1980	1990
Housing	10	1980	1990
Agriculture	5	1979	1984
Business	5	1982	1987
Manufacturers	5	1982	1987
Mineral Industries	5	1982	1987
Transportation	5	1982	1987
Governments	5	1982	1987

The actual techniques used in collecting census data are quite complicated and vary with each of the eight studies. The bureau hires and trains the interviewers and also runs sampling checks to verify the information being collected. Each respondent (individual or firm) is guaranteed that his/her replies will be kept confidential. A brief description of the key data contained in each census follows.

Census of Population: This study provides a vast amount of detailed information on the population makeup of states, counties, cities, and towns. The 1980 census counted inhabitants of every locality and obtained information on age, sex, race, citizenship, education, family composition, occupation, and income.

The much criticized 1980 Census of Population cost in excess of $1 billion—more than four times the cost of the 1970 Census ($248 million). The Bureau of the Census sent out 86 million questionnaires in 1980, and used more than 270,000 full-time and temporary workers to gather and analyze the data.

Census of Housing: Dealing with the characteristics of the nation's housing and made in conjunction with the Census of Population, the Census of Housing covers type of housing unit, value of property, size of mortgage, even type of heating and number of bathrooms in the units. For cities of 50,000 and over, these data are available by individual blocks.

Census of Agriculture: The Bureau of the Census and the Department of Agriculture combine efforts for the collection of these statistics. Information is obtained on such topics as farm ownership, number of acres, crops harvested, number and type of livestock, equipment, and facilities. This information is broken down to the county level.

Census of Business: This census covers three segments of business establishments—retail trade, wholesale trade, and selected services. The statistics pertain to nature of the business, location, dollar sales, payroll information, legal form of organization, etc. In addition to this general information, specialized data relating to each of the three segments also are collected. Retailers are classified into groups according to the nature of their businesses, and data on their total sales by merchandise lines and leased departments are available. Wholesalers are classified by the nature of their facilities and equipment and their sales receipts, as well as information on other aspects of their businesses.

Census of Manufacturers: Included here is information about all manufacturing establishments with one or more paid employees. These data provide benchmarks for many of the bureau's other statistical programs. The study covers approximately 450 industries and 6,500 commodities in terms of the value and quantity of individual products shipped, employment and payroll dollar volume, and expenditures for plant and equipment.

Census of Mineral Industries: Covering a wide variety of minerals including fuels, metallic ores, sand and gravel, and stone and clay, information such as capital expenditures, man hours, value added in mining, and quantity and value of individual products is provided.

Census of Transportation: The newest of the census studies, it was first conducted in 1963 and is really a series of four surveys. These surveys cover passenger transportation, truck inventory and usage, commodity transportation, and motor carriers. Each survey gives in-depth statistics on the movement of people and products throughout the United States.

Census of Governments: The basic purpose of this study is to identify and list all governmental units in the United States. The information collected includes such topics as the number and type of government, value of property owned, revenues, expenditures, and size and payroll of their work forces.

Because of the length of time between census studies (5 to 10 years), the bureau publishes updated census reports. For example, in conjunction with the *Census of Business*, more timely but less detailed information is collected by surveying a small sample of retail, wholesale, and selected service operations. These survey findings are released in a series of weekly, monthly, quarterly, and annual reports. Similar studies are carried out in the other census areas and result in such publications as *Annual Survey of Manufacturers, Current Industrial Reports,* and *Current Population Reports.* Anyone seeking updated census data should use the *Monthly Catalog of U.S. Government Publications* to determine which studies have been performed.

The major shortcoming of census data is the length of time between data collection and release of the information. It was almost 30 months after its collection before most of the information from the 1977 Census of Business was made available to the general public. By the time it is released, much of the data is already dated.

Additional federal government information

Various federal government agencies such as the Departments of the Interior and Health and Human Services also provide reports containing information of possible use to marketing researchers. The Department of Agriculture is especially prolific in the amount of reports it provides. Since this department does a lot of work involving the growing, canning, preparation, and even display of food products, it provides a wealth of information for food processors, wholesalers, and food retailers. Once again, the old reliable—*The Monthly Catalog of U.S. Government Publications*—is the best source to use in tracking down these government publications.

Information coming from state and local government agencies

The majority of this information is really "registration data." These are data collected as part of legal requirements—records on births, deaths, marriages, sales tax payments, auto registrations, new home starts, property improvements, etc. These data are collected on the local level and then passed on to state agencies where they are accumulated and published in a statistical summary for the state.

The County Recorder's Office, the Motor Vehicle Office, the County Planning Office, as well as their municipal counterparts, are the main sources of the registration data useful to business. For example, the Motor Vehicle Division has information on the number and make of new cars sold every week within the city as well as the transfer of ownership of secondhand cars. This is information of interest to banks, loan agencies, and car dealers.

In addition to registration data, state and local agencies compile useful data needed for their everyday operations. The City Engineering Office, in its studies of traffic lights and stop signs, collects information on the traffic flow past various locations. This information is useful to firms selecting new plant or business sites.

Certain state and city commissions, as well as Chambers of Commerce, also publish information sheets wherein they proclaim their virtues and give reasons why people or industries should choose a particular locale. While much of this descriptive information is quite biased, these reports also contain a great deal of useful statistics on schools, population, average temperatures, etc., and thus can be of use to researchers.

There are two publications that provide examples of ways in which government statistics can be acquired and used by business firms: *A Handbook for Business on the Use of Government Statistics* prepared by Eleanor May, 1979 and available through the Taylor Murphy Institute at the University of Virginia; *Measuring Markets: A Guide to the Use of Federal and State Statistical Data*, prepared by the Department of Commerce and sold through the Government Printing Office.

Little known sources for specialized information

In addition to the well-known information aids and reports listed in the previous sections, researchers can glean more specialized data from the following Washington D.C., sources.[2]

Information from Capitol Hill: This information monitors federal legislation and provides data to firms investigating an industry, a competitor, or a product. The Bill Status Office can pro-

---

[2]The information in this section is condensed from a presentation by Matthew Lesko, "Pinpointing Washington Information," Business Proceedings Series #42, American Marketing Association, Spring 1978, pp. 81–85.

vide information on any bills in the present or recent past sessions of Congress on a particular topic. If the topic is currently being considered, the Bill Status Office can obtain a copy of the bill and all the testimony surrounding it. Furthermore, over the years Congress has held investigations on almost every subject area. At the conclusion of hearings, documents of all relevant source data and expert testimony can be obtained from the Government Printing Office.

Information on Competitors: Many people believe the best source of information on a firm is a Dun & Bradstreet report. Besides being expensive, these reports can be of questionable accuracy since much of the background information is provided by the firm's executives.

Therefore, the best information on corporations can be found in the legal documents corporations are required to file at federal and state offices. Following are the major sources of such data.

Securities and Exchange Commission — Has information on all companies whose stock is publicly traded. Corporations must file both annual and quarterly reports. The drawback is that while there are 1.9 million corporations in the U.S., only 10,000 are required to file with the SEC.

State corporation filings — These documents cover the remainder of the 1.9 million firms not covered by the SEC. They are found in each state in which the firm does business and include complete balance sheets and profit and loss statements. The data can be obtained through the secretary of state in each state.

Federal and state regulation — Other agencies, e.g., Civil Aeronautics Board, Interstate Commerce Commission, Housing and Urban Development, require certain firms to file financial reports. Complete financial statements on tax exempt firms can be obtained from the U.S. Internal Revenue Service.

International information: The Department of Commerce provides a wide variety of information on market conditions in foreign countries. Its services range from mailing lists on overseas companies to providing free export promotion aid. The types of data and the specific sources in the Department of Commerce are too numerous to list in this section.

Commercial sources

A business firm can either use its own personnel to obtain the desired data or it can turn to outside agencies that gather information for a fee. In 1975 there were over 1,000 such private research firms operating throughout the United States. Most were marketing-oriented operations. The data emanating from these agencies can be either secondary or primary data, depending upon the nature of the undertaking. The following two examples will illustrate the difference.

Firm X has developed a new type of shaving lather. Before it starts production, the firm wants to obtain consumer reaction to the product. It hires Acme Research to conduct test markets and consumer interviews in selected cities. This research undertaking was specifically designed for Firm X. Thus, the information obtained originated with this study and is really primary data.

Firm Y has a wide variety of products on the market and it subscribes to the A. C. Nielsen Retail Index to keep tabs on how well its products and those of its competitors are doing in various markets. In this case, the research firm collects information on a continuing basis for a number of clients. This information does not originate in a specific project for any one firm and is thus viewed as secondary data.

This section lists firms providing information to clients on a subscription fee basis.

A. C. Nielsen Co.

This is the largest commercial research firm in the world. Its estimated income from research in 1976 was around $174 million. Much of its revenue is obtained from two major research undertakings, a retail index and a radio-television index.

Nielsen Retail Index: A series of studies is conducted every 60 days among food stores and drug outlets. The food study covers the sale of client products in a sample of 1,300 stores throughout the United States. Nielsen employees count packages on the shelves and cases in the back room, examine delivery invoices, note cents-off deals, and record special displays, shelf prices, and other promotional activities. Only clients' products are counted, but since this involves the top 50 food producers in the country, the study includes most store offerings except produce and fresh meat. The coverage or depth of these reports varies with the fee paid by the client. Annual costs to a firm for one product category would be between $60,000 and $100,000.

Nielsen Television Index (NTI): These data are collected through an electronic device called the instantaneous audimeter. They are installed in TV sets in approximately 1,200 households in the United States. The audimeter records when the TV set is turned on, what channel it is tuned to, and when it is turned off. It is tied into a central computer and twice a day the information is transferred to the computer where it is analyzed. The results can be made available to sponsors and networks within the next 24 hours.

They also have a separate panel of 2,100 households that are monitored by a less sophisticated device attached to their TV sets (recordimeter). This group also keeps diaries identifying the age and sex of viewers watching TV at a given time. It is hoped this information is filled out by participants every 30 minutes. These results are available to clients about two weeks after the measurement period.

These sample results are then projected to the entire United States to determine each show's viewership based on percent of total households and percent of households watching TV at a given time (audience share). These results are used by networks and stations to establish advertising rates for shows. They are also used by sponsors to determine the nature of the audience for certain shows and thus guide their decisions of which shows to sponsor.

Market Research Corporation of America

This firm, better known by its initials MRCA, uses a consumer panel consisting of 7,500 families to obtain information on what, when, and where families buy. Every week the families submit detailed diaries of their purchases of such product lines as food, drugs, clothing, and household supplies.

A panel enables information on consumers that is missed in store audits to be obtained. These data show the economic levels of purchasers, their educational backgrounds, and the incidence of brand-switching. Since the composition of the panel remains fairly constant over a given year, it provides insight into consumer purchasing patterns.

MRCA provides its clients with a monthly report plus a more comprehensive quarterly summary. It charges anywhere from $25,000 to more than $60,000 per year per product class. The size of the fee depends on the frequency of product purchase and the number of competitors in a product class.

Selling Areas—Marketing Inc. (SAMI)

SAMI provides data on the movement of products to retail food stores from wholesalers, chains, and rack jobbers in 36 major market areas. It provides information every four weeks on the movement of each brand in over 400 product categories. Clients can purchase data for one or all of these product categories.

Data provided by SAMI are quite similar to that in the Nielsen Retail Index, except that SAMI covers individual markets in depth whereas Nielsen covers them through samples. On the other hand, Nielsen data pertain to the consumer purchase level while SAMI pertain to store purchases from warehouses.

Other commercial research firms

Along with Nielsen, MRCA, and SAMI, some other firms are also prominent in the commercial research field. The Audits and Survey Co., Inc., collects retail sales information using the store audit method. It uses a probability sample of business blocks in cities across the country and then audits every store within the selected blocks. About 5,300 stores are generally involved, and they represent all types of retail outlets from supermarkets to gas stations.

Pulse, Inc., interviews radio listeners across the country to obtain information on which stations they listen to and at what times. They can then develop audience profiles for stations and programs—information of great importance to sponsors or would-be sponsors.

Starch Advertisement Readership studies the readership of advertisements in general magazines, business publications, and newspapers. Approximately 100,000 readers are personally interviewed annually on ads from over 100 different publications. Those people indicating that they have read a certain issue are asked questions about the ads in that issue to determine whether they merely "noted" the ad, read a portion, or read over half of it. From this information, each ad in the publication under study is given a readership rating, which can be compared to the ratings of all other ads in the same issue.

Simmons and Associates Research is primarily involved in developing profiles of the readers of magazines. It conducts personal interviews among 15,000 households and identifies 22 demographic variables of each magazine's readers.

Other well-known research operations are Market Facts, Inc.; National Family Opinion (NFO); Burgoyne Indexes; R. L. Polk Company; and the Roper Public Opinion Research Center. The number of such commercial research firms will continue to increase in the near future since the trend among business firms is to seek more and more about less and less. Whereas in the 1950s and 1960s companies sought data about the "average American housewife," today they want to know about married women in Pennsylvanian households with incomes between $10,000 and $15,000 and with all children under age 10.

This interest in specialized information has led many firms to concentrate on rather narrow research areas. One East Coast firm specializes in conducting research on the medical market and others concentrate on teen markets or leisure markets. There are even some commercial firms specializing in the gathering of secondary data for clients. They retain a large collection of data potentially useful to business firms, and a staff of quasi-librarians will peruse secondary sources on subjects requested by clients.

This category includes myriad information sources that exist to primarily serve their own industries. These publications range from general industry articles published in trade magazines to annual reports published by individual firms.

Industry sources

Trade publications

Each major industry has one or more magazines specifically aimed at its member firms. For instance, a tremendous amount of information about the grocery industry can be found in such trade publications as *Chain Store Age, Progressive Grocer*, and *Food Topics*. Information about the electric sign industry is contained in *Sign and Display Industry* and *Signs of the Times*.

A researcher should be aware of the various trade publications, and an index entitled *Business Publication Rates and Data*, published monthly by the Standard Rate and Data Service, Inc., will be of great help in identifying these publications. The previously cited *Ayer Directory of Publications* will also help.

Professional and trade association publications

Another key source of secondary information can be professional and trade associations. The coordinating offices of such operations generally compile and publish useful data for their member firms. The *Encyclopedia of Associations*, published by the Gale Research Company of Detroit, Michigan, lists associations' names, addresses, staff, number of members, and, most important, their publications.

Publications of individual firms

Many of the larger business firms furnish financial reports to the public. These annual reports are prepared primarily for stockholders or potential stockholders and can be obtained from the home office of these firms. In addition, some firms develop publications intended primarily for their own employees. Some examples are: *Monsanto*, published by Monsanto Company; *Ideal Cement Mixer*, a monthly publication by Ideal Cement Company; and *U.S. Steel News*, published by personnel services department of the U.S. Steel Corporation.

Other sources of secondary information

This is a "catch-all" category since it covers those data sources that can be useful to marketing researchers but don't fit neatly into any of the three previous categories. These include reports coming out of institutes, individual research undertakings in the academic world (theses, dissertations, and monographs), and the output of various research centers (business research centers on college and university campuses).

Some indexes for these sources were presented in an earlier section of this chapter, but it would be well to cite some of the more important ones again. The *American Doctoral Dissertation Index* is a yearly publication that includes abstracts of recent doctoral dissertations. The *Index of University Publications of Business and Economic Research* is the best source for reports published by some of the academically affiliated bureaus.

There also are many potentially useful published materials such as charts, reports, pamphlets, and monographs that generally do not have wide appeal and thus are not publicly circulated. Most libraries keep such material classified by subject in a "Vertical File." The library usually does not keep a formal record of these materials, which means the investigator must search through files to find potentially useful data. There is a *Vertical File Service Catalog* found in most libraries which lists some of these materials by subject headings.

A FORMAL SEARCH PROCEDURE

At this point the reader probably feels a little overwhelmed by the tremendous amount of business-oriented secondary data. If nonbusiness sources are then added to this total, the task facing the person searching for secondary information becomes downright awesome. That is why it is so important to follow a formal search procedure.

A formal search for information involves four basic steps: identifying the information needed, seeking possible secondary sources for this information, collecting the secondary information, and identifying information gaps (see Figure 5-4).

Steps in the Compilation of Information   **Figure 5-4**

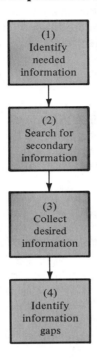

Identify information needed

The first step in any information search is identifying the types of information needed to accomplish the study's objectives. This information could be of a fairly general nature (e.g., annual sales of soft drink industry) or it could be fairly specific (unit sales of soft drinks in the state of Iowa).

In situations where the researchers are unfamiliar with the general research topic, their initial search will generally be for fairly general information. Then as they become more knowledgeable about the topic, they will narrow these needs to information that applies specifically to the study's objectives.

Search for information

Once the information needed has been identified, the search begins. It should be assumed at the outset that the desired information may already exist in one of many secondary sources.

Although the researcher will not be able to find all the secondary data pertinent to the topic, he/she can minimize search time and maximize the value of the findings if the indexes, directories, and other search tools are effectively used.

Collect secondary information

After the information sources have been identified, the researcher starts compiling the desired information. In recording these data, it is important to retain specifics on each source (name of publication, author, date, page number, etc.) so that they can be cited in the study or easily traced at a later date if accuracy must be checked.

Identify information gaps

Secondary data may satisfy only part of the information needs. The information gaps will then have to be filled through the generation of primary data, a topic covered in the next chapter.

Example of formal search – electronic games

Mary Jones is on the marketing staff of Acme Electronics, an Ohio based manufacturer of electronic equipment. She has been given the responsibility of investigating the electronic games industry to determine what role, if any, Acme might play in the rapidly growing sales area. Her starting point is to identify the information needs for such an assessment. Table 5-2 lists the type of information desired and the secondary sources she feels might provide this information.

STRENGTHS AND LIMITATIONS OF SECONDARY INFORMATION

Thus far, a list of those secondary data sources that will be of most use to the business researcher has been presented with no attempt made to evaluate their worth. It is now time to step back and assess the value of secondary information in comparison with primary information.

Strengths

The primary advantage of secondary data is its cost. The amount of money spent acquiring secondary data is generally a great deal less than that needed to obtain primary data. The various secondary data existing in libraries can be perused at no cost and most government publications can be obtained for little or no cost.

Information Needs and Sources – Electronic Games   Table 5-2

Information Desired	Sources of Information			
State Of The Art Trends in the development of consumer electronic products Technological developments in the toy/game industry Future Directors	*U.S. Government* National Technical Information Service (Dept. of Commerce) National Bureau of Standards (Dept. of Commerce) Office of Technical Assistance (Dept. of Commerce) Consumer Products Safety Commission Department of Energy	*Trade and Professional Organizations* Electronics Manufacturers Assoc. Toy Manufacturers of America Semi-Conductor Equipment Materials Institute	*Consumer/Business Press* Merchandising Electronic News Consumer Reports Popular Electronics Solid State Technology Electronic Products Magazine Toys Magazine Toy & Hobby World Appliance Manufacturer Mart Magazine	*Business & Technical Indexes,* Services, Directories Underwriters Laboratories D.A.T.A. Book Electronics
Market Trends & Developments Size & potential growth of electronic toys & games Current principal categories & likely future categories Marketing merchandising & advertising practices compared to traditional toys & games	Census of Manufacturers (Dept. of Commerce) Survey of Manufacturers (Dept. of Commerce) Current industrial reports (Dept. of Commerce)	Electronics Manufacturers Assoc. Toy Manufacturers of America Electronic Representatives of America National Electronics Distributors Assoc. Western Electronic Manufacturers Assoc.	Merchandising-Statistical Issues Appliance Manufacturer Mart Magazine Electronic News Electronic Business Electronics Retailing Toys Magazine Toy & Hobby World Appliance Magazine Mart Magazine Business Week Forbes Magazine	Leading National Advertisers Publishers Information Bureau Standard & Poor's Industry Reports Value Line Investment Service
Role of Government Federal rules & regulations likely to affect the toy industry	Reports of Congressional committees Consumer Products Safety Commission National Bureau of Standards (Dept. of Commerce)	Consumer groups Electronic Manufacturers Assoc. Toy Manufacturers Assoc.	Articles appearing in electronic, toy and trade magazines	
Competition Relative strength of the competition Competitive selling strategies	Forms 10-k, 10q (SEC) Reports of state governments	Electronic Manufacturers Assoc. Toy Manufacturers Assoc.	Wall Street Transcript Barron's The Wall Street Journal Financial World Dun's Review Forbes Articles appearing in electronic, toy and trade magazines	Electronic Engineers Master Standard & Poor's Corporation Records Reports of Investment brokerage firms National Investment Library Annual report Disclosure, Inc annual report Dun & Bradstreet reports Value Line Investment Service Fortune 500 Directory Moody's Industrial Manual Toys Directory
Consumer Behavior Level of household penetration Demographic skews Consumers' perception of these products				Directory of U.S. & Canadian Marketing Surveys & Services by Charles H. Kane Co. Finex-Directory of Market Research Reports. Studies & Surveys-Find-SVP

Source: Natalie Goldberg, "How to use external data on marketing and research," *Marketing Communications*, March 1980, p. 78

Even the seemingly high cost to subscribers of Nielsen and MRCA information can be a bargain compared to the expenses an individual firm would incur if it tried to go out and conduct national studies on store sales or consumer preferences.

Much of the secondary data (excluding the ongoing studies of commercial research firms) are "instant" since they already exist and merely need to be discovered. Thus, the time accumulating secondary data is largely search time and usually involves only a matter of hours or days. On the other hand, the collection of primary data can take weeks or even months.

An individual investigator usually cannot match the quality or size of the firms that obtain much of the existing secondary data. The federal government has thousands of trained personnel specializing in data gathering. Likewise, information coming from academic areas is the result of many months and even years of research by an individual who really becomes an authority on the subject. Another aspect of secondary data is that these often include information not accessible to individual investigators or research groups. While business firms are willing to provide their trade associations with information on their sales, expenses, and production output, they generally are unwilling to release these same data to individual investigators.

For the same reason, the government census studies obtain information of a somewhat private nature from individuals and business firms, since these groups are required to provide such information.

Limitations

Researchers must remember that secondary data were developed for purposes other than their particular projects. Thus, certain limitations can impair the data's usefulness.

The existing data might not fit the researcher's study because of differences in definitions. The researcher might be doing a study on some aspect of chain food store sales and would like to use some of the excellent sales data found in *Chain Store Age's Annual Sales Manual.* However, the researcher defined a chain as comprising 11 or more stores, whereas *Chain Store Age* views two or more similar stores as a chain operation and collected their statistics on this basis.

A researcher may want to use secondary data in a study comparing retail opportunities in two cities—Dubuque, Iowa, and Waterloo, Iowa. The most recent income and population data may come from their respective Chambers of Commerce. But Waterloo's income data are broken down on the basis of households, whereas Dubuque's are in terms of families.

While the census studies provide a great deal of useful information, they are conducted only every 5 or 10 years. Thus, a researcher in 1975 doing a project on the average rent being paid by various ethnic groups in the Los Angeles area would be foolish to build the study on data from the *1970 Census of Housing.* There is no rule of thumb as to when information becomes obsolete, but the researcher should realize that in these volatile times, data more than 5 years old is of questionable value.

"Secondhand" information refers to situations where existing data are found in a second study and your only contact with the data is through this second study. Assume the Bureau of Business Research at the University of Iowa does an in-depth study on the average number of hours per day worked by farmers in five selected Iowa counties. This information is published by the bureau and then incorporated into a newspaper story by *The Denver Post* on the changing patterns of rural life. These data as they exist in *The Denver Post* story are now secondhand data.

The major problem associated with secondhand data is the inaccuracies arising from the recording and transferring of the original data. In switching statistics from one study to another, $2,345,500 can become $3,245,500. In transferring information the second user also can arrange statements out of context, which will greatly alter the original intent of the person or source being quoted.

Whenever possible, the researcher should bypass secondhand data and seek the original source to make sure he/she is not building a study on somebody else's mistakes.

The facilities or capabilities of the agency that originally gathered the data might be questionable. The study may have been performed by a firm or individual with limited funds, forcing them to cut corners and thus affect the accuracy of their results. Doctoral dissertations and masters' theses generally suffer from this weakness since the researcher usually is strapped financially and cannot do all the traveling, interviewing, or experimenting necessary for maximum accuracy.

If the original document doesn't include some statements as to the methods used to obtain the information, when it was obtained, and from whom it was obtained, a researcher should be leery of using the study's findings. Most responsible sources will include statements explaining and defending their procedures.

The user of secondary information should always be cognizant of the intent of the original study and judge the validity of the results accordingly. As indicated in many statistics books, you can twist results to defend almost any side of an argument, depending upon the whims of the person gathering and using the data. In the mid-1960s during the cancer–tobacco controversy, both the tobacco industry and the American Cancer Society could cite statistics to defend their respective positions.

SUMMARY OF SECONDARY DATA SOURCES

Too often when the need for information arises, researchers immediately start thinking about conducting surveys or setting up experiments. They assume their information needs are unique and thus require the accumulation of new data. Actually, the majority of requests for information can be satisfied through secondary data. The awesome amount and variety of secondary data available make it essential that researchers be familiar with the major sources of secondary data, and, more importantly, how to effectively search out these data.

Secondary data come either from within the firm (internal data) or from some outside source or agency (external data). The continual development of marketing information systems within firms will provide these firms with greater access to internal data. The bulk of secondary information is external data, coming from government agencies (federal, state, and local), as well as commercial, industry, and academic sources. To successfully use external data, the researcher must know how to systematically use the various indexes, directories, abstracts, and guides that identify these data.

The biggest collector and disseminator of information is the federal government, with its major data gathering agency being the Bureau of the Census. Registration data coming from state and local governments provide information of a more localized nature.

Businessmen can also solve some of their information needs with data from their industries' trade publications. Commercial firms syndicating data for a fee can be valuable sources to clients needing regional and national information.

While secondary information can usually be obtained quickly and at little expense, the user should also be cognizant of its key limitations: inaccuracies may exist with the data; the data may be dated; or it may not fit the specific information needs of the study.

STANDARD INDUSTRIAL CLASSIFICATION

Although the Standard Industrial Classification System (SIC) is not a secondary data source comparable to those already presented in this chapter, business researchers should understand its purpose and coverage to maximize their data gathering skills. Thus, this special section is intended for those with little or no knowledge of the SIC.

The SIC was developed in 1945 under the sponsorship and supervision of the Office of Statistical Standards of the Bureau of the Budget. The purpose of the system is to facilitate the collection, tabulation, presentation, and analysis of data relating to various business establishments. Such a system enables the various statistical data collected by governmental agencies, trade associations, and private research organizations to be assembled and presented in a uniform manner.

The SIC is basically a numerical system that separates the total economy into specific industry segments. This system classifies establishments by industry on a two-, three-, four-, up to a seven-digit basis, depending upon how fine a breakdown is desired.

Makeup of the SIC

The two-digit identification is designated as a "major group" breakdown and is the foundation for the entire system. It starts at 01 and presently goes up to 94. For example, major group 08 covers forestry; major group 31 covers leather and leather products; major group 50 covers wholesale trade; major group 82 covers educational services; and major group 94 covers international government. These are just a few of the more than 80 major group classifications.

The third digit separates the major group into more homogeneous segments. While major group 50 identifies wholesale trade, the number 501 identifies the motor vehicle and automotive equipment segment of wholesale trade and 504 identifies the grocery segment. Major group number 32 identifies the stone, clay, and glass products industry, and 325 identifies structural clay products.

The fourth digit is a more finite classification. The number 5014 identifies establishments primarily engaged in the wholesale distribution of rubber tires and tubes for passenger and commercial vehicles while 5043 identifies those establishments primarily engaged in the wholesale distribution of dairy products. The number 3253 identifies establishments primarily engaged in manufacturing ceramic wall and floor tile while 3255 covers those establishments manufacturing clay firebricks.

The listings in the SIC manual do not go beyond the four-digit code. The fifth, sixth, and seventh digits, where used, identify products and groups of products within an industry. There are at present very little published data available to this degree of refinement, although the code framework does exist and will probably become more important in future years.

A company with multiple plants, each producing different products and services, would have separate SIC numbers for each of these establishments. If a firm performs two or more distinct activities at the same physical location, each activity might be viewed as a separate establishment. This assumes that they prepare separate reports on salaries, output, purchases, etc., for each activity area.

Use of SIC   Dun and Bradstreet uses the SIC in its descriptive coverage of firms. For instance, in the *Dun and Bradstreet Million Dollar Directory*, it lists six SIC numbers for the Sheller-Globe Corporation of Ohio (3069, 3429, 3461, 3714, 2522) to identify the firm's various operations. In this era of consolidations and mergers, a firm's name is not necessarily an accurate indicator of its actual lines of business, but its SIC identification pretty well pins down its operations.

Many government publications use the SIC code to arrange their data. *County Business Patterns*, an annual publication of the Department of Commerce, groups every business establishment in the U.S. by its SIC number. It provides information on types of businesses conducted within the boundaries of each county, number of employees per type of business, and their payrolls. These statistics can be used for developing market and sales potentials, studying a region's industrial structure, assigning sales quotas, and allocating advertising expenditures.

QUESTIONS AND EXERCISES

1. Why should researchers thoroughly investigate secondary sources before developing the tools for collecting primary data? In what type of research situations wouldn't secondary sources be first consulted?

2. Why are so many "internal" data wasted, or even worse, duplicated?

3. Under what conditions would a firm use the services of A. C. Nielsen or MRCA? Under what conditions would it perform its own research on product sales?

4. Your firm is contemplating developing storage facilities for products that move by barge on the Mississippi River. Two towns have been identified as possible sites—Dubuque, Iowa,

and Davenport, Iowa. As the firm's research director, you have been asked to develop a brief report containing key statistics about each town. They want the report in two days so that means all the data must come from secondary sources. Where would you look? What data would you provide? Develop a brief one-page report on each city.

5. You have been asked to compile a bibliography of articles pertaining to "the impact of solar energy on the heating industry in 1985." Develop a list of possible topic headings for your library search. Develop a list of the trade magazines most likely to carry articles on solar energy for heating buildings.

6. Refer back to the Retail Florists Delivery case at the end of Chapter 4. What general topics would be used to guide the search for secondary data? What trade magazines would probably carry articles pertaining to the delivery expenses of retail florists?

7. Which of the following secondary sources would be used to answer each of the following questions?

Sources of Information
    1. *Statistical Abstract of the U.S.*
    2. *American Statistical Index*
    3. *Encyclopedia of Associations*
    4. *Standard and Poor's Industry Survey*
    5. *Survey of Buying Power*
    6. *Monthly Catalog of U.S. Government Publications*
    7. *Census of Retail Trade*
    8. *Editor and Publisher Market Guide*
    9. *Funk and Scott Index of Corporations and Industry*
   10. *Business Periodicals Index*
   11. *Standard Rate and Data Service*
   12. *Dun and Bradstreet's Million Dollar Directory*

a. What was the per capita consumption of refined sugar in the U.S. in 1976?

b. What is the projected growth for the copying and duplicating equipment industry over the next five years?

c. What is the Buying Power Index for the San Diego Metropolitan Area?

d. In 1975 the Department of Commerce published a document on marketing in Sweden. Where would information on this document be found?

e.   Who is the executive vice president of American Marketing Association? Who is the executive vice president of Sheller-Globe of Toledo, Ohio?

f.   How many retail bakeries are in the SMSA of Topeka, Kansas?

g.   What are the principal shopping days in Fort Collins, Colorado?

h.   What is the most recent Spot Market Price Index of Fats and Oils in the United States?

i.   What commission does *Menswear News* give to ad agencies?

j.   What articles have appeared in newspapers about Shell Oil Co.?

6

Methods for obtaining primary data—Surveys

The following questionnaire was mailed to randomly selected households throughout the United States under the auspices of the National Right to Work Committee. The survey results indicated the "American public" was concerned about the increasing power of unions. Do you get the feeling the survey might be a "wee" bit slanted?

Please answer the questions below and return this form at once in the enclosed envelope. Your name will not be used without your written permission.

1. Do you feel there is too much power concentrated in the hands of labor union officials? ____ Yes ____ No

2. Are you in favor of forcing state, county, and municipal employees to pay union dues to hold their government jobs? ____ Yes ____ No

3. Are you in favor of allowing construction union czars the power to shut down an entire construction site because of a dispute with a single contractor . . . thus forcing even more workers to knuckle under to union agents? ____ Yes ____ No

4. Do you want union officials to decide how many municipal employees you, the taxpayer, must support? ____ Yes ____ No

5. Should all construction workers be forced into unions through legalized picketing, thus raising the cost of building your schools, hospitals, and homes? ____ Yes ____ No

6. Would you vote for someone who had forced public employees to join a labor union or be fired? ____ Yes ____ No

Once the researcher has determined the types of information needed to accomplish the study's objective, decisions must be made as to which sources can best provide these data. As stated in Chapter 5, the researcher first should thoroughly search various secondary sources to make sure all existing data pertinent to the study have been discovered. If after this investigation the necessary information is still lacking, primary data must be generated.

Primary data can be produced in only two ways: by questioning people or by observing selected activities. But in marketing research a third method is also included — experiments.

1. *Survey Methods.* Data are collected by asking questions of people thought to have the desired information. Questioning can be conducted through personal interviews, telephone interviews, or mail questionnaires.

2. *Observational Procedures.* The researcher observes the objects or actions of interest. These observations can be made either with mechanical devices or by individuals. For example, cameras can be used to record the eye movement of shoppers as they move through store aisles in supermarkets to determine which displays attract attention first. Or, someone could be stationed near these displays personally observing shoppers' reactions.

3. *Experimental Procedures.* In experiments the researcher introduces selected stimuli into a controlled environment and then manipulates these stimuli. In other words, the experimenter purposely influences the action, intending to measure the effect of these manipulations. Raising and lowering prices on a given product to determine what influence these price changes have on sales is a common type of experiment.

Some disagreement exists as to whether experiments are actually a distinct method for gathering primary data. Many researchers feel that experimentation is merely a special form of either the survey method or the observation method since results are obtained by questioning or observing. Experimentation is given separate classification in this book because it is felt that the manipulation and control aspects employed in experiments distinguish them from typical surveys or observations where information is usually gathered under reasonably normal conditions.

The remainder of this chapter and all of Chapter 7 deal with surveys. Chapter 8 is devoted entirely to the observational and experimental methods.

SURVEYS   In marketing research, surveys are probably the most used and most abused means of obtaining primary data: most used because they are an extremely flexible method of obtaining information on the actions and attitudes of people; most abused because many surveys are conducted where questions are biased or poorly stated, interviewers are poorly trained, or the sample interviewed is not really representative of the population.

The statement "Something beats nothing all to hell!" implies that any action, no matter how poorly performed, is still better than no action at all. This can be a dangerous assumption when surveys are involved since a poor survey might provide faulty data and lead a decision maker into a costly mistake. Thus, it is important that researchers know how to carry out effective surveys and that decision makers be able to evaluate the quality of surveys and the data they are provided.

Some terminology   To fully understand the material presented in this chapter, readers should be familiar with some terminology commonly associated with surveys.

Disguised-undisguised surveys

In a disguised survey the actual purpose of the questioning is hidden, whereas in an undisguised survey its purpose is obvious. An example of a disguised survey would be: a group of women are asked to open a number of canisters of unbranded potato chips, taste them, and then answer a number of questions about each product's taste. A few questions are also asked about the different packages and the ease of opening each style of canister. This latter information is of real concern to the researcher, and the taste questions are used merely as a cover.

Structured-unstructured surveys

In a structured interview a formal questionnaire is used and the interviewer closely follows that format. In a nonstructured interview, the interviewer has more freedom since only general questions or general topic areas are listed. This latter type of interview is the most difficult to conduct and should be carried out only by well-trained interviewers.

Most survey formats fall somewhere in between these two extremes. The questionnaire may be comprised primarily of multiple-choice questions or simple yes-no questions, but it may also include some open-end questions that enable the interviewer to probe or let interviewees phrase answers in their own words.

TYPES OF SURVEYS

Telephone surveys

There are several advantages to telephone surveys: costs are especially low when the survey is limited to a local area. Even when regional or nationwide interviews are involved, the availability of WATS lines (Wide Area Telecommunications Service) keeps cost fairly reasonable. For example, a Denver firm would pay approximately $2,900 a month for a nationwide WATS line. This would provide 240 hours of calls per month. (Rates will vary slightly from state to state.)

The speed advantage is obvious in that travel time between interviews is not needed, nor is time lost waiting for returned questionnaires (mail surveys). Telephone surveys are the most effective method when data are needed in a short period of time.

Telephone surveys provide uniformity in the questioning process and control over the interviewers. In telephone surveys the respondent's only impression of the interviewer comes from that person's voice so there is no bias created by the interviewer's presence, a weakness of personal interviewers. In many surveys telephone interviews are conducted from a central facility by groups of interviewers. This enables supervisors to monitor selected calls to ensure that prescribed questioning procedures are being followed.

There are also, however, disadvantages to this type of survey:

Incomplete universe — In the past the claim had been made that telephone owners were in higher income brackets than nonowners and therefore were not really representative of the entire population. Today, this criticism is considerably weakened since the majority (94 percent) of homes in the United States have telephones.

A recent study of 7,500 U.S. households disclosed that although some differences do exist between owners and nonowners of phones, these differences are modest and should not significantly bias the results of surveys based on telephone interviews.[1]

There are other conditions, however, that also influence the representativeness of telephone surveys:

---

[1]Lee Wolfe, "Characteristics of Persons With and Without Home Telephones," *Journal of Marketing Research*, August 1979, pp. 421-425.

1. *Directory Obsolescence.* Since over 20 percent of the U.S. population moves annually, the accuracy of any phone book rapidly diminishes during a given year. Since this is the source most frequently used for obtaining numbers, a significant part of the audience (mobile types) can be missed.

2. *Unlisted Telephone Numbers.* It is estimated that approximately 18 percent of all telephone numbers in the United States are unlisted. This percentage varies greatly in different parts of the country (in Los Angeles 34 percent are unlisted; in New York 26 percent are unlisted). At one time it was assumed the unlisted numbers were primarily high-income people, which meant this income segment was not properly represented in any sample developed from telephone directories. Recent studies have shown that the real difference between listed and unlisted numbers was not size of income, but rather marital status and sex. (Large numbers of unlisted numbers occur among divorced/separated people, women, and nonwhites.)[2]

Can't use visual aids — Some surveys require the interviewee to react to a picture, an ad, a design, etc. Unless these are mailed beforehand, such reactions can't be obtained. Similarly, questions that require a selection on a seven-nine point scale are difficult to use unless the respondents have a card before them.

Length of interview — It is difficult to keep interviewees on the phone for any length of time if the survey is not of keen interest to them. Thus, surveys of a general nature and with a general audience must be brief. There have been successful telephone surveys requiring 25 to 30 minutes, but their acceptance has been due to primarily to the fact they were well devised and pertained to a subject of major interest to the interviewee.

Other disadvantages — Since the interviews are being conducted by telephone, it is difficult for the interviewer to validate the information obtained. The interviewer must take the interviewee's word on questions related to income, products owned, nature of residence, etc. In personal interviews, the interviewer can actually observe and judge the accuracy of some of the interviewee's statements.

Another problem associated with telephone interviews is that in recent years a number of firms selling products or services use such interviews as a gimmick to gain original contact with people. During the "fake" interview they switch to a sales pitch for

---

[2]A. B. Blankenship, "Listed versus Unlisted Numbers in Telephone-Survey Sampler." *Journal of Advertising Research*, February 1977, pp. 39-42.

their products. This experience has occurred often enough that many would-be interviewees are reluctant to participate in any telephone surveys.

The most effective way to increase responses to phone surveys is to send a letter or card in advance notifying a person of the upcoming call and its general purpose.

Random digit dialing (nondirectory sampling)

One solution to the problems caused by unlisted numbers or outdated directories is the use of random digit dialing. This technique develops lists of possible numbers either by a random or systematic process. For example, in a community with two exchanges, 484 and 492, the four remaining numbers can be generated from a table of random numbers or from a computer. This process can also be used when central calling facilities are being used for a nationwide telephone survey.

In a typical random digit dialing situation starting with previously identified prefixes, 73 percent of all numbers developed were nonworking. So while this procedure may increase the representativeness of a telephone survey, it also adds to the time involved in contacting potential interviewees.

More sophisticated methods have been introduced that cut down on the amount of nonworking (nonassigned) numbers dialed. One such method is to divide the final four numbers into clusters of 1,000, and randomly select within those, clusters that have a reasonable proportion of working numbers. Telephone companies tend to assign numbers into the same hundred and thousand series (e.g., the company may begin assigning the 1,000 series first and fill that up before going to the next thousand). Where more sophisticated selection methods have been used, random selections resulted in 56 percent working numbers.[3]

'Right to privacy' issue

The increasing desire among people to protect their privacy may greatly inhibit the use (or value) of telephone surveys in the future. Households already can place their names on lists that prevent them from receiving "junk mail." There is also the possibility that in the near future telephone owners may be able to put their names on a list that identifies them as not wanting to receive any commercial-oriented calls.

---

[3]Robert Groves, "An Emperical Comparison of Two Telephone Sample Designs," *Journal of Marketing Research*, November 1978, pp. 622-631.

Mail surveys   Of the three survey methods, mail interviews have received the greatest amount of attention. Robert Ferber stated: "The mail questionnaire has been the subject of extensive controversy over the past two decades. Some have hailed it as the ultimate data collection technique while others have condemned it as an instrument of the devil."[4] Actually, mail questionnaires fall somewhere in between these two extremes.

Advantages

Wide distribution—The mail travels to all parts of our country; therefore if a proper mailing list can be obtained, all potential sample members should be reached. This also means there is not an over-representation of "desirable" neighborhoods or an ignoring of "bad" neighborhoods, as often occurs when personal interviews are involved.

No interviewer bias—The respondents are not influenced or inhibited by the presence of an interviewer. They also are more willing to answer somewhat personal questions.

Cost—It can be an inexpensive way to obtain information, especially when the potential interviewees are spread over a wide geographic area. But, the expenses must be evaluated on the basis of "cost per response." For example, assume the total cost for an individual mail questionnaire is 24¢ (20¢ stamp and 4¢ for paper and printing) plus the cost of a prepaid return (23¢ for metered postage or 20¢ for prestamped envelope). If questionnaires are mailed to 5,000 people, the cost to reach each person is only 24¢, or a total mailout cost of $1200; but the cost per response is much higher. If only 10 percent of the 5,000 people respond, the cost per response comes to $2.63 ($1200 + 500 × 18¢ per return = $1,315/500). As the rate of response increases, costs per response go down rapidly. If follow-up letters are used to increase responses, their costs must also be included when determining "cost per response."

Possibility of more accurate reply—Persons responding to mail questionnaires can do it at their own leisure and thus may give more thought to their answers or seek help from others on questions about which they are in doubt.

---

[4]Robert Ferber, Donald Blankertz, and Sidney Hollander, *Marketing Research* (New York: Ronald Press Company, 1964), p. 248.

Disadvantages

Time involved — It can take anywhere from two to four weeks before a majority of the returns are in. If follow-up letters are used, the return period is further lengthened.

Nonresponse bias — In any questionnaire that does not obtain 100 percent response, a question arises as to whether the respondents are truly representative of the universe under study or, instead, are a unique group. A number of years ago, during the height of publicity about unidentified flying objects, a questionnaire about visits to earth by creatures from other planets was sent to a representative sample of Coloradoans. A surprisingly large percentage of the respondents indicated that they felt that there had been visitors from other planets. How representative of all citizens were these respondents? Those people who were unusually interested in the UFO phenomena chose to respond, whereas people with little or no interest in the subject tended to ignore the questionnaire. This problem of "selection by the respondent" exists whenever mail questionnaires are used.

How do you cope with nonresponse bias? One method is to use follow-up calls or follow-up interviews with a limited number of the nonrespondents. Their replies are then compared with those obtained from the original respondents. Tests are then applied to see if there were significant differences in the responses of these two groups. If none are found, it may be assumed that the original respondents are representative of the universe.

"Structural shortcomings" — (1) The questions must be simple and easily understood since there is no one present to clarify them for the interviewee. (2) The questionnaire must be relatively short if a decent rate of response is to be realized. There tends to be an inverse relationship between the length of the questionnaire and the percentage of responses to it. (3) When open-end questions are used, their results are hard to tabulate. This means that the use of open-end questions in mail interviews should be minimized when a large number of respondents are involved.

Bias due to faulty samples — Bias also occurs when the sample chosen to be surveyed is not really representative of the population. This type of bias is not unique to mail questionnaires, however, since it can exist in any type of survey as well as in observations and experiments.

Increasing response rate to mail surveys

In the last decade, there has been a vast amount of research on ways to increase response rates to mail surveys. In most cases, a study dealt with such a narrow or limited situation that the author(s) usually added the caveat that the study's findings were not necessarily applicable to other mail surveys.

A few findings recurred often enough that they could be accepted as tested methods for increasing response rates to mail surveys. Following are some of these findings.

Follow-ups — Follow-ups or reminders are almost universally successful in increasing response rates. Since each successive follow-up results in added returns, a well-financed and persistent researcher can achieve a high total response rate. The value of the additional information obtained from follow-ups has to be weighed against their added costs.

Sending the follow-up requests by "special delivery" or "certified mail" is an effective method to catch the potential respondent's attention and increase the response rate. It should be noted, however, that these "urgency" techniques can backfire if they are not successfully delivered and the recipient has to make a special trip to the post office to pick up this "important" piece of mail.[5]

Preliminary notification — Advance notification, particularly by telephone, is effective in increasing the rate of response and also speeds up the rate of return. However, follow-ups appear to be a better investment in terms of cost and results.

Monetary Incentive — Including some type of monetary reward with questionnaires does increase the response rate. It should be noted that a reward of 25¢ to 50¢ generally is cost-effective. Although larger sums also increase responses, their cost tends to exceed the value of the additional responses.

It should be noted too, that although a monetary inducement usually improves the response rate, it does not necessarily improve the accuracy of the results. The respondents feel less personal commitment to the study and they answer less accurately and also leave a higher share of unanswered questions.[6]

---

[5]Arthur Wolfe and Beatrice Treiman, "Postage Types and Response Rates on Mail Surveys," *Journal of Advertising Research*, 19 February 1979, pp. 43-48.

[6]Robert Hansen, "A Self-Perception Interpretation of the Effects of Monetary and Nonmonetray Incentives on Mail Survey Respondent Behavior," *Journal of Marketing* 17 (February 1980), pp. 77-83.

Additional techniques that will increase response are:

- Inclusion of return envelopes. Metered return envelopes are less expensive, but placing placing stamps on the return envelopes results in a higher response rate.
- Using multiple stamps on the outside of the original mail envelope rather than a single stamp (two 4¢ stamps plus a 12¢ stamp will get greater response than a single 20¢ stamp).
- Individually addressing the envelopes is more effective than using address labels.
- Depending on the audience, third-class postage may be just as effective as first-class mailouts. There can be major delays in the delivery of the third class-mail, however.
- Survey sponsorship by a recognized and respected agency will increase response. University sponsorship usually results in highest return, followed by government and then private firm sponsorship.

Cover letter

A major influence in obtaining a reasonable response to mail surveys is the quality of the accompanying cover letter. A cover letter should provide three types of information to the recipient: (1) the purpose of the survey, (2) why he/she was chosen, and (3) why he/she should participate. In telephone surveys the introduction used by the interviewee should provide the same three bits of information.

Attempts to personalize the cover letter have had mixed results in terms of increasing responses. A personally typed cover letter will increase response, but personally signed form letters or personalized greetings over a form letter seem to be of little value.

The letterhead should adequately identify the agency sending out the surveys, and the signature on the cover letter should list that person's position with the firm or agency (see Figure 6-1.)

Approaches to use in cover letter — There are four basic appeals used in most cover letters to entice participation in the survey.

(a) *Ego appeal*: Emphasizes how crucial the person's participation is to the study, how valuable that input will be — "Your opinions are crucial to . . . ."

(b) *Social Utility*: Emphasizes how the person's input will aid others—"Your response will enable other consumers to . . . ."

Figure 6-1   Example of Cover Letter

College of Business

Colorado State University
Fort Collins, Colorado
80523

May 28, 1976

Dear Parent(s) of CSU Student:

A problem facing many rural Colorado communities is—What can be done to entice 18-25-year-olds to remain in rural areas? The purpose of this questionnaire by the College of Business is to provide some answers to this question.

You were selected for this survey because: (1) Your family residence is in rural Colorado, and (2) you have a child at CSU who soon will have to decide where he/she will live and pursue a career. Last month a similar questionnaire was sent to your son/daughter at CSU, and their responses are presently being tabulated. We intend to compare the students' answers (as a group) to parents' answers to see whether the two generations differ in their attitudes towards rural life and their suggestions for improving it.

Due to limited finances, a fairly small sample (less than 300 families) was selected to receive this questionnaire. Thus, your response is very important to the project's success. A self-addressed return envelope is enclosed for your convenience. Thank you for your help.

Sincerely yours,

George Kress

George Kress
Professor of Marketing

jak

Enclosures 2

(c) *Aiding the Sponsor*: Emphasizes how input will benefit the sponsoring firm—"We need your help if we are to . . . ."

(d) *Combination approach*: Combines two or more of the above appeals—"Your knowledge as a consumer can be used to aid other consumers . . . ."

The most effective approach varies according to the firm sponsoring the survey. The most effective appeal for a university seems to be "social utility" whereas the "ego" approach seems most successful for commercial sponsors. Overall, the social utility approach seems to be the least successful.[7]

Mailing lists

The sources of names most frequently used in marketing research are telephone directories, city directories, membership lists of associations, and subscription lists of publications. There is also a large variety of more segmented lists available from firms specializing in the development and sale of such lists. Virtually any time people register for something or send in for something, their names are placed on some type of list. For instance, there is a list of the children who purchased the "G.I. Joe" toy and sent in money to join his fan club. There are lists of those children who purchased ant farms—they comprise a nature-oriented audience. A list exists of over 200,000 "outdoor" types developed from registrations at camping sites.

In developing lists, individual names rather than titles should be sought. For example, "James White, Personnel Director" will receive greater response than a questionnaire sent "Attention: Personnel Director." The extra time and effort it takes to obtain specific names is rewarded by improved rates of return.

Advantages

Versatility-flexibility—This method enables the researcher to obtain maximum information. It can be used to obtain the interviewees' reactions to pictures, products, props, etc. It also enables the interviewer to validate answers by observation or by continual probing. In addition, the interviewer can use unstructured questioning and longer questionnaires.

Personal interviews

---

[7]Terry Childers, William M. Pride, and O. C. Ferrell, "A Reassessment of the Effects of Appeals as Responses to Mail Surveys," *Journal of Marketing Research*, August 1980, pp. 365-370.

Disadvantages

Expensive—This method results in the highest cost per response. The major expense involves the cost of the interviewer, which can vary from $4 an hour up to $500 a day depending upon the skills needed. Generally, a more highly qualified interviewer is needed for personal interviews than for telephone surveys. Another key cost item is the travel time and expenses associated with moving from interview to interview.

Influence of interviewer—In an attempt to impress the interviewer, the interviewee may not give completely honest answers. In addition, the personal interests and attitudes of interviewers can cause them to interpret responses differently.

The success of personal interviews is closely tied to the skills of the interviewers. If they are well trained, conscientious, and can develop rapport with interviewees, the interviews will be a success. But if the interviewers are careless or have trouble communicating with people, the survey will be jeopardized.

Group interviews   Marketing researchers began using group interviews in the early 1950s as part of the discipline's increased involvement with "motivational research" techniques. This survey process was originally criticized as being unscientific by those in the research establishment who condemned anything associated with motivational research. Nevertheless, group interviewing became widely used and today is an important tool for marketers. The end-product of group interviews will not be neat tables of quantitative data that can be used by managers in their decision making. Instead, the main purpose of group interviews is to generate hypotheses for further testing or to obtain reactions to concepts or potential products.

Focus group interviews vs. nondirected group interviews

In focus group interviews the conversation of the group centers around a particular topic. The moderator knows beforehand (and oftentimes so do the participants) the general type of information that is being sought, i.e., reaction to the concept of a facial skin cleanser for men; reaction to the concept of colorless whiskey.

Nondirected or nonfocused interviews on the other hand are largely freelance undertakings in which the group is given relatively free reign in terms of topics discussed. This type of interview is generally used to generate new ideas or product concepts, whereas focus group interviews are intended to obtain reactions to an existing idea, concept, or even a real product.

A more extensive discussion of group interviews is found in Chapter 11, "Data Collection," where strengths and limitations of this method are described, along with the conditions leading to their successful conduct.

Telephone vs. personal interviews

Approximately 55 to 60 percent of interviews are carried out over the telephone. Door-to-door interviews account for around 10 percent, and the remaining 20 to 30 percent are carried out at central research facilities or shopping centers.[8]

Studies indicate that personal interviews generally provide higher quality data. Telephone surveys tend to result in greater evasiveness by respondents to questions, especially when they are income related. It is also more difficult to obtain lengthy or detailed information via the telephone.[9]

Telephone interviews must be faster paced than personal interviews since constant talk is necessary to maintain the respondent's interest and attention. There is also a feeling that the telephone call is an imposition on the interviewee, and thus it becomes more difficult to develop a rapport or to be casual in the interview.

A capsule comparison of the strengths and limitation of each of the three survey methods is provided in Table 6-1.

Regardless of the survey method used, some type of questionnaire must be developed if the desired information is to be obtained. In a structured survey, the questions are precisely stated and laid out in a desired order. Even in unstructured surveys some type of questioning format is followed. Therefore it is imperative that researchers be able to develop effective questionnaires since their quality is so crucial to a survey's success. This section describes eight steps that should be followed in constructing a questionnaire (Figure 6-2).

DEVELOPING THE QUESTIONNAIRE

[8]Frederick Wiseman and Phillip McDonald, 'Noncontact and Refusal Rates in Consumer Telephone Savings," *Journal of Marketing Research*, November 1979, pp. 478-484.

[9]Lawrence Jordan et al., "Response Styles in Telephone and Household Interviewing: A Field Experiment," *Public Opinion Quarterly*, 1980, 80-0044-210.

Table 6-1   Comparison of the Three Survey Methods

Criterion	Mail	Telephone	Personal
1. Ability to handle complex questionnaires	Poor	Good	Excellent
2. Ability to collect large amounts of data	Fair	Good	Excellent
3. Accuracy on "sensitive" questions	Good	Fair	Fair*
4. Control of interviewer effects	Excellent	Fair	Poor*
5. Degree of sample control	Fair	Good	Excellent†
6. Time required	Poor	Excellent	Fair
7. Probable response rate	Fair	Fair	Fair
8. Cost	Good	Good	Poor

*Excluding computer-conducted interviews
†Excluding shopping mall interviews
SOURCE: Donald Tull and Del Hawkins, *Marketing Research* (New York: Macmillan, 1980), p. 131. Used with permission.

Determine the specific information needed and how it will be used

One of the saddest statements a researcher can make is, "I wish I had asked. . . ." Once the questionnaires are sent out or the various interviews conducted, it's too late to include another question. Thus, before a questionnaire is developed, the researcher must identify all the specific information needed to accomplish the study's objective(s), and decide how this information is going to be used. Will the data be analyzed using only a simple cross-tabulation method or will a statistical procedure such as chi-square, regression analysis, or analysis of variance be applied? Too often researchers don't concern themselves enough with these questions and fail to gather data in the form suitable for the desired analytical technique.

Select the interviewing process

Will a personal interview, mail questionnaire, or telephone survey be used to obtain the data? The decision is tied to three key elements: the type of information sought, the types of respondents to be included, and the funds available.

Information sought—Can the information sought be obtained through a formal, structured questionnaire or must it be obtained via an unstructured, in-depth questioning process?

Respondents—Who will be surveyed and where are they located? The geographical scope of the study, the position of the persons to be interviewed, and their accessibility and willingness to participate all have to be considered.

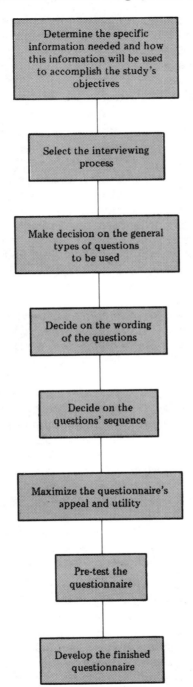

Cost and time factors — What the researcher would like to do may differ greatly from what he/she is able to do because of financial restraints. The researcher may desire to conduct in-depth interviews with the sales managers of a number of large firms but can't afford the necessary travel expense. Time is also a crucial factor since the data may have to be obtained immediately, i.e., within four days. This time restraint would necessitate using telephone interviews.

Select the general types of questions to be used

In developing the questionnaire, certain standards should be established for each question to be included. Is the question pertinent? Does it relate to the study's objectives? Could the same information be obtained by some other method?

Because the space on a questionnaire is so valuable, it is important that each question provide useful data. The exception would be in situations where a seemingly useless question is included at the beginning of a questionnaire for the sole purpose of enticing participation.

The ability of the interviewee to answer the question should also be considered. Is it within the respondent's experience? "Which shoes do you feel wear better — leather, suede, or Corfam?" If the subject has never had the opportunity to use Corfam shoes, such a question is out of his experience. Also an event may have happened so long ago that the accuracy of the answer is limited. "What was the first type of deodorant you used?"

The researcher should not ask questions that require a great deal of effort on the part of the respondent. "What was the volume in tons that your company sold in 1970 for each of the following 10 product categories?" In this particular case, the effort needed to answer this question could lead the respondent to discard the entire questionnaire or at least skip that particular question.

All questions asked fall into one of three categories: open-end questions, multiple-choice questions, and dichotomous questions. The researcher must decide which type or types to use.

Open-end questions — Respondents can answer these questions in their own words and express any ideas generated from the questions itself. The required answer could be quite brief ("How many salesmen do you have?") or could be fairly lengthy ("What methods do you use to train your salesmen?").

Since open-end questions do not suggest alternative answers, they tend to have less influence on the actual answers obtained than do multiple-choice or dichotomous questions. Thus, a weakness of open-end questions in mail questionnaires is the possibility the respondent will misinterpret the type of information sought. In a multiple-choice question, the possible answers are included with the question, and this gives some insight into the answer.

Another disadvantage of open-end questions is the problem of tabulating responses. Many answers will be phrased in such broad terms that they are difficult for the researcher to summarize. Open-end questions also give more weight to replies from better educated people. This group is more articulate and thus can more effectively communicate their ideas.

Multiple-choice questions — Here the respondent is offered a number of specific alternatives from which one or more answers can be chosen. If possible, the alternatives listed should be mutually exclusive. A category "other" should also be included to allow all possibilities to be covered.

Multiple-choice questions enable quick answers and thus are more appealing to potential respondents. Their tabulation is greatly simplified, and the alternative answers guide the respondent as to the general type of answer expected.

A shortcoming of multiple-choice questions is that bias can occur because of the order of alternative answers. Respondents who do not have strong feelings on a particular question tend to choose the first answer on the list. The possible bias caused by the position of possible answers on questionnaires can be overcome by alternating the order in which the answers are listed in different sets of questionnaires. This is called the "split-ballot" approach and can significantly increase the cost of producing the questionnaires.

When the possible answers are numbers, the nature of the bias changes because people who are undecided tend to select the middle numbers rather than the extremes. It is hard to overcome this particular shortcoming by rotating numbers on different questionnaires, since respondents are confused if numbers are presented out of their normal sequence.

A third type of potential bias involves situations where letters A, B, C are used instead of real brand names, store names, etc. — e.g., Store A or Store B. Those people who tend to be "undecided" will often choose the brand or store identified by the letter A because it connotes higher quality. Such letter bias does not exist when other letter combinations such as H, L, M are used.[10]

---

[10]Kenneth Coney, "The Special Case of Letter Preference," *Public Opinion Quarterly*, Fall 1977, pp. 385-388.

*Dichotomous questions—*A dichotomous question is an extreme form of the multiple-choice type where only two choices are offered: Yes–No; Spray–Roll-on; Cash–Credit. Since very few questions have only two possible responses, a third category, "other" or "don't know," should be included.

Regardless of the type of question used, there should be an opportunity for respondents to provide an answer to every question. If numerous questions are left blank because the respondents felt the answers provided did not apply to their situations, the study's findings will be weakened.

Decide on the questions' wording

If the questionnaires are going to the general public, the questions should be phrased in easily understood language. If the desired respondents comprise a specific group such as engineers, physicians, or teachers, the language can be more technical.

Each question should be quite explicit. For instance, "What brand of dog food do you feed your dog?" might confuse the respondent. Does the question mean "feed regularly" or "feed occasionally"?

Decide on sequence of questions

The opening few questions should be fairly easy to answer, with the more difficult or personal ones placed deeper in the body of the questionnaire. The questions should be in a logical order, and this means *logical to the respondents*. Does it flow smoothly from one question to another? Are all questions pertaining to similar subjects grouped together?

Maximize the questionnaire's appeal and utility

Mail questionnaires should be reasonably appealing to the eye and brief enough to entice answers. They should be laid out in such a manner that it is easy for either the interviewer or the interviewee to follow the sequence of the questions. They should also be structured in such a way as to enable easy tabulation.

Conduct a pretest

Before a questionnaire is ready for use, it has to be pretested. The purpose of the pretest is to check whether the ideas in each question are clear to the respondent. The pretest may show that some questions should be reworded, or in the case of multiple-choice questions, different or additional alternatives may have to be included. The people interviewed in the pretest should be quite similar to those who will be included in the final study. The sample size for the pretest can be quite small, around 30. If after the first pretest, a number of significant revisions are made in the questionnaire, a second pretest may be necessary.

When no further revisions are needed, the questionnaire that is going to be used for the formal study can be structured, placed in printed form and distributed to the selected interviewers or interviewees.

A Caveat

In the previous section, the steps involved in developing questionnaires were each described in a relatively brief manner, in keeping with the general thrust of this text. Developing a good questionnaire is actually a very difficult and time consuming task, and some research texts devote entire chapters to this topic. A beginning researcher may wish to refer to some of these texts for additional guidance in developing a questionnaire.[11]

Develop and distribute the finished questionnaire

Primary data are generated by either questioning people thought to have the desired information or by observing selected activities. This questioning can occur through personal interviews, telephone calls, or by mail. Each of these survey methods has certain strengths or limitations that influence its usage in any given situation.

   Telephone surveys are relatively inexpensive per contact and can be conducted in a brief time. Mail surveys enable wide distribution at a reasonable cost per response and eliminate interviewer bias. Personal interviews provide maximum opportunity for in-depth information as well as enabling a variety of questioning procedures to be employed by the interviewer.

   A special type of survey occurs when people are interviewed as a group. This process enables the participants to interact with one another, providing opportunities for new ideas or the reinforcement of existing ones. The results of group interviews are difficult to analyze due to their highly qualitative nature.

   Regardless of the survey method used, some type of questioning format is needed. In mail surveys, the questionnaires must be highly formalized. In personal interviews questionnaires can be less structured but still must cover certain key points.

   In developing questionnaires the researcher must first determine the specific types of information needed. Once this is iden-

SUMMARY

---

[11]Two such texts are *Marketing Research*, second edition, written by Donald Tull and Del Hawkins and published by Macmillan Publishing Company, Inc., 1980; and *Marketing Research—Test and Cases*, fifth edition, written by Harper Boyd, Ralph Westfall, and Stanley Starch, and published by Richard Irwin, Inc., 1981.

tified, the decision is made on who the desired respondents are and which survey tool can effectively and efficiently reach them. The questions are then developed, their wording is attuned to the level of the desired respondents, and they are placed in an appealing and logical sequence. The questionnaire is then pretested to uncover any major deficiencies, and the finished product is sent to the desired audience.

QUESTIONS AND EXERCISES

1. Why are experiments identified as a third method for obtaining primary data when they actually involve the use of either surveys or observations?

2. How do mail, telephone, and personal interviews differ in terms of costs, administrative control, and flexibility?

3. What are some actions that can be taken to effectively increase the response rate to mail surveys?

4. In 1936 a poll was conducted by telephone to determine which candidate people were going to vote for in the upcoming presidential election in which Alf Landon, a Republican, ran against Franklin Roosevelt, a Democrat. The results from the large random sample indicated Landon would win although Roosevelt actually won by a landslide. What is a possible explanation for this huge error in the survey's results?

5. What types of bias can occur when telephone directories are used to develop a sample?

6. How can interviewer bias in personal interviews be minimized?

7. How would mailing lists be developed for surveys aimed at each of the following audiences?
   (a) Sportscar owners
   (b) Racquetball players
   (c) College marketing teachers
   (d) Skiers

8. What conditions best lend themselves to the use of focus group interviews? How do focus groups differ from group dynamics?

CASES

Case 1

The 1980 Winter Olympics were held in Lake Placid, New York, and drew worldwide attention to that small community. Some Denver business and government officials are thinking of organizing a group to make a bid for the 1988 or 1992 Winter Olympics. They are aware that Coloradoans voted in 1972 to reject the 1976 Winter Olympics even though Denver had already been selected to host them. They are interested in determining how strong this "No Olympics" sentiment still is among Coloradoans, especially after residents had an opportunity to watch the 1980 Olympics on television.

You have been given the assignment to survey a representative number of Colorado residents to obtain this information.

The objective of this survey will be to determine the present attitude of Colorado residents toward their decision in 1972 to turn down the Winter Olympics. You will have to make the following decisions: Who should be surveyed? What survey method will be used? and What types of information will you seek from the survey? Develop a one-page survey that will accomplish these objectives. Also develop a brief cover letter, identify the audience you would try to reach and the aproximate cost of such an undertaking.

Case 2

Evaluate the following questionnaire and its accompanying cover letter. What are its strengths and weaknesses? Review it question by question, making changes you think would improve it. The questionnaire was intended to identify dog foods presently being used, the owners' knowledge of their dogs' nutritional needs, and factors that influence their selection of dog foods. The questionnaire was sent to people who had licensed their dogs. This list was available from the city clerk's office. What bias might exist in such a list?

Kandid Research
P.O. Box 1793
Dubuque, Iowa

Dear Dog Owner:

This questionnaire is part of a research project on dog foods being conducted to [a] find out more about the feeding procedures followed by dog owners and [b] determine the attitudes of dog owners toward existing dog food products. Your cooperation and participation in this study should enable dog food manufacturers to better meet your dog's food requirements.

Your name is not required in this study since we are only interested in aggregate replies. Enclosed is a stamped, self-addressed envelope for your convenience when returning the questionnaire. Your prompt cooperation in this study will be greatly appreciated.

Sincerely,

John Tensfeldt

John Tensfeldt

Enclosure

1. How many dogs do you own? _____

2. List each dog's breed and estimated dollar value; then check the category that most closely describes the dog.

		Description of Dog			
Breed	Estimated Value	Hunting Dog	Show Dog	Just a Pet	Other
[1]					
[2]					
[3]					

Some of the following questions deal with four types of dog food.
1. Table Scraps—leftover or excess meat, vegetables, and potatoes from family meals.
2. Dry Dog Food—dog food that comes in granular, pellets, milkbones, etc., sometimes used with water and sometimes without, e.g., Gravy Train, Gaines Meal.
3. Semi-Moist Dog Food—foods that come in packaged form such as Gaines Burgers.
4. Canned Dog Food—for example, Alpo, Pooch, Kal Kan, etc.

3. Check the approximate percent of each type of dog food used in your dog's weekly diet [i.e., how often you feed each type of food to your dog].

	Never 0%	Seldom 1-30%	Frequently 30-70%	Usually 70-90%	Always 90-100
Table Scraps					
Canned					
Semi-Moist					
Dry					

4. List the brand(s) of dog food you presently use (e.g., Gaines Burgers, Alpo). _____

5. What is the major health benefit to your dog from each of the following dog food nutrients? [Check "don't know" if applicable.]

Vitamins   (a) Benefit _____   (b) ☐ Don't know the value
Minerals   (a) Benefit _____   (b) ☐ Don't know the value
Fats   (a) Benefit _____   (b) ☐ Don't know the value
Proteins   (a) Benefit _____   (b) ☐ Don't know the value
Carbohydrates
             (a) Benefit _____   (b) ☐ Don't know the value

6. Select the two nutrients you feel are the most important requirements in your dog's diet.

☐ Carbohydrates   ☐ Vitamins
☐ Minerals   ☐ Proteins
☐ Fats   Don't know what value
                   [if any] each has

7. If you buy a canned dog food, indicate how important each of the following factors is in your buying decision.

	No Influence	Some Influence	Important	Very Important
Price				
Contents [% of meat, etc.]				
Brand Name [Alpo, Friskies]				
Who the Mfg. Is [e.g., Swift, Rival]				
Nutritional Value of the Dog Food				

8. What type of meat do you think is generally used in most canned dog food?

____ Same quality of meat that is sold for human consumption.
____ Meat that can't pass inspection for human consumption.
____ Inedible by-products [e.g., intestines, bones, etc.]
____ Horse meat, goat meat, etc.
____ Don't know.
____ Other _____

9. Do you feel canned dog foods meet the daily nutritional needs of your dog?

☐ Yes   ☐ No   ☐ Don't know

10. Do you feel each breed of dog requires its own special dog food?
     ☐ Yes   ☐ No   ☐ Don't know

11. Do you supplement your dog's diet with vitamin drops or pills?
     ☐ Yes   ☐ No   ☐ Don't know

12. Who usually purchases your dog food?
     ____ Male head of household
     ____ Female head of household
     ____ Children

13. From the following list of brand names select the two that you feel would contain the highest quality dog food. [These are not actual brand names. We merely want your opinion as to which names give you the image of highest quality.]
     ____ Swift & Co. Dog Food   ____ Monfort Dog Food
     ____ Champion Dog Food   ____ Pedigreed Dog Food
     ____ Blue Ribbon Dog Food   ____ Hormel Dog Food

14. What change or improvement would you like to see in canned food? [Contents, can sizes, etc.] _____
     _____

15. In order that we can analyze the relationship between owner income and their dog's diet would you please indicate the approximate income of your households.
     ____ 0-$5,000
     ____ $5,000-$8,000
     ____ $8,000-$12,000
     ____ $12,000 and over

Case 3   The following survey was carried out in four West Coast shopping centers. Interviewees were selected at random as they passed the research booth set up in the center. They were asked the questions as stated by the interviewer. Toward the end of the interview, the respondent was shown a new dental floss holder that was also a toothbrush. Evaluate the questions and determine how well their results would enable a market potential for the product to be developed.

Questionnaire

1. Do you go to a dentist on a regular basis?
    ____ Yes   ____ No   ____ Don't know/no response

2. [If Yes] does your dentist have you on a preventive dentistry program?
    ____ Yes   ____ No   ____ DK/NR

3. Have you had your teeth cleaned in the last six months?
   ____ Yes   ____ No   ____ DK/NR

4. Have you ever used dental floss?
   ____ Yes   ____ No   ____ DK/NR

5. [If Yes] can you remember if it was waxed?
   ____ Yes   ____ No   ____ DK/NR

6. Are you now using dental floss?
   ____ Yes   ____ No   ____ DK/NR

7. Does anyone else in your family use dental floss?
   ____ Yes   ____ No   ____ DK/NR

8. [If Yes] how frequently?
   ____ Yes   ____ No   ____ DK/NR

9. Is there anything in particular you dislike about using dental floss?
   ____ Yes   ____ No   ____ DK/NR

10. Have you ever used a dental floss holder?
    ____ Yes   ____ No   ____ DK/NR

11. [If Yes] was it recommended by your dentist?
    ____ Yes   ____ No   ____ DK/NR

12. Does anyone else in your family use a dental floss holder?
    ____ Yes   ____ No   ____ DK/NR

13. Would you purchase this dental floss holder for $3.49?
    ____ Yes   ____ No   ____ DK/NR

14. Family size:
    ____ 1-2   ____ 3-4   ____ 5 or more

15. Gross family income:
    ____ Under $5,000
    ____ $5-7,999   ____ $12,500-14,999
    ____ $8-9,999   ____ $15,000-24,999
    ____ $10-12,499   ____ $25,000 and over

16. Age:
    ____ Under 18   ____ 35-49
    ____ 18-24   ____ 50-64
    ____ 25-34   ____ 65 over

7

Methods for obtaining primary data on attitudes

Reprinted by permission of Marvel Comics Group.

Marketers initially viewed surveys as tools to provide answers to "who," "what," "where," and "when" type questions. But in recent years an additional question, "why," became increasingly important. This complicates the demands made on surveys, since "why" or attitude questions seek qualitative data, and some critics question whether surveys can effectively perform such a task.

Much of the controversy centers on the types of numerical data generated by attitude surveys and the meaning of these numbers. Thus, before presenting the techniques used to measure attitudes, the reader should first be made aware of the different types of numerical scales. This background will also provide greater understanding of the limitations of various statistical tools discussed in later chapters of this book.

PROPER USE OF NUMBERS

Numerical measurement is a more complicated process than researchers often realize. "... we may say that measurement, in the broadest sense, is defined as the assignment of numerals to objects or events according to rules. The fact that numerals can be assigned under different rules leads to different kinds of scales and different kinds of measurement."[1] This statement is from an article by S. S. Stevens in which he identified four basic measurement scales: nominal, ordinal, interval, and ratio. These four scales encompass all types of numerical data.

Nominal scale

These are numbers assigned to objects for the purpose of identifying them. Most adults have a social security number; college students are assigned registration numbers; and all football players wear a number on their jerseys. In some cases these numbers can provide insight into some aspect of time, position, or location. For example, zip codes not only identify territories, but they also can be used to determine geographical locations. Numbers on football jerseys identify general position of players. In most instances, though, nominal data are really of limited interpretative value since they have no meaning other than to identify an object. Finding the mean value for the jersey numbers of the Denver Broncos will not provide any useful data to opposing coaches, fans, or statisticians.

---

[1]S. S. Stevens, "On the Theory of Scales of Measurement," *Science*, Vol. 103, 1946, 677.

Ordinal scale   This scale provides for the ordering of objects with respect to some attribute. Thus one object may have "more of" or "less of" something than another object. In ranking salesmen in terms of their 1981 net sales, John Jones was number one, Pete Brown was number two and Gene Smith was number three. While an ordinal scale allows the researcher to compare rankings of objects (knowing Jones was number one meant he had higher sales in 1981 than Smith), this type of measurement doesn't enable the researcher to say to what extent Jones outperformed Brown. Ordinal scaling enables ranking of the data, but it doesn't allow an evaluation to be made between these rankings.

Interval scale   Here, specific values are assigned to objects, and the intervals between these values are equal. For example, in the Fahrenheit temperature scale, the common measurement value used is the degree. When comparing two temperatures—80 degrees and 20 degrees—the following statements can be made: A temperature of 80 degrees is warmer than a temperature of 20 degrees; the total difference between these two temperatures is 60 degrees. But, in evaluating this difference, it can't be stated that 80 degrees is four times warmer than 20 degrees. This same limitation applies to measuring attitudes. A person who gave a product a rating of 4 is not necessarily twice as favorable toward that product as a person who only gave it a rating of 2.

   The reason for this inability to rate differences is the fact that these scales are built on an arbitrary zero point which means that such mathematical activities as multiplication and division cannot be performed.

Ratio scale   In a ratio scale an absolute zero exists. Because of this, relative comparisons can be made between data. For instance, if Salesman A sells 12 units per day and Salesman B sells 24 units per day, it can be stated that B's output is twice that of A. This same type of comparison can be made when such factors as weight, length, velocity, time, light intensity, etc., are involved.

Summary of these scales

In reviewing these four scales it can be seen that in moving from the nominal scale to the ratio scale the information becomes more powerful. Whenever possible the researcher should seek to obtain and use data that fit into ratio scales. There is general agreement that procedures have not as yet been developed that enable ratio scales to be used to measure the attitudes and aptitudes of people. Many social scientists feel that such factors as IQ scores and attitude scales don't even meet the standards for an interval scale. This inability to employ ratio scales for much of the qualitative data in the social sciences is the primary hurdle to its being able to develop the invariable relationships (laws) found in the physical and natural sciences.

The key point to be made in this section is that the researcher must realize what can and cannot be done with data. When data are tied to ordinal scales, researchers can only cite such differences among the data as "less than" or "greater than." With data tied to interval scales, references to the difference among the data can only be made in terms of the size of the interval. It is only when a ratio scale of measurement is involved that the relative differences between the data can really be determined.

METHODS FOR MEASURING ATTITUDES

Most of these methods descended from a brief era when motivational research was the "in" type of marketing research. As so often happens when something becomes faddish, it gets carried to extremes, and this certainly was the case in the late 1950s with motivation research. A backlash set in leading to negative feelings toward motivation research, and these prevailed in business during the early 1960s. The pendulum swung to the middle again, with an accompanying shakeout of many of the questionable behavioral testing methods. Following are some of the surviving methods which are viewed today as important marketing research tools.

Rating Scales

These techniques are probably the ones used most frequently by marketing researchers in their attempts to measure attitudes. The interviewees are asked to provide their personal impression of a product, service, firm, ad, etc. They are not asked to compare the item with others, instead the interviewee of that subject has to derive his/her own standards.

How do you like this peanut butter?

Like it very much	Like it	Have neutral feelings	Dislike it	Dislike it very much

The advantages of these techniques are the ease with which they can be developed and the simplicity of their usage by the interviewees. The major drawback is that the criteria the interviewee used when making his/her rating are not known.

This method was developed in the 1930s by Charles Osgood. It involves having each respondent indicate his or her attitude toward a given subject through a series of bipolar adjectives. Following is a portion of such an evaluation using a florist's retail store as the subject. Five to seven levels of intensity are generally used to separate each set of adjectives.

Figure 7-1   **Semantic Differential Used for Measuring Attitudes of People Toward a Retail Florist**

	1	2	3	4	5	6	7	
Expensive	___	___	x	___	___	___	___	Inexpensive
Wide selection	___	___	x	___	___	___	___	Very limited selection
Reliable	___	x	___	___	___	___	___	Unreliable
Friendly	___	___	___	x	___	___	___	Unfriendly
Modern	___	___	x	___	___	___	___	Old fashioned
Convenient	___	___	___	___	___	x	___	Inconvenient

Semantic differential

The seven gradations for the first set of adjectives were assumed to be: extremely expensive, very expensive, slightly expensive, neither expensive nor inexpensive, slightly inexpensive, very inexpensive, or extremely inexpensive.

For a number of years a controversy existed as to whether the scales used in semantic differential were *ordinal* or *interval*. Today, increasing numbers of researchers accept these scores as *interval* scaled and apply analytic methods involving a *mean*. Profile analysis is the technique most frequently used since it enables semantic differential ratings to be compared among different individuals and groups. Figure 7-2 is a profile of two dif-

Figure 7-2   **Profile of Two New York Florists Developed from Semantic Differential Scores of 100 Consumers**

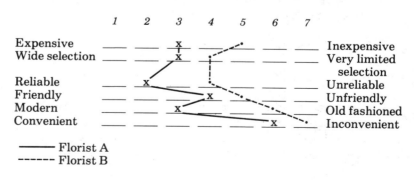

———— Florist A
------ Florist B

ferent florists in city A using results from semantic differential scores of 100 consumers.

The major advantage of semantic differential is its simplicity and versatility—it can be adapted easily to a wide variety of subjects. Its drawback is the lack of precision it provides when evaluating its results.

Staple scale

This technique differs from semantic differential in that it uses just one term and asks the respondent to describe how well that word describes the concept (Figure 7-3). Circling +3 means the respondent feels the waiters are very capable. The results can be used to develop profiles (as in Figure 7-2). This technique is simple to construct, but since it is not widely used at present, the respondent may not really understand how to use it.

Figure 7-3

Acme Restaurant

	+3		+3		+3
	+2		+2		+2
Capable	+1	High	+1	Reasonable	+1
Waiters/	−1	Quality	−1	Prices	−1
Waitresses	−2	Food	−2		−2
	−3		−3		−3

Likert attitude scales

In the Likert method a series of statements is provided and the interviewees are asked to rate each statement on the basis of the strength of their personal feelings toward it: strongly agree (+2); agree (+1); indifferent (0); disagree (−1); and strongly disagree (−2).

The numbers in parentheses are numeric values associated with each possible answer. When analyzing the results, the signs on these numbers are reversed when a statement is unfavorable. For "I would not give flowers as a gift for any occasion," the numerical signs would be reversed since an interviewee indicating a "strongly agree" with this statement has a negative attitude toward the subject.

The statements used in the survey are selected from a larger list that had been evaluated by a panel of judges. The statements finally chosen are those for which there is greatest agreement among the judges in terms of the scores assigned.

Assume that the following group of figures represents the Likert ratings of three interviewees on seven statements about flowers.

| | Interviewee | | |
Statement	A	B	C
1	+1	−1	0
2	+2	−1	+1
3	+2	−1	+1
4	0	−2	0
5	+2	0	−1
6	+2	−1	+2
7	+1	−2	+2

Remember when evaluating the responses that the five possible choices from "strongly agree" to "strongly disagree" are reversed for those statements deemed negative by the judges during the prejudging. Interviewee A's score is +10, B's score is −8, and C's score is +5. Thus A is the most favorably disposed toward flowers. These three can now be placed in an order on the basis of their attitudes toward flowers. It should be emphasized that the scores obtained via the Likert method can only be used to rank interviewees (ordinal data).

Another form of analysis that can be employed with Likert scales is separating all the respondents into three groups on the basis of their total scores — favorable, somewhat neutral, unfavorable. For example, if there were 16 statements one would be placed in the favorable category if his/her total score was 24 or less. Or all scores could be separated into quartiles, with the top quartile being the "most favorable" group and the last quartile the "least favorable" group. Each group could then be analyzed on the basis of its demographic makeup or some other characteristic to see what similarities may exist among group members.

Number and nature of choices

In the preceding techniques, respondents were provided with a number of alternative choices (words, statements, numbers) and asked to select the one that most closely describes their attitude toward the subject. When using these techniques, the researcher must decide how many choices to include as well as their wording.

Number of categories — Researchers disagree as to the ideal number of categories (choices) that should be offered to respondents. Four to eight categories appear to be the range most acceptable to researchers, with five the number used most often. Having more than eight categories requires too much refinement in answers from the respondent, whereas less than four categories does not provide enough preciseness.

Odd vs. even choices — There is also disagreement on whether there should be an even or odd number of choices. An even number of choices forces the respondent to declare a position, whereas an odd number usually provides a middle position for those situations where the respondent really cannot identify his/her feelings. The drawback of including a neutral position is that this choice attracts many respondents who do not have strong feelings on an issue, and thus does not allow the researcher to discriminate between answers. Without this middle point, however, the respondents who truly have neutral or mixed feelings become frustrated since they feel they are being forced into a positive or negative position.

Forced choice — This is related to the issue of "odd vs. even" number of choices. Should the respondent be forced to make a choice? Providing a "neutral" category does not necessarily handle this issue. There are many situations in which respondents truly do not have an opinion or do not know enough about the situation to have formed one. A "neutral" feeling and "don't know" are not the same thing. Thus if there is a possiblility the situation being evaluated is not within the experience of the respondent, a "don't know" choice should be given.

Wording of choices — Should the choices include an equal number of favorable and unfavorable statements? In most situations, they should. Responses can easily be biased if the majority of choices are either favorable or unfavorable. A situation in which an unbalanced set of categories might be used is when prior information indicates the people being surveyed all hold an extreme position — i.e., all are loyal users of the product. Then by using the following unbalanced set of choices, more preciseness in answers can be obtained: (1) Outstanding, (2) Well above average, (3) Above average, (4) Average, and (5) Below Average.

The combination of choices should be consistent. For example, the following combinations use phrases that blend together: (1) Well Above Average, (2) Above Average, (3) Below Average, and (4) Well Below Average. On the other hand, this combination is inconsistent and difficult to use by the respondent: (1) Well Above Average, (2) Good, (3) Below Average, and (4) Awful. Extreme terms such as "awful," "terrible," or "great" should be avoided.

Appropriateness of choices — Do the available choices relate to the question being asked? A problem often occurs when a series of statements is grouped and the same set of choices is used for each statement. The possible answer for a statement related to the "quality of salespeople" may not be appropriate for a statement involving store hours. In the following example, the choices available do not make sense when used with the question on store hours.

	Excellent	Above Average	Average	Below Average	Well Below Average
How do you rate the quality of our salespeople?	——	——	——	——	——
How do you feel about our store hours?	——	——	——	——	——

Thurstone differential

In this method interviewees are asked to select those statements they agree with from a total list of 20 to 25 statements. These statements are derived from an original list of 100 to 200 statements that are evaluated by a panel of 15 to 20 judges. Each judge is asked to place those statements in 11 nearly equal piles. These piles represent the judgment of these panel members as to which statements are "most favorable" and which are "least favorable" about the subject. A sixth or middle pile is the "neutral" position.

Mean scores for each of the original 100 to 200 statements are determined on the basis of the piles they were placed in by the judges, and the 20 to 25 statements with the smallest dispersion are chosen to be included in the survey. From this list of 20 to 25 statements the interviewee is asked to check only those with which he agrees, enabling a mean score for each interviewee to be derived. This score supposedly quantifies the attitude of each interviewee toward the subject under study. The word "supposedly" is used because critics of the Thurstone differential feel that the number values obtained can only be used to place the interviewees in a sequence or order (ordinal scaling) based on the intensity of their overall attitude toward the subject. They don't feel these values can be used to make comparisons between the interviewees in terms of the degree of difference in their attitudes (interval scale).

The 20 to 25 statements used in the Thurstone differential must all deal with the same subject. Therefore, if attitudes toward a variety of subjects (firm's products, its personnel, its credit policy, etc.) are sought, this technique becomes quite cumbersome since a separate list of statements would be needed for each subject.

Following are a few of the statements included in a survey using the Thurstone differential to measure interviewees' attitudes toward fresh flowers. The interviewee checked each statement he/she agreed with.

_____ 1.   A man should not wear a flower unless a specific occasion calls for it.

_____ 2.   Brides who wear fresh flowers distract from the true beauty of the wedding.

✓ 3.   Fresh flowers remind me of springtime.

_____ 4.   I would be embarrassed if a stranger gave me fresh flowers.

_____ 5.   A funeral without flowers would seem stark and cold.

✓ 6.   A flower is one of the most beautiful forms of nature.

✓ 7.   I would send fresh flowers to a friend who is hospitalized.

Each of the above statements was assigned a number based on its original rating by the judges.

        Statement 1 – 7.2

        Statement 2 – 8.6

        Statement 3 – 2.6

        Statement 4 – 7.1

        Statement 5 – 4.0

        Statement 6 – 1.8

        Statement 7 – 3.0

Interviewee A chose Statements 3, 6, and 7 as the ones with which he agrees. His average score was 2.6 + 1.8 + 3.0 ÷ 3, or 2.5. If Interviewee B chose Statements 3, 4, 5, and 7, his average score would be 2.6 + 7.1 + 4.0 + 3.0 ÷ 4, or 4.2. Thus Interviewee A would be ranked higher (the lower the number, the more positive the attitude) than B in terms of his attitude toward flowers (ordinal rating). But what other comparison can be made between the attitudes of A and B? Does A's mean score of 2.5 indicate he prefers flowers twice as much as B whose mean score was 4.2? No! Advocates of this procedure feel it enables a researcher to develop interval data from what previously was ordinal data. But most statisticians feel that all this process has done is develop a more sophisticated set of ordinal data.

Projective methods

The basic premise of these methods is that the best way to obtain the true feelings and attitudes of people is to enable them to indirectly present data about themselves by speaking though others. Two examples of projective methods are cartoon techniques and word association.

Cartoon techniques

Here, the respondents are shown a picture of people (usually two) in a situation related to the subject under study (see Figure 7-4). They are then asked to describe what is occurring or to answer a question stated by one of the cartoon characters. The characters are generally drawn to be as neutral as possible (no smiles or frowns). One study discloses that the projections are more accurate if stick figures are used in the cartoon.

Figure 7-4   The Use of Cartoon Technique

Picture frustration (putting one of the cartoon characters in a frustrating position) and Thematic Apperception Tests (depicting more general situations than the frustrating method) are the two most frequently used cartoon tests. Since actual uses of these tests and the analyses of their results can be quite complicated, these methods require a trained interpreter.

Word association and sentence completion

In word association a respondent is given a series of single words and then asked to match it with one of his/her own. The goal is to entice quick and unrestrained answers.

Rose	Smell
Florist	Funerals

Sentence completion follows somewhat the same procedures, except that ideas rather than words are used:

My favorite flower is _____

Men who buy flowers are _____

Conducting these tests can be relatively uncomplicated, thus they can be given by a semi-trained interviewer. The interpretations of the answers, however, require a highly trained person and this is one of its shortcomings.

Story completion, role playing, and reactions to lists

Story completion — This is a more lengthy version of sentence completion in which participants are presented partial scenarios and asked to complete the story.

Role playing — Participants are asked to assume the role of another person and behave in the manner they feel that person would act. For example, to identify peoples' attitudes towards life insurance salesmen, five people are asked to provide the conversation they feel would occur between five such salesmen discussing methods they use to increase sales.

Use of lists — Lists of various products or activities are shown to participants, and they are asked to describe the type of person who would have used such a list. Their answer will shed light on their feelings about the items on the list and what type of people such items appeal to.

The success of any projective technique depends on participants being willing and able to effectively describe actions. Success is also contingent upon having a skilled interpretation of their response. If properly used, these techniques can provide insight into attitudes and feelings not usually obtained through direct questioning.

METHODS FOR MEASURING SALIENCE

In determining a person's *overall* attitude, it is necessary not only to identify his/her attitude toward various attributes of a company, product, advertisement, etc., it is also important to measure how important each of these attributes is to the person. The techniques described in the previous section all dealt with valence – the degree to which respondents feel something (product, person, etc.) possesses a certain attribute. The second component of attitudes is salience – the importance of a given attribute to a person.

In measuring attitudes toward a new type of tennis racket, for example, the respondent might use semantic differential or Likert scaling to measure the racket on each of the following attributes: price, looks, weight, durability, quality of material in the racket. While it is important to obtain the respondent's impression on the degree to which the racket possesses all of these attributes, it is also necessary to determine how important each attribute is to the respondents when they evaluate tennis rackets.

The following model expresses the relationship between valence and salience that, when combined, determine a person's overall attitude toward an object.

$$A_j = \sum_{i=1}^{n} I_i P_{ij}$$

$j =$ Object being evaluated: tennis racket

$A_j =$ Person's overall attitude toward the object

$i =$ Object's attributes or characteristics

$I_i =$ Importance the person attaches to the attribute (salience)

$P_{ij} =$ Individual's perception of the extent to which Object j possesses the attribute i (valence)

How can the individual values in the above formula be determined? The methods described in the previous section (Likert, semantic differential, etc.) can provide the information needed for P_{ij}, but there is less agreement over how to measure the importance value – I_i. Following are some techniques that have been used.

A list is prepared of the object's attributes, and the respondents are asked to identify how important each is to them in their final attitude (decision to purchase) toward the object. The following table refers to the tennis racket.

Itemized approach

Attributes	Very Important	Fairly Important	Somewhat Important	Not Important
Price	x	___	___	___
Weight	___	x	___	___
Durability	___	x	___	___
Material Used	x	___	___	___
Looks	___	x	___	___

This respondent is primarily interested in price and the type of material used. But the other three attributes also were rated high. This profile illustrates the chief weakness of this method: people tend to identify most attributes as being fairly important. Thus, they should be forced to make some type of comparison or trade off between the attributes.

This method forces the respondent to rate the attributes on the basis of their relative importance to him/her. For example, the respondent could be requested to: "Divide 100 points between the following five attributes in a tennis racket in terms of the relative importance of each to you when selecting a new racket." The more attributes to be rated, the more difficult it becomes for the rater.

Comparative weights

Price	___
Weight	___
Durability	___
Material	___
Looks	___
Total	100

The respondent is presented with two objects at a time and asked to select one on the basis of some criterion as "most tart," "most attractive," "most modern." The number of comparisons the respondent must make depends on how many items or products are in the groups. If there are eight items, 28 comparisons [$n(n-1)/2$] will be necessary.

Paired comparisons

Since each set of comparisons can deal only with one attribute, if more than one product attribute is involved, the number of comparisons will greatly increase. Taste and aroma would be two different attributes and would double the number of comparisons needed from 28 to 56. This rapid increase in comparison limits the usefulness of this technique.

Table 7-1 presents the results from 100 respondents comparing five brands on one attribute. In the comparison between Brand A and Brand B, 81 out of 100 preferred Brand B. Seventy-four out of 100 preferred Brand A to Brand D.

Table 7-1   **Number of Respondents Preferring Each Brand**
(100 Respondents Queried)

	A	B	C	D	E
A	–	81	68	26	37
B	19	–	28	8	14
C	32	72	–	15	26
D	74	92	85	–	57
E	63	86	74	43	–
Total	188	331	255	92	134
Rank Order	3	1	2	5	4
M_p	0.476	0.762	0.61	0.284	0.368
Z_j	−0.06	0.71	0.28	−0.57	−0.34
R_j	0.51	1.3	0.85	0	0.23

A visual analysis discloses that Brand B is preferred over every other brand since its total of 331 greatly exceeds the total of any other brand. The data in Table 7-1 can be used to place the five brands in a rank order. The data could also be converted into an interval scale by employing Thurstone's Law of Comparative Judgment or a method developed by Guiliford called the composite-standard method.[2] Guiliford's method will be used because it is much easier to compute.

Converting to intervally scaled data

The first step in the "composite-standard" method is to calculate the means for each column using the following equation:

---

[2]J. P. Guiliford, *Psychometric Methods* (New York: McGraw-Hill, 1954), p. 170.

$$M_p = \frac{C + 0.5N}{n(N)} = \frac{188 + 0.5(100)}{5(100)} = 0.476$$

M_p = Mean proportion of each column

C = Number of times chosen

The Z values are then determined from each M_p value. If the M_p value is less than 0.5, use the actual M_p value in the Z table to determine the Z value. (Example: For Brand A, $M_p = .476$ provides a Z value of 0.06. Since it was less than 0.5, add a minus sign, -0.06.) If the M_p value is greater than 0.5, subtract this M_p value from 1 and use the difference to determine the Z value. (Example: For Brand B, $1 - 0.762 = 0.238$, which provides a Z value of 0.71.)

The R values are determined by setting the smallest Z value equal to 0 (-0.57 in our example) and then adding its absolute value to every other Z value. These R values are assumed to be intervally scaled data and can be used to evaluate the comparative differences between each brand. For example, respondents felt there was a greater difference between A and B ($1.30 - 0.51 = 0.79$) than there was between B and C ($1.30 - 0.85 = 0.45$).

Advantages and disadvantages of paired comparisons

If only a few objects are involved, it is fairly easy for respondents to participate and give reasonably accurate responses. This lends itself well to comparisons between ads, packages, and products. When the number of objects or attributes increases, however, the comparison becomes lengthy and the respondents' ability to discern differences rapidly declines.

Paired comparison results can be a little misleading because an item may do poorly when compared with others but may still have solid potential. It may have a unique taste that is enjoyed by a limited audience, but will this audience make major efforts to obtain it? This was the case for a toothpaste with a very sharp taste which fared poorly in paired comparison tests because the majority did not like it, but it strongly appealed to a small, but profitable, segment.

Trade off analysis (conjoint analysis)

This is a technique concerned with the joint influence of two or more independent variables on the rank ordering of a dependent variable. A cigarette manufacturer is interested in determining the relative importance of these four attributes to cigarette buyers: type of package (softpack vs. box), length of cigarette (80 mm, 100 mm, 120 mm), taste (mild vs. strong), and flavor (menthol vs. nonmenthol).[3]

In conjoint measurement consumers' preferences on the different combinations of the above attributes are obtained. Such data may be collected by showing the respondent a series of cards, each describing a cigarette having all four attributes but in different combinations. For example, Card One depicts a 80-mm, strong, menthol cigarette sold in a soft pack. Card Two depicts a 100-mm, strong, nonmenthol cigarette in a soft pack. All possible combinations (24) are placed on cards and the respondent is asked to rank the cigarettes (cards) on the basis of some criterion such as preference or likelihood of purchase.

The collected data can be submitted to specially designed computer algorithms (Krushals' MONA-NOVA) to derive a set of scale values for each of the four attributes. This data can then be placed in graphic form as shown in Figure 7-5.

Figure 7-5   **Depiction of Relative Utility to Respondents of Key Attributes of Cigarettes**

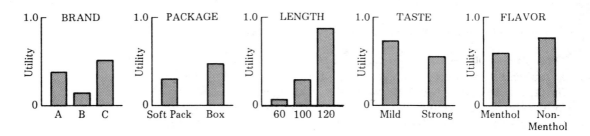

This exhibit indicates that length is the most important attribute. A switch from one length to another will have a greater impact on total utility than a change in any other attribute. If these results were to be used to develop a new product, the best combination would be a mild-tasting, nonmenthol, 120-mm cigarette sold in a crush-proof box.

Another way of handling this same situation would be to

---

[3]Much of this material is taken from a brochure published by the research firm Elrich and Lavidge, *Marketing Today*, Vol. XIII, No. 3, 1975.

have each respondent identify the trade off he/she would make between various combinations of attributes.

	Soft Pack	Box
80 mm	5	6
100 mm	1	2
120 mm	3	4

The above matrix shows one respondent's trade off between type of package and length of cigarette. The results show that length is consistently more important to that person than is the type of package. Similar matrixes could be prepared for each combination of the four attributes.

This latter trade off technique has been successfully used to identify a suggested design for a high-rise condominium using these four attributes—prices, number of bedrooms, view, and floor location. It has also been used to study intercity air travel, markets for office equipment, and demand for financial services.

Multi-dimensional scaling

This term encompasses a "family" of techniques that enable the researcher to take a series of single dimension relationships and transform them into one multidimensional relationship. These techniques have only recently been used by market researchers to identify and measure the perceptions and preferences of people. A major advantage of multidimensional scaling is that it enables relationships to be shown pictorially (in space) rather than just numerically.

A depiction of the end result of multidimensional scaling is found in Figure 7-6. There are a number of different ways in which such a scale can be developed, but only one (the use of paired comparisons) will be presented in this text.

Assume the previously mentioned cigarette manufacturer wanted to determine consumers' overall perceptions of seven brands of cigarettes. One procedure would be to ask consumers to compare each of the seven brands on six different attributes— taste, safety, harshness, reputation, price, and consistency. Each respondent would therefore be making 21 comparisons for *each* attribute.

$$\frac{n(n-1)}{2} = \frac{7(7-1)}{2} = 21$$

Table 7-2   Comparison of Seven Brands
of Cigarettes

	A	B	C	D	E	F	G
Brand A		7	9	4	13	19	11
B			12	3	2	14	11
C				17	1	5	8
D					10	20	21
E						18	15
F							16
G							

Table 7-2 shows one respondent's comparisons of the seven brands based on just one attribute — taste. The respondent feels Brand C and Brand E have the most similar taste, and Brand D and Brand G have the least similar taste.

The multidimensional scaling process enables one person's evaluation of all six attributes to be compressed into the minimum number of dimensions needed to maintain the order of those relationships. The ideal result is one that can be depicted in just two dimensions (Figure 7-6).

Figure 7-6   **Two-Dimensional Presentation of Cigarette Brands**

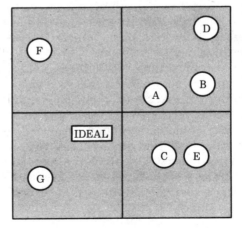

From Figure 7-6 we see that one respondent views Brands C and E as quite similar, with G very dissimilar from D. The "ideal" square depicts the combination of attributes this respondent feels is best. He should be smoking Brand A, which is closest to that ideal. The attribute or characteristic that each axis represents has to be determined by the researcher.

This has been an overly simplified description of a very complicated scaling technique. The main strength of multidimensional scaling is that the maps produced can provide insight into the combination of preferred attributes, the salient attributes of a particular product, products that are viewed as substitutes and opposites, and potential market placement of new products.

Marketers are constantly seeking ways to improve their understanding of buyer behavior. Although the techniques described in this chapter are the ones most frequently used to identify and measure attitudes, they do have certain limitations. **Limitations of attitude measurement**

1. Attitude measurement is imprecise. Unlike data on a person's income and age which can be accurately quantified, the nature and intensity of his/her attitudes are difficult to identify, let alone assign a numerical value.

2. There is still disagreement among some researchers as to the nature of data provided by such techniques as semantic differential or Likert scales. Are the resulting data ordinal or internal?

3. Attitudes of individuals are subject to frequent change, although such changes are offset within groups. For this reason, information about the attitudes of a group is generally more useful to marketing managers than is information about attitudes of individuals.

4. Although it is important to research attitudes, it must be remembered that attitudes are merely one factor influencing behavior. Economic conditions, competitors' actions, government regulation, etc., also significantly affect buyers' activities.

SUMMARY

With the increased emphasis on obtaining and using qualitative data, it is important that both researchers and clients become familiar with the techniques used to obtain attitudinal data and, even more important, that they understand how to interpret it properly. All numerical data fit into one of four scales:

1. Nominally scaled data are merely numbers used to identify objects, and any mathematical exercise performed on them such as adding or subtracting is meaningless.

2. Ordinally scaled data involve the ranking of objects, but do not allow any in-depth evaluation to be made between these rankings.

3. Intervally scaled data occur when number values are assigned to objects and it is assumed the intervals between these values are equal. But since the intervals do

not stem from a base zero, only limited mathematical analysis can take place.

4. The most powerful type of numbers are those built on ratio scales. They are derived from an absolute zero enabling all types of statistical analyses to be performed.

The methods most frequently used by marketing researchers to measure attitudes are semantic differential, Thurstone's comparative judgments, statements using Likert scales, and projective techniques in which indirect methods are used to obtain the true feelings and attitudes of people.

These methods all provide information on the degree to which people feel something possesses a certain attribute (valence), but this is only one element of their overall attitude. It is also necessary to determine how important each of these attributes/objects is to them (salience). This type of information is harder to ascertain since methods for identifying salience are fairly new and there is disagreement among researchers as to which actually do provide such a measure. Paired comparisons, comparative weighting, and conjoint analysis are the most widely used of these techniques.

QUESTIONS AND EXERCISES

1. Evaluate the following advertising claim. Which statements can legitimately be made?

   New Super Spiffo gets your clothes 30 percent brighter than Old Spiffo. Even for your white clothes you can use water temperatures 20 percent lower than needed for Old Spiffo. Most importantly, New Spiffo allows you to use 30 percent less detergent.

2. What is the main thing to keep in mind when making statements pertaining to ordinally scaled data?

3. Use (a) paired comparison, (b) constant sum, and (3) rank order to measure students' attitudes toward the following beers: Schlitz, Budweiser, Hamms, a local or regional beer, and Miller.

4. Why do some experts feel Thurstone differential is a more powerful attitude measurement than the Likert scale?

5. What is the difference between valence and salience? Why are they both necessary when the overall attitudes of respondents are sought?

A paired comparison test was used by Kandid Research to **CASES** evaluate the perceptions residents in Dallas, Texas, had of three local department stores. One attribute measured was "quality of **Case 1** merchandise." The following table shows the choices of 78 respondents. Which store was perceived to have the highest quality merchandise? Convert the results to intervally scaled data and make statements about the relative differences in ratings for the three stores.

Stores	A	B	C
A	–	29	47
B	49	–	44
C	31	34	–

Interviews were conducted by a motivational research firm to **Case 2** determine the reasons why people buy or fail to buy bedding plants. In addition to a series of questions on their gardening activities, each respondent was shown the following two pictures and asked these two questions:
1. Which family do you feel leads the more exciting existence?
2. Which family do you feel is more modern?
   a. What do you think the responses were?
   b. What criticisms would you have of the scenes shown in terms of giving insight into attitudes toward growing flowers?

S

R

Case 3 Your research firm has been contacted by the Department of Agriculture to develop a survey instrument that will enable a comparison to be made between the attitudes of rural adults and urban adults toward living in rural areas. This study is to provide insight into ways that might be used to entice more urban people to move to rural areas.

1. Develop a set of 8 to 10 statements using Likert scales that can be used to identify attitudes of both groups toward rural living.

2. Develop an analytic method that can be used to distinguish between respondents who are "pro" rural living, "neutral" rural living, and "anti" rural living.

8

Methods for obtaining primary data— Observations and experiments

"Do you like Cher?" "No!" That was the reply most subjects gave in a test conducted by Dr. Sidney Weinstein. Men thought she was a "floozy" and women didn't like her because she wore see-through blouses.

However, while their lips may have been saying "No," their brains were saying "Yes!" Each of the subjects was attached to sophisticated electronic equipment that enabled their brain patterns to be studied, and Cher made their brain waves "go bonkers."

The network sponsoring the study relied on the verbal response and turned down her "special." That "special" became a major success on another network that gave more credibility to the brain wave findings.

The implication of this finding—whenever some aspect of morality is involved, surveys will often not provide the most accurate data and probably should be replaced with a more penetrating method of data collection.

Excerpted from "Madison Avenue's Ultimate Brainstorm," TWA Ambassador, August 1980.

One of the weaknesses of the survey method is that much of the information obtained is based on interviewees' statements describing past actions or their expected future actions. In the case of past actions, the interviewees might be in error in trying to recreate what happened, especially when quite a bit of time has elapsed since the event occurred. Their intended actions may also differ significantly from what actually occurs. This is especially true when people are asked about their plans for future purchases—autos, homes, or major appliances. Many intended purchases never come to fruition due to changes in economic conditions, changes in attitudes, etc. The observation method does not suffer from these shortcomings.

OBSERVATION METHOD

The observation method involves the personal or mechanical monitoring of selected activities. It records actions as they occur; it records "what is." Thus, there is no loss of accuracy due to an interviewee's faulty recollection of past actions or poor estimate of future ones.

In the physical and natural sciences the observation method is heavily used because these disciplines usually deal with inanimate objects, plants or animals, subjects that cannot give a response. In the social sciences, surveys are emphasized because the studies tend to focus on people, and they are able to write or state their responses.

Limited coverage in texts

The observation method is a far more important marketing research tool than implied by the scant coverage it receives in books or articles. A possible reason for this lack of attention is that the observation technique is such an intricate part of our everyday activities that many authors may feel there is no need to dwell on the subject. We are constantly observing. We observe another person's reaction to what we say. We observe how much money is dropped into the collection basket at church on Sunday. We observe the type of car a person drives.

There is great variation in the complexity of observation methods used in marketing research projects. An example of low-level observation would be to have the dishwasher in a restaurant serving group luncheons observe what types of food come back untouched. This indicates a particular group's (Kiwanis, D.A.R., Rotary) likes or dislikes of certain meal combinations and can be used in developing future menus. A more complicated example of an observation method occurs when a variety of ads are shown to people, and their responses to the ads are measured by wiring key parts of their bodies to disclose physiological reactions to each ad. Most observational techniques fall somewhere in between these two in terms of complexity.

When to use the observation method

The observation method should be used when a high degree of accuracy in the results is mandatory. In the past many firms merely described a product idea to interviewees or displayed a model of a new product to obtain their reactions. "How much would you pay for this item?" "Would you buy this item if it were available in grocery stores?" "Which of these two packages do you prefer?" They found they were often misled by the answers since such questions required only verbal commitments from the respondents, not monetary ones.

A more accurate test of customer reactions is having the product available in selected outlets under normal buying conditions and recording sales of the product. This requires a monetary commitment by customers, which is a much more accurate depiction of their real attitudes toward the product.

The observation method is also used when existing information might be in question. For example, questionnaires might have been given to residents of Fayette, Iowa, to determine church attendance. The results indicate that 85 percent of the families in the community attend church regularly; actual church attendance figures differ significantly from this percentage. Thus, to get an accurate picture, it is necessary to actually observe families over a given period of time and record their church attendance.

The nature of the information needed may also dictate the use of observation techniques. For example, information on traffic patterns can only be obtained through traffic counts. The work patterns of salesmen must be observed if they are to be properly evaluated. The routes shoppers travel in supermarkets have to be witnessed.

What type of observation procedures should be used?

Once the decision is made to use the observation method, a series of other decisions must then be made related to the specific procedures to employ.

Controlled vs. normal environment

Ideally it is best to observe an activity under normal conditions, i.e., shoppers' usage of new two-tiered shopping cart in supermarkets. But, since some activities just don't lend themselves to this type of format, it is often necessary to observe an activity or event in a controlled environment, e.g., to bring people into a specially equipped room in order to observe the difficulties they encounter when opening three new types of plastic containers.

Disguised vs. open observation

Should the people be aware they are being observed? In some cases this awareness will have little effect on their normal actions. The existence of traffic counters at a particular site does not influence the amount of automobile traffic passing that site. But there are many situations in which people alter their activities if they know they are being observed. Salespeople in a clothing store may be especially polite to customers if they know their performance is being evaluated.

Structured vs. unstructured observation

In a structured situation the observers are told what to observe and how to observe it. They may even be given a formal checklist to record what specifically takes place. Structured methods are needed when a hypothesis is to be tested or a causal study is involved.

In an unstructured observation the observer is given a great deal of freedom in terms of what to note. This is most useful in research of an exploratory nature. A chain supermarket with an unusually high rate of shoplifting has a security expert spend a few days in selected stores just looking for general conditions that might shed light on the reasons for this unexplained rate of theft.

Manual vs. mechanical observation

In recent years a variety of mechanical devices have been introduced that can be used for observing the actions or responses of people.

A *psychogalvanator* measures a person's emotional reactions to various stimuli by measuring changes in his/her perspiration rate; it is used to measure people's reactions to different ads. The *pupilometer* measures changes in the size of a person's pupils as he/she is looking at an ad, a package, or a product design. A change in pupil size supposedly reflects the person's interest in the subject being viewed. *Eye cameras* study a person's eye movements while reading. This allows a precise analysis to be made of the procedures followed when reading copy. It identifies the parts the reader perceived first, the parts dwelled on, and the amount of copy actually read.

A fairly new technique is the study of brain patterns to measure the recall and recognition impact of ads. Such patterns can be identified by attaching small electroids to the subject's head and then identifying the amount of right and left brain activity occurring while the subject views an ad.

Most of the above techniques deal with a somewhat similar situation, the evaluation of ads. But there are other mechanical devices with broader usage — traffic counters, turnstyles, audiometers for TV sets, and cameras used to supplement human observations.

While mechanical devices usually can provide greater accuracy, there are certain extras that only human observers can add. A mechanical traffic counter can identify how many cars passed a location, but it can't identify the number of people in the car or the state or county the car was from. An audiometer on a TV set can record what channel the set is turned to, but it can't evaluate the viewers' degree of interest in the program or even the number of people in the audience.

One fairly simple observation method is called "response latency." It measures the amount of time a person takes to answer a question. Quick answers indicate certainty of preference. If a participant is asked to choose between Product A and Product B and quickly chooses Product A, it can be concluded he/she has a strong preference for that product. Conversely, if he/she hesitates in the choice, no strong preference exists. This observation technique is especially useful in telephone interviews since latency can be measured with voice stimulated stop watches.

Steps in using the observation method

If the observation method is to be used successfully, the activities to be observed must be ones that can be precisely identified. Subjective judgment by the observer as to what is actually occurring must be minimized. To ensure maximum success in the use of the observation method, the following procedures should be carried out in the listed order.

1. Make general decisions about who or what is to be observed and where these observations will take place.

2. Choose the specific method or methods for recording results. Will the information be recorded at the time of observation? Will mechanical equipment be used? Will those being observed be aware of the study?

3. Choose the categories or specific characteristics to be observed. This is a crucial step since it is necessary to precisely define activities to be observed in order to minimize the observer's subjectivity.

4. If human observers are to be used, properly train them, making sure they are consistent, critical, and careful in their observations. They should be just as precise in these observations at 4 P.M. as they were at 10 A.M. that same day.

The most effective way to tie this section together is to list the strengths and weaknesses of the observation method as a data-gathering technique. The potential advantages of using the observation method are: (1) Increased accuracy can be obtained if the observation method is well planned and executed. (2) Data usually can be gathered under typical or normal conditions. (3) What is actually happening is recorded, not past history or future intentions. (4) It does not depend on the subject's communication abilities, a condition crucial to the success of many surveys.

Summary of observation techniques

The potential shortcomings of using the observation method include: (1) The actions being observed may occur infrequently; and much time can be wasted waiting for a particular activity to take place. (2) People, knowing they are being observed, may act in an abnormal manner. (3) There are inherent weaknesses associated with observers. These include the tendency to tire over a period of time, the observers' inability to discern what is actually occurring, personal carelessness in recording events, etc. (4) There are certain activities that can't be observed because of their intimate or private nature. (5) Only the final action is observed, and little insight is provided into the factors influencing such a decision. Thus it may be necessary to supplement observation with some type of survey.

The observation method can be a valuable tool to researchers, but it is a mistake to look upon it as an "easy" way to obtain information. Proper planning prior to its use, accompanied by careful, consistent, and critical gathering of data are necessary to ensure success.

EXPERIMENTS

Experiments are really a special form of survey or observation methods, since people are asked questions about some controlled conditions or their reactions to certain controlled conditions are observed. But it differs in one significant way from these two methods. In experiments, the researcher manipulates selected independent variables and measures the effect of these manipulations on the dependent variables. In the survey and observation methods, the information is usually obtained under normal or near-normal circumstances, and the researcher intervenes only to gather data, not to alter the environment.

Experimentation is the most conclusive of the procedures for gathering primary data. It is viewed as "the hallmark of scientific research," and most researchers are reluctant to accept the validity of any cause-and-effect relationships unless they have been verified by experimentation.

The use of experiments in marketing

Researchers may select one of two possible goals for their study. They may seek to explain the relationships that exist between certain variables or they may study the nature of the changes resulting from the relationships. Marketing research is generally involved with the latter type of investigation since many changes occurring involve human decisions, and attempts to explain all the underlying causes of these decisions are usually futile.

Components of experiments

All experiments involve three basic components: (1) the variable being acted upon, called the "test unit," "dependent variable," or "subject"; (2) the actual alteration, called the "treatment"; (3) the results of the treatment, which are given a variety of labels— "outcomes," "observation," "change," "effect," etc.

The Dayton Manufacturing Company wanted to determine what effect introducing music into work areas would have on the output of its employees. The work areas comprise a number of different buildings with different activities performed in each building. It was decided, however, to test the effect of music in only a few selected work sections. In this experiment the workers in the selected sections are the "test units"; piping in music is the "treatment"; and the amount of worker output under these altered conditions is the "outcome."

Additional terminology

In addition to the above three components, there are some other frequently used terms associated with experiments.

Test or experiment group—This is the group to which the treatment is being applied. It is the group under study.

Control group—This group is similar in makeup to the test group, but does not receive the treatment. It represents what would have occurred among the test group if the experiment had not been introduced.

Field experiment—An experiment conducted in a "real world" environment. In an experiment measuring tire wear, for example, various makes of tires are put on cars driven by state troopers, and the tread remaining on each tire after 20,000 miles of road usage is measured.

Laboratory experiment—An experiment conducted in a carefully controlled environment. An experiment measuring tire wear is carried out in a specially designed laboratory in which actual driving is simulated on a treadmill and each of the tires is measured for wear after 20,000 miles.

Reliability—A measure of the stability or consistency of the experiment's outcome. If the same treatment would be repeated a number of times, will the outcome be reasonably similar? Many researchers do not give proper attention to the reliability aspect because it requires repetition of experiments, a costly and time-consuming activity.

Validity—Refers to how well the experiment measures what it claims to measure. Was the treatment totally responsible for the outcome, or did some other factor also have some major impact? Validity is such an important element of an experiment, that it is covered at greater length in the next section.

Since experiments use results from samples and project them to the universe, these results must be both internally and externally valid.

Validity of experiments

Internal validity—Was the experiment treatment solely responsible for the changes occurring, or did some outside or extraneous factors also influence these results? If there were outside influences, what was their total impact?

External validity—Do the results of this experiment apply to the real world? There is little point in performing an internally perfect experiment if the results obtained have no application to real world situations. A prime shortcoming of many economic models is that they ignore the influence of extraneous factors with the assumption of "ceteris paribus," i.e., "all things being equal."

Examples of validity

Experiments can be performed either in the field or under controlled laboratory conditions. Establishing internal validity for field experiments can be quite difficult. However, in a laboratory experiment, great control exists over all variables with the result that its internal validity is usually quite high.

Field experiments generally are externally valid since they are conducted under normal or real world conditions. Laboratory experiments on the other hand may lack external validity because of the controlled environment under which they were conducted.

Many tests or experiments involving new products are conducted under laboratory conditions. For example, three different tuners for television sets may be tested to determine how well each holds up under similar stress conditions. In a laboratory a machine is attached to each set, turning it on and off up to 300 times an hour. In a one-week span each set would have been turned on and off over 10,000 times, which would be comparable to its usage in an average home over a four-year period.

While the above experiment is internally valid (it shows which tuner can stand up longer under these off-on conditions), it is not externally valid. In actual home usage over a four-year period, the sets would be subjected to differences in heat, humidity, dust, etc., that can't be duplicated in a lab test condensed into a one-week period. In fact, the tuner that held up best in the laboratory may be the weakest one in terms of being able to withstand actual usage in the home.

Even with this limitation, lab experiments may still have to be used due to time constraints. If the firm tested each tuner for four years before incorporating it into its sets, the tuner would be either outdated or inappropriate for the new sets being produced. This means the researcher must weigh the importance of internal validity against external validity in deciding whether to conduct the experiment in the field or under laboratory conditions. This is not meant to imply that researchers must be satisfied with only one type of validity. In many experiments, both internal and external validity can be achieved, but the researcher should always be aware of the limitations related to "where" the experiment is conducted.

The term "laboratory" conjures up an image of white-coated scientists mixing chemicals in test tubes or a room filled with cages of little white mice. In marketing research, a lab can be any environment in which outside or extraneous influences can be eliminated or at least controlled. It could be a room specifically designed to observe people's reactions to products or advertisements. It could be a special area set up in a shopping center into which people are brought to make taste tests. Or it could be a specially equipped movie theatre where groups of people view commercials and identify the parts they like or dislike.

Using a laboratory can provide some very important advantages to the researcher. It enables the experimental process to be carried out in a condensed time span and thus speed up the testing process; it enables the standards or conditions under which the experiment is conducted to be rigidly controlled; it permits constant observation. And, finally, if the firm is continually conducting experiments, the existence of a laboratory can save money on its experiments over a period of time.

Extraneous factors (uncontrollables)

The key questions related to an experiment's internal validity are what influence did the treatment have on the actual outcome and what was the possible influence of extraneous factors? Extraneous factors are outside factors that affect the test unit/subject and thus affect the outcome. These factors can take a number of forms:

Impact of history and maturation – The changes associated with the passage of time are described as history and maturation. The influence of history is exemplified by changes in current events external to the experiment but which still may have affected its outcomes. In the Dayton Manufacturing Company example, a number of things might have happened during the test period to affect worker output. The state may have switched to daylight saving time, providing more hours of daylight working time and thus improving lighting within the work area. There may have been some changes in the machinery used in the manufacturing process during the test period. The impact of history becomes greater as the length of time encompassed by the experiment increases.

Maturation is primarily concerned with changes occurring within the individual subjects. Some workers recently hired may have improved their performance during the test period merely because they became more familiar with their jobs. Or a major change in the company's fringe benefits may have placed the workers in a better mood and increased their output. Thus, part or all of the increased output may have had nothing to do with the inclusion of music.

The influence of repeated testing—This does not apply to the Dayton example, but it does occur in experiments where the same people are tested a number of times. As they become familiar with the testing or experiment procedures, their performances may change solely because of this familiarity. For instance, some consumers on a panel are being tested on their reactions to certain messages in TV commercials. After this initial test, they become more conscious of ad messages in general. The next time they are tested, they show a greater awareness of the ads' contents, but their improved content knowledge in the second test period may have had little relationship to an ad's quality.

The impact of the researchers themselves—The researchers themselves may cause some of the change. They may improve their recording ability, or they may improve their use of the recording devices as the period of experimentation continues. Or, their very presence may influence the actions of the subjects being observed.

The mortality of participants—A problem with experiments carried out over a long period is that some of the original subjects may drop out. For example, 10 stores may have been lined up to run an experiment on a specially designed point-of-purchase display. Midway through the test period, 2 stores withdraw from the test. This problem of dropouts also occurs in consumer panel experiments. There is no way of knowing whether the test units lost would have responded similarly to the treatment as those units that remained.

Selection errors—These errors occur when the test units are chosen in a manner that biases the results. They may not be representative of the desired universe, or the treatments are assigned to them in such a way that it influences the outcome. We assume that people can volunteer for one of three time periods in which the experiment will be run—9 to 11 A.M., 1 to 3 P.M., and 7 to 9 P.M. Thus those who volunteer for the morning session could be different in a variety of ways from the evening group, and these differences could distort the outcomes.

Miscellaneous factors—This includes all other factors that can have an influence on the experiment's outcome but over which the experimenter has little or no control. For example, in test markets, the pricing and promotional activities of competition can greatly influence sales of the product being tested. No two situations involving human subjects are identical, and allowances must be made for such differences in order to obtain a true picture of the experiment's results.

An experimental design acts as a blueprint for the experiment since it defines the pattern that will be followed in applying the treatments to the test units. These designs can be placed in two broad categories – informal and formal designs.

Experimental designs

Informal designs

When informal designs are used, many of the effects related to the experiment can be quantified. But because of the fairly loose way in which they are structured, the changes specifically caused by the treatment cannot be isolated by means of statistical tests. There is a lack of randomness in the manner in which the treatment is assigned to the test units and also in the way the test units are chosen. In spite of these restrictions, informal designs are still useful for marketing research because they usually are less costly and easier to use than formal designs.

Before-after without control – The simplest informal design to use is the "before-after without control." This involves measuring the test unit (dependent variable) before and after it has been subjected to the treatment.

The Dayton Manufacturing Company and its attempt to measure the influence of music on worker output will be used to demonstrate this design. For one month prior to the inclusion of the music, the daily unit outputs of the 27 workers to be studied were recorded. The average departmental unit output has been 537 units. During the fifth week music was channeled into the work area, and a record was kept of the workers' daily output under this new condition. The daily output with music turned out to be 582 units.

Period 1: Worker output prior to music – 537 units (O_1)
Period 2: Worker output with music – 582 units (O_2)

$$O_2 - O_1 = \text{effect of the treatment}$$
$$582 - 537 = +45 \text{ units per day}$$

Seemingly, the inclusion of the music had a positive effect in that daily output increased by 45 units. This assumes that any changes in units produced were due solely to the introduction of music. Realistically, at least part of the difference could have been caused by such extraneous factors as changes in the weather or improved skills of the workers.

Before-after with control—In this informal experimental design, a control group is set up and studied during the experimental period. This can be illustrated by an example involving the sale of cut flowers in a supermarket chain. In the past, the chain's stores had displayed cut flowers in buckets on a display stand. In four of their stores they are experimenting with a new type of "open top" cooler for displaying cut flowers. They want to see what influence this more elaborate type of display facility has on flower sales. They also want to have some measure of the extraneous factors, since cut flowers are quite dependent on moods of buyers, the weather, the quality and price of the flowers, the season of the year, etc.

To give the chains a more accurate picture of the actual influence of this new display case during the experimental period, they also keep track of the cut flower sales in stores still using the regular bucket type of display. This latter group acts as the control unit.

Sales in experiment stores prior to introduction of new display case (EX_1)
Sales in control stores (C_1)

Sales in experimental stores during period in which new display cases are used (EX_2)
Sales in control stores during test period (C_2)

The subscript 1 or 2 identifies the period in which sales were measured. *EX* identifies experimental stores, whereas *C* identifies control stores.

$$EX_1 \text{ Sales } = 172 \text{ bunches} \qquad EX_2 \text{ Sales } = 212 \text{ bunches}$$
$$C_1 \text{ Sales } = 168 \text{ bunches} \qquad C_2 \text{ Sales } = 181 \text{ bunches}$$
$$EX_2 - EX_1 = \text{ total change in sales in experiment stores over two periods}$$
$$212 - 172 = +40 \text{ bunches}$$
$$C_2 - C_1 = \text{ total change in sales in control stores over two periods}$$
$$181 - 168 = +13 \text{ bunches}$$
$$(EX_2 - EX_1) - (C_2 - C_1) = \text{ treatment effect}$$
$$40 - 13 = +27 \text{ bunches}$$

The assumption here is that the change in sales in the control stores (+13 bunches) over the two periods was caused by something other than the experiment, and these changes should be taken into consideration when determining the real effect of the new display case. The major assumption in the design is that the control and experiment units are both influenced in a similar manner by extraneous factors. The control units chosen should be quite comparable in makeup to the experimental units.

After only with control—This experimental design is the one most frequently used by marketing researchers. It is intended to eliminate the influence of "pretesting," therefore no "before" measurements are taken between either of the two groups.

$EX - C = $ effect of treatment
$\quad EX = $ measurement of experimental group after the treatment
$\quad\quad C = $ measurement of control group in the same period

A firm wanted to test the success of free samples as a method of stimulating sales for its product. It mailed small sampler packages of its detergent to selected homes in a specific neighborhood. A month later it mailed coupons offering 25¢ off on the purchases of a large package of its detergent to this same group of homes. These coupons were also mailed to a control group from a comparable neighborhood but which had not received the free sample. The coupons were coded to enable a count to be made of the number of coupons redeemed by each group. The experimental group redeemed 121 coupons and the control group redeemed 76 coupons. The difference (45 coupons) was felt to be the result of the sampler.

$$121 - 76 = 45$$
$$EX - C = \text{effect of treatment}$$

While this design neutralizes the impact of "pretest," it does not allow any measurement or analysis to be made on the total change that occurred, a situation handled well in the "before-after with control" design.

Ex post facto design—This is a variation of the "after only" design. The difference between the two is that in the "ex post facto" design, neither the experimental nor control groups are chosen until after the treatment is actually applied. This design attempts to create equivalent experimental and control groups but identifies each only after they have been exposed to the experiment.

A group of people who read a certain issue of *Esquire* magazine are contacted. Those who said they read a certain ad in that edition on radial tires would be the experimental group; those who didn't read this ad would be the control group. Both would be asked questions about some attribute (safety or durability) of different types of tires, and the difference in the two groups' ratings of radials would determine the ad's success. The advantage of this design over the "after only with control" design is that the experimental variable will have exerted its influence in a natural setting, enabling the researcher to study a group which by choice was exposed to the treatment, rather than having been selected to receive the treatment.

Formal designs

In formal designs the researcher *randomly* assigns treatments to *randomly* selected test units. (In the previously described informal designs this careful assignment of treatments was *not* followed.) Therefore, statistical tests (usually analysis of variance) can be applied to the results of experiments using formal designs. Analysis of variance enables the researchers using an experiment on a sample to determine whether one factor (treatment) significantly influences another factor or whether the observed association could have been due to chance or some other factor.

A more extensive discussion of analysis of variance is provided in a later chapter, "Analysis and Interpretation of Data." This section will describe various formal designs and when they should be used. It is important to recognize that these are designs, not statistical tests.

Completely randomized design—This is the simplest of the formal designs. Treatments are assigned to test units on a random basis, and analysis of variance is then performed to determine whether these treatments caused a significant difference in outcomes among these test units. Due to its rather basic structure, however, it can only measure one type of variance—that occurring between treatments.

Example: A supermarket chain is selling antifreeze in all of its stores but it doesn't know what is the most effective price to charge. It tests three different prices per gallon—$2.89, $3.09, and $3.29 – and records the sales from each. It randomly assigns these prices to the nine experimental stores, three using each price (see Table 8-1).

Number of Cases Sold at Various Prices   **Table 8-1**

Week	$2.89	$3.09	$3.29
1	19	9	15
2	16	13	20
3	22	20	9
4	24	18	12
Total	81	60	56

The analysis would focus on the average amount of the product sold at each price. It could disclose whether the difference in sales at the lower price was a significant one or whether sampling error could have been involved. It fails to take into consideration, however, the influence of such extraneous factors as weather, size of store, or competitors' prices.

Thus this design presupposes that the extraneous variables have had an equal impact on all of the test units, which was the shortcoming of *informal* designs. Such an assumption might be acceptable in a laboratory experiment where the researcher controls most of the conditions, but it is a dangerous assumption to make for experiments conducted in a real world environment. Thus, this design is not widely used for field experiments.

Randomized block design – This type of design is used when the researcher wants to isolate *one* major source of variation in addition to the treatment's influence. In the previous example where three different prices were tested in nine different stores, no allowance was made for the difference in the sizes of the stores, a potentially important influence on the actual sales obtained.

The randomized block design enables one extraneous factor to be separated from the total experimental error, providing a truer picture of the treatment's actual impact. It is necessary that this additional variable be identified and measured at the time of the experiment.

Example: Building on the previous example of different prices for the antifreeze, assume the researcher wants to identify the actual impact of store size. The nine stores used are broken into three blocks:

Block 1, those stores with weekly total store sales in excess of $100,000, *Block 2*, those stores with weekly sales of $65,000 to $100,000, and *Block 3*, stores with weekly sales of less than $65,000.

Because this second variable (store size) has been added, it is also necessary to increase the number of stores involved to keep the number equal in each cell. Twenty-seven of the chain's stores were selected (nine in each store size), and the prices used were randomly assigned within each of three blocks (see Table 8-2).

Table 8-2   **Randomized Block Design**

Block Store Size	No. of Cases of Antifreeze Sold at Various Prices		
	$2.89	$3.09	$3.29
1 $100,000+	135	92	89
2 $65,000—$100,000	68	61	50
3 below $65,000	42	25	20
Total	245	178	159

When analysis of variance was applied to these results, it disclosed that the lower price ($2.89) resulted in significantly greater sales. It also disclosed that the sales resulting from different prices were not related to the stores' sizes, which showed that this extraneous factor did not significantly affect the treatment.

Latin square design—This design is more powerful than the randomized block design. It enables the researcher to isolate *two* major sources of extraneous variation in addition to measuring the experiment's impact. This is a rather complex design to set up and can be costly and time consuming to use. The added efficiency it provides must be weighed against its additional costs and the greater expertise needed by the user. This design assumes that there is no interaction between the factors being measured.

Example: Expanding on the previous antifreeze example, assume that the manufacturer wishes to test the impact of different prices (treatment) on sales, and wishes to control the impact of store size and the type of chains doing the selling—Chain A, Chain B, and Chain C.

When Latin square is used, the number of extraneous variables to be controlled must be equal in number to the number of treatments (three in this case). Thus, three levels of store size are needed, and stores from three different chains will be involved. The rows and columns of the resulting matrix contain the extraneous variables. The treatment (different prices) is assigned so that each price level occurs only once in each row and column (Table 8-3).

Latin Square Design

Table 8-3

Chain	Size of Store (Weekly Sales)		
	+$100,000	$65–$100,000	Below $65,000
A	Price 2	Price 3	Price 1
B	Price 1	Price 2	Price 3
C	Price 3	Price 1	Price 2

Latin square designs are particularly useful in experiments where it is important to establish controls for the effect of store size, type of store (supermarket vs. drugstore), or time period.

Its limitations are as follows: (1) It requires an equal number of rows, columns, and treatment levels; this can pose a problem when four or five treatments are involved. (2) Regardless of the number of treatments, it can still only control *two* extraneous variables. (3) It assumes that the extraneous variables don't interact with each other or even with the treatment, a questionable assumption in many marketing experiments.

Factoral design — In the previous designs it was assumed that one or two major sources of variation existed and the researcher wanted to separate them from the total variance. No allowances were made for the possibility that some factors might interact with one another. In the antifreeze experiment, the researcher might want to see if stores serving higher-income clientele have greater success with the higher prices than those stores serving lower-income clientele.

The factoral design measures the influence of interacting variables on the dependent variable; for example, improved sales associated with both the income of a store's clientele and any change in the store display used, or a change in sales related to a change in the product's package and the type of display used. The actual design used can be a randomized block or a Latin square, but a more complicated form of analysis of variance is applied to the results. Because of its complexity, no additional information on factoral design will be provided in this book. An outstanding source to consult for more information is the book *Experimentation in Marketing* by Seymour Banks.[1]

---

[1]Seymour Banks, *Experimentation in Marketing* (New York: McGraw-Hill, 1965), pp. 149-179.

Summary of designs

The decision of whether to use a formal or informal design depends on the researcher's own resources—time, money, and statistical know-how. Formal designs enable the variance associated with experiments to be statistically analyzed. They enable one or two extraneous factors to be isolated, and in the case of the factoral design, even the interaction among certain independent variables can be measured.

The design used should enable the desired standard of accuracy to be obtained with the smallest expenditure of time and effort. "There is no special merit in either a complicated experimental plan or a highly refined technique if equally accurate results can be secured with less effort in some other way. A good working rule is to use the simplest experimental design that meets the needs of the occasion."

TEST MARKETING— THE ULTIMATE FIELD EXPERIMENT

Before a new product is introduced nationwide or before a major change in the marketing mix is implemented, business firms often will test these changes on a small, representative portion of the market. This action, called test marketing, is the most common type of field experiment.

The two primary uses of test marketing are: (1) to obtain the reactions of the marketplace to a new product and (2) to evaluate alternative marketing mixes (market plans) for new or existing products.

It must be emphasized that because of its high costs, test marketing should be restricted to those products or marketing plans that have already passed rigorous testing and evaluation. Strong evidence should already exist that a product or plan will be a success, with the test market acting only as the final and most exhaustive investigation.

Cost of test marketing

There are both direct and indirect costs associated with test marketing. Direct costs are those specifically tied to the production and promotion activities of the test. A key factor increasing these costs is the firm's inability to realize economies of scale since everything used in the test market can only be produced in small amounts. For example, a pilot plant may be needed to produce the limited volume of the "new" product; only limited amounts of point-of-purchase materials will be developed, higher trade allowances might be needed to entice outlets to handle the product. All of this results in unusually high costs considering the number of products to be sold or the size of the market reached. In the late 1970s the cost of a typical two-city test market was around $300,000; and if additional cities were added, it could exceed $1 million.

Indirect costs do not involve direct dollar outlays, but are losses that can accrue because (a) the test market may give your competition a warning that you have a new product or (b) the testing requires an inordinate amount of your own management's time and energies.

Guidelines for test marketing

The following generalizations about test marketing are derived from various articles on the subject and a specific survey of firms engaged in test marketing.[2]

1. Test marketing is a costly undertaking—the cost of an effective test is rarely less than $300,000 and can run to four or more times that figure. Therefore, test markets should not be used to test the acceptability of a broad product concept. Companies should use these tests only for products they feel have a good chance of being successful.

2. Tests typically cover a 10-month period, or the length of time needed to evaluate repeat sales.

3. Three geographic test areas are generally used.

4. A combination of store audits and consumer surveys are most effective since you need to know how many units were sold, but more importantly who bought the product and what was the buyer's reaction.

5. The most common uses of test marketing are to identify the market acceptance of a new product, test various price levels, compare the effectiveness of promotions such as "cents off coupons" vs. "free samples," and compare consumer reactions to different ads and different levels of advertising.

6. Test marketing will enable firms to *minimize* losses, but it will not enable them to *maximize* profits.

---

[2]Some of these findings are taken from a presentation made to a Midwest Conference on Successful New Marketing Research Techniques by V. B. Churchill, Jr., "New Product Test Marketing—An Overview of the Current Scene," March 3, 1971.

When not to use test marketing

Test marketing should not be used in the following circumstances.

1. *Financial loss from a product's failure is fairly low.* Because of the huge costs associated with test marketing, a firm should determine the possible costs if the product did fail. Tests should not be used if such costs are reasonably close to the cost of carrying out the test marketing.

2. *Product is similar to one the firm already has successfully put on the market.*

3. *Product is tied to a "faddish" condition.* If the product is one arising from a condition of a short-lived phenomena (popularity of "Star Wars" movie and its accompanying games, shirts, toys), it has to be on the market fast and can't wait for test results since the fad will have passed or be on the downslope by the time the test results are obtained.

4. *Product has unique concept but one that can be easily copied.* If a firm may lose lead time in hitting the market or competition might be able to produce a similar product, it should be cautious about test marketing.

5. *Product to be tested is expensive to produce in small numbers.* Some product technology requires the same sort of facilities to produce one unit or a thousand units. (This drawback can be overcome if the product can be temporarily produced by an outside firm.)

Competitors' reactions to test marketing

A key factor in deciding whether to test market is how much competitors may benefit from information they can obtain from your firm's testing. If you run tests in areas where firms such as Nielson are running audits, your product's sales results will become available to other firms.

It is not unusual for a firm to make an accurate evaluation of a competitor's test market results and eventually reach the national market at the same time with a reasonably similar product. General Foods audited Lever Brothers' year-long test marketing of "Mrs. Butterworth" and was able to introduce a buttered syrup nationally at about the same time Lever-Brothers introduced its syrup. Thus, if your product can be easily copied, you might be surrendering any lead time advantage if test marketing is used.

Competitors sometimes attempt to negatively influence the test market results. They can do this by altering the promotional or pricing activities on their own products in the test areas to distort the test results. Some firms have even bought up all or a large share of their competitors' test products so no realistic sales information could be obtained. Vicks Chemical once influenced tests Colgate was running on a new cough syrup by distributing 25,000 samples of Nyquil into two of the test markets.

To overcome some of these problems, firms can run their tests under controlled conditions. In a normal test market the firm will reach the market through its regular distribution channels. In a controlled test market, outside research firms are placed in charge of distributing, shelving, and pricing the test items; they usually choose smaller cities for these tests and even pay a fee to the stores for handling the products. This controlled condition enables close tabs to be kept on the product and competitors have a difficult time obtaining any useful information. If properly performed, a controlled test may also cut down on the amount of time needed to run the test.

Normal vs. controlled conditions

When choosing cities to use for test markets, the following criteria apply:

Selecting test markets

1. A market should be large enough to provide meaningful results, but not too large to make testing overly expensive.

2. A market should be self-contained in terms of media and shipment of merchandise. The major part of the media's circulation should not go outside the test area. Ads on the test products shouldn't be reaching a large audience outside the market where the product is not available because a great deal of confusion and ill will could arise among consumers. Self-containment in terms of shipping applies primarily to chain warehouses. You don't want them shipping test products to their stores outside of the test area. This problem can be overcome by using "controlled" test markets.

3. A market should be "normal" in terms of not being dominated by any single industry or institution.

4. A market should be demographically representative of the larger market to eventually be reached—income, age, family size, ethnic breakdown, etc.

5. A market should complement the product being tested. A butter substitute should not be tested in Wisconsin where people are unusually loyal to dairy products. Air filters for homes should not be tested in the clear atmosphere of Arizona.

Firms involved with frequent test marketing know the particular cities that best meet their test needs. For those firms that are undertaking their first test market activity, lists of "favorite" test cities can be obtained from major advertising agencies. For example, one New York ad agency will provide (for a $200-$300 fee) a list of 45 preferred test cities, their demographic characteristics, media data, names and location of major retail outlets, and history of previous test market activities within that city.[3]

Overview of test marketing

In a test market situation a firm is trying to duplicate the plan it intends to follow on a national basis. This is rarely accomplished, especially in promotional efforts. Usually the amount of advertising or sales promotion dollars used in the test areas could never be matched on a national basis. Thus, unless these factors are properly monitored, the test results can be misleading.

General Mills tested three new products—Bugles, Whistles, and Daisies—in six paired test cities.[4] These products sold so well they couldn't produce enough to keep shelves stocked so they were forced to drop some of the test cities. These unusual results led them to go national with the three products even before the tests were completed. If they had waited for the total test results, they would have discovered that the sales were primarily the result of the promotional campaign and not due to consumers being enamored with the products. In fact, most consumers did not repurchase the items, a condition not discovered in the abbreviated test markets, and the three products had problems over a longer selling period.

A test market is also important in a situation where a firm's new product may cannibalize sales of one of its existing products. Cadbury Limited, a British firm that produces candy and grocery products, was the first firm to introduce a rum and raisin chocolate bar.[5] The firm developed another liquor flavored chocolate

---

[3]"Finding the Right Market," *Sales and Marketing Management*, November 17, 1980, p. 22.

[4]"How a New Item is Born," *Progressive Grocer*, August 1967, pp. 54-59.

[5]Cadbury, N. D. "When, Where, and How to Test Market," *Harvard Business Review*, May-June, 1975, pp. 96-105.

bar but didn't know whether the new product would expand the market segment for all such bars, or merely cannibalize sales of its other liquor flavored bar. Only a test market could determine this. The test indicated that the second bar would expand the market, and thus Cadbury was willing to add the bar to its line.

The marketer should realize that test marketing will not guarantee that all winners and all losers will be identified. A lot of new products have failed nationally, even though they had successful test markets. But test markets do provide additional bits of evidence on the potential sales of a new product or potential success of a planned marketing program.

Finally, it is important to recognize that product managers and researchers differ in their attitudes toward the purpose of test markets. Product managers will usually want to market the product if it *doesn't* perform poorly in the test. Researchers, on the other hand, want to keep the product off the market unless it has a very *positive* test result. Remember, product managers are evaluated on the number of their successful products, whereas researchers are evaluated on their ability to prevent costly product failures.[6]

Simulation— another alternative

The high costs of test marketing have led some firms to use laboratory simulation as an inexpensive substitute. A shopping environment is simulated (partial supermarket set up in lab or truck) and the consumers' buying actions or use of promotional materials are then observed and recorded. The results are then used to project the product's expected success. While such simulations are superior to mere concept testing, they do not provide an environment as realistic as a good test market.

SUMMARY OF METHODS FOR OBTAINING PRIMARY DATA

The three methods available to the researcher for gathering primary data are surveys, observations, and experiments. When survey methods are used, data are obtained by questioning the people who can provide the desired information through telephone, mail, or even direct personal interview. A number of factors influence which technique(s) to use: *Time*, or How fast are the data needed? *Cost*, or How much money does the researcher have available? *Know-how*, or What methods is he/she capable of

---

[6]Klompmaker, Jay, et al. "Test Marketing in New Product Development," *Harvard Business Review*, May-June 1976, pp. 128+.

handling? *Accuracy sought*, or How accurate must the data be? If the need for accuracy is critical, this would eliminate using mail questionnaires and would necessitate personal interviews, or it might even require observations rather than surveys.

In the observation method, information is obtained by observing specific actions. The strength of the observation method is that activities are studied as they occur—What is! It doesn't have to rely on people to accurately describe their past actions or future intentions, as is the case with surveys.

A third method for obtaining primary data is through experimentation. Here, the researcher manipulates certain conditions in an environment and then measures the impact of these manipulations. Experiments can be conducted under laboratory conditions or out in the field. The problem with field experiments is that outside factors often influence the experiment's results. If a formal research design is used in the experiment, the influence of some of these extraneous factors can be measured through analysis of variance.

Formal designs can be complicated to develop and use; thus many researchers use informal designs with control groups. Although the use of control groups in informal designs enables allowances to be made for extraneous factors, the overall nature of these designs does not enable statistical tests to be applied.

Test marketing is the most elaborate type of field experiment. It is used to identify the markets' reaction to a new product or to evaluate alternative marketing mixes. Test marketing does not guarantee that all successes or failures will be identified, but it does provide managers with additional information enabling them to make better decisions.

QUESTIONS AND EXERCISES

1. Give an example of (a) a disguised, structured observation carried out in a normal environment, and (b) an undisguised, structured observation in a controlled environment.

2. Why is it often necessary to supplement mechanical observation with surveys?

3. What simple observation procedures would you use to obtain the following types of information?
   a. Type of clientele using two record stores located on the same block. The intention is to determine whether they appeal to different groups of customers.
   b. The drawing power of a carnival sponsored by the Downtown Merchants' Association.

   c. The potential of a site for a fast food restaurant that is located two blocks from a huge manufacturing plant.

4. What are the key limitations or shortcomings associated with the observation method?

5. Distinguish between internal and external validity. In trying to maximize the internal validity of an experiment, why is its external validity generally endangered?

6. What role do extraneous factors play in experiments?

7. How do the terms "history" and "maturation" differ?

8. What is the chief difference between informal and formal experimental designs?

9. What role do control units play in experiments?

10. Set up an experimental situation using a "before-after with control" informal design.

11. The Acme Research Company wants to determine what is the most effective way to increase responses to its mail questionnaires. The three possibilities to choose from are:
   1. Including 50¢ in each letter to compensate respondents for their time in filling out the questionnaire.
   2. Including a coupon for two cheeseburgers at their local McDonalds.
   3. Having them sign their name and addresses to the completed questionnaire. Thereafter, they will then be mailed a check for $1.50.
Set up an experiment in which these incentives can be tested and the preferred method identified. Assume they will mail out a total of 4,500 surveys in three different cities.

12. Howser Bottling Company is contemplating introducing two new fruit flavors to its soft drink line. It has four possible flavors to choose from. Set up an experiment that will help the company identify the two flavors it should choose. It will sell the soft drinks in supermarkets, convenience stores, and liquor stores.

13. Which of these situations lend themselves to test marketing?
   a. The bottler of Burp Cola is thinking of adding two noncarbonated fruit flavors to the soft drink line.
   b. The creators of the "pet rock" have come up with another novelty idea for a gift product—a "personal enemy." It is a pillow-like device that is almost indestructible and people can hit it and throw it against walls, etc., to relieve their frustrations.
   c. The Society of American Florists wants to develop a new flower holiday—"Be-Nice-to-a-Friend" day. Should it go

national with a promotional campaign or try it out in a limited area first?

d. A firm manufacturing water-related products (shower heads, water jet toothbrushes, foot massages) has developed a very simple device that can be used in a bathtub as a "whirlpool."

14. Evaluate the city in which you live in terms of its potential as a "test city."

9

Sampling—Its role in research

The major TV networks spent two years and $20 million getting ready for the 1980 election-night broadcasts. In the end, the main event—the presidential race between Reagan and Carter—was in doubt for little more than an hour of their broadcast time.

At 8:15 p.m. (New York Time) NBC News formally projected a Reagan victory, a time at which West Coast voters still had almost two hours left to cast their votes. Carter himself conceded at 9:52 p.m. (New York Time), even though people were still voting.

NBC used "exit polls" conducted among thousands of voters as they left their polling places, and combined this with voting returns in key East Coast precincts to make its prediction. This graphically illustrates the important role sampling plays in the predictive efforts of researchers.

"Electronic Anticlimax," *Broadcasting*, November 10, 1980, pp. 33–34.

Regardless of the method used to obtain the primary data (experimentation, observation, or survey), the researcher has to decide whether the information will be collected from every unit of the population under study, or whether only a portion of the population will be used.[1] This latter approach, known as sampling, plays a key role in research undertakings. This chapter presents some of the key elements of sampling with which researchers should be familiar. This information will not make the readers sampling experts, but it will give them greater insight into its strengths and weaknesses, along with a better understanding of its role in research.

SAMPLING—A COMMON ACTIVITY

Before purchasing a novel, the reader will generally first peruse a few of its pages to get an indication of its contents. When buying a spray cologne, the shopper will squirt some on his or her hand to see if it is the fragrance he/she is seeking. We submit to blood tests as part of physical exams since the few drops we surrender provide a lot of information about our health. We form opinions on civic organizations, various ethnic groups, and even educational institutions based on our contact with only a small segment of their membership. Thus, the sampling process plays an important role in the daily lives of most people.

Although the sampling methods presented in this chapter will be of a more formalized nature than the preceding examples, the purpose of all sampling is the same—to obtain information about a population using data selected from only a portion of that population.

Advantages of using samples

The factors that make sampling such a desirable method of obtaining information are described under the five following headings:

Reduced costs — A much lower cost results from gathering information from only a portion of a population than would be incurred if a study of the complete population were undertaken. It

---

[1]The words "population" and "universe" will be used interchangeably in this text. They describe the total group (people or things) which the researcher wishes to study.

is less costly to survey 150 people than it is to survey 15,000 people.

Greater speed — Data can be collected and summarized more quickly when a sample is used. This condition is especially important in projects where time is a key factor. The Nielsen TV studies exemplify the need for speed, since their results must be available in short order so sponsors and networks can make decisions about altering or dropping certain programs.

Greater accuracy — This seems to be a contradiction. How can results taken from a sample be more accurate than those taken from the entire population? The increased accuracy occurs because a smaller, better trained, and better supervised work force can be used to obtain information if sampling is involved. (This assumes a rather large population is being studied.) If each adult member of a large community had to be questioned about his/her television viewing habits, a huge number of interviewers would be needed. This means people of marginal skills might have to be used as interviewers with a resulting decline in the quality of the data obtained.

Greater depth of information — Since a smaller group of respondents is involved when a sample is used, the researcher may decide to get more information from each respondent. The consumer panel approach is a good example of this process. Here a limited number of housewives might be interviewed regularly on their attitudes toward certain products or stores; because of the small number of participants, these interviews can be quite lengthy, allowing more in-depth information to be obtained.

Preservation of units — There are some situations where the testing process involves the actual consumption or destruction of products. This applies to quality control studies involving such items as ammunition, matches, tires, etc. Unless these types of tests were conducted on only a portion of the population, there would be no product remaining for eventual sale or distribution.

Problems associated with sampling

Since the data are obtained from only a portion of the population, sampling is not feasible in any situation where *precise* knowledge about each unit in the population is needed. Public utility companies cannot bill their individual customers on the basis of an "average" drawn from a sample of electricity users. Banks likewise cannot reduce the checking accounts of their individual customers on the basis of "average withdrawals" obtained via samples.

Even in those situations where sampling procedures are applicable, certain problems exist with which the researcher should be familiar. These problems generally are related to how well the sample results depict the population or universe from which they were taken. The accuracy and reliability of sample data is affected by two different types of errors; sampling errors and data collection errors.[2] The influence of both of these can best be shown by means of the following formula: $P = S \pm e_s \pm e_{dc}$ The S represents the values or results obtained from the sample and the P represents the true, but unknown, characteristics of the population. The e_s are discrepancies due to sampling errors and e_{dc} are discrepancies caused by data collection errors. Thus, the variation between the actual population values and the resulting sample values is tied to the size of e_s and e_{dc}.

Sampling errors

It is highly unlikely that any sample will be a perfect miniature of the population from which it is drawn. The discrepancy between the unknown population values (parameters) and the values obtained from the sample (statistics) are sampling errors.

Assume that a study is made of a certain college's students to determine what portion they personally contribute to their total education expenses. A random sample of 200 from the student body is surveyed, and the results indicate that they earned 37.5 percent of their own educational expenses. Now assume that a study of the entire student body is made and the results show that they pay 40.2 percent of their educational expenses. The difference between the parameter (40.2 percent) and the statistic (37.5 percent) is a sampling error. It was not due to inappropriate sampling procedures but merely to the fact that the sample of 200 was not an exact miniature of the entire student body.

If a probability sample is used, statistical procedures can be applied to estimate the size of these sampling errors. A more extensive discussion of these procedures is contained in the next chapter.

---

[2]In many statistics and research texts the authors go to great lengths to distinguish between such terms as "precision" and "accuracy." The two terms are used interchangeably in this text.

Data collection errors

There are a variety of conditions that distort the sample values from the actual values of the population. These errors, unlike sampling errors, do not "average out" to the actual population values regardless of the sample size.

1. *Nonresponse errors.* In most surveys not all members of the sample can be reached, and many that are contacted may refuse to participate. These nonrespondents may differ significantly from those who do respond in terms of their attitudes, actions, and overall characteristics.
2. *Selection errors.* This includes situations where improper procedures were used to select the individual sample units, or else the entire list (frame) from which the individual sample units were drawn is of questionable representativeness.
3. *Measurement errors.* These result from such factors as bias caused by the interviewer's presence or the way the questions are asked; errors made in the recording of data by either the respondent or interviewer; errors arising when the data are edited or coded.
4. *Surrogate information errors.* When predictions of future activities are involved, substitute information must often be accepted because of respondents' inability to provide precise information.

How to handle e_s and e_{dc}

Referring to the model $P = S \pm e_s \pm e_{dc}$, it is evident that the combined impact of sampling errors and data collection errors could significantly influence the sample's results. As previously stated, the amount of sampling error can be estimated if a probability sample was used, but what can be done about data collection or nonsampling errors?

There are three different ways of dealing with nonsampling errors: (1) ignore them, (2) estimate them, (3) measure them by means of follow-up surveys or control groups.[3]

---

[3]This information on nonsampling errors is taken from Donald Tull and Gerald Albaum, *Survey Research* (New York: Intext Educational Publishers, 1973), pp. 59-80.

Ignore errors — This is the most widely used of the three methods. It assumes that effective data collection methods had been used, and while some nonsampling error probably exists in the data, it will not significantly alter the results. This approach assumes proper monitoring of the data collection procedures will keep nonsampling errors to a minimum.

Estimate errors — This strategy uses formal procedures to estimate possible ranges of error for each of the sources that could cause nonsampling error (i.e., refusals, measurement, etc.). These individual assessments are then combined into an overall estimate of the nonsampling error. This is a fairly complicated and highly subjective procedure.

Measure errors — This method uses follow-up surveys among selected members of the original sample to determine the amount of nonsampling error. Results from both the original and follow-up surveys are compared, with any unusual variations evaluated as nonsampling errors.

In the last few years researchers have given more attention to ways of dealing with nonsampling errors, as witnessed by an increasing number of articles in academic journals; but most of their models are very complicated to understand and often require some questionable major assumptions. Most researchers still feel the best way to handle nonsampling errors is to minimize their chances of occurring by using the appropriate data collection procedures.

SAMPLE DESIGNS

The method used to select the individual sample members determines whether it is a probability or a nonprobability sample. These two types are really nothing more than samples objectively selected (probability) and samples subjectively selected (nonprobability).

Probability samples

A probability sample is chosen in such a way that each member of the universe has a known chance of being selected. It is this condition — *known* chance — that enables statistical procedures to be used on the results to estimate sampling errors. Probability samples should be used in any study involving sample data where the accuracy of the results has to be at least partially defended by statistics. The most frequently used probability samples are simple random samples, systematic samples, stratified samples, and cluster samples.

Simple random samples

In a simple random sample each member of the population has a *known* and *equal* chance of being selected. A selection tool frequently used with this design is the table of random numbers. Table 9-1 is a portion of such a table.

Suppose Proctor and Gamble wants to determine the attitudes of its salesmen toward existing remuneration policies. Assume that there are 2,500 such salesmen in the organization and a simple random sample of 250 is to be used. One random selection procedure that might be followed would be to assign a number from 0 to 2,499 to each employee. Then a table of random numbers could be consulted using only four-digit numbers. The researcher is free to use any of a variety of methods to choose the desired amount of numbers from these tables.

In our example we will start with the first four columns on Table 9-1 and work downward. Only those four-digit numbers below 2,499 will be used from the table, so it will require a rather lengthy selection process. Starting at the top, 4,934 is too large so we ignore it. The next number is 0156, which is less than 2,500, so we include it as one of our 250 sample numbers. The employee who was assigned that number will now be included in our sample. We don't run across another number less than 2,500 until we come to 1,883. This then is our second sample member. This process is continued until a total of 250 numbers and the employees they represent have been chosen.

Another random method for selecting sample members is assigning each employee a number, placing these 2,500 numbers in a container, and then randomly drawing out 250 numbers. A major assumption of this process is that the numbers have been thoroughly mixed within the container so that the sequence of number's placement in the container will not affect the probability of its being drawn. After a number is drawn out, it is then placed back into the container so that the probability of any number being selected remains known and equal. Computer programs now exist which can be used to generate the desired amount of random numbers.

Systematic samples

In this sample design the members are chosen in some systematic manner from the entire population. Each member has a *known* chance of being selected, but not necessarily an equal one. To

Table of Random Digits **Table 9-1**

```
49344  33448 34945  22704 66567  30722 06148  81139 53308  14483
01565  63683 95791  95254 10324  95952 93544  57515 90896  51772
45906  70975 73203  32961 96695  53678 44046  54054 90040  34785
83459  35685 07769  93214 00710  53857 66118  42274 77031  07622
92735  35048 62889  96468 44148  39783 70408  70499 71823  67041

47019  80469 03538  88628 26423  75962 38536  31216 77099  19365
61368  93270 64631  39496 04404  96681 38984  01883 84856  11917
48072  06002 87096  88383 33341  88461 95866  23735 80950  88576
64913  26273 31344  37751 46301  67602 70440  07056 68791  24448
45104  51726 02912  75688 98726  39605 67033  08026 16081  01095

18833  00839 59643  02764 26120  93217 24393  28615 62828  25217
50036  66634 64327  41672 18148  97047 13655  89572 67320  77405
29840  26164 98840  91773 72584  82187 23688  94165 39714  12687
75637  33488 84531  92203 18124  56614 47340  17734 62161  22768
54581  12473 81761  62984 58169  96305 41467  62127 28160  62715

46718  30101 95947  78632 50692  93664 01953  39231 86649  48634
68347  23612 52831  41755 90630  52182 12860  55284 10109  92970
92684  87323 99855  03427 79473  42282 17108  65655 54995  73161
11944  34009 51650  94274 23127  80111 08532  54826 79951  74711
87793  37576 32387  10209 47829  21125 93110  11206 81644  70227
```

illustrate this technique we will use our previous example involving the 2,500 salesmen.

We want to select a sample of 250 from the universe of 2,500 employees, or 1 out of every 10:

$$\frac{n}{N} = \frac{250}{2500}$$

We randomly select a digit between 1 and 10, say 7, and then select every 10th name after 7. Thus, we would select from our list of names the 7th, 17th, 27th, . . . 2,447th names.

The systematic procedure is often used in selecting names from city directories, from telephone books, or from almost any type of list. It is much less work and can be developed much faster than a simple random sample. In both cases it is necessary that a list exist of all units of the population. If such a list is nonexistent or cannot be developed, neither systematic samples nor random samples can be used.

Possible bias — The major weakness of this selection process is that the system used may create a bias in the results. A study was made in 1972 on the need for a second bowling alley in Fort Collins, Colorado. One part of the investigation involved interviews with some of the league bowlers using the existing alley. Team rosters were available and every "nth" name from the various team rosters was selected. Because of the arrangement of names on these rosters the "nth" person always turned out to be a team captain. The usage of, and demand for, bowling facilities by typical team captains far exceeds those of the average bowler. Thus, the results from this sample could have been badly biased if this peculiar pattern had not been discovered.

Monotonic trend—Another problem along these same lines is that a monotonic trend may exist in the order of the population list. A good example of this is found in *Survey Sampling*, an outstanding book on sampling procedures by Leslie Kish.[4] A study was to be made on the average value of mortgages held by a large lending institution. A list of 20,000 mortgages granted by the institution to home buyers was numbered in the precise order they were granted over a 15-year period. During those 15 years, the average mortgage value increased due to inflation. Also, the amount of mortgage debt remaining on the loan would be reduced over the 15 years. These two factors caused the mortgages of more recent years to be higher than those of earlier years. Assume that a systematic procedure is used to obtain a sample from this entire population—every 100th name. If a low number were chosen in selecting the first sample unit (7, 107, 207, etc.), the mean value of mortgages would be much smaller than a sample where a higher number was used at the outset (84, 184, 284, etc.). Thus, a monotonic trend can affect results obtained via a systematic sample when the variables to be sampled are in some ascending or descending order based on their value.

Stratified samples

A stratified sample is used when the researcher is particularly interested in certain groups within the total population. The universe is divided into strata on the basis of recognizable or measurable characteristics of its members—age, income, education, etc. The total sample then is comprised of members from each stratum so that the stratified sample is really a combination of a number of smaller samples.

---

[4]Leslie Kish, *Survey Sampling* (New York: John Wiley & Sons, 1965), pp. 120-121.

In a study to determine salesmen's attitudes toward travel allowances, it is felt that attitudes on this subject are closely related to the amount of traveling done by the person. Thus, a stratified sample could be used with "miles traveled per month" as the characteristic determining the makeup of the various strata. Table 9-2 shows such a breakdown.

Classification of Salesmen According to Miles Traveled Monthly   **Table 9-2**

Miles Traveled per Month	Number of Salesmen	% of Total Salesforce	Number in Sample
Less than 200 miles	250	10	25
201–500 miles	1250	50	125
501–750 miles	825	33	82
More than 750 miles	175	7	18
Total	2500	100	250

The salesmen in each of these four strata would seemingly be more homogeneous in terms of their attitudes toward travel allowances than the 2,500 salesmen in total. Thus, it is possible to increase the accuracy of the results by taking a sample from *each* stratum, rather than using a sample selected from the entire population. The stratified sample will be a probability sample as long as the individual units are chosen from each stratum in a random manner.

It is important to realize that the use of stratified samples will lead to more accurate results only if the strata selected are logically related to the information sought. For instance, in the previous study placing salesmen in strata on the basis of their weight or color of their eyes would add nothing to the findings. On the other hand, using strata such as years with the firm or geographic area served could be meaningful.

Proportionate stratified samples—The breakdown of members per stratum can be done on either a proportionate or disproportionate basis. A proportionate stratified sample is one where the number of items in each stratum is proportionate to their number in the universe. Thus, since 10 percent of the previous universe is comprised of salesmen driving less than 200 miles monthly, this group will comprise 10 percent of the sample. The same relationship holds true for the other three strata. The column "Number in Sample" in Table 9-2 is a proportionate stratified sample.

Disproportionate stratified samples — In some cases the composition of various strata is such that if a proportionate sample were used, very little information would be obtained about some of the strata. Assume a study is to be made concerning characteristics of car owners, with the type of car owned being the basis for stratification While there are a large number of Chevrolet, Ford, and Plymouth owners in most cities, there are relatively few Lincoln and Cadillac owners. Thus, if a proportionate stratified sample of 400 car owners were to be obtained in a typical city, there might be only 2 Lincoln and 4 Cadillac owners in the sample. (Assume that Lincoln owners comprise 0.5 percent of car owners, with Cadillac owners comprising 1 percent of the total.) With such small representation, little could be learned about the characteristics of these two types of car owners.

In this situation, a disproportionate stratified sample should be used. This means that in some of the strata the number of units would differ greatly from their real representation in the universe. A smaller number of Chevrolet and Ford owners would be included in the sample than their number in the universe warrants. Conversely, a large number of Lincoln and Cadillac owners would be included.

A disproportionate stratified sample should also be used when there appear to be major variances in the values within certain strata. With a fixed sample size, those strata exhibiting greatest variability are sampled more heavily than strata that are fairly homogeneous. Thus, using a disproportionate stratified sample necessitates that the researcher have some previous knowledge about the population being studied.

Improved accuracy — Although stratified random sampling will almost always provide more reliable estimates than simple random samples of the same size, this gain in accuracy will often be rather small. This means the researcher has to weigh the additional time and effort involved in stratification against the additional accuracy obtained. Statistical procedures for determining the amount of this gain can be found in texts concentrating on sampling procedures.

Cluster samples

In this sampling design the various units comprising the population are grouped in clusters and the sample selection is made in such a way that each cluster has a known chance of being selected.[5]

A cluster sample is useful in two situations: (1) when there is incomplete information on the composition of the population or universe; and (2) when it is desirable to save time and costs by limiting the study to specific geographic areas.

Example: A study of consumers is to be made among households in the Milwaukee Standard Metropolitan Area. Because people are constantly moving, no up-to-date list is available on the composition of Milwaukee households. Yet if the researcher wants to carry out a probability study, every household must have a known chance of being selected in the sample. Cluster sampling enables this condition to be met.

The total Milwaukee Standard Metropolitan Area can be divided into clusters on the basis of civil divisions or combinations of Milwaukee census tracts. Figure 9-1 illustrates the geographic breakdown used in a consumer analysis of Milwaukee residents. A total of 40 clusters were established which were felt to be reasonably similar in terms of residential characteristics.

Since in cluster sampling only a small portion of the total population is included, it is necessary to select certain clusters from the total group for further study. Each of the 40 clusters in Figure 9-1 is assigned a number from 1 to 40. A decision then has to be made as to how many clusters will be included in the sample. If the researcher desires that a total of five clusters be involved, a table of random numbers can be used to select these five. If the five number selected from the table were 8, 14, 21, 27, and 38, the five clusters represented by these numbers would be included in the sample (see Figure 9-1).

Since there are a large number of households in each of the five clusters, it is necessary to narrow each cluster down further so that a count of its households can be made. This is accomplished by establishing the actual city blocks that exist in each of the five selected clusters. (This information on blocks can be obtained from the city or county engineer's office.)

Figure 9-2 contains a fictitious breakdown of the blocks in Cluster 8. Each block in this cluster is assigned a number. Then, some of these blocks (assume a total of seven) are randomly selected from each cluster for more extensive investigation. The

[5]In some statistics and research texts this sampling process is called area sampling and they consider cluster sampling to be a specific type of area sampling. They interpret a cluster sample as one where a selected geographic area (a block, a precinct, or a street) is sampled in its entirety.

Figure 9-1   Community Boundaries for Milwaukee, Wisconsin

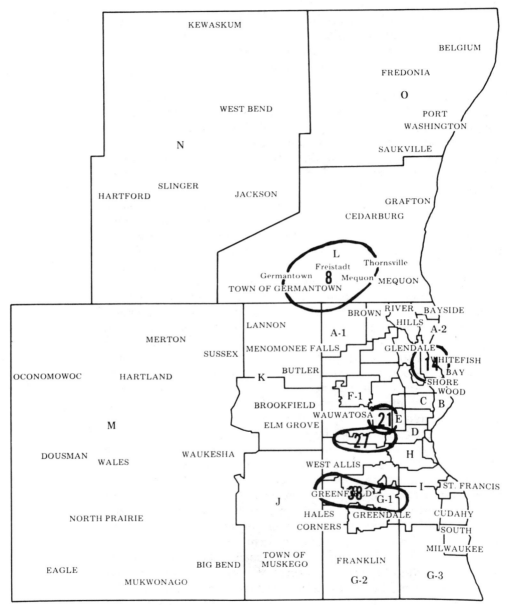

The 40 community areas are civil divisions or combinations of Milwaukee city census tracts, which are reasonably similar in residential characteristics.

Economic Areas: Areas with heavy black lines (A-1, A-2, B, C, etc.) are combinations of community areas.

Households in Cluster 8

Figure 9-2

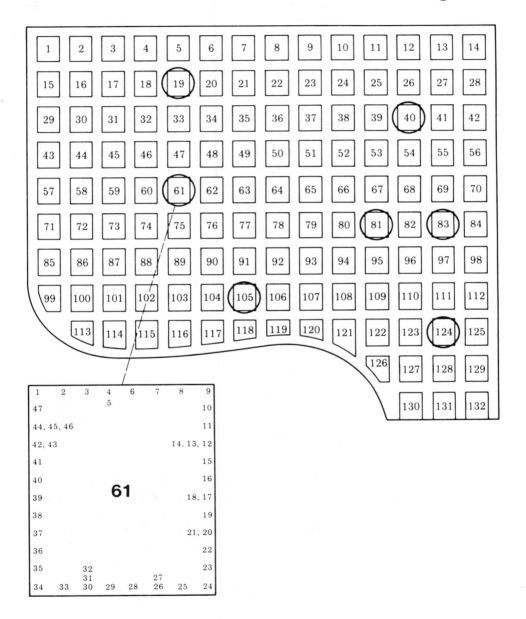

seven randomly selected blocks in each cluster are then can-
vassed and each of the cluster's households is assigned a number.
Figure 9-2 illustrates the numbering of households in one of the
chosen blocks in Cluster 8. There were 47 households in this
block. If there were a total of 300 households in the seven blocks
of Cluster 8, each of these households would be assigned a number from 1 to 300. This same numbering procedure would be carried out in clusters 14, 21, 27, and 38.

Using portions of the block's population — The total sample
size desired for our consumer study is 250 households. The selection of these specific sample members can be done in two ways:
(1) An equal number of households can be selected from each of
the five clusters, i.e., 50 each; or (2) each cluster can be represented in the sample on a somewhat proportionate basis.

If an equal number were to be taken from each cluster, a separate selection process would be undertaken in each cluster enabling 50 households to be randomly selected. If proportionate
representation is desired, a weighting procedure must be followed
so that the 250 sample members proportionately represent the
number of households in each of the five clusters. Table 9-3 contains a proportional depiction of the five sample cluster.

Table 9-3

	Number of Households	Cumulative Number of Households	Cumulative Numbers
Cluster 8	300	300	01–300
Cluster 14	270	570	301–570
Cluster 21	330	900	571–900
Cluster 27	280	1,180	901–1,180
Cluster 38	220	1,400	1,181–1,400

A total of 1,400 households has been identified in the five
clusters. Each household can be assigned a number from 1 to
1,400. Three hundred numbers with a value less than 1,401 are
then randomly selected. If number 577 were chosen from a table
of random numbers, a household from Cluster 21 would be included. Using this procedure each cluster should have proportional representation in the final sample. This means that close to
220/1,400 or 16 percent of the sample of 250 should be from
Cluster 38.

Using block's entire population — Another cluster sampling
method is to assign numbers to each block of the five selected
clusters. No attempt is made at this time to count the households
in these blocks. A certain number of blocks are then randomly se-

lected from each area. The final step is to include in the sample every household of these selected blocks. This technique minimizes the amount of information needed for sample selection since the only specific data required are the block breakdowns for the five clusters that comprise the sample.

The previous example pertained to selection of a sample from geographical areas. But cluster sampling can be used in other ways; for example, cluster sampling is feasible in preparing sample estimates from data contained in a large volume of punch cards. If the cards are stored in a number of drawers, each drawer can be considered a cluster. Several drawers can then be picked at random, and either all or a designated portion of cards from each drawer can be used in the sample.

Advantages of cluster sampling — The major advantage of cluster sampling is that complete information about the population is not needed at the outset of the study. By constantly narrowing down the components of the clusters, complete information on any one cluster can be postponed until the last stage.

A second advantage of cluster sampling is that it saves time and money when personal interviews are used. Since the sample units are usually found in rather compact geographic areas, the interviewer does not have to leap-frog back and forth across what could be a rather large geographic area.

Main shortcoming of cluster sampling — The major drawback of cluster sampling is that it leads to a substantial loss in precision, since units within each cluster tend to be rather homogeneous. For instance, when block clusters are used to select households for a study, the members of the households within each block tend to be quite similar in income, ethnic background, and, in many cases, even in their general types of employment.

Thus, for maximum precision, clusters should be formed so that the individual units within a cluster vary as much as possible. If clusters are internally heterogeneous, the clusters will tend to be similar to one another. This is the ideal condition, but it is difficult to attain when clusters are developed around geographic areas.

Summary of cluster sampling — The use of cluster samples is appropriate when total information on the universe is missing or if personal interviews are to be used and the researcher wants to minimize the amount of traveling needed to obtain these interviews. The sample is generally selected in stages, and in each succeeding stage more information is required on the makeup of the cluster. Because units in a cluster tend to be homogeneous, the results obtained from a cluster sample are less precise than those from a simple random sample. In deciding whether to use a cluster sample, the researcher has to weigh the loss of precision in the results against the lower costs and extra time gained from its use.

Nonprobability samples

In nonprobability samples the chance of any particular unit in the population being selected is *unknown*. Thus, since randomness is not involved in the selection process, an estimate of the sampling error cannot be made. But this does not mean that the findings obtained from nonprobability samples are of questionable value. If properly conducted, their findings can be every bit as accurate as those obtained from probability samples. The three most frequently used nonprobability designs are judgment samples, convenience samples, and quota samples.

Judgment samples

A person knowledgeable about the population under study chooses sample members he/she feels would be most appropriate for the particular study. A supermarket owner is thinking about including a delicatessen in his store but first wants to learn the attitudes of his customers toward such a service. He feels the people who would use this service most often are those families where both the husband and wife work. He knows that these people tend to shop on Friday nights when they can combine their shopping with the cashing of their weekly paychecks. Thus, he interviews only Friday night shoppers. In his "judgment" these are the people who could best provide the desired information.

One type of judgment sampling is called "snowballing." Its name is derived from its similarity to the situation of a snowball gaining additional mass and momentum as it rolls down a hill. No frame is needed initially. Rather, a list of names for a special population is developed by finding some members of that group and using them as sources for additional names. For example, owners of unique stereo equipment can generally identify others with the same expensive equipment, and they in turn know others. A frame can be developed from a series of such inquiries.

Convenience samples

These sample units are chosen primarily on the basis of their convenience to the investigator. If 50 adults from the city of Waco, Texas, are to be interviewed, the investigator goes to a convenient location in Waco (shopping mall) and selects the sample units. Even if a "random" method of selecting the people is used — each person crossing a particular spot at 10-minute intervals — there is no way of determining the probability of each adult in Waco being selected. For example, people living or working near the interviewing site would have much greater probability of being selected than other Waco adults.

Quota samples

This sample design is similar to the stratified sampling method since the universe is divided into strata on the basis of certain characteristics of the population. The sample units are chosen so that each stratum is represented in proportion to its importance in the population.

If 100 heads of households in Toledo, Ohio, are to be interviewed on their attitudes toward a proposed city tax, the researcher might want to structure the sample on the basis of household income. Suppose that 28 percent of the Toledo households have annual incomes below $8,000; 59 percent have incomes between $8,000 and $20,000; and the remaining 13 percent have incomes exceeding $20,000. The sample of 100 households would then be comprised of 28 units from the "less than $8,000" income category; 59 from the "$8,001 to $20,000" category; and 13 from households with "incomes exceeding $20,000."

Up to this point, the quota sample is similar to a proportionate stratified sample. However, in the quota sample the units for each stratum are chosen in a nonrandom manner. The interviewer might go into three different residential areas and haphazardly interview households until the quota for each stratum has been met. Thus, in this selection process, each member of the universe does not have a known chance of being chosen.

An example of the potential complexity of sampling

The previous sections contain information about alternative sample designs and some of the problems that can emerge when choosing a sample. The following question and answer format is used to illustrate the variety of decisions that must be made in one sampling situation — a shopping center used as the locale for personal interviews.

Shopping centers are becoming increasingly popular as locations for consumer interviews because the cost of facilities is reasonably low, travel is minimized, and visual materials can be included in the questioning process. A shortcoming of many studies conducted in these centers, however, is the haphazard way in which interviewees are selected.[6]

Q. Are shopping centers used by the "average" consumer?

A. Recent studies indicate that 90-95% of all adults shop at a shopping center at least once a year, but its usage is less among lower income or older households. Also, the types of persons using the center can be affected by the center's size and location.

Q. How should interviewees be selected?

A. The alternatives are to interview people as they enter/exit the center, or as they are moving around within the center. Exit interviews are more difficult because of packages being carried or the person's time commitments.

Q. If using entry interviews, how should the entrances be selected?

A. Using just one entrance could bias results. For instance, if the entrance is by a bus stop, it could greatly distort the economic and geographic characteristics of the sample. All entrances might be sampled on a proportionate basis, determined by the number of people entering over a given period of time.

Q. What about using a single location within the center?

A. Again, a sample bias can occur since centers are usually anchored by major stores, and each might attract demographically different customers. A single location would be affected by such stores; therefore it is preferable to sample from multiple locations within the center.

Q. What time of the day should the interviews take place?

A. The types of people visiting a center will vary by season, day of the week, and even hour of the day. Therefore, interviews must be conducted over a variety of time periods to ensure a representative sample is involved. Again, the number of interviews per time period can be proportioned to the amount of customer traffic at each period.

---

[6]Much of this data is from an article by Seymour Sudman, "Improving the Quality of Shopping Center Sampling," *Journal of Marketing Research*, November 1980, pp. 423-431.

Q. How can the representativeness of the sample be improved?

A. To minimize the bias in the sample results, the data should be weighted using information obtained from the interviewees, e.g., length of time they were in the center, how often they visited the center in the past four weeks, etc.

This series of questions and answers was included to emphasize that sampling is a complicated activity and requires a great deal of planning prior to its undertaking.

SUMMARY

Probability sampling is the only method where the sampling error can be estimated. This enables a more precise estimate of universe values to be made. (The specific techniques for making such estimates are presented in Chapter 10.) It also allows the relative efficiency of various sample designs to be evaluated. You can compare the relative costs and statistical efficiency of simple random samples with those of a stratified sample.

This method does not always require detailed information about the universe; basically all that is needed is some method for identifying every unit of the universe along with information on the total number of universe elements. The latter information is not even needed when a multistage cluster sample is used.

There are some basic disadvantages associated with probability sampling that limit its wider usage. Probability sampling requires a fairly high degree of skill on the part of the person designing the sample. This can be quite complicated, and not many businessmen have the necessary background to use anything other than relatively simple sampling methods.

Setting up and using a probability sample can be both time-consuming and costly. The cost per observation or contact is generally much higher for a probability sample than for a nonprobability one.

Nonprobability samples, on the other hand, can usually be developed in less time and at less expense than probability samples. If properly conducted, the findings from nonprobability samples can be as accurate as those obtained from probability samples. However, because of the procedures used to select individual members, the sampling error among data collected from nonprobability samples cannot be estimated.

In selecting a sample design, the researcher has to weigh the various advantages associated with each type of design against the additional time, dollar outlay, or loss of precision that might occur from its usage. As will be shown in the next chapter, the statistics involved in some sampling decisions can become quite complex. Thus, the businessman or the "occasional" researcher should seek advice from a qualified statistician or a person knowledgeable in sampling procedures. The help these people can give in selecting and setting up the sample design will more than offset the costs of their services.

QUESTIONS AND EXERCISES

1. What is your reaction to the statement, "Sampling error is an inherent part of the sampling process; it can't be eliminated"?

2. How do sampling errors differ from data collection errors? Why are data collection errors so difficult to quantify?

3. Under what conditions would a disproportionate stratified sample be used?

4. What is the major advantage associated with using a probability sample?

5. Provide examples in which a quota sample and a proportionate stratified sample are used. What is the major difference between these two types of samples?

6. John Jones is a marketing researcher for a large chemical company. In a recent conversation with a researcher from another company, Jones stated, "I won't put any faith in survey data collected with a nonprobability sample. It can't be relied on." How would you defend nonprobability samples to Jones?

7. There are over 4,000 names listed alphabetically in the American Marketing Associations membership roster. What method would you use to: (a) develop a random sample of 300 of these members; (b) develop a stratified sample of 400 of the members on the basis of whether they were in (1) education; (2) in a manufacturing industry; and (3) in a service industry?

8. Explain the procedures you would use to develop a cluster sample of 600 for the city in which you work or go to school. What is the key shortcoming of cluster sampling?

10

Developing the sample

WHEN RANDOM SELECTION IS NOT RANDOM

On April 24, 1980, the number 666 won the Pennsylvania state lottery. Winning numbers for this lottery were chosen in the following manner: a large number of ping pong balls were released over jets of compressed air until three of the balls were sucked into selection tubes. A single number between 0 and 9 was written on each ball. Thus the winning three digit number was the combination of the numbers on the three "randomly" selected ping pong balls.

This time, however, the numbers weren't randomly selected. Shortly before the drawing, someone injected a clear liquid into all the balls except those numbered 6. When the air was turned on, only the unweighted balls jumped toward the selection tubes—thus the number 666.

Six people were eventually indicted for fraud, including the lottery's number caller. The fixers had purchased $1.2 million worth of tickets on number 666.

"Their Lottery Number Was Up," *Newsweek*, September 29, 1980, p. 30.

The previous chapter provided information on the strengths and weaknesses of sampling and a description of the most frequently used sample designs. With this background, the reader is now provided with a list of the six specific activities that should be performed when developing and using a sample.

1. The population from which the sample is to be drawn is defined.
2. A frame is developed.
3. The sample design is selected.
4. The sample size is determined.
5. The specific sample members are selected.
6. The estimated sampling error is adjusted on the basis of data obtained from the sample.

The degree of difficulty in step four depends upon whether a probability sample is used. The activity described in step six is conducted only when the sampling error is to be estimated for the collected data. This chapter is devoted to a discussion of each of the six steps.

DEFINING THE POPULATION OR UNIVERSE

When a sample is used, the first thing that has to be done is to define the population from which the sample is to be drawn. The population or universe is the specific group of people, firms, conditions, activities, etc., that is to be the focal point of the study.

In many projects the population can be easily defined. For instance, assume that a theatre owner is investigating the movie-going habits of college students from the local university. This population can be defined as any student presently enrolled and carrying more than eight hours at the university. There is no question about who should be included in this population since records exist in the registrar's office indicating each student's present class load. Another example of a population might be all of a company's customers that are "slow payers"—do not pay their bills within a specified time after receiving the goods. Once again the definition is quite specific and population members can be easily identified.

In many situations though, identifying the population members can be quite difficult. For instance, a study is to be undertaken on the educational backgrounds of the unemployed in Omaha, Nebraska. Here the precise composition of the population unemployed in Omaha is quite hazy. Who are the "unemployed"?

Definitions from various government publications or from economics texts could be used or the researcher might even set up his own definition. But regardless of the definition used, there will still be many isolated cases of "Should they or shouldn't they be included?" Should college students be included? How about people who are just moving into the area and do not have a regular job yet? How about the people who don't want to be employed? The researcher must define the population in a way that will minimize doubts about who (or what) should be included.

In defining the population, the researcher should also make sure that if the information collected from the sample is to be compared to existing secondary data, the two populations are consistent with one another. For instance, existing government data on households in Des Moines, Iowa, cannot be compared with primary data collected from a sample of Des Moines households unless both studies used the same definition for "households." In a similar vein, "household" data from Study A cannot be compared with "family unit" data of Study B since two different populations are involved.

In summary then, it is mandatory that the population under study be precisely defined to ensure the development of a meaningful sample.

DEVELOPING THE FRAME

After the population to be studied has been specified, the next step is to develop a frame of this population. A frame is a listing of the general components or the individual units that comprise the defined population. In a study involving the car owners of Linn County, Iowa, a frame would be a list containing the names of these car owners. Such a list is available in the Motor Vehicle Division of the Linn County Court House. This list is quite accurate since it is compiled in conjunction with state requirements for licensing motor vehicles.

In many cases the available frame is not as encompassing. If a study is to be made on the dog-feeding habits of dog owners in Fort Collins, Colorado, the population might be defined as: "All families or household units in Fort Collins owning dogs." Since all dogs in the city of Fort Collins must be licensed, and therefore registered at the City Clerk's Office, this list would be a logical frame for the study. But since many dog owners ignore this licensing requirement, the frame may not contain a major share of the defined population. In this case, the researcher might choose to redefine the population as: "All families or household units in Fort Collins that have licensed their dogs." The assumption the researcher makes in using this new definition is that the feeding habits of licensed dog owners are representative of all dog owners, a questionable assumption.

A frame does not always have to be a list of names; it can also involve a definite location, a boundary, an address, or a set of rules by which a sampling unit can be delineated. For example, in an agricultural study involving crop yields, the sample units may be plots of ground. The frame would be sets of coordinates used for selecting these various plots.

Decisions involving the first two steps of the sampling process are closely intertwined. When defining the population, the researcher must also be concerned with whether a frame exists or can be developed for such a population. If no frame exists, what would be the cost of developing one? Would this cost exceed the benefits derived from sampling such a population? If a frame does exist, how well does it represent the population? Will it be necessary to improve or update the existing frame?

Close tie between steps one and two

In many sampling studies, the frame used by the researcher will have certain weaknesses and limitations. It might be dated—developed a year or two prior to your study; it might be only partially inclusive—the example of the licensed dog owners; or it might be somewhat inaccurate—a list of restaurants might also include taverns serving lunches. The researcher should be cognizant of these possible conditions and what effect they might have on the study's results.

Since the development of a good frame generally takes a lot of effort and ingenuity, the researcher should seek out all possible sources that might be of help. Many of the secondary sources listed in Chapter 5 of this text will provide either the desired lists to be used as frames or give insight on where such lists might be obtained or developed.

The selection of the sample design really involves two decisions. The researcher first has to decide whether to use a probability or a nonprobability sample. The decision then has to be made about which specific sample design to use in collecting the data.

SELECTION OF SAMPLE DESIGN

In the previous chapter the advantages and disadvantages of both probability and nonprobability designs were presented. It was pointed out that the researcher's choice will be affected by the following considerations.

1. If the researcher wants to estimate the sampling error of the results, a probability sample should be used.

2. If the researcher will be required to defend the randomness in the selection of sample units, a probability sample should be used.

3. If a frame does not exist and one cannot be developed, a nonprobability sample should be used.

4. If the researcher has only limited knowledge concerning the statistical aspects of sampling, a nonprobability sample should be used.

5. If the factors of time and money are crucial, the researcher may be forced to use a nonprobability sample.

These are by no means the only influencing factors, but they should be considered when deciding between a probability and a nonprobability sample.

Once this decision has been made, the researcher must choose the sample design that will best enable the research objectives to be accomplished. Each sample design has unique strengths and weaknesses, and the researcher has to weigh the attributes of a particular design against some of the restrictions controlling the study. For instance, if the researcher is doing a study in a large city for which there is no accurate frame, the desire for maximum representation obtained with a stratified or a simple random sample may have to take a back seat to the need to minimize costs and collect the information as quickly as possible—advantages associated with cluster sampling. Conversely, the need to know about some particular characteristics of the population—the relationship between incomes of consumers and their propensity to purchase private brands—might require the use of a stratified sample even though the cost and time factors are also crucial.

Regardless of the design finally chosen, the researcher may have to defend this design when the study's results are ultimately presented. Thus, the researcher should feel confident that the sample used provides an accurate depiction of the universe from which it was drawn.

SELECTING THE SAMPLE SIZE

The population has been defined, the frame has been developed, and the specific sample design has been selected. The task now facing the researcher is deciding how large the sample should be. The complexity of this decision depends on whether a probability or a nonprobability sample is involved.

As previously stated, the main reason for using a probability sample is that it enables the researcher to estimate the amount of sampling error that might exist in the sample results. The size of the sample directly influences the estimates since as the sample size increases, these estimates generally become more precise. Thus, researchers are faced with a dilemma: they want the sample to be large enough to provide a relatively precise estimate of population values, yet they don't want to squander funds on a sample that is larger than is really necessary. How can they decide on the correct sample size?

Statistical techniques exist that enable researchers to accomplish both goals: maximizing precision while controlling sampling costs. A few of these procedures are presented in the following sections of this chapter. It should be noted, however, that these techniques pertain specifically to simple random samples. If other probability sample designs (stratified, cluster, etc.) are used, slightly different statistical procedures are needed. Nevertheless, the broad concepts described herein are applicable to all probability samples, and if researchers understand them, they will have a good grasp of the techniques to use in determining a sample's size.

Probability samples

For the remainder of this chapter it is assumed that the reader has some background in elementary statistics and is familiar with such terms as mean, standard deviation, normal distribution, and variance. If the reader is a little hazy on these concepts, it would be wise to obtain an introductory statistics book and brush up on them before proceeding any further into the chapter.

The size of a probability sample is so closely tied to the precision sought in estimating population values that the first step in determining sample size is to establish a desired degree of accuracy for the sample results. This means that the person or agency requesting the study must state the limits of error that will be tolerated in the sample results.

For example, if a study is to be made on the movie-going habits of male adults in Toledo, Ohio, the researcher might be seeking the average number of movies attended per month by this group. The firm requesting this information wants the sample results to be within ±0.5 movies per month of the real population figure, 95 percent of the time. Or the Safeway food chain may want to know the average weekly food expenditures made in its stores by young marrieds (ages 21 to 30). It wants the dollar figures obtained to be within ±$5 of the real population value in 99 out of 100 samples.

In both of the above examples the degree of precision desired for the sample results was first established. Once this was set, it could then be determined how large a sample would be needed to obtain that precision. This is the procedure described in this chapter. That is why the next few pages are devoted to a discussion of such terms as standard error of the mean, standard error of the proportion, and confidence intervals. All of this information is then tied together, and the reader is shown how a statistically defensible sample size is developed.

Nonprobability samples

It should be reiterated that the statistical methods apply only to probability samples. In a nonprobability sample, the probability of any member of the population being selected is unknown. This means that the central limit theorem or the principles of normal distribution do not apply.

The decision on how large a nonprobability sample should be is usually made in a rather subjective manner. The researcher selects that sample size felt to give a reasonably accurate depiction of the population. The decision may also be influenced by the financial resources available. In fact, the cost factor is often the single most important determinate of sample size for nonprobability samples. A certain amount of money may be allocated for sampling activities ($5,000), and the researcher chooses a sample size accordingly.

Some statistics and research texts state, "The sample size should never be less than thirty" or "The sample size should be around one-tenth of the population size." The final decision about what is a proper sample size really depends on whether the researcher feels reasonably secure that the sample is large enough to accurately depict the population.

Example: In order to better illustrate some of the ideas being presented in this section, an imaginary study involving a college town will be used. River City College is located in River City, U.S.A. It is a private, coeducational liberal arts college with an enrollment of 5,000 students. The college is presently going through a building expansion program, and the administration is planning to solicit some of the funds from townspeople. One promotional tool used will be to show the townspeople—especially the merchants—the economic impact that the college has on River City. As part of this major study, a sample of students will be surveyed to determine their monthly expenditures in the community. These results will be used to estimate the expenditures for the entire student body.

Throughout this example it will be assumed that the sample size has already been determined. By making this assumption, it will be easier for the reader to understand the various processes involved in ultimately selecting a sample's size. In the River City College survey, a random sample of 400 students was used to obtain the desired information. They were asked a variety of questions, but the key information obtained from all students was the amount of money they spent monthly with the local merchants. The survey disclosed that the average student in the sample ($n=400$) spent \$49.50 monthly with various River City merchants. This figure is then viewed as the average for all 5,000 River City College students.

Is this a valid assumption? If another random sample of 400 students was surveyed, would its average monthly expenditures also be \$49.50? Probably not! If a large number of samples all numbering 400 were used, a different mean value for each sample would emerge. The reason for these differences is that old bugaboo—*sampling error.* A sample is rarely an exact replica of the population from which it is drawn.

Although sample values differ somewhat from their population values, an important relationship exists between the means of samples ($\bar{x}$) and their population's mean (u). *If a number of probability samples are taken from a population, their means are normally distributed around the mean of the population from which they were drawn.* In fact, the mean of all these sample means is the population's mean. This relationship enables an estimate to be made on the size of sampling error. (This relationship applies only if all the samples are the same size.)

It should be pointed out that this relationship between sample means ($\bar{x}$) and their population's mean (u) assumes a sample of "reasonable size." The more irregular the distribution of the population, the larger the sample size must be if a normal distribution is to be attained. The reason for this is that the more items there are in the sample, the greater will be the opportunity for extremely large and small values to offset each other. Statisticians generally agree that a sample size of 30 or more is usually adequate to enable such a normal distribution to occur.

Figure 10-1 illustrates how the means of samples form a normal distribution around the universe mean. Since the sample means are normally distributed around the population mean, if a very large number of samples were taken, approximately 68 percent of these samples' means would be within one standard deviation (σ) of the universe mean (u). The term "standard deviation" applies to the deviation of units of the population around that population's mean. In the situations involving the deviation of

Sampling error revisited

Figure 10-1   Distribution of Monthly Expenditures of All 5,000 Students

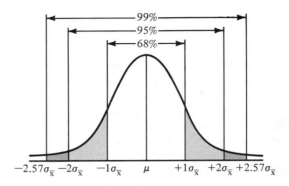

Possible Values of Sample Means

sample means, a slightly different interpretation is made. Instead of using the term "standard deviation" (σ), the term "standard error of the mean" ($\sigma_{\bar{x}}$) is used to describe the deviation of sample means around their population mean. Thus, 68 percent of the sample means will be within $\pm 1.0\sigma_{\bar{x}}$ of the population mean; 95 percent of the sample means will be within $\pm 1.96\sigma_{\bar{x}}$ of the population mean; and 99 percent of the sample means will be within $\pm 2.57\sigma_{\bar{x}}$ of the population mean.

Standard errors of the mean vs. standard errors of the proportion

Two general types of characteristics can be measured in samples. One type can be expressed as a numerical value such as average height, weight, dollar expenditures, etc. We call this "sampling for variables." When variables are involved, the standard error of the mean ($\sigma_{\bar{x}}$) is sought. A second type of characteristic is expressed in dichotomous terms: good or bad, heavy user or light user, yes or no, etc. This is called "sampling for attributes." When attributes are involved, the standard error of the proportion (σ_p) is sought. Examples of both types of samples will be provided in the following sections.

Computing the standard error of the mean—The formula for deriving the standard of the mean is

$$\sigma_{\bar{x}} = \frac{\sigma}{\sqrt{n}}$$

However, if the sample (n) involves more than 5 percent of the population it is recommended that a correction factor be included. The formula for the correction factor is

$$\sqrt{\frac{N-n}{N}}$$

The correction factor makes allowances for the fact that as a sample becomes larger relative to the population, the size of the sampling error will decrease. When $n=N$, there won't be any sampling error because the sample and the population are identical. Thus, if the sample involves more than 5 percent of the population, the total formula for determining the standard error of the mean is

$$\sigma_{\bar{x}} = \frac{\sigma}{\sqrt{n}} \cdot \sqrt{\frac{N-n}{N}}$$

Estimating standard error from sample data—A rather questionable assumption is made in the previous formula. This assumption is that the standard deviation of the population (σ) is known. If that were the case, the mean value of the population would also be known and the researcher would not even have to be concerned with estimating sampling errors. Since in the vast majority of cases the population mean *is* unknown, the standard error must be estimated from the same sample data used to estimate the mean of the population. The reasoning here is that since sample data can be used to estimate the population mean, sample data also can be used to estimate that population's standard deviation. The following formula is generally used to derive the value for the standard error of the mean.

$$s_{\bar{x}} = \frac{s}{\sqrt{n}} \cdot \sqrt{\frac{N-n}{N}}$$

$s_{\bar{x}}$ = standard error of the mean using sample data
s = standard deviation derived from the sample
n = sample size
N = population size

Referring back to the survey involving the 400 River City College students, it was found that the average student in this sample spent \$49.50 monthly with various River City merchants. The standard deviation of this group's expenditures was \$14.50. Using this information, the standard error of the mean $(s_{\bar{x}})$ can now be estimated.

$$s_{\bar{x}} = \frac{s}{\sqrt{n}} \cdot \sqrt{\frac{N-n}{N}}$$

$$= \frac{\$14.50}{\sqrt{400}} \cdot \sqrt{\frac{5{,}000-400}{5{,}000}}$$

$$= \$0.696 \quad \text{or} \quad \$0.70$$

ESTABLISHING CONFIDENCE INTERVALS FOR POPULATION MEANS

The whole purpose of sampling is to make estimates of population values. The fact that samples usually are not perfect replicas of the populations from which they were drawn means that the researcher is never sure how close the sample value is to the population value. While sample data won't determine the exact population value, the data can be used to establish an interval which is felt to contain the population value. This interval is called a "confidence interval" and its size depends upon the degree of confidence desired in the sample's results by the researcher.

The confidence coefficients most commonly used are 95 percent and 99 percent. Confidence coefficients are related to the dispersion of values in the form of a normal distribution. It was shown in Figure 10-1 that 95 percent of the sample means will be within ± 1.96 standard errors of their population mean, and 99 percent of the sample means will be within ± 2.57 standard errors of their population mean.

The formula for constructing a confidence interval is:

$$\bar{x} \pm 1.96(s_{\bar{x}}) = 95\% \text{ confidence interval}$$
$$\bar{x} \pm 2.57(s_{\bar{x}}) = 99\% \text{ confidence interval}$$
$$\bar{x} = \text{sample mean}$$
$$s_{\bar{x}} = \text{standard error of the mean of the sample}$$

Plugging in the sample data obtained from the River City study, the following 95 percent confidence interval results:

$$\bar{x} = \$49.50 \qquad \bar{x} \pm 1.96(s_{\bar{x}}) = 95\% \text{ confidence interval}$$
$$s_{\bar{x}} = \$0.70 \qquad \$49.50 \pm 1.96 \ (\$0.70)$$
$$\$49.50 \pm \$1.37$$
$$\$48.13 \longleftrightarrow \$50.87$$

What does this 95 percent confidence interval of $48.13 to $50.87 mean? It means that if a large number of probability samples (all size 400) were taken among the River City College student body, 95 percent of these samples would contain the actual mean of the universe within an interval of ± 1.96 standard errors of their mean values. It is assumed that this sample with a mean of $49.50 is among those 95 percent.

What about a 99 percent confidence interval? This interval would be derived in the following manner:

$\bar{x} \pm 2.57(s_{\bar{x}}) = 99\%$ confidence interval
49.50 ± 2.57 ($0.70)
$49.50 \pm $1.79
$47.71 \longleftrightarrow $51.29

Thus, the 99 percent confidence interval is $47.71 to $51.29. This higher confidence coefficient results in a larger interval. Therefore, if researchers wish to increase the user's confidence in their findings (99 percent vs. 95 percent), they will either have to increase the size of the confidence interval or increase the size of the sample.

Applying findings to the population
The 95 percent confidence interval ($48.13 to $50.87) can now be applied to the entire student body. Based on information obtained from the sample of 400 students, it is estimated that the River City College student body of 5,000 spends between $240,650 and $254,350 monthly with River City merchants. This estimated range of expenditures was obtained from the following computations: 5,000 $\times$ $48.13 = $240,650 and 5,000 $\times$ $50.87 = $254.350.

If a 99 percent confidence interval had been used, the estimated monthly expenditures of the 5,000 students would have been between $238,550 and $256,450 (5,000 $\times$ $47.71 = $238,550 and 5,000 $\times$ $51.29 = $256,450).

Standard error of the proportion—s_p

Thus far, the discussion has centered around a situation where the characteristic being measured was a variable – the dollar expenditures of River City College students. There also are many studies concerned with attributes, and since this involves proportions or percentages, the concept of standard error of the proportion (s_p) is used.

The formula for deriving the standard error of the proportion is:

$$s_p = \sqrt{\frac{p \cdot q}{n} \cdot \frac{N-n}{N}}$$

s_p = standard error of the proportion
p = proportion of sample possessing a certain
attribute
q or $(1-p)$ = proportion of sample not having that attribute [1]

The River City College study also can be used to illustrate how to derive the standard error of the proportion. One question in the survey asked the sample members to evaluate their overall shopping experiences with the River City merchants. From the sample of 400, it was found that 88 of the students (22 percent) had favorable attitudes toward the merchants while 312 (78 percent) held unfavorable ones. Based on this information, what would be the 95 percent confidence interval depicting the attitude of the entire student body toward their shopping experiences with River City merchants?

The formula for a 95 percent confidence interval when attributes are involved is $p \pm 1.96$ (s_p). In order to determine the confidence interval, it is first necessary to find the value for the standard error of the proportion (s_p).

$$s_p = \sqrt{\frac{p \cdot q}{n} \cdot \frac{N-n}{n}} \qquad\qquad s_p = \sqrt{4.29 \times 0.92}$$

$$= \sqrt{\frac{(22)(78)}{400} \cdot \frac{5{,}000 - 400}{5{,}000}} \qquad = 1.99\%$$

p = 22% with favorable attitudes
q = 78% with less than favorable attitudes
n = 400

This s_p value can now be used to construct a 95 percent confidence interval depicting the attitudes of students toward the River City merchants.

$$\begin{aligned}
95\% \text{ confidence interval} &= p \pm 1.96(s_p)\\
&= 22\% \pm 1.96\,(1.99\%)\\
&= 22\% \pm 3.9\%\\
&= 18.1\% \longleftrightarrow 25.9\%
\end{aligned}$$

What does this interval of 18 percent to 26 percent mean? It means that if a large number of samples were taken from the col-

---

[1]The formula is usually presented in the following form:

$$S_p = \sqrt{\frac{P \cdot Q}{n} \cdot \frac{N-n}{N}}$$

P=proportion of population possessing a certain attribute
Q=proportion of population not having that attribute
But as previously stated, population data of this nature are seldom known, which means a formula using sample data exclusively is usually needed.

lege's student body, 95 percent of these samples would contain the universe mean within ±1.96 s_p of their mean values. It is assumed that this sample ($p = 22$ percent) is one of those 95 percent. Based on these sample data it is felt that only 18 percent to 26 percent of the River City College students have a favorable attitude toward the River City merchants.

This section of the chapter was supposed to deal with step four of the sampling process, how the researcher determines the sample's size. So far the presentation has touched on everything *but* this aspect. It was stated at the outset of this section, however, that the information on $s_{\bar{x}}$, s_p and confidence intervals had to be covered first to provide the reader with a better understanding of the various factors determining the sample's size.

Using standard errors of the mean to determine sample size

The formulas for determining $s_{\bar{x}}$ and s_p are used in choosing the sample size, but they have to be altered so that the sample size (n) becomes the formula's focal point. Situations involving variables (s_x) will be used initially to illustrate the procedure. The correction factor $\sqrt{\frac{N-n}{N}}$ is eliminated in this example since it merely complicates the computations without improving the findings to any significant extent. Following is the process used to arrive at the desired formula:

(1) $\quad s_{\bar{x}} = \dfrac{s}{\sqrt{n}} \cdot \sqrt{\dfrac{N-n}{N}}$

(2) $\quad s_{\bar{x}}^2 = \dfrac{s^2}{n}$ $\qquad$ (2) Eliminate the correction factor and square the entire formula.

(3) $\quad n = \dfrac{s^2}{s_{\bar{x}}^2}$ $\qquad$ (3) Transpose the terms.

The procedures used to determine the sample's size (n) can be illustrated by the following example. The Society of American Florists (SAF) is interested in obtaining information about the flower-buying activities of young adults. One group in which they are particularly interested is male college students. For this part of their study they select a typical Midwest university – Ball State – and will sample a portion of the male students. SAF wants to determine the amount of money a typical male student spends annually for fresh flowers as gifts or for personal use. Ball State has approximately 18,000 students of which 8,300 are male.

SAF wants to be reasonably confident that the dollar figure obtained will be within ±$2 of the average male student's real expenditures. How large a sample will be needed to achieve this precision? Since this situation involves sampling for a variable, the formula involving standard error of the mean ($s_{\bar{x}}$) will be used.

Finding the s^2 value

$$n = \frac{s^2}{s_{\bar{x}}^2}$$

The above formula presents a problem to the researcher in that it contains three unknown values. Thus, before a value for n can be derived, values for s^2 and $s_{\bar{x}}^2$ must be found. The first step is to establish the s^2 value. This can be done in one of three ways.

The researcher might have information from a somewhat comparable study and use that study's standard deviation for inclusion in this formula. This procedure is based on the rather questionable assumption that the standard deviations for both samples are about equal.

A more acceptable method is having the researcher conduct a small survey ($n = 30$) among the population under study. A standard deviation is computed from this subsample and used as the s value in the formula.

A third method can be used when a range of values for the variable under study can be reasonably estimated. This range is then divided by six, and the resulting figure is the standard deviation. The key assumption in this method is that in a normally distributed set of values, the range encompasses approximately three standard deviations (plus or minus). Thus, by dividing this range by six, the result is a reasonable estimate of one standard deviation.

$$\text{Estimated } s = \frac{\text{total estimated range}}{6}$$

In our example we will use this third method. The researcher is fairly confident the range of annual expenditures for flowers by male students at Ball State is from $0 to $80. Thus, $s = \$80 \div 6$ or $13.50. So one figure in the formula is now established.

$$n = \frac{(13.50)^2}{s_{\bar{x}}^2}$$

Determining the $s_{\bar{x}}^2$ value

The next step is to find the $s_{\bar{x}}$ value. This has been identified for the researcher by SAF's statement on the degree of precision they desire from the sample's results. They want to be 95 percent confident that the sample mean will be within ±$2 of the actual mean of the population. Using this request as the guideline, the $s_{\bar{x}}$ value can be deduced. The logic used to obtain this value is as follows.

A 95 percent confidence interval involves $1.96s_{\bar{x}}$. In this example that means $1.96s_{\bar{x}} = ±\$2$ or a total range of $4.

$$\therefore s_{\bar{x}} = \frac{2}{1.96}$$
$$= \$1.02$$

Thus, the second figure of the formula is established.

$$n = \frac{(\$13.50)^2}{(\$1.02)^2}$$

If SAF desired greater confidence (99 percent) that the sample mean would be within ±$2 of the population's actual mean, the $s_{\bar{x}}$ value would be determined as follows:

99% confidence interval involves $2.57\ s_{\bar{x}}$

$$\therefore s_{\bar{x}} = \frac{\$2}{2.57}$$
$$= \$.78$$

It is important to recognize a key point in using the above procedure for determining $s_{\bar{x}}$. Be sure you understand the degree of accuracy sought in the collected data. If it is requested that the actual population figure lie within a total range of $6, this means the actual interval consists of ±$3. If the total range requested is $10, then the actual interval is ±$5. The degree of confidence employed will usually be either 95 percent or 99 percent.

Using the formula—Returning to our original problem, enough information now exists to determine the sample size.

$$n = \frac{(13.50)^2}{(1.02)^2}$$
$$= \frac{182.25}{1.04}$$
$$= 175$$

Thus, to be 95 percent confident that the sample mean will be within ±$2 of the population mean, a sample of 175 male students must be contacted.

Increasing precision—Impact on sample size—If SAF desired greater precision, i.e., a smaller interval of ±$1, a larger sample would be needed. A 95 percent confidence interval of ±$1 would require a sample of 701 students.

$$1.96 s_{\bar{x}} = \$1 \qquad \therefore s_{\bar{x}} = 0.51$$

$$n = \frac{(13.50)^2}{(0.51)^2} = \frac{182.25}{0.26}$$

$$= 701$$

This small change in precision sought (±$1 vs. ±$2) requires almost a fourfold increase in the size of the sample needed. This demonstrates the importance of weighing the value of added precision against the much higher costs of the larger sample needed to provide that precision.

Shortcut for determining sample size

If the reader understands the logic involved in the previous formula, then the following *one-step* formula could be used to determine the sample size.

$$n = \frac{Z^2 s^2}{e^2}$$

$Z =$ number of standard errors associated with the desired level of confidence
$s =$ standard deviation of sample data
$e =$ allowable error

Referring to the previous example, assume the firm desires a sample large enough to provide a 95 percent confidence interval of ±$1. The standard deviation is still $13.50.

$$n = \frac{1.96^2 \cdot \$13.50^2}{\$1}$$

$$n = 701$$

Adjusting *n* on basis of population's size

If the n value generated by the above procedure is more than 5 percent of the population ($\frac{n}{N} > 5\%$), the sample size should be revised downward. The downward revision would take the following form:

$$n_a = \frac{n}{1 + n/N} \qquad n_a = \text{adjusted sample size}$$

In our example with the Ball State male students, the sample size required was 175. This is only 2 percent of the total 8,300 male students so no downward adjustment is necessary. But if the sample size had been determined to be 701, this would have been about 8.5 percent of the population, enabling a downward adjustment.

$$n_a = \frac{701}{1 + 701/8300}$$
$$= \frac{701}{1.085}$$
$$= 646$$

It is important to recognize that the sample size indicated in the previous procedures is really the number of respondents from whom data will be obtained. Therefore, if a mail survey is to be used, an estimate of the rate of response will have to be made so that the sample size of 175 will be achieved. If only 40 percent response is expected, 438 surveys will have to be mailed out.

Sample size in surveys—a key point

$$\frac{175}{0.40} = 438$$

If a smaller response (25 percent) is expected, an even larger number (700) will have to be used. Emphasizing this point again, the sample size indicates the number of participants needed. The actual number of people that must be contacted originally is determined by the expected rate of response.

Finding sample size when attributes are involved

Assume that the Society of American Florists (SAF) wanted to know the proportion of male college students who spend more than $20 a year on fresh flowers. They want to be 95 percent confident the sample's value will be within ±6 percent of the true mean. How large a sample would be needed to provide this precision? In this situation the formula involving standard error or the proportion (s_p) would be used.

It is important that the reader understand why in this situation the standard error of the proportion (s_p) is used rather than the standard error of the mean ($s_{\bar{x}}$). Since the characteristic being measured is a proportion (percentage of male students who spend more than $20 annually on fresh flowers), the data involve "attributes."

The researcher has to look closely at the characteristic about which information is sought and determine whether this characteristic is a variable (height, weight, dollar expenditures, years of schooling, etc.) or an attribute (good or bad, pro or con, regular or irregular, etc.). When this has been determined, the formula to use in determining sample size becomes evident.

In the SAF example the researcher has to determine how large a sample is needed to develop a 95 percent confidence interval of ± 6 percent. The researcher transposes the s_p formula following the same reasoning as used in the $s_{\bar{x}}$ formula.

$s_p = \sqrt{\dfrac{p \cdot q}{n}}$ (1) Ignore the correction factor to simplify computations.

$s_p^2 = \dfrac{p \cdot q}{n}$ (2) Square both sides to eliminate square root sign.

$n = \dfrac{p \cdot q}{s_p^2}$ (3) Transpose terms.

Determining p value

A small sample of the male students could be surveyed to obtain an estimated p value. If this is impossible or undesirable, a value of 50 percent can be assigned to p. Allowing p to equal 0.5 guarantees the maximum sample size needed for a desired degree of precision; if the cost factor is crucial, this technique should *not* be used.

In this example it will be assumed that a preliminary study is made among 40 students, and 13 (32 percent) of this sample indicates they spend $20 or more annually for fresh flowers.

Determining s_p value

Since the Society of American Florists desires a 95 percent confidence interval of ± 6 percent, the s_p will be 3.06.

A 95 percent confidence interval involves 1.96 s_p.

$$1.96 \, s_p = \pm 6\%$$
$$1 \, s_p = 6\%/1.96$$
$$= \pm 3.06\%$$

Using the formula—The researcher now has all the information needed. The s_p and p values can be plugged into the formula identifying the sample size required for the desired precision.

$$s_p = 3.06$$
$$p = 32\%$$
$$q = 68\%$$
$$n = \frac{p \cdot q}{s_p{}^2}$$
$$= \frac{(32)(68)}{(3.06)^2}$$
$$= \frac{2176}{9.4}$$
$$= 231$$

A sample of 231 students would be needed to enable a 95 per-cent confidence interval of ±6 percent. If a confidence interval of ±3 percent is desired, the sample size will increase to 967.

$$s_p = \frac{3\%}{1.96} \qquad\qquad n = \frac{(32)(68)}{(1.53)^2}$$
$$= 1.53\% \qquad\qquad = \frac{2176}{2.25}$$
$$= 967$$

In the above situation, when the confidence interval was halved from ±6 percent to ±3 percent, the sample size was in-creased over fourfold from 231 to 967.

Assigning p a value of 50 percent

If previous information is not available on the value of p, the researcher is forced to assign p a value of 50 percent. This action guarantees that the sample will be large enough to provide the desired confidence interval no matter what the real value of p might be. If SAF wanted a 95 percent confidence interval of ±6 percent and p is assigned a value of 50 percent, the sample size needed is 266.

$$n = \frac{p \cdot q}{s_p{}^2}$$
$$= \frac{(50)(50)}{(3.06)^2}$$
$$= \frac{2500}{9.4}$$
$$= 266$$

Formula when *N* is known and small

An analysis of the above formula discloses that the resulting sample size totally ignores the size of the original population since it depends solely on the values of p and s_p. Thus, $n = 266$ would result regardless of whether the actual population size was 8,300 or 400. When the population size is known and is reasonably small (less than 1,000), the following formula might be more appropriate.

$$n = \frac{p \cdot q}{\dfrac{e_s^2}{z^2} + \dfrac{p \cdot q}{N}}$$

n = sample size
N = population size
p = proportion of sample possessing a given attribute (50%)
$q = 1 - p$
e_s = allowable error ($\pm 6\%$)
z = confidence level in terms of s_p (1.96)

To illustrate how the use of this formula can affect the sample size, it will be assumed that the male student population of Ball State is 830 instead of its actual size of 8,300.

$$n = \frac{(50)(50)}{\dfrac{(6)^2}{(1.96)^2} + \dfrac{(50)(50)}{830}}$$

$$= \frac{2500}{\dfrac{36}{3.84} + \dfrac{2500}{830}}$$

$$= \frac{2500}{12.4}$$

$$= 201$$

This compares to the value $n = 266$ determined when the population's size was not taken into consideration.

When the actual population size is fairly large ($N >$ the value of $p \cdot q$ using whole numbers), using this formula will have little or no impact on altering the sample size. Tables that are available in some statistics books give the necessary sample size for specified levels of precision and population sizes when attributes are involved.

Important factors affecting sample size

There are four key factors to be kept in mind when determining the actual sample size needed.

1. The sample size obtained from the formulas is the actual number of responses needed. If a sample size of 276 is needed for a mail survey, the researcher has to estimate the number of questionnaires that have to be sent out to obtain these 276 responses. If it is felt that only 1 out of 5 questionnaires will eventually be returned (20 percent response), 1,380 questionnaires must be mailed out to achieve the necessary sample size of 276.

2. A confusing aspect for many beginning researchers is that the formulas presented in this chapter will indicate the sample size needed to develop a confidence interval. But this confidence interval applies only to the specific population characteristics obtained from one question on a survey. In other words, the confidence coefficient associated with a given sample size does *not* pertain to the results of the entire study. Generally, a study is not carried out to answer only one question since the researcher is interested in several values. This means that the researcher will attain less precision on some questions than may be desired.

The previous example involving the florists' survey of male college students illustrates this point. It was determined that a sample of 175 was needed if a 95 percent confidence interval of ±\$2 was to be established for the students' annual expenditures for fresh flowers. If another question in the survey asked the students how much they spent annually on another gift item— candy—a completely different $s_{\bar{x}}$ value would be involved. The sample of 175 might be too small to enable the same preciseness on the students' candy purchases as was obtained for their flower purchases.

In light of this, when a questionnaire is used, the researcher should select the one question (or characteristic) felt to be most crucial to the study. The desired confidence interval for answers pertaining to that question should be established, and this will determine how large a sample is needed.

3. The formulas given in this chapter apply only to simple random samples. Other probability samples such as stratified samples or cluster samples require somewhat different methods for determining their sample sizes. The general principles described in the use of the simple random formulas also apply to these other formulas. Researchers should consult a research or statistics book or, better yet, a sampling expert if they are not sure of the formulas that fit their particular sample design.

4. Whenever a sample size is to be determined, the researcher has to weigh the costs of various sample sizes against the increased precision obtained via larger samples. Generally a compromise will have to be made between the two.

SELECTION OF SPECIFIC SAMPLE MEMBERS

The population to be sampled has been defined, the frame developed, the sample design chosen, and the sample size determined. Now it is necessary to select the specific units that will comprise the sample.

In the previous example, it was determined that a sample of 175 males from the entire student body of 8,300 was needed. A selection process using random numbers could be applied to a list of names obtained from the school's registrar. Each male could be assigned a number from 1 to 8,300, or their actual school ID numbers could be used. Then the names could be obtained by using a table of random numbers or by having these numbers generated from a computer.

Not all units selected for the sample will participate. Some may no longer be in school; others may just refuse. So whether the survey is done by mail, telephone, or personal contact, allowances should be made to incorporate enough members into the sample to guarantee the 175 respondents.

Since the problem of nonresponse is tied so closely to the actual data gathering, the presentation of methods for coping with nonresponse and the selection of substitute sample units is covered in the next chapter.

REVISING PRECISION LIMITS IN LIGHT OF SAMPLE RESULTS

This final step involves the adjustments that should be made in light of the data actually collected from the sample. Chronologically, this activity follows the data collection and data tabulation steps of the total research process. But it is presented now because it is tied so closely to choosing confidence intervals and sample sizes.

The previous example involving the florists' (SAF) analysis of the flower purchases of male college students will be used again. It will be recalled that previous computations indicated that 175 male respondents were necessary to provide the SAF with a 95 percent confidence interval ($\pm$\$2) of the average male students' annual flower expenditures. In determining the sample size needed for this desired preciseness, the standard deviation used in the computations was an estimated value of \$13.50.

Assume now that 175 male students were contacted and information obtained on their flower expenditures. The researcher must now make adjustments in light of the data actually collected. While the standard deviation prior to the sample was estimated to be $13.50, the actual standard deviation was $14.85. In light of this, either the confidence interval (±$2) or the confidence coefficient (95 percent) will have to be adjusted. The researcher must decide which of the two should be maintained.

If the decision is made to maintain the ±$2 interval, then the confidence coefficient will be affected. The new standard deviation ($14.85) must be incorporated into the original formula.

Confidence interval maintained

$$s_{\bar{x}} = \frac{s}{\sqrt{n}}$$

$$= \frac{\$14.85}{\sqrt{175}}$$

$$= \$1.12$$

The ±$2 interval $= \frac{\$2}{1.12} = 1.78 s_{\bar{x}}$

$1.78 s_{\bar{x}} = 92.5\%$ confidence coefficient (obtained from z table)

The confidence coefficient has been lowered from a desired 95 percent to 92.5 percent because of the difference between the actual standard deviation ($14.85) and estimated standard deviation ($13.50). Although this is a fairly small percentage change, in many studies it can be as great as 5 to 10 percent.

If it is decided to preserve the 95 percent confidence coefficient, then the size of the interval will be altered.

Confidence coefficient maintained

$$s_{\bar{x}} = 1.12$$
$$95\% \ \text{CI} = \pm 1.96 \, (s_{\bar{x}})$$
$$= \pm 1.96 \, (1.12)$$
$$= \pm 2.19$$

As in the previous example, the change (±$2.19 instead of ±$2.00) was not very dramatic, but there are many instances where the change in value could be quite large.

Adjustments when sample size differs

It was originally determined that a sample size of 175 was needed to provide the necessary confidence interval (±$2) at the 95 percent level. If only 142 male students actually participated in the study, allowances would have to be made for this smaller sample. Assume the standard deviation of their expenditures was $14.20.

$$s_{\bar{x}} = \frac{s}{\sqrt{n}}$$

$$= \frac{\$14.20}{\sqrt{142}}$$

$$= \$1.19$$

If the 95 percent confidence coefficient is to be maintained, then the interval must be adjusted.

$$95\% \text{ CI} = \pm 1.96 \, (s_{\bar{x}})$$
$$= \pm 1.96 \, (\$1.19)$$
$$= \pm \$2.33 \text{ (new interval)}$$

If the $\pm\$2$ interval is to be maintained, then the confidence coefficient would be altered.

$$\pm\$2 \text{ interval} = \frac{\$2}{1.19} = 1.68 s_{\bar{x}}$$

$$1.68 s_{\bar{x}} = 90.6\% \text{ confidence coefficient}$$
$$\text{(from } z \text{ table)}$$

Adjustments involving attributes

If the study involved attributes (s_p) instead of variables $(s_{\bar{x}})$, similar adjustments must be made. A second phase of the florist study was to determine what proportion of the male students spend more than $20 annually on flowers. The florists wanted to have the resulting figure be within a 95 percent confidence interval of ± 6 percent. The sample size needed for this preciseness was 231. This figure was based on an assumed p value of 32 percent. If the actual p value was 28 percent, the following adjustments could be made.

$$\text{actual } p = 28\% \qquad \text{assumed } p = 32\%$$
$$\text{actual } s_p = 2.95\% \qquad \text{assumed } s_p = 3.06\%$$

$$s_p = \sqrt{\frac{p \cdot q}{n}}$$

$$s_p = \sqrt{\frac{(28)(72)}{231}}$$

$$s_p = 2.95\%$$

Based on the actual sample data, the adjusted 95 percent confidence interval now becomes ± 5.8 percent $(1.96 \times 2.95 s_p)$. This is an improvement over the ±6 percent originally sought.

If it is desirable to maintain the ±6 percent interval, the confidence coefficient can be raised.

$$\pm 6\% \div 2.95 = 2.03 s_p$$
$$\pm 2.03 s_p = 95.2 \text{ confidence coefficient}$$

The adjustments made in light of the actual data collected from the sample can either improve or lower the preciseness of the results. If the actual standard deviation is larger than originally estimated or the actual number of sample respondents is less than originally needed, the study's preciseness will be negatively affected. If the opposite situation occurs (smaller standard deviation or larger response than expected), the study's preciseness will be improved. If adjustments of the results are necessary, a decision has to be made on which trade off will take place—protect the interval and change the coefficient, or maintain the coefficient and alter the interval.

Summary on adjusting data based on sample results

The researcher can follow either of two approaches when determining the sample's size or the preciseness of its results. A desired precision can be specified in advance, and the sample size needed to achieve this precision is then determined. This is the approach emphasized in this chapter. On the other hand, the sample size can be arbitrarily or judgmentally chosen, and when the results are obtained (assuming a probability sample is used) their preciseness can be determined by applying the appropriate formulas.

In either case, there are three key factors to consider when determining how large the sample should be.

TWO GENERAL APPROACHES TO SAMPLING

1. *Cost*—How many dollars are available for sampling? What sized sample is affordable with these dollars? The sample size desired by the researcher will often have to be scaled down to meet the financial restraints of the project.

2. *Representativeness*—Does the sample mirror, in a reasonable manner, the population under study? While no sample can be an exact miniature of its population, it should be large enough so that it adequately represents the key segments comprising that population.

3. *Adequacy*—Is the sample large enough to evoke confidence in the findings? Both the researcher and the data

user should feel comfortable that the results depict what is taking place within the population.

SUMMARY   The starting point for any sampling activity is to define the population to be studied. The researcher must feel that the units to be surveyed or observed will give data relevant to the study's objectives. Since a frame enables the individual population members to be identified, it may be necessary to alter the definition of the population to suit an existing frame.

Once the population to be studied has been defined and an accompanying frame obtained, the researcher chooses the sample design that will provide the best information in light of (1) the stated objectives of the study, (2) the representativeness and preciseness sought, and (3) the financial restraints imposed on the study.

In developing the sample design, the researcher must first decide whether a probability sample or a nonprobability sample will be used. Results obtained from probability samples are more easily defended since the amount of sampling error can be estimated. Nonprobability samples are used in those situations where time and cost are of the essence or where sample members cannot be objectively selected.

Following the decision on whether to use a probability or a nonprobability sample, the researcher selects the specific sample design. In the use of probability samples, the choice usually will be from among simple random samples, systematic samples, stratified samples, or cluster samples. This decision hinges on the funds and time available, the nature of the information sought, and the capability of the data-gathering team.

Once the sample design has been chosen, the researcher determines the size of the sample needed. When a probability sample is used, statistical procedures exist for selecting the sample size necessary to achieve a stated level of preciseness. This means such limits of precision must be established prior to selection of the sample's size. In the case of nonprobability samples, the selection of sample size generally depends on the researcher's subjective judgment.

Once the sample size is chosen, the actual sample members are selected and the data are then collected. The original precision limits may have to be revised to properly reflect these data.

It is paramount that businessmen understand proper sampling procedures since many of the decisions they make will be based solely on sample data. As stated at the outset, the purpose of these chapters was not to make the readers experts in sampling, but rather to provide insight into its strengths and weaknesses as a tool for gathering data.

---

1. Which comes first—defining the population or developing the frame?

2. How do you defend the sample size when a nonprobability sample is involved?

3. What is the purpose of the correction factor?

4. Are there statistical procedures for eliminating sampling error?

5. What is the key relationship between samples and population that enables sampling errors to be estimated?

6. What is the difference between standard deviations and standard error of the mean?

7. How do you distinguish between "attributes" and "variables" when deciding which formula to use in determining standard error?

8. Explain what is meant by "The 95 percent confidence interval of the amount of money spent monthly on cosmetics by the typical St. Louis adult female is $3.92 to $4.78."

9. How does switching from a 95 percent interval to a 99 percent interval affect the results? (Assume sample size remains the same.)

10. "I am 95 percent confident in the results of this questionnaire." Evaluate this statement.

11. How will the following situations affect the results obtained from a sample (assume all other data remain the same). What adjustments must be made in the collected data?

    a. The expected rate of response to a survey was 25 percent. Actually, 30 percent of those in the sample responded.

    b. The standard deviation used to determine the $s_{\bar{x}}$ value was $6. When the data were actually obtained, the standard deviation was found to be $7.90.

    c. A p value of 10 percent was assumed. The actual results disclosed a p of 21 percent.

    d. A p value of 0.5 was used.

QUESTIONS AND EXERCISES

CASES

Case 1

Brown and Williamson (cigarette manufacturers) are interested in finding out more about the smoking habits of college students. They want to determine how many cigarettes the average student smokes a day. They also want to be 95 percent confident this figure is within a total range of one cigarette of the true mean for all college students. They have chosen the University of Minnesota as their test campus. How large a sample is needed to provide this degree of accuracy?

A random survey of 40 students disclosed the average student smoked 5 cigarettes a day with a standard deviation of 5.5 cigarettes. Thirty-seven percent of this sample stated they were "heavy" smokers.

Case 2

Acme Products, a components manufacturer with a large nationwide sales force, is contemplating leasing cars for its salesmen rather than giving them a $300-a-month car allowance, the method now being used. Before making the decision, it needs to know how many miles its average salesman drives per month. Acme will obtain this information in a mail questionnaire sent to a sample of its salesmen. The person making the decision wants to be sure (99 percent) that the real figure is contained in a total interval of 30 miles.

An informal study conducted among 20 salesmen disclosed that they drive an average of 835 miles a month with a standard deviation of 112 miles. How large a sample is needed to provide the desired accuracy?

Case 3

Beauty Products, a Chicago cosmetics firm, is thinking of developing a sales program aimed at increasing sales on college campuses. It plans to hire 2 to 3 female students on campuses where there are at least 8,000 students. They will have part-time assignments helping out with special promotions and finding other ways to bring the company's products to the attention of female students.

Before they undertake such a program, however, they want to obtain more information on the students' expenditures on cosmetics. A random sample of 300 female students at the University of Illinois disclosed that 75 percent of them spent more than $5 a month on cosmetics. The survey also disclosed that their mean yearly expenditure on cosmetics was $48.32, with a standard deviation of $24.

Based on this information, develop a 95 percent confidence interval on the amount of money the school's 7,500 female students spend annually on cosmetics.

Jody Koehler, a recent college graduate, feels that the town of Greeley, Colorado, could support another bookstore. There are three such stores already in the city, but she feels there is enough business so that a fourth store could easily survive.

Before going further in her plans for such a store, she decides to sample a portion of the adult population to obtain a figure on total book purchases by residents in the past year. (Obviously, the three existing stores would not provide her with their sales figures.)

A random sample of 200 households disclosed that 54 of them feel there is a need for a fourth store. The survey also disclosed that the mean yearly expenditure among the households for books (hardcover and paperbacks) was $18.40, with a range from $0 to $92.

a. Develop a 95 percent confidence interval on the amount of money that 12,000 households spend annually on books.

b. Assuming Jody could obtain 15 percent of the book business the first year, estimate her potential sales.

11

Data collection

The jury has heard the complicated antitrust case and has now retired to begin its deliberations. Behind the one-way mirror, the same lawyers who had argued the case observe the jurors as they discuss the case in the jury room. While this would be illegal under normal circumstances, this is a "practice jury," a new technique being used by lawyers to improve their chances in the courtroom.

The mock jurors discuss the case and arrive at a decision. The lawyers observe the deliberations and learn what things are important to the mock jurors in deciding the case. Thus, when the actual case is tried in the near future, they will know which points to emphasize and which to play down. Does the procedure seem familiar? It should, since it is a modified version of two techniques frequently used by marketers to obtain consumer reactions to a product or concept — test marketing and focus groups.

This example is taken from the following article, "Trials by Trial Jury," *Newsweek*, March 19, 1981, p. 84.

The major activities leading up to the collection of the data have been completed: objectives were identified; tools for gathering the data were developed; and sampling procedures were chosen. The researchers now can begin data collection. Much of the effort and dollars expended on the previous tasks will be wasted unless appropriate collection methods are followed.

This chapter identifies the problems most frequently encountered in this activity and provides guidelines for dealing with them. In addition, special emphasis is given to two collection techniques frequently used in marketing—test markets and group interviews.

DATA COLLECTION ERRORS

In the previous chapter on sampling, reference was made to the existence of two categories of errors that occur when surveys, observations, and experiments are involved. One category was labeled "sampling errors." These are the differences that arise between the statistics (sample) and the parameter (population) because the sample is rarely an exact miniature of the population from which it was drawn. In probability samples the size of this sampling error can be estimated.

The second category of errors was "data collection errors," or differences between the statistics and the parameters caused by problems incurred in the actual collection of data. Some of the more common causes of data collection errors are (1) nonresponse, (2) improper sample coverage, and (3) influence of the interviewer. These were touched on briefly in Chapter 9; each is now covered in greater detail.

Nonresponse

Who is a nonrespondent?

Although researchers agree nonresponse occurs in almost all surveys, these same researchers cannot agree on who should be labeled a nonrespondent. This problem stems from the fact that there is no one method used by all researchers to determine the "rate of response" to a survey.

Figure 11-2 indicates the variety of outcomes that could occur with telephone surveys. It also illustrates the variety of ways in which the response rate could be determined. Should such a rate be based on all original sample members? Should it be based only on "eligible" sample members? Or, should it be based only on those sample members who were successfully contacted? Until the researchers adopt a single definition for determining response rates, it will be very difficult to compare the nonresponse aspects of different surveys.

The author merely intends to alert the reader to these definitional problems and does not want to get bogged down in the semantic problems of the research industry. For the remainder of this text nonrespondents will be viewed as those people/households from the eligible sample that for any reason do not participate in the survey.

Nonresponse — personal interviews

Persons originally selected to be personally interviewed might not respond for any of three reasons:

1. They can't be contacted or located.
2. They refuse to cooperate (refusals).
3. They are "unsuitable" to interview (ill people, senile people, recent death in family, etc.)

The incidence of "unsuitables" is usually beyond an interviewer's control, but the number of "can't locates" and "refusals" can be influenced with proper field procedures.

Potential interviewee can't be located — The number of people in the sample who "can't be located" varies by the time of the day, day of the week, and season of the year.[1] Oftentimes, the households that can't be contacted during the hours from 9 A.M. to 3 P.M. have something in common — the female head works part-time or full-time. As the number of working wives continues to grow (48 percent of all households in 1980), the number of "not-at-homes" will also increase.

Some findings of value to marketing researchers are:

- Retired persons are home more than anyone else and are very receptive to being interviewed.

- People between the ages of 14 and 29 are very difficult to find at home, and phone appointments are about the only way to reach them.

- The probability of finding someone at home is greater among low-income families because they have fewer places to go, and less money to spend.

- People in northern states tend to be home more in the winter than in summer months when travel is easier.

---

[1]Harper W. Boyd and Ralph Westfall, *Marketing Research: Text and Cases,* 5th ed. (Homewood, Ill.: Richard Irwin, 1981), p. 370.

- "Can't locates" are more likely to occur in urban areas than in rural areas. A fairly high percentage (50 to 80 percent) of the first attempts to contact interviewees in large cities result in failures.

- Saturday is the best day of the week to find a respondent at home during the day, but both Friday and Saturday evenings are the least productive times to call.

- In setting up a "cold canvass" type of interview schedule, the most productive hours for interviewers would be 5:00 to 9:00 P.M., Sunday through Friday and 10:00 A.M. to 5:00 P.M., Saturday.[2]

All of these conditions illustrate why the researcher can't take for granted that people contacted are representative of the "not-at-homes."

While some "can't contact" or "not at home" will always occur, the interviewer can influence its size as indicated by the variation among experienced and inexperienced interviewers. The experienced interviewers scheduled their callbacks more effectively by uncovering possible reasons for the potential interviewee's absence and then adjusted their callbacks on the basis of this information. Advance appointments made by telephone also aid in reducing the incidence of "not-at-home."

Number of callbacks—Callback policies will vary among firms, but most research organizations feel that three callbacks (a total of four calls) will bring the "can't contacts" down to an acceptable level. Figure 11-1 depicts the cumulative response rate to typical nationwide surveys involving personal interviews and telephone interviews.

As shown, three callbacks (total of four calls) with personal interviews resulted in 83 percent of the sample being contacted, but only 67 percent of contacts in telephone surveys. But the greater efficiency of the personal interview is more than offset by the much lower cost-per-call of telephone contacts.

Figure 11-1 also illustrates that significantly fewer personal callbacks are needed to contact 100 percent of the households than is the case for telephone interviews (7 personal callbacks versus 16 telephone callbacks). This difference occurs because the personal interviewer can gather additional information about the sample member from neighbors to aid in making more productive callbacks. Telephone interviewers have no comparable information source available to them.

---

[2]M. F. Weeks et al., "Optimal Times to Contact Sample Households," *Public Opinion Quarterly*, Summer 1980, pp. 101-114.

Figure 11-1   Cumulative Percentage of Households Contacted
                                Based on Number of Calls Made
                                Personal and Telephone Surveys

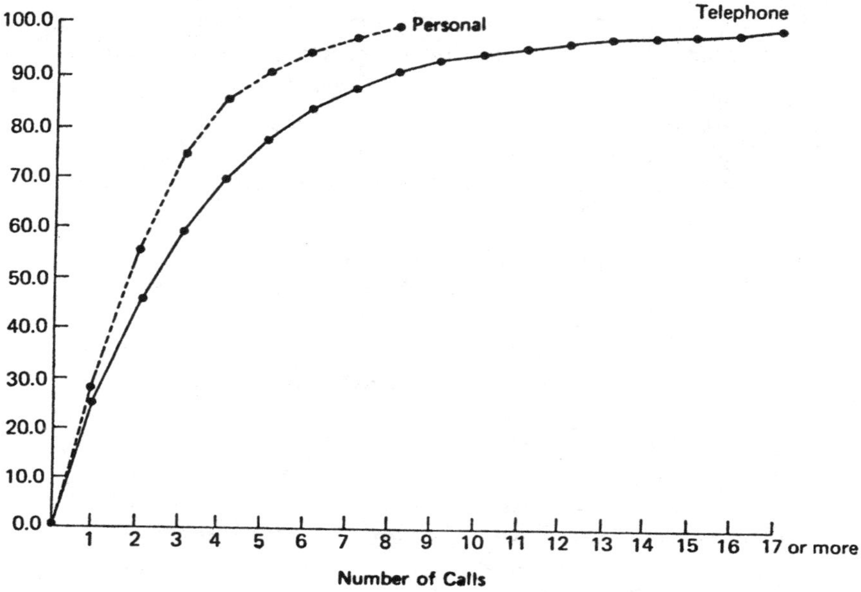

SOURCE: Robert M. Groves and Robert L. Kahn, *Surveys by Telephone* (New York: Academic Press, 1979), p. 59.

It is possible to handle "not-at-homes" without using call-backs by employing a method developed by Politz and Simmons.[3] Individuals who are interviewed are asked to indicate the number of times they have been at home during the period all the interviews were being conducted. The respondents are then divided into groups according to the number of times they were at home. This supposedly will reflect the probability that an individual would be interviewed when calls were only made once. To allow for those who are not interviewed, the responses of those with the lowest probability of being interviewed (seldom at home) are

---

[3]A. Politz and W. Simmons, "An Attempt to Get the 'Not-at-Home' into the Sample Without Callbacks," *Journal of the American Statistical Association,* 44 (March 1949), pp. 9-31.

weighted more heavily than the responses of persons with higher probability of being interviewed.

One method that should not be used is to substitute another unit in the neighborhood for the "not-at-homes." All this does is add another "at-home" unit and increases the problem of getting proper representation of the "not-at-homes" group.

*Refusals—personal interviews—*The percentage of sample members refusing to participate in personal interviews will vary from project to project, rising to 20 to 30 percent in some studies. In addition to those situations where the respondent won't answer any questions, others may refuse to answer specific questions asked in the interview, especially those of a highly personal nature. Just as the interviewers can influence the number of "can't contacts," they can also influence the number of "refusals."

A portion of the refusal rate is tied to an increasing reluctance among people to allow strangers into their homes for reasons of personal safety. Some of this can be overcome by having the interviewer carry proper identification or a letter of authorization.

In one major study sponsored by the federal government, the two reasons most frequently cited by individuals for refusing to participate in a survey were: the survey was an invasion of privacy or they had had an unfavorable experience as a survey respondent.[4]

*The unsuitables—*Since many potential interviewees are randomly selected, there is no way of predetermining their suitability for inclusion in the study. Upon making contact, the interviewer may discover that the person or household selected is unsuitable. They may have an illness or injury that prevents them from being interviewed or certain conditions have occurred that make them no longer appropriate for the study, i.e., a man recently married when the study involves only single people. This writer was once assigned an interview address and upon arrival discovered the house was on fire. Needless to say, this potential interviewee would not have been receptive to an interview at that time.

Thus, the incidence of "unsuitables" is usually beyond the control of the interviewer.

---

[4]Theresa J. DeMaio, *"Refusals: Who, Where and Why," Public Opinion Quarterly*, Spring 1980, pp. 225-232.

Nonresponse – telephone surveys

As shown in Figure 11-2, the same three categories of nonrespondents – "can't contacts," "refusals," and "unsuitables" – occur when telephone surveys are used. Potential respondents might not be contacted for any number of reasons: not at home, doesn't get to the phone in time, line is busy, no number available, etc.

If contacted, they may refuse to participate or be immediately rejected because they do not possess the necessary characteristics (e.g., households with a working wife may be the only ones to be surveyed). Even after they are involved in the interview, they may refuse to answer all the questions or additional information might disclose that they are not really eligible for the survey.

A major study undertaken by Wiseman and McDonald obtained input from 32 firms that regularly made use of telephone surveys. These firms had compiled noncontact and refusal rates from a total of 182 surveys. They found that median noncontact rate for telephone surveys was 39 percent and the median refusal rate was 28 percent. The refusal rate ranged from 17 percent to 32 percent depending on the length of interview, geographic boundaries, and nature of the product category included in the survey.[5]

In the case of noncontacts, some type of systematic substitution can be used. Before substitutes are introduced, however, at least two attempts on different days and at different hours should be made to reach the original sample member. Some firms will use as many as six to eight callbacks before substituting.

Since it is easier for the sample member to refuse a telephone survey than to turn down an interviewer in person, it is crucial that proper telephone etiquette be followed by interviewers to increase the chance of each member's participation.

Nearly 80 percent of the refusals occur at the end of the introductory remarks; therefore these remarks must concisely justify the research and the respondent's role in it, legitimize the research firm, and convince the respondent of his/her importance to the survey.

Telephone interviewers should have reasonably pleasant voices, be easily understood, and attempt to sound spontaneous even though they will be reading most of their presentation.

---

[5]Frederick Wiseman, and Philip McDonald, "Toward the Development of Industry Standards for Response and Nonresponse Rates," Report No. 80-101, 1980, Marketing Science Institute, Cambridge, Massachusetts.

Figure 11-2

Possible Outcomes When Using a Telephone Survey

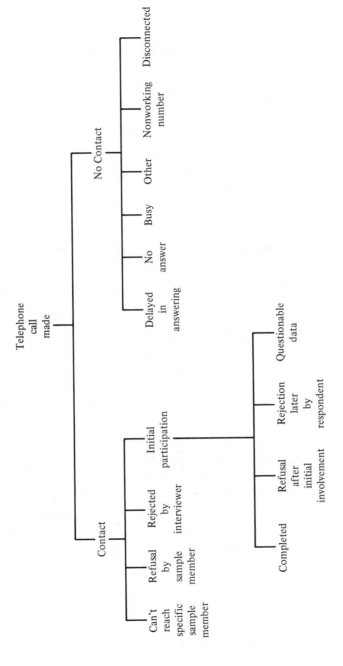

(Format adopted from model in Wiseman and McDonald, p. 29).

Nonresponse—mail surveys

"Can't locates" will always occur in mail surveys, but their number will be kept to an acceptable level if an accurate, up-to-date mailing list for the frame is used. In the past it was usually assumed the "can't locates" were reasonably similar to those who did receive the questionnaire, so no adjustments were made for them when interpreting the results. It should be recognized, however, that in the 1980s, almost 25 percent of the population moves annually, and a significant portion of that movement occurs among low-income households. Thus, there may be a stronger tie than previously thought between "can't contacts" and household income.

"Refusals" or nonrespondents are the chief problem in mail surveys. Their percentage can vary from as high as 95 percent in some national surveys to as low as 5 to 10 percent in some local surveys where numerous mail and telephone follow-ups are used. In Chapter 6, dealing with mail surveys, some guidelines were provided for making the mail questionnaire more appealing so the recipient is more prone to participate.

Numerous articles also exist in research journals dealing with the impact that such incentives as money, gifts, or gift certificates can have on increasing the response to mail surveys. No one type of incentive has been shown to be consistently most effective in enticing participation since each has had varying success among different groups. Advance postcards, along with follow-up letters, have also been successful in significantly improving response.

Methods for handling nonresponse to mail surveys—Since nonresponse will always occur in mail surveys, a decision must be made at the outset on how it will be handled.

1. *Ignore it.* In this instance the researcher assumes that no major differences exist in the answers received from respondents and those sample members who did not respond. This is a rather naïve and dangerous assumption to make without some type of supportive evidence.

2. *Substitute for nonrespondents.* A second wave of questionnaires can be mailed to all those who did not respond to the original one. The responses to this second wave are viewed as representing the original nonrespondents. If comparisons show no significant differences exist between the original respondents and second wave respondents (in demographics or nature of answer), then the researcher can downplay the potential impact

of nonresponse bias. (Chi-square tests are frequently used for this analysis; they are discussed in Chapter 14.)

3. *Survey sample of nonrespondents.* Assuming nonrespondents can be identified, a small group (20 to 30) could be surveyed by telephone and their responses compared to those of the original respondents. If this method is used, the entire subsample chosen to represent the nonrespondents should be contacted.

4. *Weighting for nonresponse.* This is illustrated by the following example. A survey of adults is taken to obtain their perceptions of discrimination against women in business. The survey is sent to 500 men and 500 women. Responses are received from 60 percent of the women and 40 percent of the men. In addition, a higher proportion of women (75 percent) than men (35 percent) feel that discrimination against women exists.

It is obvious that the underrepresentation of men among the respondents will bias upward the results for the entire population. Consequently, weights should be developed to give each sex representation in the sample proportionate to its representation in the population.

Because the arithmetic procedures for this weighting are quite lengthy, no attempt will be made to cover it in this text, but good examples of its usage can be found in articles by Carol Fuller and Lewis Mandell.[6] In addition, tables do exist that can be used to calculate the impact of nonresponse bias on results when proportions are involved.

Noncoverage errors

A second cause of data collection errors is improper coverage of the population. Noncoverage errors occur when (1) some units or entire groups are not included in the original sampling frame or (2) once the sample is selected, some units in this sample are not contacted in appropriate amounts.

Incomplete frames

All three survey methods—telephone, mail, and personal interviews—are dependent upon a listing of the units in the population under study. In many instances this list or frame is incomplete, which means samples developed from them may not cover all key segments.

---

[6]Carol H. Fuller, "Weighting to Adjust for Survey Nonresponse," *Public Opinion Quarterly*, 38 (Summer 1974), pp. 239-46. Lewis Mandell, "When to Weight: Determining Nonresponse Bias in Survey Data," *Public Opinion Quarterly*, 38 (Summer 1974), pp. 247-52.

The telephone directory, for instance, does not provide a complete frame of a city's population. Since every household does not have a phone and others have unlisted numbers, any list drawn from a telephone directory will exclude some units. While unlisted numbers can be handled through random digit dialing (discussed in Chapter 6), their names cannot be included in any mailing list developed from the directory. The real problem occurs when these "unlisted" numbers or nonowners of telephones have characteristics different from the households included in the directory. A study previously cited in Chapter 6 indicated that while the households with unlisted numbers did not differ from regular households in terms of income, they did differ in marital status and sex, since a disproportionate number of the unlisted numbers were held by women and divorced or separated people.

There is little question that a disproportionate number of the households not having phones are from lower-income segments, which means any mailing list developed from directories underrepresents low-income households.

Following is an example of the problems encountered when trying to develop a frame of dog owner. A dog food company was interested in learning what criteria dog owners use in choosing dog foods. One city was selected for this study. A list of dog owners was obtained from the city clerk's office, but this list contained only the names of people licensing their dogs. The city clerk estimated this number to be only 35 to 45 percent of all dog owners. This would seem to be a questionable frame to use, especially since there was probably a link between owners' income and their willingness to pay the fee to register their dogs. The firm doing the research felt the households licensing their dogs were also the ones most likely to spend money to feed their pets commercial dog food. Thus, although the frame was incomplete, in this instance the researchers felt justified in using it because it provided a list of names of households of greatest potential for higher-priced commercial dog foods.

Checking the frame—In the previous example, it was obvious at the outset that the frame of dog owners was incomplete. But in many situations, such a condition is not so evident. A good way to check on the frame's representativeness is to use some outside criterion—census data, association data, other studies on comparable studies, etc. Comparing these data with the frame's makeup should disclose any unusual differences between the two groups. In most cases, simply knowing how the names in the frame were compiled, will enable the researcher to evaluate its representativeness.

Handling noncoverage—Since the bias resulting from non-coverage is not a sampling error, it can't be estimated in the usual standard error formulas; nor will increasing the sample's size reduce its impact. It can best be handled by recognizing its existence, working to improve the sampling frame, and, where possible, making allowances for the frame's imperfections by applying weighting procedures to the results.

Noncoverage of sample members

This involves situations where the listed sample units are not contacted. While this is most likely to occur in personal interviews, it can occasionally also be a problem when using telephone surveys.

Interviewers often are guilty of the common human frailty of seeking the path of least resistance. When conducting interviews in the field, they will attempt to minimize visits to lower income/higher-crime areas of the city. They will choose those households that are easy to reach and relatively free from any type of potential "unpleasant" situations. This problem is especially prevalent when the interviewer is given a geographic area to survey rather than a specific list of addresses. But even when addresses or sites (e.g., 4th, 9th, and 16th household starting at southeast corner of each block) are designated, interviewers may occasionally ignore such instructions and choose the most accessible units.

In telephone surveys the interviewer might ignore orders to make at least three callbacks to "no answer" households, and instead substitute immediately for them. They may pass off the information obtained from the substitute unit as being from a member on the original list. One study carried out to catch interviewer errors discovered that of 2,186 interviews checked for accuracy 1 out of every 25 (4 percent) did not actually take place with the identified respondent.[7] This rate occurred among surveys where the interviewers knew some follow-up checks would be made. The rate is no doubt higher in surveys where the interviewers know their field work will *not* be checked.

Handling the problem—The most effective way to handle the problem of inappropriate sample coverage is to limit the interviewer's freedom in choosing interviewees. Designate the specific addresses or persons he/she is to contact. Where that is not possible, have a precise system to be followed in selecting interviewees

---

[7]Peter Case, "How to Catch Interviewer Errors," *Journal of Advertising Research*, Vol. II, No. 2, April 1971, p. 41.

and their substitutes. A second step is to let the interviewer know follow-ups will be made among a sample of his/her cases. Once questionable field practices are uncovered, severely sanction the guilty interviewers. A large share of the interviewing problems are concentrated among a relatively small group of interviewers, so being tough with the few guilty parties will weed out many of the problems![8]

Measurement errors and interviewer influence

A third factor that can cause errors in the data is the influence the interviewer has over the respondent's answers and actions. This is most prevalent in personal interviews and, to a more limited extent, in telephone surveys. Included are such things as the interviewer's voice inflections when asking questions; how closely the interviewer follows the suggested questioning format; the interviewer's personal appearance; and the interviewer's accuracy when interpreting and recording the respondents' answers. Also included are any questionable practices (cheating) that the interviewers might employ.

Voice inflections — Since interviews involve a social relationship between the interviewer and the respondents, the respondents will oftentimes adjust their actions or replies to what they consider is proper for the situation. Thus, a simple thing such as the inflection of the interviewer's voice when asking a question could cause interviewees to give a reply that they feel is more socially acceptable to the interviewer than one that depicts their actual feelings or actions.

Characteristics and appearance of interviewers — Usually the more characteristics the interviewer and the respondent have in common, the greater the chance of a successful interview. Thus, if members of a certain ethnic group are to be surveyed, more successful interviews will take place if the interviewers are of the same ethnic background. This also holds true for interviews among different age groups or different sexes.

While it is desirable to match interviewees and interviewers, it is unrealistic to assume that this can always be accomplished. The next best thing is to use interviewers with reasonable acceptance among the majority of the designated interviewees. Middle-aged women have a high acceptance level among many different groups and thus are widely used as interviewers. In addition,

---

[8]Ibid., p. 43.

they are the group most often available for part-time employment, another plus factor.

Accuracy in recording—If the questionnaire is quite lengthy, or if there are a number of open-end questions involved, the interviewer might have difficulty in accurately recording the respondent's answers. If too much time is spent in writing down the responses, the interviewee loses interest. On the other hand, if too sketchy an answer is recorded, the real meaning of the respondent's answer might be lost.

Many researchers advocate the use of tape recorders to ensure accurate answers. Another benefit of recorders is that they enable a check to be made of the questioning procedures being used by the interviewer. Some researchers feel the presence of tape recorders inhibits some respondents. One of the few studies done on this subject indicated the use of tape recorders slightly increased the accuracy of the survey's findings and did not inhibit most interviewees.[9] If recorders are to be used, the interviewee's permission should be asked and they should never be used in a covert manner (hidden microphone).

Cheating by interviewers—This involves situations where the interviewer fills out a totally fictitious interview or fills in portions of a survey to save time or meet a deadline. The chief causes of cheating are surveys that are unusually long or difficult to complete, unreasonable deadlines, or respondents who are difficult to locate. The best way to minimize interviewer cheating is to eliminate the previously mentioned conditions that cause low morale.

Interviewee errors—The researcher should also recognize that there are certain inherent factors affecting the accuracy of the interviewee's replies.[10]

1. As the length of time between the occurrence of an event and the interview increases, there is a tendency toward underreporting of information about that event (e.g., the number of visits to a doctor are understated, the greater the length of time between the last visit and the interview).

---

[9]William Belson, "Tape Recording—Its Effect on Accuracy of Response in Survey Interviews," *Journal of Marketing Research*, Vol. IV, August 1967, pp. 253-260.

[10]Charles Connell, Lois Oksenberg, and Jean Converse, "Striving for Response Accuracy: Experiments in New Interviewing Techniques," *Journal of Marketing Research*, Vol. XIV, August 1977, pp. 306-315.

2. Events that are more important to the individual are reported more accurately than events of less importance.
3. The reporting of an event is likely to be distorted in a socially desired direction (underreporting of secondary loans on automobiles, overreporting on the size of contributions to United Fund).
4. The accuracy of interviewees' answers is directly related to the problems they encounter in coming up with the answers. If the information is readily accessible or can be easily recalled, the answers are much more accurate.

Guidelines for interviewers

While most users of this book will not do a great deal of personal interviewing, there may be occasions in their research activities when some interviewing may be necessary. In those circumstances, or when instructions must be given to other interviewers, the following steps should be emphasized.

1. Whenever possible, arrange the interview time beforehand.
2. Be familiar with the questionnaire.
3. Establish rapport with the interviewee.
4. Follow the instructions given to you.
5. Be a skillful interviewer.
6. Accurately interpret, record, and tabulate the response.
7. Attain a proper exit.

Set up interview time

After the interviewees have been designated, it is usually necessary to make some preliminary arrangements to set up these interviews, especially if they involve people at their jobs. The advantage of preliminary arrangements is that they can aid in securing privacy and eliminate interruptions. They also minimize the "not at home" or "not available" problems so prevalent in personal interviews.

Be prepared

Be familiar with the questions or outline to be used. Understand what each question is seeking. Know the steps or procedures to be followed. Don't learn the questionnaire procedure during an actual interview; practice on noninterviewees—such practice not only will improve the interviewer's finesse but might uncover some flaws in the questionnaire that were not discovered in the pretests. Even if an informal interview is to be used, prepare the general question format in advance.

Establish rapport

Rapport exists when the interviewee seeks to give the interviewer the necessary information. In most cases it is not too difficult to get a positive reception from interviewees, since the interviewer is offering them an unusual opportunity in that their ideas, feelings, and attitudes are being sought.

Follow instructions

The instructions given in the survey should be closely followed. Ask each question exactly as it is worded in the questionnaire unless directions allow some latitude. Ask questions in the order in which they appear on the survey. Ask every question unless the directions state it may be skipped or its inclusion was dependent on a previous answer.

Be a skillful interviewer

If allowed in the instructions, it may be necessary to sometimes probe the respondent's original answer to obtain a more accurate reply or his/her true feelings.

Interviewer: "Mr. Jones, suppose your son decided to become a lawyer. Would you approve such a decision?"

Respondent: "Lawyers are worse than card sharks."

Did he answer the question? Although he seems to dislike lawyers, he still might approve of his son becoming one. Therefore it is necessary to probe to get a precise answer to the question. You may also have to probe to handle "Don't know" or "I can't remember" responses.

Interviewer: "When did you buy your automatic washer?"

Respondent: "Gee, it was so long ago, I can't remember."

Interviewer: "Were you living in this house at the time you bought the washer? Do you remember the occasion or special event which led you to buy it?"

Interviewer: "Do you feel that your company is fair in the way it compensates its salespeople?"

Respondent: "Why, I don't really know."

What does he mean? He may be afraid to truthfully answer the question, so he avoids it. Or, if he has not given any previous thought to this matter, he may not know all the facts and thus can't make a judgment on the company's personnel policy.

Interviewer: "I realize you may not be familiar with the overall compensation policy of your company, but what are your feelings on those situations you are aware of?"

Respondent: "Well, like I said, I really don't know about the whole company, but in our department it seems to me the salespeople don't receive a high enough commission on their sales."

A note of caution should be injected here. In probing for answers, the interviewer should be careful not to instill an attitude (hostile or friendly) where none may have existed—some people may actually have neutral feelings.

Accurately interpret, record, and tabulate the responses

Accurately recording the respondent's replies is a major problem for interviewers. Some use shorthand; others may do no writing during the interview because they feel it distracts the interviewee. They recommend sitting down immediately after the interview and trying to recall what was said. Still others may use tape recorders exclusively.

The method most frequently followed is one in which the interviewers write down key data in rough notes and then expand these notes immediately after the interview. It is critical to record the essential points made by the respondent at the time they are made, since after a lengthy interview some earlier statements become hazy.

Attain a proper exit

Leave the interviewees with the feeling that they have really contributed something and that their cooperation is appreciated. Leave them in such a frame of mind that they will be willing to participate in future interviews with other legitimate interviewers.

Although this chapter has dealt only with the data collection errors in surveys, these errors also occur within observations and experiments. Observers may be careless in recording events or even cheat when filling out observation data. People, knowing they are being observed as a part of an experiment, may alter their activities. If mechanical equipment is used in the observation or experiment, it may malfunction, causing errors in the results.

The researcher must realize that data collection errors are an inherent part of obtaining primary data. Unlike sampling errors, they don't "average out," which means that statistical procedures usually can't be employed to assign ranges of possible values to them. As stated in Chapter 9, in recent years increased attention has been given to ways for compensating for data collection errors, but most of these methods are complicated to use; they also require some major assumptions that weaken their acceptance. Most researchers feel that the best way to handle data collection errors is to take measures that will minimize their chances of occurring—development of representative frame; using top quality trained interviewers; giving them appropriate instructions; and using checkup methods.

Data collection errors—an overview

This method for obtaining primary data was covered briefly in Chapter 6. Because group interviews have become an increasingly important research tool, it is important that marketing researchers (and their clients) have a fairly solid understanding of their capabilities, limitations, and procedures.

GROUP INTERVIEWS

- The group may vary from 5 to 12 participants with 7 or 8 being the most prevalent. Five may not be large enough to get diverse ideas and 12 may be too large and stifle some conversation.
- The interviews usually last from 90 minutes to 2 hours.
- Group interviews may require the use of some type of incentive—gift certificate, actual product, or even money—to entice people to participate. The incentive used should not influence the eventual responses of the participants during the interviews.
- Availability of appropriate facilities and equipment is necessary. This includes a room large enough to handle the

Typical group interviews

group along with any equipment (tape recorders, cameras, two-way mirrors, etc.) needed to record or view the sessions.

- This requires a moderator (interviewer) who is trained in handling small groups. This person's skills are critical to the interview's success.

- Additional focus groups should be used until it is felt no new ideas are being provided. Generally this will occur after the third or fourth focus group.

Major contributions of group interviews

Brings client closer to data sources — The client or firm requesting the data can either witness the actual interview or hear the taped results. This provides firsthand contact with potential customers, whereas information from other sources is usually provided in a written report comprised of cold facts and figures. If two-way mirrors are used in the interview room, the client can watch the participants' responses to a new product or package. The client might even choose to sit in as a silent member with the group.

Stimulation of ideas — Participants often stimulate each other into areas of thought that may not have occurred in individual interviews. A participant may find security in the group and be more willing to express ideas and attitudes after hearing others express similar attitudes.

Flexibility in obtaining data — In mail surveys, a number of individual questions are asked, but it is difficult to link these individual findings or events together. Group interviews (and also personal interviews) can develop such a linkage: "You said you like to sit down and talk on the phone to friends, but oftentimes feel guilty when you have other work to do. What if you could have a device that would enable you to do your housework while talking on the phone?"

A skilled moderator can also direct the discussion into areas of potential interest to the client as new ideas are generated by the participants.

Drawbacks of group interviews

Success depends on moderator's skills — The moderator has to stimulate participants, direct the nature of the conversation, and where tape recordings are not used, even record the results. His/her actions can bias the results, cause the discussion to go in areas of little interest, and he/she can misinterpret statements by participants when analyzing the results. Thus, this technique requires a highly skilled individual.

Quirks of the participants — One or two people may dominate the interview. Some people may be shy or unable to verbalize their ideas. Personality conflicts may arise between participants and negatively affect the whole interview. These shortcomings can be minimized by a skilled moderator.

Concept oriented — Users of group interviews should recognize that these sessions are designed to get reactions to concepts or to develop hypotheses. Group interviews should not be used as substitutes for test markets, surveys, or other procedures for gathering primary data.

Since the primary function of group interviews is to generate ideas or obtain broad reactions to concepts, a client expecting hard statistical results will be disappointed. The final report will not be a set of tables containing figures as to the number of people favoring a particular action; instead, the results will be a set of tapes or a report containing quotes from participants, along with the analyst's interpretation of the group's responses.

High cost per respondent — Focus groups can involve a number of expenses — contacting and paying participants, cost of interview facilities and equipment, fees and expenses of moderators, and data analysts. A single session with consumers can cost over $1,000, and a session with managers/executives could cost over $2,500.

Requisites for successful group interviews

The number of groups and sessions conducted depends on the topic being considered, the audience to be covered, along with time and expense considerations. But regardless of these previous factors, there are certain conditions that should be met to enhance the success of group interviews.[11]

Be aware of "dos" and "don'ts" in selecting participants — Concentrate on population segments that will give the most meaningful information. Because of the small sample size, recognize that all possible segments can't be covered. Get as much commonality as possible in a group. Don't put full-time housewives

---

[11]Myril Axelrod, "Ten Essentials for Good Qualitative Research," *Marketing News* (March 14, 1975).

with single working women. Don't put teens, college students, or pre-teens together. Unless really necessary don't interview men and women together. Seek respondents who are likely to give spontaneous, honest answers. Be leary of people who have participated in other group interviews—"professional interviewees."

Conduct interviews in relaxed atmosphere—If possible conduct interviews in a home environment. If a formal session room is used because filming or client observation is necessary, this room should provide an informal atmosphere.

Moderators must be prepared—They should identify beforehand all possible areas to be discussed and the best possible ways to get to these areas. This is a delicate situation since moderators want to ensure spontaneity among the respondents, but also want to ensure that the interview covers the designated topics.

Moderators must control sessions—Moderators must control the interview while still giving the impression that they are part of the group, i.e., they must control dominant respondents; keep the discussion from getting bogged down; and get total participation. Don't let people merely say, "I agree." Probe them, "What makes you feel that way?"

Interpreting results—A major problem of group interviews is deriving some key findings. While this survey process doesn't lend itself to clean, precise conclusions, something concrete should emerge. At its conclusion the client should not wind up wondering "What did we really learn from all of this?"

Focus group vs. group dynamics

Although focus group interviews are basically unstructured, the respondents are asked to center (focus) their discussion on a specific subject. In "group dynamics," on the other hand, the discussion is allowed to wander. The participants can unburden themselves of frustrating experiences or share happy ones. Such sessions are largely exploratory in nature and require a great deal of skill by the moderator and analyst if any useful information is to emerge. These are most prevalent in searching for unsatisfied needs or insight into possible new avenues for promotion.

Overview of group interviews

Group interviews contradict many of the principles of sound research. The samples are small and the members are often chosen in a manner that raises a question about their representativeness; questions are asked differently in each session; results are often impossible to quantify. Their success depends heavily on the skills of the moderator and analyst. With all of these drawbacks, why are they so widely used? They still are the most effective survey method for obtaining reactions to new ideas or concepts, and they also effectively serve to develop hypotheses for more rigorous investigation.

To generate hypotheses for further study[12]

Examples of the use of group interviews

Example: A series of focus group sessions were carried out among bank customers to obtain their reactions to electronic bank tellers. The discussions in these sessions disclosed that the participants felt teller stations should somehow be personalized; the secret code number should be made easy to remember; and incentives would probably be needed to get people to use them. These hypotheses were then tested.

To aid in structuring questionnaires

Example: A soft drink company wanted to identify the needs people were trying to satisfy with soft drinks. Twenty group sessions were conducted throughout the country to develop an all-encompassing set of needs. These were then incorporated into a questionnaire.

To obtain reactions to new product concepts

Example: A telephone equipment producer used group interviews to obtain housewives' reactions to a device that could be used to enable them to converse on the phone even though they were 12 to 20 feet away from it.

To generate new ideas for existing products

Example: Group interviews disclosed that one segment of the market — mothers-in-law — was being missed in flower promotions. These women had the ideal characteristics for flower users, but other than birthdays and anniversaries there were few special occasions when flowers could be given to them. Thus a new flower holiday was promoted.

---

[12]Danny Bellenger and Barnett Greenberg, *Marketing Research — A Management Information Approach* (Homewood, Illinois: Richard D. Irwin, 1978), pp. 177-183.

Typical group interviews

There is no one "best" format to follow when conducting a focus group interview, but the following scenario would be fairly typical. Assume the purpose of this focus group is to obtain women's reactions to a new method for packaging the fresh flowers sold in supermarkets.

The interview is conducted in a specially designed room located in a major shopping center. Each of the 10 participants was previously screened to ensure each had the necessary characteristics—a housewife between 30-50 years of age who had purchased fresh flowers from a supermarket in the last three months.

The participants and the moderator go through a brief warm-up period in which they introduce themselves to the rest of the group, and the ground rules for the session are explained. They then are asked to discuss their flower purchase habits, their past experience with fresh flowers, and their feelings about flowers in supermarkets compared to those at florists.

The new product (or concept) is introduced to the group and each is asked for her reactions to it. Additional discussion on different aspects of the product also takes place. When the discussion is completed, each participant is asked to identify what she felt was the group's general attitude toward the product.

Before leaving, each participant may be asked to fill out a form providing some demographic information. (Some firms ask for this information prior to the session.)

SUMMARY

A lot of sound planning for research is negated because of mistakes made in the collection of the data. While data collection errors will always occur, their impact can be minimized by the researcher through appropriate measures. Data collection errors arise primarily from nonresponse, noncoverage of the population, and mistakes in measurement.

Nonresponse occurs in personal interviews because the desired respondents can't be located, refuse to participate, or are unsuitable for the survey. Interviewers can cut down on the number of "can't locates" through appropriate callback methods. They can influence the number of "refusals" by developing proper rapport with the interviewees and effectively probing during the interview. Interviewers have little influence over the "unsuitables."

Nonresponse in mail surveys can be partially handled by multiple mailings or personally contacting a representative portion of the nonrespondents and obtaining replies from them. Some researchers use weighting measures to make allowances for nonrespondents.

Noncoverage errors occur when either the frame does not adequately represent the defined population or the listed sample units are not contacted. The most effective method to ensure that interviewers make the necessary contacts is to assign them specific addresses or telephone numbers and then make them aware that spot checks will be made among a portion of their respondents.

Interviewers can influence the survey's results in the way they ask questions, their actions in the presence of interviewees, and their accuracy in recording the results. Specific instructions should be provided to each interviewer on the procedures they are expected to follow. Cheating is also a problem, and the way to minimize its occurrence is to keep interviewer morale high through reasonable work assignments.

Focus group interviews are used to generate hypotheses for additional study, aid in developing the direction for larger surveys, and generate new product concepts or new ideas for existing products. The success of these interviews depends on having a competent moderator, an environment conducive to discussion, and a group of participants willing to exchange ideas and attitudes. The end-product of group interviews will not be a document comprised of facts and figures, but rather it will describe the group's reactions to the topic discussed. This lack of a precise finding is often a cause of disappointment to sponsors of these interviews.

QUESTIONS AND EXERCISES

1. Interviewers have little influence over the amount of nonresponse occurring in personal interviews. What is your reaction to this statement?

2. The increase in crime in cities has made people reluctant to allow strangers into their homes. What future implications does this hold for personal interviewing as a survey tool? What can be done to overcome this negative condition?

3. Develop an introduction which telephone interviewers can use to get survey participants for the following situation: a firm conducting telephone interviews to determine the attitudes of housewives toward soft drinks for their children.

4. What actions should be taken when attempting to obtain interviews with business people during their work hours?

5. Why is it beneficial to provide interviewers with precise instructions on who should be interviewed and guidelines to follow when substituting for "can't contacts."

6. Why are middle-aged women commonly used for personal interviews in homes? Would they be equally appropriate for business interviews?

7. Many products that have been test marketed fail. How then can this costly research method be defended? Why test market?

8. Why is the person leading group interviews called a "moderator" whereas the person carrying out a single interview is called an "interviewer"?

9. What drawbacks of group interviewing should clients be cognizant of before approving this type of data gathering tool?

10. Set up a group interview with five to seven other people. You act as moderator. Choose a topic of potential interest to a business firm, for example: one-way bottles for soft drinks; the importance of brand names to shoppers in supermarkets.

12

Processing the collected data

Not everyone responds willingly to a survey!

To the student who wrote the dumm questionare.

How can the university waste us taxpayer's money on such stupid stuff. I always new the university was full of dope fends and communist reds, but I don't want my tax dollars to be used on such dumm things.

How did you get my name anyhow? I bet the stupid post office (a bunch of freeloders) sold it to you didn't they.

No wonder the U.S. is in such bad shape becuz people like you (our futur leaders—ha, ha) are doing such dumm things in your classes. I bet you never were in the army were you? Rich kids like you never have to do nothing that will help the U.S. get better.

So Im not going to anser your questions for those reasons. I hope no one else does ether.

A good taxpayer who
don't waste tax money

The above response was received to a student research project. Around 1 percent of all responses to university-student surveys will contain comments of this nature.

Once the data have been collected, they usually must undergo some processing prior to analysis. This processing involves three activities: editing—inspecting, correcting, and modifying the collected data; coding—assigning numbers or other symbols to each answer, or placing them in categories to prepare the data for tabulation; and tabulating—bringing together similar data and totaling them in an accurate and meaningful manner.

EDITING

When data are obtained via surveys, the questionnaires usually must be edited both in the field and later in a central office. Field editing is especially important when personal interviews are involved, since it is difficult for the interviewer to properly fill out the entire questionnaire during such interviews. Brief notes or symbols are frequently used to originally record the answers; then, as soon as possible after the interview, each form is reviewed, corrected, and made more specific by the interviewer.

In major surveys where teams of interviewers are involved, the supervisor of each team is generally responsible for some quick field editing to ferret out any unusual problems among the interviewers under his/her control. At this time the supervisor might also make spot checks among a sample of the respondents to ensure the quality and honesty of the interviewer's work.

Office editing occurs at some central point where the interviewers' reply forms or all returned mail or telephone surveys are brought together. Office editing is especially critical for mail surveys. Whereas in personal or telephone interviews many editing problems are handled by interviewers either at the time of the interview or in their field editing, mail questionnaires have not gone through any previous processing and are returned in an unabridged form.

Following are some basic problems editors will encounter in their editing activities.

Fictitious interviews

This problem, which pertains to personal interviews and telephone surveys, was touched on in the preceding chapter. Its existence can sometimes be detected by editors when answers either show unusual uniformity or peculiar inconsistencies—small children reported in every household; interviews in a predominantly Polish section of the city showing only an "average" number of Catholics. Open-end questions are the most difficult to fake, so if cheating is suspected these responses should be closely studied.

Occasional checks can be made with randomly selected interviewees by telephone or post cards to authenticate whether the actual survey was conducted. Letting interviewers know that such sample checkups will be made usually lessens their inclination to cheat.

Inconsistent or contradictory replies

In one part of the returned questionnaire it might be stated that a household had no children. In a later section the ages of two children in the household are listed. The editor can adjust the answer to the first question since the respondent's listing of the specific ages seemingly implies that the first answer was a mistake. In situations like this, the more precise information has precedence.

Responses that aren't legible

If the handwriting on a mail survey can't be read, the editors may have to throw it out. If this occurs in personal interviews, the interviewer responsible for it can be contacted to decipher the writing. The larger the number of open-end questions included in mail questionnaires, the more prevalent the problem of sloppy or illegible responses.

Incorrect answers

A completed questionnaire states the time of the day the respondent watched a particular TV show. Other evidence exists that he did indeed watch the show, but the editor knows the date cited is not correct. The viewing date can be changed on the basis of this knowledge.

Incomplete answers

An interviewee is asked to name all brands of television sets he is familiar with but fails to mention the one he presently owns. When asked to describe his educational background, a respondent lists a master's degree in business but does not include the fact that he possesses an undergraduate college degree or high school degree. In both cases, the editor could add the necessary information.

'Don't know' and 'no answer'

A "don't know" is just what its name implies; the respondent acknowledges that he/she doesn't have an answer or opinion to the question posed. A "no answer," on the other hand, occurs when the respondent leaves a question blank in a mail questionnaire.

In some surveys, the number of "don't knows" and unanswered questions is so small that once acknowledged in the results, they are then forgotten since they are of no real importance to the findings. But in many situations a large number of "don't knows" and unanswered questions occur and can be critical to the outcome. This is especially true in political polls. In 1976, one poll disclosed the following breakdown of pre-election opinions of voters on two presidential candidates. "Don't knows" would eventually determine the election's outcome.

Ford	42%
Carter	45%
Don't know	13%

"Don't knows" usually fall into three categories which follow.

"Legitimate" don't knows — These exist in the above example. At the time they were interviewed, many voters really didn't know which candidate they would eventually vote for.

"Confused" don't knows — The interviewee may not understand the meaning of some of the terms in the questions (e.g., manufacturer's agent, discount store) and thus checks "don't know" or leaves the question blank.

"Reluctant" don't knows — The respondent doesn't want to answer the question and is hiding behind a "don't know" answer. "What do you think of the policies your firm follows in assigning sales territories?" A salesman might use "don't know" as the easy way out, especially if the survey is conducted by the company's sales manager.

Handling 'don't knows' and unanswered questions

It is best to show the number of "don't knows" and unanswered questions in your formal results.

A	30
B	25
C	30
No opinion	12
No answer	3
	100

Some researchers advocate dividing the "no opinion" or "no answers" on a ratio based on existing answers. Thus, the 15 "no opinions" and "no answers" would be distributed in this manner: 30/85 × 15 would be assigned as an A answer, 25/85 would be assigned as a B answer, with the remainder assigned to C. This is a highly questionable technique since it assumes the "don't knows" will eventually follow the pattern of those people who already have a preference. In actuality, the "don't knows" could be a very homogeneous group and eventually act in unison when making their final decisions.

Other editors follow the policy of throwing out any return that is not completely filled out or contains some illegible response. This is a foolish practice since it eliminates a large number of questionnaires containing valuable information. "Don't knows" and unanswered questions will always occur and should be anticipated by the researcher.

Specific instructions for editors of surveys[1]

- Be familiar with the editing instructions, as well as the instructions given to interviewers and coders.

- When editing, do not write over the original entry, making it illegible. Make the needed changes, but retain the original response.

- Initial all changes made and date each survey after editing it.

- Make all editing changes in some distinctive color and follow a consistent pattern in the way these changes are made.

- Editing should take place as soon as possible after receiving the surveys so that if clarifications are needed from the original interviewers, the data will be recent enough that they can be helpful.

CODING As stated at the outset of this chapter, coding is assigning numbers or symbols to the answers to prepare them for tabulation. When computers are to be used for the tabulation, it is necessary to replace the answers given on the returned printed questionnaire with code numbers that can be transferred to punch cards. Even for hand tabulation, it is usually better to code the replies rather than maintaining the answers in their original survey form.

---

[1]C. William Emory, *Business Research Methods* (Homewood, Ill.: Richard D. Irwin, 1980), p. 371.

In some cases, coding of the questionnaires can be done simultaneously with the editing activity. But this will be an inefficient procedure if numerous alterations in categories may eventually result from editing changes. Generally, it is best to postpone coding activities until the editing is complete.

The data must be placed in categories that will provide the information needed to meet the study's objectives. In many cases these categories merely follow the pattern of the questionnaire. Assume that the respondent is asked to "Check the dollar figure that identifies the gross income of your household last year."

Establishing categories for quantitative data

_____ [1] Less than $5,000

_____ [2] $5,001-$8,000

_____ [3] $8,001-$14,000

_____ [4] $14,001-$20,000

_____ [5] More than $20,000

These five categories would then be used in coding the responses.

But what if the question had read: "What was the approximate gross income of your household last year?" *$18,400.* This open-end question would result in a variety of answers. For coding purposes, how should these replies be handled? Each respondent's reply *could* be recorded in the original form—the $18,400 would be placed on the coding sheet. Or each answer could be changed into ranges (in this case it would be included in [4] $14,001-$20,000). Depending on the type of analysis to be performed on the collected data, it may be necessary to use both methods for recording the income figures. This dual coding provides the researcher with greater flexibility when it comes time to analyze the data. If any questions exist about which statistical techniques will eventually be used with the data, it is best to keep the data in the most disaggregated form.

Categories should be developed only after a representative sample of the replies has been reviewed. This review will provide a "feel" for the pattern of answers and thus determine what categories best represent the answers.

When numerical data are involved (income, dollar sales, frequency of use, miles traveled, number of hours of TV watched, etc.) and it is necessary to place the data in intervals or ranges, the following guidelines should be followed.

Developing categories/ ranges for coding quantitative data

- Know what types of analysis will be performed. Build the categories and their intervals around the study's objectives and hypotheses.

- Set intervals so that the numbers most frequently cited are near the interval's mid-point. In a survey on TV viewing habits, a number of respondents state they watch television 20 hours a week, and a number of others state they watch it 30 hours a week. The intervals established should be: 16-25 hours, 26-35 hours, etc. Using intervals of 20 to 29 hours, 30 to 39 hours would not properly depict the majority of the respondent's replies.

- Establish categories so that the intervals are mutually exclusive: 16 to 25 hours, 26 to 35 hours, 36 to 45 hours do *not* overlap; 15 to 25 hours, 25 to 35 hours, 35 to 45 hours *do* overlap and can confuse the respondents, as well as coders and analysts.

- Establish categories that coincide with categories used in other studies with which you intend to make comparisons. If you intend to compare the incomes of Bank A's customers with the average incomes of *all* households for the city in which Bank A is located, both sets of income categories should be similar. Or, if you intend making comparisons with other cities (e.g., the income breakdowns found in Sales Management's *Survey of Buying Power*), set up comparable categories.

- It is better to have too many categories than too few. Numerical data can always be combined into fewer categories at a later time if so desired. But if too few categories are used at the outset, their numbers can't be increased without going back and recoding all the original surveys. For example, if the categories used to depict weekly TV viewing are based on three-hour intervals 0-3, 4-6, 7-9, etc., these could easily be combined into fewer categories of larger intervals 0-9 hours, 10-18 hours, but if the data were originally recorded in these 9-hour intervals and smaller intervals were later desired, it would be necessary to go back and recode all the original surveys.

- Use multiple categories when doubt exists about how the data will be analyzed. Using the example of TV viewership again, a respondent's answers would be recorded two ways: their specific answer on how many hours per week they watch TV, and this answer placed in the appropriate interval. If respondent A watches TV 20 hours a week, then this 20 hours would be recorded. This figure would also be recorded in the appropriate interval: (a) 0-8, (b) 9-15, (c) 16-25, etc. He would be placed into the (c) category.

When qualitative data are involved (type of occupation, brand of toothpaste used, type of car driven, etc.), the researcher should keep these suggestions in mind.

Establishing categories for qualitative data

- As with quantitative data, the final decision of which categories to use in the coding process should be made after a representative number of responses have been reviewed.

- Use categories that enable comparisons to be made with other comparable data.

- Use categories that are precise and mutually exclusive. The response should not be able to be placed into more than one of the identified categories.

"Where do you buy the majority of your cigarettes?"

_____ Grocery stores

_____ Tavern or restaurant

_____ Vending machine

_____ Gas station

Some people may buy the majority of their cigarettes from vending machines in taverns. How do they answer? How do you accurately code their answers?

- Include all possible answers. This does not mean that each answer has to be specifically identified by a numerical code, but they should fit reasonably well into the available categories. Using a category entitled "Other" provides coverage for rather esoteric responses.

- In mail surveys to the general population, it is usually preferable to obtain information about the respondents' occupation through an open-end question (What is your occupation?) rather than to ask them to check a category. Figure 12-1 indicates a list of occupational categories issued by the Department of Labor.[2] If such a list were included in the survey, many respondents would not know which category to check as their occupation. A barber, for example, might check either craftsman or service worker. Thus, these errors can be avoided if the respondents are just asked to identify their occupation and the coder assigns the proper category for computer purposes.

Figure 12-1   Broad Categories of Occupations

            1 – Professional or technician
            2 – Farmer/rancher or farm/ranch manager
            3 – Manager, proprietor or official
            4 – Clerical worker
            5 – Salesman
            6 – Craftsman or shop foreman
            7 – Operative – semiskilled workers
            8 – Service worker
            9 – Laborer – nonagricultural
           10 – Farm laborer
           11 – Retiree
           12 – Military
           13 – Housewife

- Life cycle categories are an efficient way to combine information on age of parents, age of children, and marital status. As in the case of occupation data, respondents should not be asked to select their appropriate life cycle category, rather it should be assigned by the coder when reviewing each respondent's demographic information. Life cycle categories should not be used on the coding sheet to *replace* other demographic data, rather they should be used *in addition* to that data.

Figure 12-2   Life Cycle Categories

            (1) Young single
            (2) Young married – no children
            (3) Married – young family (all under 6 years)
            (4) Older married – children at home
            (5) Older married – no children at home
            (6) Older married – retired
            (7) Sole survivor – working
            (8) Sole survivor – retired

---

[2]These are over 20,000 possible occupations. This means that if the occupation of each respondent is to be coded and placed on the computer, a series of broad categories must be used.

Altering established categories

The categories used in the original questionnaire will usually also be used when coding the collected data, but it is often necessary to make further alterations in these categories prior to the actual data tabulation.

As previously stated, the only way to ensure that the proper categories have been chosen is to examine a random sample of the returned questionnaire. For example, assume that the following question was asked of college students: "What is your favorite form of entertainment?" (This is a dangerous question to ask this group!)

The alternatives listed were:

_____ Movies

_____ Skiing

_____ Boating

_____ Watching TV

_____ Other [describe] _____

A large number of students from schools in the western United States wrote "horseback riding" in the "Other" category. In fact, such a large number mentioned this activity that it was provided a separate category.

Precoded questionnaires

Coding can be greatly simplified if "precoded" questionnaires are used. (See Figure 12-3.) The coder uses the section on the right border of the questionnaire when going through the replies checking the proper code number. The advantages of precoding are speed, accuracy, and ease of reading by the keypuncher or tabulators. The major drawback of precoded forms is that all possible answers must be anticipated prior to sending out the questionnaire. For example, in the previous case how would "horseback riding" be given a code number where none existed on the precoded form?

One way of handling this problem is to include extra numbers which can be used when new categories emerge. The following example illustrates this point.

"What is your favorite form of entertainment?"

#8

_____ Movies   1. _____

_____ Skiing   2. _____

_____ Boating   3. _____

_____ Watching TV   4. _____

_____ Other [describe] _____   5. _____

_____   6. _____

If no one answer was described very often in the "Other" category, then each questionnaire with "Other" checked would be assigned the number 5 by the coder. If, as in the case described earlier, a large number wrote in "horseback riding," requiring that it be given separate listing, then number 6 could be used for all those indicating "horseback riding." Number 5 would still be used for those filling in the "Other" category but not citing horseback riding.

Figure 12-3   **Example of a Precoded Questionnaire**

	PAGE [1] Do Not Write In This Space	PAGE [2]	PAGE [3]
Answer **each** of the following questions to the best of your ability. Use a check to designate your answers.			
	#1	#7	#11
1. Are cut flowers presently being sold on a regular basis through mass marketing outlets in areas served by your firm? ____ Yes ____ No ____ Uncertain	____ 1 ____ 2 ____ 3 ____ 4	____ 1 ____ 2 ____ 3	____ 1 ____ 2 ____ 3 ____ 4
	#2		
2. Has your firm been contacted in the last six months by mass market outlets to provide them with cut flowers? ____ Yes ____ No	____ 1 ____ 2 ____ 3		

**Figure 12-3
(continued)**

3. Is your firm presently involved in any way in the mass marketing of cut flowers?

_____ No

_____ Yes, we are selling cut flowers to mass marketing outlets. [How many such outlets? _____]

_____ Yes, we are leasing space in mass market outlets and selling flowers ourselves. [How many such outlets? _____]

_____ Yes, other. [Describe] _____

#3
_____ 1
_____ 2
_____ 3
_____ 4
_____ 5

#8
_____ 1
_____ 2
_____ 3
_____ 4
_____ 5

#12
_____ 1
_____ 2

4. What effect has mass marketing had on your firm's sales of cut flowers?

_____ Increased our cut flower sales.

_____ Hasn't really affected our flower sales.

_____ Decreased our cut flower sales.

#4
_____ 1
_____ 2
_____ 3
_____ 4

#9
_____ 1
_____ 2

#13
_____ 1
_____ 2
_____ 3

5. What proportion of your firm's current sales of cut flowers go to mass markets?

_____ None

_____ Less than 10%

_____ 10-35%

_____ 36-50%

_____ More than 50%

#5
_____ 1
_____ 2
_____ 3
_____ 4
_____ 5
_____ 6

#10
_____ 1
_____ 2
_____ 3
_____ 4

6. How do you rate the quality of the cut flowers generally sold through mass marketing outlets?

_____ Comparable to the quality of flowers sold by florists.

_____ Slightly inferior to the flowers sold by florists.

_____ Greatly inferior to the flowers sold by florists.

_____ No opinion.

#6
_____ 1
_____ 2
_____ 3
_____ 4

Figure 12-3 also illustrates another time-saving device involving coding. If the questionnaire is fairly long, it can be produced in such a way that the right side of the pages overlap—page 2 wider than page 1. This allows the person doing the tabulating or card-punching to obtain the necessary results without leafing through the questionnaire. This short cut obviously can't be used when questionnaires are printed on both sides of a page.

Coding procedures when computers are used

When the data is to be tabulated on computers, all answers must be converted into a numerical form adaptable to punch cards. Figure 12-4 is a page from a questionnaire sent to dog owners to determine the factors guiding their selection of canned dog food.

Three hundred forty-seven dog owners responded to this questionnaire. Since it is fairly short, the responses from each dog owner could be placed on a separate punch card. Thus, the information from all of these questionnaires can be transferred to a data deck of 347 computer cards. In situations where a long questionnaire is involved, each respondent's answers may exceed the 80 columns provided on normal computer cards, necessitating the use of two or more cards. In those cases, it is important that each respondent be assigned an ID number and that number be placed on each computer card containing his/her responses. This will save a lot of time if the data deck is ever dropped or the cards get out of order.

Questions 9, 10, and 11 pose no coding problems. The answers to each can be covered in four rows on the punch card. For instance, in question 9 the four possible row entries would be "Yes," noted in the first row; "No," noted in second row; "Don't know," noted in row 3; and if no answer is given, this would be acknowledged in the fourth row. It is emphasized again that an unanswered question (see question 11), should not be treated as a "Don't know."

The hand-written numbers on the border of this questionnaire were placed there by the coder. In the case of question 10, the 24-2 means column 24, row 2. In question 11, the "No response" was designated as row 4. These numbers would then be transferred to a coding sheet. Card punching from the coding sheet is much faster than having the card puncher work from each individual questionnaire. (Figure 12-5 shows how these answers are transferred to a punch card.)

Sample Questionnaire Illustrating Coding Methods   **Figure 12-4**

6. Check the approximate percent of each type of dog food used in your dog's weekly diet (i.e., how often you feed each type of food to your dog).

	Never %	Seldom 1-30%	Frequently 30-70%	Usually 70-90%	Always 90-100%	
Table Scraps	_____	✓	_____	_____	_____	14-2
Canned	_____	_____	✓	_____	_____	15-3
Semi-moist	_____	✓	_____	_____	_____	16-2
Dry	_____	_____	_____	_____	_____	17-6

7. If you buy a canned dog food, indicate how important each of the following factors is in your buying decision.

	No Influence	Some Influence	Important	Very Important	
Price	_____	_____	✓	_____	19-3
Contents (% of meat, etc.)	_____	_____	✓	_____	19-3
Brand Name	_____	✓	_____	_____	20-2
Nutritional Value of the Dog Food	_____	✓	_____	_____	21-2

8. What type of meat do you think is generally used in most canned dog food?

_____ Same quality of meat that is sold for human consumption.
_____ Meat that can't pass inspection for human consumption.
___✓___ Inedible by-products (e.g., intestines, bones, etc.)   22-3
_____ Horse meat, goat meat, etc.
_____ Don't know.
_____ Other _____.

9. Do you feel most canned dog foods meet the daily nutritional needs of your dog?
_____ Yes   _____ No   ___✓___ Don't know   23-3

10. Do you feel each breed of dog requires its own special dog food?
_____ Yes   ___✓___ No   _____ Don't know   24-2

11. Do you supplement your dog's diet with vitamin drops or pills?
_____ Yes   _____ No   _____ Sometimes   25-4

12. From the following list of brand names select the two that you feel would contain the highest quality dog food. Write "1" by your first choice and "2" by your second choice.

__1__ Swift & Co. Dog Food		_____ Monfort Dog Food	26-1
_____ Champion Dog Food		_____ Pedigreed Dog Food	27-6
_____ Blue Ribbon Dog Food		__2__ Hormel Dog Food	

13. What change or improvement would you like to see in canned dog food?

The food should be in bigger cans

In question 6 (Figure 12-4), each of the four different types of dog food is given a separate column. "Table scraps" is designated column 14, and the answer selected is placed in row 2. Since "Dry" was left blank by this respondent, it was given a designation of row 6 – "No answer."

Some coders prefer to use a consistent numbering system for unanswered questions and use the zero row on the punch card to identify nonresponses for all questions.

Question 12 seeks two answers from the respondent along with a rating of their replies. Column 26 is used to identify the respondents' first choice and column 27 for their second choice. Another way of handling this would be to assign each of the six names a column with three rows: Row 1 – First choice, Row 2 – Second choice, and Row 3 – Not selected. The shortcoming of this method is that it uses more columns on the punch card and also requires six coding actions as opposed to the two now used.

Question 13 is an open-end question and poses a special coding problem. How can numbers be assigned to a series of rather lengthy answers? The best way is to read through a representative number (20 to 25 percent) of the returned questionnaires to become familiar with the general nature of the replies. Usually, only a limited number of responses are cited by the respondents and once these are noted, numbers can be assigned to the ones most frequently mentioned. In the example from Figure 12-2, the request to "sell in bigger cans" was written in often enough that it was given separate identification, in this case number 6. The replies identified by only a small number of respondents may all be placed in the "other" category.

The key thing to remember about coding is that *all replies have to be acknowledged and recorded in some manner.* Coding can be a laborious task, but problems can be kept to a minimum if proper attention is given to potential coding problems prior to the actual administration of the questionnaire.

Personalized coding sheets

Computerized coding sheets (Figure 12-5) require that the coder be very accurate when transferring data from the questionnaire to the coding sheet. In those situations where the coding procedures are fairly complicated or where the person codes only on an infrequent basis, the coder may feel more comfortable with his/her own coding sheet.

Sample Coding Sheet and Punch Card of
Data from Figure 12-2

Figure 12-5

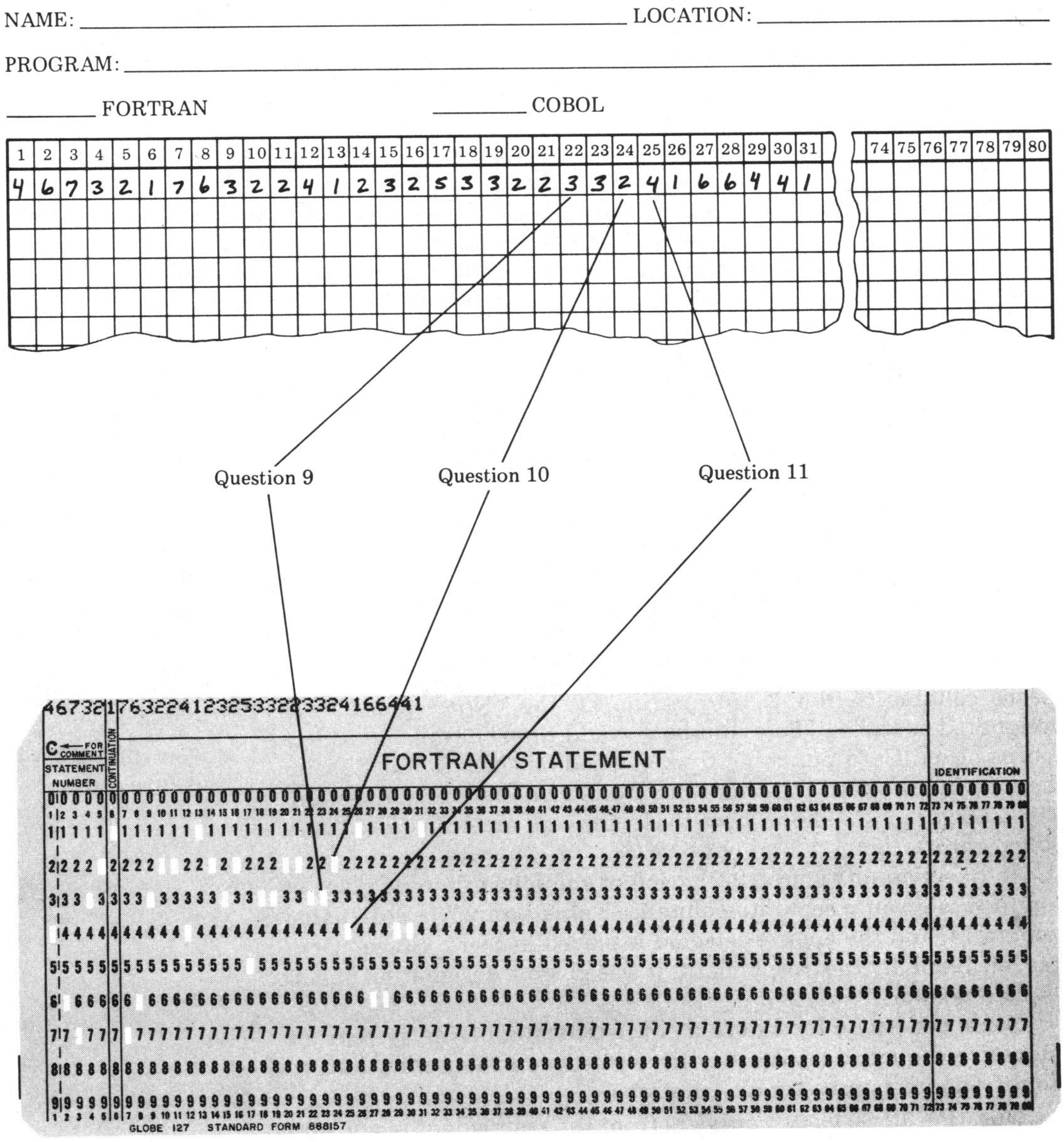

Figure 12-6 illustrates a portion of a personalized coding sheet developed for the sample survey found in Figure 12-4. Note how each item that is to be coded is identified by some term or phrase to ensure accurate transference to computer cards. If these personalized coding sheets are properly structured, data can be key punched directly from them to the cards.

It has been this writer's experience that the coding process will be much more accurate (especially on student research projects) if personalized coding sheets are used.

TABULATING

In this step the collected data are combined and totaled. This tabulation can either be done manually or by computer. This decision should be made before the survey is undertaken so that appropriate personnel and facilities can be obtained.

Manual tabulation

This method involves manually recording the answers on some central record sheet. It is used when only a few questionnaires are involved and the researcher does not intend to undertake any complex analysis of the data.

Machine tabulation

Electronic data processing enables thousands of computations to be made per second, permits a wide variety of mathematical operations to be undertaken, and allows a vast amount of data to be stored. Computers can accomplish in seconds what previously required hours or days of manual effort. Programming is the most time-consuming and complex activity associated with computer usage, especially if a unique program is required. This text provides very little information on programming or the computer in general, since these are subjects best left to specialized courses.

Manual vs. machine tabulation

Manual method—advantages

1. Simple forms used; no mechanical equipment is necessary.
2. "Set-up" time is relatively short.
3. Work can be performed entirely in the office or other informal location.
4. The categories used to code the data are usually kept in terms of their original description rather than being translated into confusing computer language.

Manual tabulation is best suited to situations where only a small sample is involved and the analysis is limited to simple tabulations or limited cross-tabulations (bi-variate analysis).

A Portion of a Personalized Coding Sheet   **Figure 12-6**

2	14	Table scraps	(#6)
3	15	Canned	(#6)
2	16	Semi-moist	(#6)
6	17	Dry	(#6)
3	18	Price	(#7)
3	19	Contents	(#7)
2	20	Brand name	(#7)
2	21	Nutritional value	(#7)
3	22	Type of meat	(#8)
3	23	Meet nutritional needs	(#9)
2	24	Breed requires	(#10)
4	25	Supplement	(#11)
1	26	First choice	(#12)
6	27	Second choice	(#12)

Mechanical tabulation – advantages

1. The data can be tabulated with greater speed and accuracy.
2. The computer cards provide a compact record of the collected data.
3. Tabulation and statistical analysis that are too complex for manual methods can be performed.

On the whole, when the equipment is available the advantages of machine tabulation greatly outweigh those of manual tabulation. Note that cost was *not* listed as an advantage of either. A few years ago when computers were less common, it was quite expensive to develop a program and pay for computer time.

Today, increasing numbers of firms have access to computers on their own premises or through time-sharing.

Computer programs for marketing researchers

A key barrier to wider use of the computer for tabulation and analysis has been the difficulty of developing appropriate programs. Researchers were often forced to develop their own programs for analysis, a rather awesome task for anyone with only a limited computer background.

Today, this hurdle has been diminished for a number of reasons. (1) Programming is becoming less complex, especially with breakthroughs in FORTRAN and the wider availability of computers using BASIC computer language. (2) More college graduates have computer backgrounds and are not as awed by computers as were their predecessors. (3) Many firms have full-time programmers with business backgrounds. Researchers can now communicate more effectively with programmers and there is greater understanding on both sides about what the researcher really wants.

SPSS

A computer package that is especially useful to marketing researchers is the Statistical Package for the Social Sciences (SPSS).[3] This package is a set of computer programs that include regression-correlation, analysis of variance, chi-square, discriminant analysis, and many others. Its major attraction is its simplicity: the researcher does not have to program, but merely must identify the program desired and the format in which the data should appear.

SUMMARY

Data processing involves one or all of these activities: (1) *editing* — putting the data in an appropriate form; (2) *coding* — preparing the data for tabulation; and (3) *tabulating* — bringing the collected data together so that they can be easily interpreted.

[3]Norman Nie, et al., *SPSS,* 2nd ed. (New York: McGraw-Hill, 1975).

Editing can be done immediately after the data are collected or it can be performed later at some central facility. When personal or telephone interviews are conducted, both types of editing should be performed. The editors are faced with a number of problems: how to handle inconsistent or contradictory replies; what to do with unanswered questions or incomplete answers; and how to detect questionable practices by interviewers.

Too often, coding decisions are made after the data have been collected. Actually, decisions on categories to set up and how the answers are to be coded should be made when the questionnaires are developed. This is mandatory when precoded questionnaires are involved.

The final processing activity, tabulating, can be done manually or by machine. It should be done manually if only a few questionnaires are involved and only a very simple analysis is to be performed. But, if there is a large number of questionnaires or if complex analysis is to be performed, the computer should be used.

QUESTIONS AND EXERCISES

1. Why should "don't know" replies on a survey be treated differently than questions that are left blank? Why should both be acknowledged in presenting results?

2. What is the advantage of coding quantitative data in both its original form as well as in intervals?

3. Why is it important to make most coding decisions at the time the questionnaire is developed?

4. Under what conditions would manual tabulation be preferable to machine tabulation?

CASES

Edit and code the following questionnaire.

Case 1

This questionnaire is to be filled out by either the male or female head of the household. The term "fresh flowers" as used in this questionnaire means flowers in bouquets or arrangements. It does *not* include potted plants or bedding plants.

1. What is your favorite fresh flower? (Check one)

_____	Carnations	_____	Tulips
_____	Gladioli	_____	Daisies
_____	Pom Poms	_____	No favorite
___✓___	Roses	_____	Other (specify) _____

2. Which *one* of the following words do you most closely associate with fresh flowers?

_____	Tenderness	___✓___	Love
_____	Forgiveness	___✓___	Gift
_____	Fragrance		Other _____
_____	Beauty		

3. Which *one* of the following events do you most clearly associate with the use of flowers?

_____	Weddings	_____	Dances
_____	Funerals	_____	"Get well" gift
_____	Anniversaries	___✓___	Other situations (describe)

    my sister's wedding

4. Indicate how often individuals in your household purchase fresh flowers by placing a check (x) on the proper line.

	Weekly	Regularly (Once a month)	Occasionally (3-6 times/year)	Rarely (1-2 times/year)	Never
Male head	_____	_____	_____	✓	_____
Female head	_____	_____	✓	_____	_____
Other (describe)	_____	_____	_____	_____	_____

5. Approximately how much money does your household annually spend on fresh flowers?

    $ __20__

6. If your household spends less than $20 a year on fresh flowers, which statement best describes your feelings toward flowers?

_____	Don't particularly care for flowers.
___✓___	Like flowers but feel they cost too much.
_____	Like flowers but there just aren't many occasions when they can be used.
_____	Like flowers, but grow our own.
_____	Other (describe) _____

7. How often do you (or your household) purchase fresh flowers from each of the following types of outlets?

	Weekly	Regularly (Once a month)	Occasionally (3-6 times/year)	Rarely (1-2 times/year)	Never
Florist	_____	_____	✓	_____	_____
Super-market	_____	_____	✓	_____	_____
Roadside or street vendor	_____	_____	_____	_____	✓
Other (de-scribe) flower children	_____	_____	✓	_____	_____

8. What is your attitude toward retail florists?

_____ I enjoy shopping at florists and doing business with them.

✓ I am a little reluctant to buy at retail florists.

_____ I don't like to buy flowers at retail florists.

_____ I really don't have any strong feelings for or against florists.

9. Have you ever seen fresh flowers displayed in supermarkets? ✓ Yes _____ No

If yes, what are your feelings towards them?

(a) Quality of fresh flowers in supermarkets is generally

_____ Well above average in quality

✓ Slightly above average in quality

_____ Of average quality

_____ Below average in quality

_____ Well below average in quality

(b) Price of fresh flowers in supermarkets

_____ Very high priced

✓ High priced

_____ Average priced

_____ Low priced

_____ Very low priced

10. In summer months do you grow your own flowers? _____ Yes ✓ No

11. When you were young, how often did your parents buy fresh flowers?

_____ Weekly

_____ Regularly (once a month)

_____ Occasionally (3-6 times a year)

✓ Rarely (1-2 times a year)

_____ Never

Following are some questions that will give us a better understanding of what factors might explain why households buy or do not buy flowers. These questions are somewhat personal, but we need the information to better understand what distinguishes "buyers" from "nonbuyers" of fresh flowers. Check the words that describe the person filling out the questionnaire.

(a) ___✓___ Male _____Female

(b) ___✓___ Married _____ Single
_____ Widowed _____ Divorced or separated
If married, for how many years? __8__

(c) What are the ages of the people living in your household?
Male head __29__ Children __76,54,3,2,1__
Female head __25__ Other (specify) _____

(d) Check your educational background (and your spouse's if married)

	Male head	Female head
Did not complete high school	_____	_____
High school graduate	_____	___✓___
Completed some college	___✓___	_____
College graduate	_____	_____
Advanced college degree	_____	_____

(e) Occupation of male of household: TV repairman

(f) Occupation of female head of household: _____
If employed outside the home, is it for more than 20 hours per week? _____ Yes ___✓___ No

(g) What is the approximate annual income of your household?

_____ Less than $5,000	___✓___ $10,000 but less than $12,500
_____ $5,000-$7,500	_____ $12,500 but less than $18,000
_____ $7,500 but less than $10,000	_____ More than $18,000

(h) What type of community were you raised in?

	Male head	Female head
Rural (farm or farm community)	_____	_____
Small town (less than 10,000)	___✓___	_____
City (10,000-50,000)	_____	_____
Metropolitan area (50,000-200,000)	_____	___✓___
Major metropolitan area (over 200,000)	_____	_____

(i) In what type of residence do you now live?

_____ Apartment _____ Own home
_____ Mobile home _____ Condominium
_____ Rented house __✓__ Other trailer

(j) What is your religion? None of your business

(k) To what ethnic group do you belong? American

In which city do you live?

_____ Pueblo
_____ Fort Collins
__✓__ Colorado Springs
_____ Denver and vicinity

Thank you for your cooperation.

13

Analysis and interpretation of data

SHOCKING REVELATIONS ABOUT PICKLES

The harmful effects of pickles can be conclusively proven using analytic methods widely followed by government officials and commonly used in TV commercials.

Recent surveys have shown:

"..... that 86.8% of all Russian sympathizers have eaten pickles."

"..... that 79.7% of the people involved in traffic accidents consumed pickles within 14 days preceding the crash."

"..... that 63.1% of juvenile delinquents come from homes where pickles are served frequently."

Perhaps you seek evidence of long-term nature:

"Of the people born in the year 1860 who later dined on this vegetable, there has been a 100% mortality."

"All pickle-eaters born between 1890-1910 have wrinkled skin, brittle bones, and failing eyesight.

Even more convincing is the report of a noted team of medical specialists; rats force-fed 30 pounds of pickles per day for 30 days, developed bulging abdomens.

Derived from February 1963 issue of Farm Chemicals

Of the various activities that comprise the research process, the analysis and interpretation of data probably demand the greatest skill from the researcher. An old adage states that "The facts speak for themselves." In terms of research efforts, nothing could be further from the truth. Facts don't say a darn thing. They just sit there until someone gives them meaning. For instance, knowing that the per capita personal income in the Rocky Mountain states in 1981 was $6,010 is of little value unless it can be associated with other pertinent data. This income figure takes on meaning when it is compared with the average personal income figure for other regions (Far West—$6,312; Southeast—$5,479) or when it is related to income figures for the Rocky Mountain states in previous years.

That is what analysis and interpretation are all about: giving meaning to the collected data by combining them with existing information. Too often researchers view this task as a rather simple procedure. They feel the tough job (collection of data) is behind them and all that remains is to routinely interpret the collected data in light of the study's objectives; any researcher with such an attitude is rather naïve.

The purpose of this chapter is to present some guidelines and techniques that will aid the researcher in these very crucial activities. The starting point is to distinguish between analysis and interpretation. While these are two distinct activities, there is a great deal of interdependence between them.

Analysis—This is placing the collected data into some order or format so that it takes on meaning. Analysis really answers the question: "What message exists in each group of data?" It is looking at each group of collected data separately and finding the key point or points contained therein. Raw data become "information" only when placed in a meaningful form.

Interpretation—Once the data have been analyzed, these various bits of "new information" are related to one another or to other existing information. This involves drawing conclusions from the gathered data. Interpretation changes the "new information" emerging from the analysis into information that is pertinent or relevant to the study: "How do the findings from this group of data relate to the objectives and hypotheses of the study?"

Identification of relevant data

Before the collected data can be analyzed, the researcher must review it and select those items that will directly aid in accomplishing the study's objectives. In most research undertakings a lot of excess information (especially secondary data) is accumulated. This does not mean that the researcher carelessly collected information; rather, this excess information exists because the direction of the study is often times altered as the study progresses. Therefore, what were once thought to be pertinent data are of little use when the study's objective is changed.

For example, a study was initially intended to investigate the methods used to select and train managers for Indiana supermarkets. A wide variety of secondary data, and even some primary data via store interviews, was accumulated. As the study progressed, the researcher soon realized that an analysis of all Indiana supermarkets would be an awesome task. The study was then narrowed to include only chain supermarkets. Although a large amount of information pertaining to independent supermarkets had already been collected, when the study's objectives were narrowed, much of this information lost its relevance.

Too often researchers take a miserly attitude toward the data they have accumulated. They feel that since they spent the time, effort, and money to obtain it, it must be used in the study. The more data of questionable usage retained, the more cumbersome and complex the analytic process becomes, Thus, an intensive review should be made of all the collected data to identify the relevant portions.

Another advantage of this evaluation is that it forces researchers to review all the collected data and thus update their knowledge. If a research project spans a lengthy time period, the researcher often forgets about some of the data collected at its outset.

Interrelationship between analysis and interpretation activities

When defining analysis and interpretation, it was emphasized that these two activities are tied closely to one another. If either is not properly carried out, the success of the study is jeopardized.

Improper interpretation

Assume that a large detergent manufacturer—the Acme Company—makes quarterly shelf and back room counts of its sales in 1,000 retail grocery stores across the nation. These counts disclose that the sales of one of its products, Bluppo Bleach, have been steadily declining the last two years. Table 13-1 contains data on Bluppo Bleach sales since 1978, along with sales data on Acme's new detergent with extra whiteners, called Whitex.

The company's marketing manager looks at these sales data, notes the declining bleach sales along with the increasing sales of Whitex, and concludes that bleach sales are dropping because consumers are switching to detergents with the extra whiteners. He then recommends that Acme consider dropping Bluppo Bleach from its product offerings.

In reality, what was happening in the market was that two other bleach manufacturers were trying to offset the intrusion of these new extra whitener detergents by running huge promotion campaigns during the period from mid-1978 through 1979. Thus, while there was some decline in the total sales of bleach due to the introduction of the new stronger detergents, the sales decline of Bluppo Bleach was due primarily to the increased promotional efforts of the other bleach companies.

Acme's Bleach and Enzyme Sales in 1,000 Test Stores **Table 13-1**
(Sales in terms of cases; product introduced in February 1978)

		Bluppo Bleach	*Whitex*
1978	1st Quarter	137,000	900
	2nd Quarter	129,000	2,200
	3rd Quarter	114,000	10,600
	4th Quarter	103,000	25,300
1979	1st Quarter	101,000	40,000
	2nd Quarter	97,000	46,400
	3rd Quarter	88,000	53,000
	4th Quarter	81,000	61,000

The data collected from sample stores (Table 13-1) indicate that Bluppo Bleach sales were steadily declining and the new detergent's sales were increasing. In light of the data collected, a proper analysis *had* been made. It was the *interpretation* that was faulty since these data were not properly related to other information. If total bleach sales for the industry had been obtained, or a closer study made of their competitors' activities, the real cause of the decline in sales would have been discovered.

Improper analysis

The previous example illustrated a situation of *proper* analysis but improper interpretation. The following example demonstrates improper analysis. The Brown Company is trying to decide which of three ads would most effectively increase sales of its electric carving knives. It tests the three ads by running each at different times in newspapers in four different cities. Table 13-2 lists the sales supposedly emanating from each of the ads.

Table 13-2

Sales Impact of Three Different Ads

Advertisement	Total Sales Associated with Each Ad
1	2,030 units
2	1,664 units
3	1,575 units

These sales results indicate that Advertisment 1 was the most successful. The logical action flowing from this analysis would be to use Ad 1 for the company's nationwide campaign. But was the proper analysis performed on the collected data? If a two-way analysis of variance had been used, a different finding would have emerged. This analysis would have disclosed that the three ads did *not* differ significantly in sales impact. Rather, Ad 1's success was really due to unusual demand in City B, one of the test cities (Table 13-3).

Table 13-3

Sales Impact of Ads in Four Different Test Cities

Advertisement	A	B	C	D	Total
1	407	875	391	357	2,030
2	382	412	430	440	1,664
3	415	462	362	336	1,575

Although the proper interpretation of the data contained in Table 13-2 would be to select Advertisement 1 for national usage, this interpretation was based on improper analysis.

The point made at the beginning of this section—that analysis and interpretation are interdependent—is emphasized again. The most sophisticated analytic procedures will be wasted unless the resulting data are properly interpreted. Conversely, the quality of the interpretation can only be as good as the analytic procedures used allow.

Early selection of analytic techniques

A sad epitaph to any research project is "If only I had . . ." To prevent such a situation from occurring, the selection of the primary analytic technique(s) should take place when the decision is made on the types of data to be gathered. When researchers postpone the selection of their analytic techniques until after the data have been collected, the nature of the data collected dictates which analytic procedures can be used – the tail wags the dog! Thus, a researcher may want to perform a simple correlation analysis to determine the degree of association between two variables, but the data may not have been collected in a form that will enable such a technique to be used.

ANALYTIC TECHNIQUES

It is impossible for any one researcher to have a working knowledge of every technique that could be used to analyze data. Each month numerous articles are published in trade and academic journals describing new analytic models and techniques. Some of these methods have wide application and can be adopted by researchers for use in their analyses. Other models are so esoteric that they apply only to the study for which they were developed.

This book concentrates on those analytic techniques that have fairly wide usage in marketing research. Researchers familiar with these techniques will have the background needed to effectively analyze most data. If more unique or sophisticated techniques are desired, statisticians or other experts in quantitative analysis should be consulted.

Two levels of analysis

Data analysis can take place at two different levels. At the first or lower level, the collected data are sorted into categories and comparisons made between the categories. Table 13-1 displays quarterly sales of two of the Acme Company's products. Such sorting and summarization may be all that is necessary to satisfy the research objectives.

In most research projects, however, a higher level of analysis is needed since hypotheses are to be tested or inferences from sample data are to be made. This necessitates the second level of analysis – the use of statistical techniques. These techniques will be discussed later in this chapter.

Lower level analysis – When the term "analytic procedures" is used, one immediately thinks of statistical techniques using complex formulas. In reality, many research projects rely totally on a simple process called cross-tabulation for the analysis of data. Because of its importance to researchers, cross-tabulation procedures will be discussed at length in the next few sections of this text.

CROSS-TABULATION

The starting point of cross-tabulation is to develop simple one-dimensional data and then separate these data into two or more categories. The categories used in this breakdown generally are based on the objectives of the study, but some categories may also emerge from the "intuitive" searching by researchers for other possible relationships.

A cross-tabulation example frequently cited involves data obtained from an insurance company's accident records.[1] This example also illustrates some of the errors resulting from improper cross-tabulation. These original data disclosed that 62 percent of the company's policyholders had never had an accident while driving (see Table 13-4).

Table 13-4

Accident Rate of Automobile Drivers

	Percent
Never had an accident while driving	62
Had at least one accident while driving	38
	100
Number of cases	14,030

This information was then broken down on the basis of sex, to determine if there was a difference between male and female drivers. The following two-dimensional table of data emerged, much to the chagrin of men (Table 13-5).

Table 13-5

Accident Rate of Male and Female Drivers

	Men (%)	Women (%)
Never had an accident while driving	56	68
Had at least one accident while driving	44	32
	100	100
Number of cases	7,080	6,950

The results of this table suggest that all the jokes about women drivers are exaggerations, since actual accident figures show that the average woman driver is involved in fewer accidents than her male counterpart. At this point, some men might question the accuracy of the study; others might feel that while

---

[1]This example was taken from Hans Zeisel, *Say It with Figures,* 5th ed. (New York: Harper & Row, 1968), pp. 120-137.

the figures are accurate, there are additional factors that should be considered. A possible explanation might be that men have more accidents because they drive more. Thus, a third factor is added to the existing information to see if "miles driven" is important, as shown in Table 13-6.

Table 13-6

Automobile Accidents of Male and Female Drivers by Amount of Driving

	Miles Driven by Males		Miles Driven by Females	
	Over 10,000	Under 10,000	Over 10,000	Under 10,000
Had at least one accident	52%	25%	52%	25%
Number of cases	5,010	2,070	1,915	5,035

The inclusion of this third factor indicates that the higher overall accident rate among male drivers occurs because they drive more than women. While this breakdown doesn't demonstrate male superiority in driving, it does show that accidents are related to the number of miles driven, not the sex of the driver.

Selecting factors to be cross-tabulated

The above example illustrates that the success of cross-tabulation methods depends upon the researcher's ability to select those factors crucial to relationships and then construct the cross-tabulation format along these lines. The type and number of factors used vary according to the nature of the study: In simple *fact-gathering* research, the factors to be considered are usually spelled out and the researcher merely places data in the desired form. For example, if a researcher is instructed to gather information on the ownership of color TV sets in Colorado based on the age of the head of the household, the factors to be used for the cross-tabulation have been established—color TV ownership and age of the head of the household.

In *applied research*, the researcher has more latitude in choosing these factors. Assume that a large company wants to determine whether there are certain key factors related to the performance of its salesmen. These factors might include the salesman's age, years of previous selling experience, and scores on the company's aptitude tests. In addition, the researcher decides to include the following data: size of college from which employee graduated, amount of extracurricular activities in college, amount of college expenses earned through jobs while attending college. In this situation the factors cross-tabulated came from the (1) requests of the client and (2) "intuitive" searching by the researcher.

In *basic research* projects the researcher selects all the factors to be cross-tabulated. For example, in a customer analysis the researcher is free to select any factor or characteristic (age, sex, family life cycle, income, education, etc.) that possibly influences purchasing habits.

Regardless of how much freedom the researcher has in setting up cross-tabulation categories, the selection of most of these factors should be made *before* the data are actually collected. Cross-tabulating ownership of color TVs with age of the head of the household can only be done if age was part of the data originally gathered. This does not mean that other factors cannot be added later, but cross-tabulations can only be performed on factors for which actual data were obtained.

Drawing meaning from cross-tabulations

The purpose of cross-tabulating data is to uncover relationships that might exist between certain factors. The shortcoming of this technique is that if the proper factors are not included in the analysis, improper conclusions may result. Even if the proper factors are included, the researcher may use them improperly so that what appears to be a solid relationship between factors may only be a spurious one.

Assume that a study was made among River City residents to determine their movie-going habits. A random sample of 1,000 residents (all over age 12) were interviewed and 26.7 percent turned out to be "regular" movie-goers—attend at least two movies per month (Table 13-7).

Table 13-7

Movie Attendance Among Sample of 1,000 River City Residents

Regular Movie-goers	26.7%	(267)
Not Regular Movie-goers	73.3%	(733)
Total	100.0%	1,000

It was hypothesized that a larger proportion of college students were "regular" movie-goers than noncollege residents, and the data were then broken down on this basis (Table 13-8).

College Students vs. Noncollege Students in Terms of Movie Attendance

Table 13-8

	College Students		Noncollege Students		Total
Regular Movie-goers	37%	(130)	21%	(137)	267
Not Regular Movie-goers	63%	(220)	79%	(513)	733
Total		350		650	1,000

This cross-tabulation seemingly indicates that college students differ from nonstudents in terms of movie attendance. But before this hypothesis is accepted, the question is raised, "What effect does age have on movie attendance?" (Table 13-9).

Age as a Factor in Movie Attendance

Table 13-9

	23 Years Old and Under		Over 23 Years of Age		Total
Regular Movie-goers	35%	(157)	20%	(110)	267
Not Regular Movie-goers	65%	(293)	80%	(440)	733
Total		450		550	1,000

When age is introduced, it becomes evident that it is a key factor in movie attendance. Regular movie-goers tend to be younger than those who are not regular movie-goers. This leads to the question: "Do college students attend more movies because they are younger, or do younger people attend more movies when they are college students?"

Movie Attendance by Age and College Enrollment

Table 13-10

	23 Years Old and Under				Over 23 Years of Age				
	College Student		Noncollege Student		College Student		Noncollege Student		Total
Regular Movie-goers	36%	(97)	34%	(60)	22%	(17)	20%	(93)	267
Not Regular Movie-goers	64%	(173)	66%	(120)	78%	(60)	80%	(380)	733
Total		270		180		77		473	1,000

Table 13-10 discloses that the relationship between college students and high attendance at movies is really explained by the fact that most college students are under 23 years of age. When these two factors were combined, the importance of college students as movie-goers becomes secondary to the relationship between age and movie attendance. A person's age is the key factor in determining his or her movie-going habits.

Simultaneous vs. sequential analysis

The data presented in Tables 13-8 and 13-9 are examples of sequential analysis — one explanatory factor at a time. Table 13-10 illustrates simultaneous analysis: viewing two or more factors at the same time. Sequential analysis often results in misleading findings on the actual relationship between factors. Simultaneous analysis, on the other hand, can often uncover spurious or false relationships. Many conclusions have been destroyed, or at least radically changed, because simultaneous analysis was performed on the finding originally obtained from a simple sequential cross-tabulation.

Correlation vs. spurious relationship[2]

Correlation exists when there is a smooth flow from one factor to another: Factor 1 leads to Factor 2 which leads to Factor 3.

$$F_1 \rightarrow F_2 \rightarrow F_3$$

This can be illustrated by an example relating marital status of women to job absenteeism. Cross-tabulations disclosed that married women had a much higher rate of absenteeism than single women. A second analysis disclosed that an even more crucial factor was the amount of the women's home responsibilities — children, housework, etc. All three factors could be tied together — married women had more home responsibilities than single women, and women with more home responsibilities had higher absenteeism. F_1 (marriage) leads to F_2 (more home responsibilities) which leads to F_3 (greater absenteeism). $F_1 \rightarrow F_2 \rightarrow F_3$. This *one-way* flow is true correlation. The process *can't* be reversed. Higher absenteeism doesn't lead to more home responsibilities, or more home responsibilities don't lead to marriage.

In the example involving age, college enrollment, and movie attendance, a one-way flow did not exist. Being a college student, F_1, did not determine age, F_2. The actual relationship was: $F_1 \leftarrow F_2 \rightarrow F_3$ (college student $\leftarrow$ age $\rightarrow$ movie attendance). Age was a factor in both movie attendance and college enrollment.

---

[2]Many of the ideas in this section were drawn from Hans Zeisel's book, *Say It with Figures*, pp. 143-148.

True correlation is a relationship that involves a one-way flow between factors: F_1 leads to F_2 which leads to F_3. Thus, there is a direct tie between F_1 and F_3, F_1 leads to F_3. Spurious relationships on the other hand involve flows in multiple directions, $F_1 \leftarrow F_2 \rightarrow F_3$. F_2 is related to both F_1 and F_3; the relationship that seemingly exists between F_1 and F_3 is due merely to their common tie to F_2, and not because F_1 leads to F_3.

Limitations of cross-tabulations

There are two major limitations associated with cross-tabulations: (1) A fairly large sample is needed if a number of factors are to be considered, and (2) it is difficult to be sure all the pertinent factors have been considered.

Referring to the first limitation, the sample must be large enough to enable simultaneous analysis to be carried out. This means enough units are needed to give proper representation to each cell in the data matrix. If only 50 people had been included in the study on movie attendance, a meaningful simultaneous analysis could not have been carried out. There would have been too few people in each of the eight categories to provide any useful data (see Table 13-10).

Although preliminary investigation and regular contact with the situation will provide researchers with an intuitive feel for what the key factors are, they are still never sure if all such factors have been included. In the example on absenteeism among female employees, it was assumed that the link was the amount of the worker's home responsibilities. Maybe the nature of the female's family (its size and age breakdown) was even more crucial since that would greatly influence the amount of her home responsibilities.

This uncertainty as to whether all the key factors have been included prevents researchers from saying whether Factor A *causes* Factor B. Correlation does not prove cause and effect, it merely shows that an association exists between factors. Factor A is associated with Factor B, or Factor A changes with changes in Factor B. More will be presented on this point in the next chapter when correlation and regression are discussed.

Computer graphics

In this section on analytic techniques, it is important to cite a recent breakthrough in computer technology—computer graphics. Computer graphics are printouts of data in a pictorial format. For instance territorial sales data can be presented in a map using different colors or sketchings to show differences in sales among territories. Such a presentation is often more enlightening to the manager than lists of quantitative sales data. Patterns emerge in pictures that are not as evident in lists of numbers.

Computer graphics should not be viewed as an analytic technique similar to regression, cluster analysis, analysis of variance. You can't test hypotheses with graphics, nor can you project to population data from graphics. Rather it should be viewed as a process in which data are reassembled to take on additional meaning, and in that respect, it is an analytic tool.

Possible uses — The most frequent marketing applications are for analyzing markets, (identifying location of people by ages, income, education, etc.), analyzing competitors (showing densities of competitors' sales in various geographic areas), media planning (coverage of newspapers, demographics of people, boundaries of trading areas), site analyses (determining store sites based on population, competition, etc.).[3]

Using statistical tests in the analysis of data

It was previously stated that data can be analyzed at two levels. The first or lower level involves simple comparisons based on either univariate or bivariate (cross-tabs) comparisons. The development of means, medians, or modes for the collected data would also be viewed as first level analysis.

A second or higher level of analysis involves making inferences to populations based on sample data, or identifying significant differences or associations between groups based on sample data. This requires the application of statistical techniques. The remainder of this chapter and the majority of Chapter 14 describe those statistical techniques used most frequently in marketing research.

Choosing the appropriate technique

Because of the large number of statistical techniques available, the researcher may have difficulty in selecting the technique most appropriate for the situation. Following are five key questions that will aid the researcher in making this choice.

1. *What is the test intended to show?* Is it to determine whether there are significant differences between groups of data, or is

---

[3]Hirotaka Takeuchi and Allen Schmidt, "New Promise of Computer Graphics," *Harvard Business Review*, January-February 1980, pp. 122-131.

it intended to determine whether there is association between two or more variables?

Group differences		Test for association

2. *What measurement scale is involved: nominal, ordinal, interval, or ratio?* As described in Chapter 7 in "Attitude Measurement," there are major differences between the actual meaning of numbers. The nature of the numbers involved determines which tests can be used. Interval and ratio data are often identified as "metric data," whereas nominal and ordinal data are called "non-metric data."

3. *How many samples are involved?* Is a comparison being made between a sample and a population? Is a comparison being made between two or more samples? Compare characteristics of two groups of shoppers: those shopping at a center between 9 and 11 A.M., and those shopping at a center between 4 and 6 P.M.

   Is the comparison being made among units within the same sample? Compare the smoking habits of freshmen, sophomores, juniors, and seniors segmented within the same sample.

4. *If two or more samples are used, are they independent or are they related?* An example of an independent event would be one where one sample (Group A) receives a "10¢ off" coupon and a different sample (Group B) receives a "15¢ off" coupon. When the *same* group is involved twice, the two measurements are no longer independent; members of group A are observed before they receive a "10¢ off" coupon and then after they receive the coupon.

5. *How many variables are involved?* This is critical in tests for associations where criterion (dependent) and predictor (independent) variables are involved. The techniques used when just two variables are involved are known as bivariate techniques. When more than two variables are involved in the tests, multivariate techniques are used.
   Bivariate — The association between sales performance of our salesmen (dependent variable) and their scores on a company aptitude test (independent variable).
   Multivariate — Sales of flowers (dependent variable) related to life style and income of consumers (two independent variables).

These then are the five key factors affecting the researcher's choice of a statistical test.

Two charts are included in Chapter 14 that show how these five factors are used in selecting the appropriate statistical test.

DEVELOPING AND TESTING HYPOTHESES

Since the statistical tests discussed in this text are generally used to test hypotheses, it is imperative that the researcher understand both how to develop hypotheses and the procedures to follow when testing them.

Developing hypotheses

Hypotheses are statements that the researcher sets out to accept or reject based on the data collected. The hypotheses should flow from the study's objectives so their acceptance or rejection enables these objectives to be met. The researcher should state the null hypothesis (the hypothesis to be tested) in such a way that its rejection leads to the acceptance of the desired statement—the *alternative* hypothesis.

This action of trying to reject the null hypothesis stems from the fact that in marketing research the acceptance of a hypothesis can only be tentative because additional evidence may later show it to be in error. Thus null hypotheses are not really "accepted"; rather it is just a case of not being able to reject them due to a lack of enough solid evidence.

Assume the television industry wants to determine the viewing habits of different market segments. One such segment is the college market. It is felt this group watches TV less than typical adult Americans, and a survey is carried out to obtain the necessary information. Assume information exists that shows the typical adult American watches 32 hours of TV each week. The null hypothesis developed for this study is:

H_o: $\overline{X}_s \geq 32$ hours per week
The average college student watches at least 32 hours of television per week.

The alternative hypothesis would be:

H_a: $\overline{X}_s < 32$ hours per week
The average college student watches less than 32 hours of television per week.

If the data collected from the survey enable the null hypothesis to be rejected, the alternate hypothesis would be accepted.

Other examples of possible hypotheses:

H_o: There is no difference in the results produced from two sales training methods (Method A and Method B).

H_a: Sales training Method A produces results that are significantly different from the results from Method B.

H_o: The proportion of the firms using Acme computers is equal to, or less than, 5 percent.

H_a: More than 5 percent of the firms use Acme computers.

Hypotheses should be simple, precise statements. They should not contain multiple possibilities that make the task of accepting or rejecting them more difficult. The following hypothesis is too complicated.

Keep hypotheses precise

H_o: Less than 40 percent of male students and 50 percent of female students attend more than three movies per month.

Since a multiple condition exists (proportion of both male and female students attending movies), one part of this statement might be accepted but the other part might be rejected. The hypothesis should be able to be accepted or rejected in its entirety.

The hypothesis should also be based on a statement that can be quantified.

Imprecise hypothesis

H_o: "The use of 10¢ off coupons will increase sales of Acme bread." If the collected data show that Acme bread sales increased by just *one* unit, the above hypothesis would have to be accepted because of its imprecise phrasing.

Precise hypothesis

H_o: "10¢ off coupons will increase April sales of Acme bread by at least 10 percent"; or "10¢ off coupons will increase April sales of Acme bread by at least 5000 units." Both are precise statements that can be accepted or rejected based on actual population data or information obtained from samples.

The null hypothesis is either rejected or not rejected. In making this decision, however, an error *could* occur, since whenever sample data are used it is impossible to be certain the decision was a correct one.

Type I and II errors

A Type I error occurs when a true hypothesis is rejected; a Type II error occurs when a false hypothesis is accepted. The probability of making a Type I error is designated as the level of significance or alpha (α). The value of alpha depends on how much risk the researcher wants to take in rejecting a true hypothesis. The most common levels of significance are 0.05 and 0.01.

The probability of making a Type II error is labeled beta (β). These two types of errors are not complementary: alpha + beta $\neq$ 1. The probability of committing a Type II error is quite complicated to determine and will not be covered in this book. Additional information about Type I errors is presented in the following section on "Z" and "t" tests.

TESTS FOR MEASURING GROUP DIFFERENCES

The statistical tests described in this text are placed in two broad categories: (1) those used to measure differences between groups or (2) those used to determine whether groups or variables are associated. The first series of statistical techniques presents the ones most frequently used to measure group differences.

Z and t tests

Whenever sample data are involved, it is always necessary to cope with sampling error. Z and t tests are techniques for measuring differences among data while still recognizing the influence sampling error may have had on these values.

Qualifications – These tests can be used when:
- Measurement scales are at least interval.
- Observations are drawn from normally distributed population.
- Observations are independent.
- Two or less groups are involved.

Z versus t tests

If the previous qualifications have been met, the researcher then has to decide whether a Z test or a t test is most appropriate. A Z test is used under the following two conditions:

1. Information exists on the population mean and standard deviation. This population can be an actual one or an assumed one in which some parameter value is selected,

e.g., it is assumed a new product will be accepted by 25 percent of the population.
2. The sample data come from a sample larger than 30.

A t test is used when the population's standard deviation cannot be obtained, the sample size involved is less than 30, or only sample data are available on both groups. Since these latter conditions tend to prevail, in marketing research the t test is used much more than the Z test.

Like the "normal" or Z distribution, a t distribution is a continuous probability distribution. The t distribution, although symmetrical, is more widely dispersed than the normal distribution. Thus a "t" distribution has a larger proportion of its total area in its tails than the normal distribution. The t distribution is in reality a family or series of normal curves with each curve based on the size of the sample. As the sample size gets larger the t values tend to become quite similar to Z or "normal" distribution values.

Example: As an example of a Z test, the First National Bank of River City is carrying out an in-depth analysis of its customers. It wants to determine their general makeup in terms of age, income, desires for additional financial services, and overall satisfaction with the bank's offerings.

One aspect of this study deals with how the incomes of the bank's customers compare with the incomes of typical River City residents. A recent study carried out in River City disclosed that the average household income was $13,200 with a standard deviation of $1,500.

The First National Bank sampled 1,024 of its customers and found their household's average income was $14,300 (Table 13-11).

Income Data on Two Groups **Table 13-11**

	River City Households	Bank Customer Households
Number Surveyed	Total Population	1,024
Mean Income	$13,200 ($\mu_1$)	$14,300 ($\overline{x}_2$)
Standard Deviation	$1,500	$3,400

Null hypothesis — The null hypothesis to be tested is: The mean household income of the Bank's customers is equal to the mean income of the average River City household.

$$H_0: \overline{x}_2 = \mu_1$$
$$H_a: \overline{x}_2 \neq \mu_1$$

Level of significance — Since sample data are involved, it is impossible to be certain that the decision to accept or reject a hypothesis is correct because of the influence of sampling error. It is possible, however, to state the probability of rejecting a true hypothesis, a Type I error. The probability of such a mistake is called alpha (*a*) or the level of significance. The alpha value used depends on how much risk the researcher wants to take in rejecting a true hypothesis. In this example an 0.05 level of significance is used.

Formula used — The formula used for a *Z* test is:

$$Z = \frac{\text{Population or hypothesized value minus sample value}}{\text{standard error of population value}}$$

$$= \frac{\mu_1 - \overline{x}_2}{\sigma_{\overline{x}_1}}$$

In this formula the difference between the sample value (*x*) and the population value (*μ*) is expressed in terms of standard errors.

It was shown in an earlier chapter that in a given population, the means of all samples of size *n* will be normally distributed around the mean of the population from which they are drawn. The mean of all the sample means of the population of River City was known to be $13,200. The researcher is really testing to see if the income data on River City households and the data on the bank customers' households could have come from the same universe. Thus, the standard error of the mean would be computed as follows:

$$\sigma_{\overline{x}1} = \frac{\sigma}{\sqrt{n}}$$

$$\sigma_{\overline{x}1} = \frac{1,500}{\sqrt{1,024}}$$

$$\sigma_{\overline{x}1} = \$46.88$$

$$Z = \frac{\$13,200\text{-}\$14,300}{\$46.88}$$

$$= \frac{-\$1100}{\$46.88}$$

$$Z = -23.5$$

Could a difference this large (23.5 standard errors) be the result of sampling error, or does it mean a real difference exists between the two values? This decision is made by comparing the computed Z value of 23.5 with the tabular Z value associated with the 0.05 level of significance chosen for our study. (See Z Distribution Table in the appendix to this book.)

Tabular Z values using one- and two-tailed tests

The tabular value of Z at the 0.05 level of significance depends on whether a one-tailed or a two-tailed test is involved. A one-tailed test is used when the null hypothesis involves a greater than ($>$) or less than ($<$) situation. These are situations when the researcher is concerned only with determining whether one value is significantly larger or smaller than another value.

A two-tailed test is used when the null hypothesis is a statement pertaining to equality between two sets of data: H_0: $\mu = \bar{x}_1$.

If a one-tailed test is used, the tabular Z involves just one-half of the normal curve and the entire level of significance applies to that area (see Figure 13-1, Parts 1 and 2). If a two-tailed test is used, half of the level of significance is applied to each end of the normal curve (Part 3).

Since 0.05 and 0.01 are the most commonly used levels of significance, a table is developed containing their tabular values for both one-tailed and two-tailed tests (Table 13-12).

Table 13-12

Tabular Value of Z for 0.05 and 0.01 Levels of Significance (α)

$\alpha = $ 0.05 One-tailed test, $Z = $ 1.64
$\alpha = $ 0.05 Two-tailed test, $Z = $ 1.96
$\alpha = $ 0.01 One-tailed test, $Z = $ 2.33
$\alpha = $ 0.01 Two-tailed test, $Z = $ 2.58

One- and Two-Tailed Tests

0.05

0.05   0.025   0.025

(1) One-tailed test involving a "less than" ($<$) hypothesis

(2) One-tailed test involving a "greater than" ($>$) hypothesis

(3) Two-tailed test involving an "equal to" ($=$) hypothesis

Example: In the previous bank example comparing the average income of the First National Bank customer with the income of the average River City household, a two-tailed test is involved because the null hypothesis involved a statement of equality.

$$H_o: \overline{x}_2 = \mu_1$$

The tabular Z value for a two-tailed test using a 0.05 level of significance is ±1.96. Since the computed Z in our example (−23.5) greatly exceeded this tabular Z, the difference between the two mean values ($13,200 and $14,300) was too great to have been caused by sampling error. Thus the null hypothesis is rejected and the alternative hypothesis that the two means are not equal is accepted. A further interpretation would be that the average income of the bank's customers is significantly larger than the income of the typical River City household.

Example: If the data pertain to proportions rather than discrete numbers, a different formula is needed. To illustrate this situation, the bank study will be used again. Another part of that study was concerned with the proportion of bank customers owning their home compared with the proportion of home ownership among *all* River City residents.

The null hypothesis to be tested is: The proportion of home ownership among the bank's customer households is comparable to the proportion of ownership among all River City households.

$$H_o: p_B = P_R$$
$$H_a: p_B = P_R$$

P_R = proportion of River City households owning houses
p_B = proportion of Bank's customer households owning homes

In the sample, 1,024 bank customers were contacted, and 71 percent of these respondents were in a household owning/buying their own home. The data available on the proportion of home ownership among River City households disclosed that 59 percent owned their own homes.

$$P_R = 59\%$$
$$p_B = 71\%$$
$$n_B = 1024$$

The formula for deriving a Z value when proportions are involved is:

$$Z = \frac{p - P}{\sigma_p}$$

$$\sigma_p = \sqrt{\frac{P \cdot Q}{n}}$$

The formula for determining this standard error value assumes both groups are from the same overall population and includes portions of data from both the sample and the population (p value is for sample, P value is from population).

$$Z = \frac{71\% - 59\%}{\sigma_p}$$

$$\sigma_p = \sqrt{\frac{59 \cdot 41}{1,024}} = \sqrt{2.36} = 1.54$$

$$Z = \frac{12\%}{1.54} = 7.8$$

Computed $Z = 7.8$

Tabular $Z = 1.96$ (two-tailed test at 0.05 level of significance)

Since the computed Z greatly exceeds the tabular Z, the null hypothesis is rejected and the alternative hypothesis that there is a difference between the two groups in terms of home ownership is accepted.

Situations requiring t tests

The mathematics of Z tests are relatively simple to perform. For that reason, the Z test was used to illustrate the steps involved in using Z or t tests to test hypotheses. In actual marketing research situations, the t test is used much more frequently since the most common situation is one in which all the data are obtained from samples or the samples used are fairly small. Following are three different formulas for t tests, and a description of when each should be used.

1. When population data exist, but the comparison involves data from a fairly small sample, this formula should be used:

$$t = \frac{\overline{x} - \mu}{s/\sqrt{n-1}}$$

s = standard deviation of sample

2. When the data on both groups are obtained from samples and the means of the two groups are to be compared, this formula is used:

$$t = \frac{\overline{x}_1 - \overline{x}_2}{\sqrt{(S_{\overline{x}_1})^2 + (S_{\overline{x}_2})^2}}$$

$S_{\overline{x}_1}$ = standard error of the mean for sample 1

$S_{\overline{x}_2}$ = standard error of the mean for sample 2

3. When all data are obtained from samples, and the differences to be tested involve proportions, this formula is used.

$$t = \frac{p_1 - p_2}{\sqrt{\dfrac{p_1 \cdot q_1}{n_1} + \dfrac{p_2 \cdot q_2}{n_2}}}$$

p_1 = proportion of sample 1 having a given characteristic

p_2 = proportion of sample 2 having a given characteristic

In all three of these situations, a t table must be consulted to obtain the tabular t value. This value is based on the degrees of freedom $(n - 1)$ involved. When two samples are involved the degrees of freedom to consult in the t table becomes $(n_1 + n_2 - 2)$. A t table is included in the appendix of this text. As the sample size nears 120, tabular t values become comparable to normal distribution or Z values.

Steps in using Z or t tests

Remember the following key factors in determining whether Z or t tests can be used: The data must be at least interval-scaled. The observations must be independent. Two or fewer groups must be involved. The observations must come from a normally distributed population.

If these criteria are met and the researcher decides to employ a Z or t test, the following steps should be followed.

1. The null hypothesis should be developed. $H_0: \overline{x}_1 = \overline{x}_2$. (This determines whether a one- or two-tailed test is involved.)

2. The level of significance (α) should be chosen, usually 0.05 or 0.01.

3. Based on the nature of the collected data, the proper formula for deriving a computed Z or t value must be selected. (Means or proportions?)
4. The computed Z or t value is compared to the appropriate tabular Z or t value.
5. The null hypothesis is accepted or rejected based on the outcome of these comparisons.

If some of the criteria enabling the use of Z or t tests are not met, there are other tests that can be used. Although they are not as powerful as the Z or t tests, they still enable the effective testing of hypotheses.

Alternatives to Z and t tests

Mann-Whitney U test

Example: Assume that the First National Bank devises a survey which enables each customer in the sample to provide an overall rating of the bank. The bank wants to determine whether its younger customers (35 years or less) differ from older customers in terms of their attitudes toward the bank. Table 13-13 contains the attitude scores obtained from 20 customers (10 in group 1, 35 years of age or younger; and 10 in group 2, more than 35 years old). This small sample was used to make the presentation of results easier (see Table 13-13).

Customer Evaluations of Bank

Table 13-13

Attitude Scores		Ranking of Score	
Younger Group	Older Group	Younger Group	Older Group
94	78	1	14
86	75	7	15
72	84	17	9
90	88	3	5
64	83	19	10
79	80	13	12
90	81	3	11
88	92	5	2
75	67	15	18
85	61	8	20
		$R_1 = 91$	$R_2 = 116$

The third and fourth columns rank each score in terms of its standing in the total group. For example, the second individual in the younger group had an attitude score of 86, which was the seventh highest of all 20 scores. Once these rankings are assigned, the next step is to find the sum of ranks associated with each group.

Two formulas are used together to derive the Mann-Whitney U value.

$$U_1 = n_1 n_2 + \frac{n_1(n_1 + 1)}{2} - R_1$$

$$U_2 = n_1 n_2 - U_1$$

$$n_1 = 10 \qquad R_1 = 91$$
$$n_2 = 10 \qquad R_2 = 116$$

$$U_1 = (10)(10) + \frac{10(11)}{2} - 91$$

$$= 64$$

$$U_2 = (10)(10) - 64$$

$$= 36$$

The Mann-Whitney U is the smaller of the two U values obtained. In this case the Mann-Whitney U is 36. If the logic in the above formulas is studied, it becomes clear that the more similar the two groups are in their evaluations, the smaller the R values will be and thus the larger the value of U. It then follows that we are testing the probability of obtaining a value the size of the smallest of the two U values if the two groups are indeed similar in their attitudes.

H_o: There is no difference in attitudes of the two groups toward the bank

H_a: There is significant difference in the attitudes of the two groups toward the bank

significance level $\alpha = 0.05$ (two-tailed test)
computed $U = 36$
tabular $U_1 = 23$ (obtained from table showing U values in Mann-Whitney test)

In this test the computed value must be less than the tabular value to reject the null hypothesis.

Decision — Since the computed U is larger than the tabular U, the null hypothesis cannot be rejected. There is not enough evidence to reject the statement that *both* groups have similar attitudes toward the bank.

Kruskal-Wallis test

This test is another version of the Mann-Whitney U test. It is used when more than two independent samples are involved. In our bank example, it would be used if the customers were divided into three or more groups based on their age. This test, like the Mann-Whitney U test, can be used on nonmetric data.

Wilcoxon T test

This test is used when nonmetric data on two samples are involved but the samples are not independent. This is suited to pretest and post-test situations. It can also be used when two samples are involved, but the criteria necessary for a t test or Z test cannot be met.

In our bank example, the Wilcoxon T test would have been used if the bank wanted to test the effectiveness of an ad campaign intended to enhance the reputation of the bank. A group of customers would be tested during Period 1 on their overall evaluation of the bank's reputation. The ad campaign would then be launched. At the conclusion of the campaign the same group of customers is tested again on their evaluation of the bank's reputation. The Wilcoxon T test will show whether attitudes have changed significantly over the two periods.

If the reader is interested in possibly using either the Kruskal-Wallis or Wilcoxon T test, a book on business statistics should be consulted to obtain the procedures and formulas.

QUESTIONS AND EXERCISES

1. Which is most important: *proper analysis* or *proper interpretation of data*?
2. When should the key analytic techniques be chosen?
3. Explain the difference between simultaneous and sequential cross-tabulations.
4. What are spurious relationships? Give an example.
5. What do the terms "dependent" and "independent" mean when applied to sample data?
6. Why does the researcher set out to reject the null hypothesis?

7. Do recent graduates of Ohio Tech contribute more money (on the average) to the Alumni Fund than people who graduated five or more years ago? A survey of *all* graduates in the last five years disclosed their average contribution was $18.75 per year with a standard deviation of $7.80. A random sample of 400 alumni who graduated more than five years ago disclosed their average contribution was $14.50 with a standard deviation of $6.50. Is there a difference between the average contribution of the two groups? Set up the hypothesis to be tested at the 0.05 level of significance.

8. The Acme Brewing Company is seeking information about the makeup of its customers. Acme feels its beer appeals more to "higher educated" segments of the market due to the sophisticated ads used. It develops two samples. One is comprised only of male beer drinkers with college educations (Sample 1). The other is comprised of male beer drinkers with no college education (Sample 2). Each sample was randomly developed.

  college: $n_1 = 140$ 28 of these men drink primarily Acme beer

  noncollege: $n_2 = 180$ 44 of these men drink primarily Acme beer

Set up a hypothesis to be tested. Use the 0.05 level of significance and test your hypothesis.

CASES

Case 1

Educo is a firm that prepares and sells videotape educational material for industry employees. One set of potential clients Educo is interested in reaching is quality control engineers. In an attempt to learn more about the types of videotape classes these engineers are seeking, Educo surveyed 3,000 members of a national quality control association.

When a series of cross-tabulations was performed on the survey responses, a number of relationships emerged.

  — A higher portion of older employees (over 40 years of age) had advanced degrees.
  — Those engineers with advanced degrees tended to be with larger firms (annual sales in excess of $58 million).
  — Over 80 percent of larger firms had on-site videotape facilities whereas only 22 percent of smaller firms (sales less than $50 million) had such facilities.

What relationship exists between the age of engineers, the nature of their degree, and their access to videotape facilities? Are the relationships real or spurious? Do these findings suggest any strategy for Educo in terms of marketing its videotape courses?

14

Analysis and interpretation of data, continued

WHEN IS 'THE AVERAGE' NOT AVERAGE?

According to the Bureau of Labor Statistics, a married worker with three dependents had an average weekly gross pay of $237 in the third quarter of 1980. When inflation is considered, this worker appears to be worse off than was his counterpart of 1967.

In reality, this "average" worker's worsening income is more the result of a faulty statistical base than inflation. In truth, the average married worker with three dependents earned a good deal more than the "average." How can this be?

The previous figure was derived by dividing the total amount of weekly wages reported by employers by the total number of names on their payrolls. Since some persons were on more than one payroll, a strange result occurred. A worker who made $250 a week at one job and $100 a week at a second part-time job earned (according to the government) an average of $175 a week, a figure that understated his true earnings by 50 percent.

Multiply this situation by the 5 or 6 million people who have two or more jobs and it becomes evident that a statistical monstrosity has been created.

Taken from the newspaper article by Geoffrey Moore, "How About a Statistical Break?" Rocky Mountain News (Denver), February 22, 1981, p. 65.

Chi-square is the test most frequently used by marketing researchers for handling hypotheses. Since this is a nonparametric test, it can be used when the distribution of the population is unknown and when nonmetric data are involved.

The general approach in chi-square analysis is quite similar to the procedures used for the Z and t tests. That is, the objective of the chi-square analysis is to determine whether real or significant differences exist among groups of data, or whether the differences are due merely to sampling.

CHI-SQUARE ANALYSIS

The symbol x^2 is used to designate chi-square. The chi-square distribution is similar to the t distribution in that its values depend upon the number of degrees of freedom involved. In Figure 14-1, it can be seen that a chi-square distribution is very skewed when a small number of degrees of freedom are involved, and, as the degrees of freedom increase, the distribution becomes more symmetrical. In fact, as the degrees of freedom become fairly large, the distribution begins to resemble the normal curve. The chi-square table in the appendix includes the different values associated with the various degrees of freedom.

Chi-square distribution

Figure 14-1

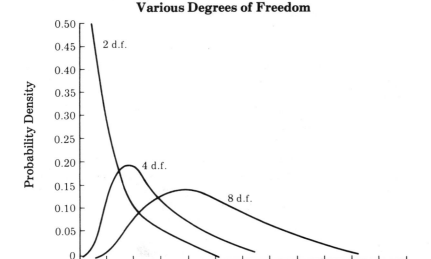

Distribution of Chi-Squares for Various Degrees of Freedom

2 d.f.

4 d.f.

8 d.f.

Probability Density

Scale of X^2

<table>
<tr><td>

Procedures for chi-square analysis

</td><td>

Chi-square tests involve a comparison of expected frequencies (f_c) with observed frequencies (f_o) to determine whether the difference between the two is greater than that which might occur by chance. There are five steps in using chi-square tests.

</td></tr>
</table>

1. The difference between each observed frequency (f_o) and each expected frequency (f_c) is computed.
2. These differences are squared.
3. Each squared difference is divided by its respective expected frequency.
4. These quotients are added together to obtain the computed chi-square values.
5. This computed value is then compared to a tabular chi-square value.

If the computed chi-square value is greater than the tabular chi-square value at a predetermined level of significance, the hypothesis that there is not a significant difference between the sets of data is rejected. On the other hand, if the computed chi-square value is less than the tabular chi-square value, there is not enough evidence to state a significant difference exists between the sets of data.

$$\chi^2 = \Sigma \frac{(f_o - f_c)^2}{f_c}$$

f_o = the various observed frequencies

f_c = the various expected frequencies

Examples of chi-square analysis

The expected frequency values used in chi-square analysis may either be arbitrarily assigned or determined mathematically from existing information.

Arbitrarily assigning expected frequencies

John Jones is marketing manager of the Acme Detergent Company. The firm is presently developing a new product and wants to choose the best package for this product. The choices have been narrowed down to four designs, and Jones wants to test whether these four are equally acceptable to the consumers. To test this hypothesis, he surveys 200 consumers and has each of them observe all four packages. They are then asked to choose the one they feel is most appealing.

If each package has equal appeal, then each should be selected by approximately 25 percent of the sample members as their favorite. The actual selections made (observed frequencies) by the sample members are shown in Table 14-1.

Selection by Sample Members of Various Packages   **Table 14-1**

Package	Number of times selected as "favorite"
A	72
B	62
C	28
D	38
	200

Table 14-1 discloses that the respondents' selection of "favorite package" was not evenly divided. The question is, was this distribution due to a real difference in opinions among the observers or did it result from sampling error?

H_o: the four packages have equal appeal to customers
H_a: the four packages do not have equal appeal to customers

Chi-square Analysis of Sample Members'   **Table 14-2**
Selection of Four Package Designs

Package	(1) Observed Frequencies (f_o)	(2) Expected Frequencies (f_c)	(3) $(f_o - f_c)$	(4) $(f_o - f_c)^2$	(5) $(f_o - f_c)^2/f_c$
A	72	50	22	484	9.7
B	62	50	12	144	2.9
C	28	50	−22	484	9.7
D	38	50	−12	144	2.9
	200	200			25.2

The computed chi-square value is 25.2, as shown in Table 14-2. This value measures the discrepancy between the set of observed frequencies and the set of theoretical or expected frequencies. Could a discrepancy this large have been caused by sampling error? To answer this, the computed x^2 value is compared to a tabular x^2. Since the x^2 value is taken from a chi-square table, the degrees of freedom and the level of significance involved must be determined.

For chi-square analysis the degrees of freedom $= (r - 1)$, where r equals the rows involved. Thus, there are three degrees of freedom in this analysis. The level of significance chosen was 0.05. On this basis the tabular x^2 is 7.8.

Since the computed X^2 (25.2) exceeds the tabular X^2 (7.8), there is a significant difference in the consumer preferences of the package design. Therefore, the null hypothesis, "The four packages have equal appeal to customers," is rejected.

Mathematically determining expected frequencies

In the previous example the expected frequencies (f_c) were arbitrarily assigned. A more common practice is to mathematically determine them. A survey on check cashing policies was conducted among 303 food chains, in which a questionnaire was mailed to each of these chains and 188 responded. The question arose as to whether these respondents were representative of the entire universe. Comparisons were made between certain characteristics of the respondents and similar characteristics of the original group of 303 chain operations. One such characteristic was the chain's size in terms of its numbers of stores. To see whether the respondents were representative of the universe, a chi-square test was used.

The expected frequency figures (f_c) used in the test were derived from a percentage breakdown of the 303 chains comprising the original population. For example, 140 chains of the original 303 had 8 to 15 stores in their operations. Based on this information, if the respondents and the original group were reasonably similar, there should have been about 87 chains of the 188 respondents with 8 to 15 stores in their operation.

$$\frac{140}{303} \times 188 = 86.8$$

All the expected frequencies listed in Table 14-3 were determined in a similar manner.

The computed chi-square value obtained was 0.39 and the tabular value of chi-square at the 0.05 level of significance was 9.5. Since the computed value is less than the tabular value, there is not a significant difference between respondents and nonrespondents based on their number of stores.

Similar chi-square analyses were made on such characteristics as: geographical location of the chains' operation; average sales per store; and type of control imposed by their headquarters. This use of chi-square analysis is an effective method for determining whether nonresponse bias exists in questionnaire results.

Chi-square with two variables involved

The previous examples using chi-square pertained to situations where only one variable was to be tested: number of stores or choice of package designs. Chi-squares can also be used to test the relationship between two variables, and this makes it ideal for analyzing cross tabulations. This use of chi-squares becomes a somewhat restricted test of association between variables, restricted in the sense that it can indicate whether an association exists between two sets of variables, but it cannot determine the strength of this association.

Results of Chi-square Analysis of Respondents Based on Their Number of Stores   **Table 14-3**

No. of Stores in Chain	Observed Frequencies (f_o)	Expected Frequencies (f_c)	$(f_o - f_c)$	$(f_o - f_c)^2$	$\dfrac{(f_o - f_c)^2}{f_c}$
8-15	84	86.8	−2.8	7.8	0.09
16-30	48	46.2	1.8	3.2	0.07
31-75	29	28.4	0.6	0.36	0.03
76-150	12	12.9	−0.9	0.81	0.06
Over 150	15	13.7	1.4	1.9	0.14
Totals	188	188.0			0.39

Computed value of chi-square = 0.39
Degrees of freedom = 4
Level of significance = 0.05
Tabular value of chi-square = 9.5

Example: The alumni office of a major university is planning a promotional campaign to stimulate donations from its alumni to the school's building fund. The office is analyzing patterns in past donations for any unusual findings to guide its new campaign. One thing it wants to learn is whether there is any association between contributions and the nature of the degree received. Sample data were obtained over the past five years on these two variables, with the results shown in Table 14-4. (The school does not give Ph.D. degrees.)

If the computations are to be carried out manually, it is easier if the information is placed in a single column. The "expected frequency" values then have to be determined for each category. This can be done for each category by multiplying its

Table 14-4   **Alumni Contributions Based on**
Nature of Degree

| | *Type of Degree* | | |
Size of Contribution	*BS/BA*	*MS/MA*	*Totals*
Less than $10	80	35	115
$10-$40	40	20	60
$41-$100	45	25	70
More than $100	35	20	55
	200	100	300

H_o: The amount of an alum's contribution is not related to the nature of his/her degree.
H_a: The amount of an alum's contribution is related to the nature of his/her degree.
The level of significance used is 0.05.

row total times its column total and then dividing by the overall total. Using the data on Table 14-4, the expected frequency for the cell of row 1, column 1 (those people with BS/BA degrees who give less than $10), would be $\frac{(200 \times 115)}{300}$ or 76.7. The expected frequency for row 2, column 2 (MS/MA gave between $10 and $40) would be $\frac{(100 \times 60)}{300}$ or 20.

Table 14-5   **Chi-square Analysis of Alumni Contributions**

| | *Observed Frequencies* | *Expected Frequencies* | | $\frac{(f_o - f_c)^2}{f_c}$ |
	(f_o)	(f_c)	$(f_o - f_c)^2$	
Less $10 by BS/BA	80	76.7	10.89	0.142
Less $10 by MS/MA	35	38.3	10.89	0.284
$10-$40 by BS/BA	40	40	0	0
$10-$40 by MS/MA	20	20	0	0
$41-$100 by BS/BA	45	46.7	2.89	0.061
$41-$100 by MS/MA	25	23.3	2.89	0.124
+700 by BS/BA	35	36.7	2.89	0.079
+700 by MS/MA	20	18.3	2.89	0.158
	300	300		$\Sigma\chi^2 = 0.85$

Computed $\chi^2 = 0.85$
Tabular $\chi^2 = 7.81$ (based on 3 degrees of freedom at 0.05 level of significance)

Therefore, the null hypothesis cannot be rejected. The evidence does not indicate whether a relationship exists between the amount of a person's contribution and the type of degree he/she obtained from the school.

When two variables are involved, the degrees of freedom equal the number of rows minus one times the number of columns minus one (see Table 14-4).

$$(r - 1)(c - 1) = (4 - 1)(2 - 1) = 3$$

Chi-square analysis can be used with nonmetric data. As in the t distribution, tabular chi-square values vary with the degrees of freedom. Chi-square analysis does not allow proportions to be used in its tables (95 percent, 82 percent, etc.), so all proportions must be changed into discrete values. There must also be at least five units in 80 percent of the observed frequency cells. The data used must come from independent samples.

When chi-square can be used

McNemar test

Variation on chi-square tests

This test is really a modified chi-square test. It can be used with either nominal or ordinal data and when the samples are not independent. Thus it is an ideal test for pre-test−post-test evaluations. Its use is limited to situations where a 2×2 frequency table is involved.

Example: The previous example of alumni donations to a university will be used. The alumni office has now mailed out a series of brochures to its alums requesting donations to its building fund. The effectiveness of this mail campaign will now be tested. It selects a sample of 300 of its alumni and records their donation patterns prior to the mailing and after the mailing (pre-test−post-test situations).

Donations of Alumni

Table 14-6

		After Campaign	
		Donated Less than $40	Donated More than $40
Before Campaign	Donated Less than $40	105 (A)	53 (B)
	Donated More than $40	19 (C)	122 (D)

H_o: Mail campaign did not significantly alter donation from alums

H_a: Mail campaign significantly altered donation from alums

Cells B and C show the changes that occurred among the alumni during the two time periods; cells A and D include those alums who did not change their donation patterns.

$$\chi^2 = \frac{[(C - B) - 1]^2}{C + B}$$

$$\chi = \frac{[(19 - 53) - 1]^2}{72}$$

$$\chi = 15.1$$

computed $\chi^2 = 15.1$
tabular $\chi^2 = 3.84$ (0.05 level of significance and $(r - 1)$ $(c - 1) = 1$ degree of freedom)

Thus the null hypothesis is rejected. The mail campaign was indeed successful in significantly altering donations from the alumni.

When more than two dependent samples are involved, the Cochran Q test is appropriate. This is described more fully in business statistics texts.

ANALYSIS OF VARIANCE

Analysis of variance is of greatest value in evaluating data obtained from experiments. "What influence did the treatment have on the dependent variable?" The general premise of this tool is that the total variance that exists among the data can be apportioned to specific factors by means of formal mathematical techniques. The size of the variance related to each factor indicates that factor's influence on the dependent variable.

The name of this process would imply that variance is the main value of concern. But what really happens is that differences between *means* are measured. These differences are described in terms of variance, thus the name, "analysis of variance."

Example: A company's research department is attempting to determine which of three package designs is the most effective for a new detergent. It tests all three designs in five different test cities to determine what influence each of the different packages has on sales. Another possible cause of variation could be basic differences between the five test cities. Therefore, two major sources of variation that should be considered are the impact of the packages and the influence of the cities. This situation means that a randomized block design should be used for the experiment.[1]

The data in Table 14-7 suggest that Package 3 is the most successful in terms of total number of cases sold. But, was the difference in sales among the three packages due to an overall preference by buyers for Package 3, or was it the result of differences in preferences among residents of the five cities? Another possibility is that since the study involved samples, the difference in sales among the three packages may have been the result of sampling error and had nothing to do with differences in preferences for the various packages.

Table 14-7

Randomized Block Design Showing Sales of Three Different Packages in Five Test Cities
(Figures are in terms of case sales)

Test Cities	Package 1	Package 2	Package 3	Mean Value of Rows
A	44	32	62	46
B	30	32	22	28
C	60	60	88	69
D	31	45	52	43
E	25	41	36	34
	190	210	260	

Treatment means $\overline{X}_1 = 38$ $\overline{X}_2 = 42$ $\overline{X}_3 = 52$ Overall mean $= 44$

Hypotheses to be tested

The following two null hypotheses will be tested:

H_0: There is reasonably similar acceptance of all three package designs among buyers.

H_0: There is reasonably similar acceptance of all three package designs among all five cities.

---

[1]As described in Chapter 8 of this book, the completely randomized design, the randomized block design, and the Latin square design, are all designs for the use of analysis of variance. The researcher's choice of any of these depends on how many sources of variation are to be analyzed.

Test procedures

The starting point for this analysis is to set up a table indicating the type of information needed and how this information will be used to derive the computed F ratios.[2] Table 14-8 contains the format for a randomized block design.

Table 14-8   **Analysis of Variance Using Randomized Block Design**

Degree of Variation	Sum of Squares	Degrees of Freedom	Mean Square	F Ratio
Between Treatments (Packages)	SSTr	$t - 1$ Number of treatments minus one	$\dfrac{SST}{t - 1} = MS(SST)$	$\dfrac{MS(SST)}{MS(SSR)}$
Between Rows (Cities)	SSC	$n - 1$ Number of rows minus one	$\dfrac{SSC}{n - 1} = MS(SSC)$	$\dfrac{MS(SSC)}{MS(SSR)}$
Residual Error	SSR	$(n - 1)(t - 1)$	$\dfrac{SSR}{(n - 1)(t - 1)} = MS(SSR)$	
Total Sum of Squares	TSS	$tn - 1$		

Following are the computations used to derive the various sums of square values. These figures were taken from Table 14-8.

SSTr = sum of squares to treatments (sum of squares of columns)
   $= 5 \ [(38 - 44)^2 + (42 - 44)^2 + (52 - 44)^2]$ (5 represents number of rows)
   $= 520$

SSC = sum of squares of cities (sum of squares of rows)
   $= 3 \ [(46 - 44)^2 + (28 - 44)^2 + (69 - 44)^2 + (43 - 44)^2 + (34 - 44)^2]$ (3 represents number of columns)
   $= 2,958$

---

[2]Thus far Z, t, and chi-square have been considered. The use of analysis of variance introduces still another type of distribution – the F distribution.

TSS =total sum of squares
   $=(44 - 44)^2 + (32 - 44)^2 + ... + (36 - 44)^2$
   =4,408

SSR =residual sum of squares (really the unexplained variation)
   $=$TSS $- $(SSC $+$ SSTr)
   $=4,408 - (2,958 + 520)$
   =930

The computed sum of squares values are then placed in an analysis of variance table so the F values can be computed for each source of variation (Table 14-9).

The computed F ratios for treatments and cities are then compared to tabular F values obtained from the F table in the appendix. The value of the tabular F depends upon the degrees of freedom in both the numerator and the denominator of the F ratio. In the F ratio for the treatment, there are 2 degrees of freedom in the numerator and 8 degrees of freedom in the denominator. If a 0.05 level of significance is being used, the tabular F value for this combination is 4.46. The computed F for the treatments (2.24) is smaller than the tabular F (4.46). This analysis indicates there was *not* a significant difference among the packages in terms of overall consumer preference.

Analysis of Variance for Randomized Block Design **Table 14-9**

Source of Variation	Sum of Squares	Degrees of Freedom	Mean Square	F Ratio
Between Treatments (Packages)	520	2	$\frac{520}{2} = 260$	$\frac{260}{116.2} = 2.24$
Between Rows (Cities)	2,958	4	$\frac{2,958}{4} = 739.5$	$\frac{739.5}{116.2} = 6.37$
Residual Error	930	8	$\frac{930}{8} = 116.2$	
Total	4,408	14		

Therefore, the first null hypothesis—"There is reasonably similar acceptance of all three package designs among buyers"

—cannot be rejected because the evidence just isn't strong enough to show that the difference in sales among the three packages was not the result of sampling error or some other variable.

The computed F for the differences between cities (6.37) did exceed the tabular F value of 3.84 for 4 and 8 degrees of freedom at the 0.05 level of significance. This means the second null hypothesis—"There is reasonably similar acceptance of all three package designs among all five cities"—is rejected. There was a significant difference among the five cities in terms of their purchase patterns of the different packages.

Thus, the analysis has shown that the difference in the appeal of the three packages was not the result of a consistent preference by all consumers, rather it was the result of different preferences for the packages among the five test cities.

Summary of analysis of variance

Analysis of variance is a very flexible statistical technique and with slight modification can be used for a variety of experimental designs. The computations involved are somewhat laborious, especially for a rather large Latin square design, but computers can be used to do all of the calculations in a matter of seconds. One restriction is that it can only be used to analyze experimental data when the treatments (packages in our example) have been randomly assigned to the various experimental units (cities in our example).

MEASURING ASSOCIATION

Regression and correlation analysis

The analytic methods presented thus far enable the researcher to determine whether significant differences exist among groups of data. There are other situations where the researcher is interested in whether a relationship exists among variables, as well as the intensity of this relationship. Regression and correlation analysis are the statistical techniques most frequently used to provide these types of information.

Distinction between regression analysis and correlation analysis

Both of these statistical techniques measure the relationship between a dependent variable and one or more independent variables, but they differ in how they present this relationship. Regression analysis identifies the relationship between variables in the form of an equation, $Y = a + bX$. This equation can also be used to estimate or predict Y values if adequate information exists on the various X (independent) variables.[3]

Correlation analysis, on the other hand, is concerned with the strength of this relationship. The term "coefficient of determination" (r^2) describes the extent of association between the variables being studied. For instance, an r^2 value of 0.37 means that 37 percent of the variation in the values of the dependent variable (Y) is explained by the variation in the independent variable (X). Note that while correlation analysis can be used to show the extent of the relationship between variables, it cannot be used to prove a cause-and-effect relationship. The reason for this limitation is that the researcher can't be sure that the correlation analysis includes all the key variables. There may be other variables that affect both X and Y, but they were not included in the formula.

This was part of the tobacco industry's argument against attempts to link smoking with cancer. Their position is that while there seemingly was a high correlation between smoking habits of people and cancer, a third physiological or psychological factor (such as nerves) could be the real link to cancer. Nervous people smoke more and nervous people may also have a higher incidence of cancer, whether they smoke or not.

Example: The floral industry wants to determine various factors that might be used to explain the variations of florists' flower sales from city to city. A study of 15 cities was undertaken and data were obtained on the flower sales of the "average" florist in each of these cities. One factor felt to be related to sales was the Buying Power Index (BPI) for each city. The BPI is a weighted index developed for each major city by *Sales Management* magazine based on three of the city's characteristics: (1) its effective buying income, (2) its percentage of U.S. retail sales, and (3) its percentage of U.S. population (see Table 14-10).

---

[3]There are a variety of regression formulas that might be used, depending upon the nature and number of variables being studied. If only one independent variable is involved, a simple regression equation can be used to describe the relationship ($Y = a + bX$). If more than one independent variable is involved, a multiple regression formula is used ($Y = a + b_1X_1 + b_2X_2. \ldots$) The number of b values in the formula depends upon the number of independent variables being studied. Both of the above formulas assume that a linear relationship exists between the dependent and independent variables. If a curvilinear relationship exists, different formulas for both simple and multiple regression are used.

Table 14-10 **Flower Sales and BPI of 15 Selected Cities**

City, *i*	(Y) Flower Sales per Florist (0000 omitted)	(X) Sales Management Buying Power Index
1	5.1	0.435
2	5.8	0.361
3	6.5	0.484
4	7.0	0.572
5	5.9	0.482
6	4.8	0.292
7	6.2	0.490
8	7.0	0.504
9	6.5	0.483
10	5.9	0.412
11	6.1	0.437
12	6.2	0.392
13	5.6	0.404
14	6.2	0.444
15	5.2	0.371
	$\Sigma Y = 90$	$\Sigma X = 6.56$

The first step is to place the data into a scatter diagram to determine the general nature of the relationship between the dependent variable (Y), flower sales, and the independent variable (X), the BPI. The scatter diagram will indicate whether the relationship is linear or nonlinear, enabling the appropriate formula to be selected. In this example, it is a linear relationship, so the formula used will be $Y = a + bX$.

Determining a and b values

The specific formulas used to develop the a, b, and r^2 values are as follows:

$$b = \frac{\Sigma XY - \dfrac{(\Sigma X)(\Sigma Y)}{n}}{\Sigma X^2 - \dfrac{(\Sigma X)^2}{n}}$$

$$a = \frac{\Sigma Y}{n} - \frac{b\Sigma X}{n}$$

$$r = \frac{n \cdot \Sigma XY - (\Sigma Y)(\Sigma Y)}{\sqrt{[n \cdot \Sigma X^2 - (\Sigma X)^2] \cdot [n \cdot \Sigma Y^2 - (\Sigma Y)^2]}}$$

The key data are taken from Table 14-10 and plugged into the three formulas.

$$\begin{aligned}
\Sigma Y &= 90 \\
\Sigma X &= 6.56 \\
(XY) &= 39.88 \\
(\Sigma Y^2) &= 545.6 \\
(\Sigma X^2) &= 2.934
\end{aligned}$$

$$b = \frac{39.88 - \dfrac{(6.56)\,(90)}{15}}{2.934 - (6.56)^2}$$

$$b = 7.88$$

$$a = \frac{90}{15} - \frac{\dfrac{15}{7.88(6.56)}}{15}$$

$$a = 2.55$$

$$r = \frac{15 \bullet (39.88) - (90 - 6.56)}{\sqrt{[15 \bullet 2.93 - (6.56)^2] \bullet [15 \bullet 545.6 - (90)^2]}}$$

$$r = 0.887$$
$$r^2 = 0.787$$

Placing these figures into the original formula results in

$$Y = a + b(X)$$
$$Y = 2.55 + 7.88(X)$$

This means that for every one unit change in X, there will be a 7.88 change in the value of Y. Therefore, in a city with a Buying Power Index of 0.675, the flower sales of the average retail florist should be approximately $79,000 dollars.

$Y = \$2.55 + \$7.88(.675)$ (remember 0000s were omitted in the computations)

$= \$79,000$

The coefficient of determination (r^2) between the city's flower sales and its BPI was 0.787. This means that 79 percent of the variation from city to city in the average florist's sales is explained by the variation in cities' Buying Power Indices.

Testing the significance of r^2

While $r^2 = 0.79$ suggests a fairly high correlation between florists' sales and the cities' BPI, the question arises as to whether this could have resulted by chance, especially since only a small number of cities was used in the test.

The formula for testing the significance of the relationship for simple linear correlation is:

$$t = \frac{r \sqrt{n-2}}{\sqrt{1-r^2}}$$

In the flower example the computed t is 6.9.

$$t = \frac{0.887 \sqrt{15-2}}{\sqrt{1-0.787}}$$
$$= \frac{3.2}{0.461}$$
$$= 6.9$$

A t table is consulted based on $(n-2)$ degrees of freedom at 0.05 level of significance. The tabular t turns out to be 2.16. Since the computed t exceeds the tabular t, the relationship between florists' sales and the city's Buying Power Index is a significant one.

Multiple correlation

If more than one independent variable is involved, a coefficient of multiple determinants (R^2) can be developed. This R^2 value represents the portion of the total variation in the values of the dependent variable explained by *all* of the independent variables included in the correlation analysis.

In the previous example involving the flower sales of retail florists, a second independent variable could have been the number of supermarkets in each city selling flowers. It would be expected that the sale of flowers in supermarkets would negatively affect florists' sales.

A complete example of the computation in multiple correlation is not provided in this text. A text on business statistics should be consulted to obtain the formulas and procedures. The user of multiple correlation should be aware of two important factors: (1) Multiple correlation models assume the independent variables (Xs) are not correlated among themselves. When such correlation exists, "multicollinearity" occurs. An example of this error would be using both "education" and "income" as independent variables (predictors), since they are highly correlated with one another. (2) An F test should be used to test the significance of the R^2 obtained. Assume in the previous example (flower sales correlated with a city's BPI and its number of supermarkets) that the R^2 was 0.72. Does this indicate a significant relationship?

$$F = \frac{R^2 / (K-1)}{(1 - R^2) / n - K}$$

$$= \frac{.72 / 2}{(1 - 0.72)} \over 12$$

$$= 15.7$$

n = number of observations

K = total number of variables

An F table is consulted using 2 degrees of freedom for the numerator and 12 degrees of freedom for the denominator.

computed F = 15.7

tabular F = 3.89 (0.05 level)

This suggests that the relationship between the dependent and independent variables (identified by $R^2 = 0.72$) is a significant one.

Partial correlation

This test is used when the influence of *more than one* independent variable is to be evaluated. It enables the researcher to determine the relationship between a selected independent variable and the dependent variable while holding the other independent variables constant. For example, in the flower study a partial correlation R^2 value might be:

$R^2_{12.3} = 0.35$

1 = flower sales

2 = BPI

3 = number of supermarkets

This indicates that 35 percent of the variation in flower sales from city to city that is not explained by the number of supermarkets is explained by the Buying Power Index.

Rank correlation when ordinal data are involved

The previous correlation tests all require that the dependent variable be metric data. Correlation can still be measured when this requirement is not met, but the tests are less powerful. Spearman's rank correlation is the test most frequently used to measure correlation among ordinal data. Its formula is:

$$r_s = 1 - \frac{6\Sigma D^2}{n(n^2 - 1)}$$

D = absolute difference between rankings
n = number of observations

Example: This procedure will be illustrated by the example of the River City Bank found in the previous chapter. You recall that the bank was undertaking an in-depth analysis of its customers. It surveyed a portion of them to obtain information on their attitudes toward the bank's offerings and overall operations. In this example the survey results from only 10 customers will be used to keep the analysis relatively simple. The bank wants to determine whether there is an association between the number of years people were customers of the bank and their overall rating of the bank. Since the customer ratings are in the form of ordinal data, rank correlation should be used.

Table 14-11
Customers' Ratings of Bank
Related to the Number of Years They Have Used Bank

Customer	Rating Score on Bank		Number of Months a Customer of Bank		D	D^2
1	42	(3)	120	(1)	2	4
2	49	(1)	115	(2)	-1	1
3	33	(9)	35	(9)	0	0
4	41	(5)	42	(7)	-2	4
5	29	(10)	14	(10)	0	0
6	46	(2)	106	(3)	-1	1
7	38	(7)	94	(4)	3	9
8	42	(3)	42	(7)	-4	16
9	37	(8)	59	(6)	2	4
10	39	(6)	72	(5)	1	1
					$\Sigma D^2 =$	40

The numbers in parentheses in Table 14-11 indicate the ranking of the number in relation to other numbers in the same column.

Customer 4's rating of the bank was 41 which was the fifth highest rating among the 10 customers sampled. The same person had been a customer for 42 months, the seventh longest period among the 10 customers surveyed.

The D values are the difference in the two rankings for each customer. For customer, 4, it is 5 minus 7 or -2. The correlation between the individuals' ratings and their years as bank customers can now be determined.

$$r_s = 1 - \frac{6 \Sigma 40}{10(100 - 1)}$$

$$= 0.76$$

$$r_s^2 = 0.58$$

Other measures of association

Contingency coefficient (value) — This test is used to measure the association between two sets of nominal data. Its chief limitation is that its upper limit cannot be 1, but rather is determined by the number of cells in the category matrix. Also, it can only be used when the number of categories is the same for each variable, i.e., number of rows = number of columns. The computed C is then compared to the maximum C, and the closer the two are in value, the greater the association

$$\text{computed } C = \sqrt{\frac{\chi^2}{n + \chi^2}} \qquad \text{maximum } C = \sqrt{\frac{(r-1)}{r}}$$

$$r = \text{number of rows}$$

$$\chi^2 = \text{chi-square}$$

If $r = 2$, then maximum
$C = 0.707$

Three emerging statistical techniques

The increased accessibility of computers has resulted in wider use of some statistical techniques that previously were viewed as being too complex or too esoteric for the analysis of research data. Three techniques especially useful to marketers are factor analysis, discriminant analysis and cluster analysis. Each of these methods is briefly described to give the reader a general understanding of its potential value as an analytic tool.[4]

Factor analysis

This term describes a group of statistical methods whose primary purpose is condensing information contained in a fairly large number of variables into a smaller set of new variables or "factors." This reduction will take place with a minimum loss of the information contained in the original variables.

Example – A questionnaire for consumers has 30 questions, each dealing with a slightly different aspect of their buying behavior. Factor analysis is used to identify some basic underlying factors shared by two or more of these original 30 dimensions. This will enable the original 30 to be reduced to a significantly smaller number of dimensions (factors), making the results more useful to researchers and other users of the data.

Factor analysis is an interdependent technique since all variables are evaluated simultaneously. The original data are not divided into dependent and independent variables.

Discriminant analysis

This technique is used when the researcher wishes to explain differences between groups or wishes to classify subjects into groups based on their scores on several variables. What distinguishes heavy beer drinkers from moderate beer drinkers? from nondrinkers?

Discriminant analysis involves deriving a linear combination of independent variables that maximizes between-group differences and minimizes within-group differences. Thus the researcher will not only learn more about how heavy beer drinkers differ from moderate drinkers, he/she will also be able to use that data to predict the beer drinking habits of other subjects based on certain characteristics of those subjects.

Discriminant analysis, like regression analysis, uses data on independent variables to estimate the value of a dependent variable. Unlike regression analysis, however, it can involve two or more dependent variables and the dependent variable can be nonmetric (nominal or ordinal) data.

---

[4]If the reader desires more information about these techniques, two sources that provide concise, easily understood explanations are *Multivariate Data Analysis* by Joseph Hair, Jr., et al., Petroleum Publishing Company, Tulsa, Oklahoma, 1979 and *Marketing Research: Methodological Foundation* by Gilbert Churchill, The Dryden Press, 1976.

Possible uses: Determine the characteristics that differentiate among
- — poor, mediocre and good salespersons.
- — purchasers of our product vs. purchasers of competitor's products.
- — light, moderate, heavy users of a product/service/facility.

Cluster analysis

Cluster analysis allows the researcher to search through large amounts of data on a number of different variables, with the goal of placing subjects with similar characteristics in clusters.

This technique is similar to discriminant analysis in that it groups subjects so that within-group similarities are maximized, and between-group similarities are minimized. Unlike discriminant analysis, however, this technique does not use independent variables to estimate dependent variables, nor are the groups/segments known beforehand.

Discriminant analysis starts with groups of subjects and then searches for similarities between each group's members. Cluster analysis, on the other hand, starts with diverse individual subjects and seeks to place them in clusters based on some discovered similarities.

This technique is ideal for situations where it is desirable to segment a market, but the basis for such segmentation is not as yet known. Cluster analysis will uncover similarities among subjects, allowing clusters (segments) to be formed. The researcher must then determine if such clusters can be used as viable market segments.

Possible uses are:

- — identify similar cities to be used for test markets.
- — cluster a market to identify potential factors to use as advertising appeals.
- — cluster subjects on the basis of activities to discover potential needs for new products/services.

A major problem confronting researchers is determining which of the many statistical tests available is the appropriate one to use. The ability to perform the mathematics isn't nearly as important to the researcher as knowing which test should be used. Compu-

SUMMARY OF STATISTICAL TESTS

ters can perform the computations, but the researcher has to select the test.

The five questions presented in Chapter 13 are the best criteria the researcher can use when selecting the appropriate statistical test.

1. What is the test supposed to do? Should it determine whether significant differences exist between groups of data or should it determine whether an association exists between two or more variables?
2. What measurement scale is involved: nominal, ordinal, interval, or ratio?
3. How many samples are involved?
4. Are the samples independent?
5. How many variables are to be measured?

Table 14-12 is a matrix in which all five of these criteria are used to categorize the various types of statistical tests when group differences are to be measured. Table 14-13 does the same thing but also identifies the tests to use when the association between groups is to be evaluated. Most of the tests listed in these tables were touched on (if only briefly) in the previous sections. But there are some that were not covered in this text and the interested researcher should consult other statistics texts to obtain more extensive descriptions of them.

Table 14-12   Tests for Group Differences

| Measurement Level | One-Sample Case | Two-Sample Case | | k-Sample Case | |
		Related Samples	Independent Samples	Related Samples	Independent Samples
Nominal	Binominal χ^2 one-sample	McNemar	Fisher exact probability χ^2 two-sample	Cochran Q	χ^2 for k samples
Ordinal	Kolmogorov-Smirnov one-sample test Runs test	Sign-test Wilcoxon matched pairs	Median test Mann-Whitney U test Kolmogorov-Smirnov Wald-Wolfowitz	Friedman two-way ANOVA	Median extension Kruskal-Wallis one-way ANOVA
Interval and Ratio	t test	t test of differences	t test	Two-way ANOVA	One-way ANOVA

Source: Adapted from S. Siegel, *Nonparametric Statistics for the Behavioral Sciences* (New York: McGraw-Hill, 1956).

Table 14-13

Tests for Association Between Groups

T = Independent Variable K = Dependent Variable		Type and Number (T−k) of Independent or Predictor Variables					
		Interval/Ratio		Ordinal		Nominal	
		T−k=1	T−k>1	T−k=1	T−k>1	T−k=1	T−k>1
Type and Number (k) of Dependent or Criterion Variables	Interval or Ratio						
	k=0		Factor analysis Cluster analysis				Factor analysis with dummy variables cluster analysis
	k=1	Regression analysis	Multiple regression analysis				Multiple regression analysis with dummy variables
	k>1		Canonical correlation				Canonical correlation with dummy variables
	Ordinal						
	k=0				Kendall's coefficient of concordance (W)		
	k=1			Spearman's rank correlation (r_s) Kendall's rank correlation (τ)			
	k>1						
	Nominal						
	k=0					Contingency coefficient index of predictive association	Contingency coefficient index of predictive association
	k=1		Linear discriminant analysis				
	k>1		Multiple discriminant analysis				Multiple discriminant analysis with dummy variables

Source: Maurice Tatsouka and David Tiedman, "Statistics as an Aspect of Scientific Method in Research on Teaching," in N. L. Gage, ed., *Handbook of Research on Teaching* (Chicago: Rand McNally, 1963), pp. 154-155.

INTERPRETA-TION OF DATA

In Chapter 13 a distinction was made between the activities of analysis and interpretation. Analysis involves placing each group of collected data into some order or format and then deriving meaning from them. Interpretation goes one step further in that it ties these various groups of analyzed data together or combines them with other existing data, resulting in "information" pertinent or relevant to the study. Thus, analysis involves dissecting the data, whereas interpretation involves synthesizing or reassembling the data into a form that enables the objectives of the study to be accomplished.

In an instructional text such as this one, attempts are made to establish a set of steps or procedures to be followed to successfully perform a given activity. No such neat set of procedures can be established for "interpretation" because each study requires unique interpretative activities. However, there are two conditions necessary for effective interpretation: (1) an understanding of the inductive and deductive reasoning processes and (2) objectivity in deriving conclusions.

Understanding inductive and deductive reasoning processes

The two methods used in drawing inferences from data are *induction* and *deduction*. Deductive reasoning involves moving from general premises to specific conclusions. The example frequently cited to illustrate this process is the following syllogism:

- All men are mortal (major premise).
- Socrates is a man (observed fact or minor premise).
- Therefore, Socrates is mortal (inferred conclusion).

This third statement, "Socrates is mortal," logically follows or can be deduced from the preceding two statements.

In contrast to this technique is induction. In this reasoning process, generalizations, principles, or even laws are derived by tying together a number of separate facts or observations.

- In experiment 1, water was heated and it boiled (observed fact).
- In experiment 2, water was heated and it boiled (observed fact).
- In experiment 3, water was heated and it boiled (observed fact).
- In experiment 4, . . . , etc.

From these separate instances, the following generalization emerges:

- Water, when heated, will boil.[5]

Deductive reasoning in marketing research

Deductive logic involves a set of sentences (called an *argument*) in which the truth of the last sentence (the *conclusion*) follows logically from the preceding sentences. One pitfall of deductive reasoning is that the format of the argument is sometimes overemphasized and the resulting conclusions suffer. For instance, one branch of deductive reasoning called *propositional logic* is concerned solely with the form of an argument and tends to ignore the validity of the statements:

- All men have two heads.
- Donald Duck is a man.
- Therefore, Donald Duck has two heads.

In the above example, although neither of the first two sentences of the argument is true, the form of the argument is correct. The final statement is a legitimate deduction from the first two statements. So while deduction is an acceptable way to arrive at conclusions, the usefulness of these conclusions depends upon the validity of the major premise and the accuracy of the minor premise. In business examples, these major premises oftentimes are somewhat shaky.

- When mortgage rates rise abruptly, new building starts decline (major premise).
- In 1975, mortgage rates rose abruptly (observed fact or minor premise).
- Therefore, in 1975 new building starts declined (conclusion).

In this example, the conclusion logically flows from the major and minor premises. But the actual result was quite different. Housing starts increased during 1975 because people felt mortgage rates were going to climb even higher in future years. So, while deductive reasoning can be used in business research to derive conclusions, the major premises used in the argument oftentimes are rather tenuous. This reliance on questionable ma-

---

[5]In this illustration, the amount of heat applied in each experiment was ignored since this would merely complicate the example.

jor premises restricts somewhat the success of the deductive process in business.

Inductive reasoning in market research

Inductive reasoning is concerned with developing a series of premises which are then combined with other premises to arrive at a conclusion or a generalization. These individual premises can be obtained from experiments, observations, or surveys.

- John Jones is a Ford owner and would purchase one again.
- Pete Brown is a Ford owner and would purchase one again.
- Marge Smith is a Ford owner and would purchase one again.

From these individual bits of information the following conclusion might emerge:

- The majority of Ford owners would purchase a Ford again.

The inductive method is often described as the empirical or scientific approach to learning, since any conclusions derived via this method are based on actual evidence obtained from experiments or observations. In fact, some researchers feel that knowledge can only be obtained empirically or inductively. They view the deductive process as nothing more than a form of mental gymnastics because it emphasizes the form of an argument rather than the evidence itself. This criticism of the deductive process is too harsh, especially since one of the key tools in the physical sciences is mathematics, a discipline solidly built on the deductive process.

Induction and deduction are more compatible than the previous discussion might imply. In fact, many of the major premises used in deductive arguments are derived by means of the inductive process. "The heaviest car sales occur during the summer months" might be used as the major premise in a deductive argument. The evidence for this premise could have come from the study of seasonal car sales over a period of 30 years. So, an inductively derived conclusion usually acts as the major premise in a deductive argument.

Summary of the reasoning process

There is really nothing mysterious about effective interpretation. It merely involves building up the proper evidence so that conclusions flow smoothly from this evidence. The smooth flow or logic of the conclusion must be apparent not only to the researcher; it also must be apparent to anyone presented with the same total evidence. In the case of deductive reasoning, the major concern is ensuring that the premises used in the argument are valid, whereas in inductive reasoning the central concern is that the various bits of empirical evidence are accurate.

It was pointed out in earlier chapters of this text that objectivity of the researcher is a necessary component of the data-gathering process; but this need for objectivity is even more critical in the interpretation of data. Since researchers control the data that will be included for interpretation, they may be tempted to exclude some or all of it that is alien to their own beliefs of what the study's outcome *should* be.

Objectivity in deriving conclusions

The ideal research project is one in which the researcher can hold a completely neutral position throughout the study. But, how neutral can the sales manager of Company X be when conducting a study on the attitudes of salesmen towards Company X's fringe benefits – benefits which the sales manager was instrumental in introducing? How neutral can a product manager be when carrying out a test on a new toy he has personally recommended? How neutral can an ad agency be when testing an advertisement it developed for a client?

This writer has seen studies with the following stated goals: "The objective of this study is to show that City X needs another municipal swimming pool." "The objective of this study is to show that low morale has led to a high rate of turnover among Company A's sales force." Such stated goals raise serious doubts as to whether the researcher will objectively pursue all data that could influence the results. It is best not to set out to prove a specific point – "The objective of this study is to determine whether City X needs and could support a second municipal swimming pool." "The objective of this study is to determine what factors have caused the unusually high rate of turnover among Company A's salesmen."

It would be foolish to suggest that no effective research can be undertaken unless the researcher is completely neutral. It is almost impossible for the researcher *not* to have an opinion or preference in terms of the study's outcome; but it is mandatory that the researcher subjugate these personal feelings or personal interests as much as possible. Research should not be undertaken only to prove a point. Rather, its purpose should be to objectively investigate all aspects of a condition or situation.

SUMMARY At the outset of Chapter 13 it was stated that of all the activities in the research process, analysis and interpretation demand the greatest skills from researchers. Analysis changes data into "information" by placing each group of collected data into some order or format. Interpretation involves taking these various pieces of information and combining them with other existing information so that the study's objective(s) can be accomplished.

Researchers have a variety of analytic tools from which to choose. They might rely solely on cross-tabulation methods; or they might decide to apply statistical tests to the collected data. Z or t tests, chi-square analysis, analysis of variance, regression analysis, and correlation analysis are the statistical methods most frequently used by marketing researchers in their analytic efforts. Although some of these statistical methods are rather complicated to use, the most crucial problem facing researchers is not a computational one. Rather, the most difficult task in knowing *which specific* statistical technique(s) to use. Understanding the capabilities of various statistical techniques is essential to the researcher's successful analysis. The key analytic techniques to be used should be chosen early in the research process, certainly before the data are actually gathered.

Interpretation involves synthesizing the collected data in an objective manner and then deriving conclusions or meaning in light of the study's objectives or hypotheses. There is no set procedure which, if followed, will guarantee successful interpretation.

If the data are not properly analyzed, the accompanying interpretation will suffer. Conversely, if the various groups of data are all properly analyzed but then tied together in a questionable manner, improper conclusions will result. Thus, no matter how carefully the early steps of the research process are conducted, if the analysis and interpretation of the collected data are not done properly, the entire study becomes suspect.

QUESTIONS AND EXERCISES

1. How does correlation differ from regression analysis?
2. The relationship between new car sales and disposable personal income is $r^2 = 0.71$. Explain what this r^2 means.
3. What are some of the key factors to consider when determining which statistical technique to use for analyzing the data?

4. What is the major problem in using deductive reasoning when interpreting marketing data?

5. Why must the researcher maintain a position of objectivity when interpreting and analyzing data?

CASES

Case 1

The sales manager for the Lombardi Furniture Company wants to develop a technique for accurately estimating potential furniture sales so that sales potential figures can be developed for any given region. He feels that a strong relationship exists between furniture sales in an area and new housing starts. He requests you, the firm's marketing researcher, to make such an analysis.

Furniture sales and data on new housing starts for 12 areas are contained in the following table. Your job is to (a) determine which statistical technique to use, (b) determine what the relationship is between these two variables, and (c) whether it is a significant one.

Area	Furniture Sales (Millions $) Y	New Housing Starts (Hundreds) X
1	6	18
2	4	16
3	6	30
4	9	25
5	2	10
6	4	20
7	3	15
8	6	26
9	8	27
10	7	24
11	5	20
12	8	29
	$\Sigma Y = 68$	$\Sigma X = 260$

Case 2

A sports magazine wants to measure the effect different price offerings have on new subscriptions. It tests three different blocks of customers: (1) professional men, (2) college males, and (3) businessmen. A total of 2,250 men were sent letters (250 in each of 9 cells). One-third of each group received a price offering at 85 percent of normal newsstand price, one-third received an offering at 75 percent of normal newsstand price, and the remaining third received an offering at 60 percent of newsstand price.

The following table shows the response by each group to these various offerings. Was there a significant difference in the responses to each offering? Was there a significant difference in the acceptance rate of each group? What test would be used to answer these questions? Apply that test!

Blocks	85% of Regular Price	Treatments 75% of Regular Price	60% of Regular Price
Professional men	96	114	165
College males	90	110	163
Businessmen	114	136	182

Case 3   Associated National Bank of Muncie, Indiana, mailed a survey to 2,400 randomly selected households in its community. It received 1,100 responses. The bank wants to apply some test to determine whether the respondents are representative of Muncie households or whether nonresponse bias occurred. The responses of households broken down by incomes were:

Household Income	Number of Responses
(1) Below $7,000	106
(2) $7,001-10,000	205
(3) $10,001-15,000	341
(4) $15,001-25,000	282
(5) $25,001-50,000	105
(6) $50,000+	61

The bank has access to updated census information on the income of most Muncie households. This data shows that 9 percent of the households are in income category 1, 21 percent in 2, 29 percent in 3, 26 percent in 4, 9 percent in 5 and 6 percent in 6.

What test could be used to determine whether or not the respondents are "representative"? Use the test. Are the respondents representative of Muncie households in terms of income?

15

Presentation of findings

'GOBBLEDY-GOOK'

Our third category of social variables includes ethnic-group identification of the skipper, whether or not the skipper also owned his boat, and the presence of kin ties among members of the crew, including the skipper. There was no significant difference between mean gross stocks for boats skippered by their owners or boats with hired skippers, but most New Bedford boats are in fact owned by individuals or small groups of individuals.

The above paragraph is part of a report on the New England fishing industry prepared by two social scientists. It is a prime example of how good research findings may be wasted because they are poorly presented in the final report.
From March 31, 1981, issue of Wall Street Journal, p. 1.

The final major activity of the research process is the preparation of a report of the findings and its presentation to the appropriate audience. The above example illustrates that the value of a fine research effort can be significantly diminished if a poor job is done in reporting its results. This chapter contains suggestions for making effective written and oral presentations.

The two key factors guiding the preparation of written reports should be the nature of the audience and the original objectives of the project.

WRITTEN PRESEN-TATIONS

Nature of audience

In preparing the written report, the researcher must consider the backgrounds and interests of the audience. What types of information are they expecting—in what terminology and in what depth? When these questions are answered, the resulting report will usually fall somewhere between a highly technical report and a low-level popular report.

The *technical report* is prepared for those specialists who have an interest in, and an understanding of, the technical aspects covered in the project. A report prepared for this audience will be in technical language and provide an in-depth handling of the subject matter.

The *popular report* is intended for persons with only limited interest in the technical aspects of the research methodology and findings. They want the basic findings, presented in a simple uncomplicated manner. This audience would include nontechnicians and even top executives. The style of popular reports is designed to encourage and aid rapid reading and fast comprehension by its users.

When the audience is mixed (technicians and nontechnicians), it will be necessary to develop a composite report serving a variety of segments. In such reports the more technical data may be placed in appendices, and a "highlights" section presenting the study's key findings in summary form is often included at the front of the report. This highlights section is then followed by sections or chapters providing an in-depth coverage of the study's findings.

It may even be necessary to prepare separate reports for specific audiences. For example, a firm interested in switching to a completely computerized inventory control system seeks information about other companies who have made such a change. In presenting the findings the researcher could prepare one report for executives and administrators telling them about the expenditures needed for the equipment and facilities, as well as the expected savings in time, personnel, and other costs. A more technical report would then be prepared for the accounting department, showing the various changes needed in recordkeeping if a different computer system were to be adopted. A third report might also be necessary to provide lower-level managers with information on the possible changes in their particular areas if a new computer system were installed.

Research objective(s)

The second key factor guiding the preparation of the report is the need to present the collected data in a manner that enables the project's original objective(s) to be accomplished, i.e., "The objective of this project is to provide an evaluation of four sites as potential store locations." The ensuing report should provide the information needed to make such an evaluation.

Organization of written reports

Although there is no single format which all reports should follow, there are some ingredients basic to most of them. Figure 15-1 contains those components crucial to most research reports. Each component is then more fully discussed.

Figure 15-1   **Components of Written Reports**

Initial Information
 – Title Page
 – Letter of Transmittal
 – Table of Contents
Synopsis
Introduction
Objectives – Hypotheses
Methodology
Limitations
Presentation of Findings
Conclusion/Recommendations
Appendices

Initial information

This includes all of the material that acquaints the reader with the general nature of the study.

Title page — The title of the report, information on who prepared it, who sponsored it, and the date it was completed should appear on the title page.

Letter of transmittal — This is an actual letter to the person or agency requesting the research; it describes the conditions under which the study was initiated and is a formal authorization for the study. In some cases different letters of transmittal are developed for each key person receiving a copy of the report. This letter is an important component of the report only if authorization for the study is crucial.

Table of contents — The chapters, sections, or other key headings used in the report and the pages on which each is found are listed. Readers interested only in specific parts of a lengthy report will use this table to find them. The importance of the table of contents varies with the length and complexity of the report. For very short reports, it is questionable whether one is even needed. No rule-of-thumb exists in terms of the minimum number of pages needed before a table of contents is included.

Synopsis

This section may be given any of a variety of labels — Executive Summary, Highlights, Abstract, etc. Regardless of its name, its purpose is to provide a concise summary of the study's findings, conclusions, and recommendations for those who will not read the full report.

The synopsis should be only one or two pages in length and can only be written after the total report is completed. Because of its brevity, it requires efficient use of words, and its material should be presented from a managerial rather than a technical perspective.

Introduction

This is the beginning of the actual written report and provides the reader with information on the factors necessitating the study. The length and depth of the report's introduction depend on the nature of the audience. In situations where the report will be used only by people already familiar with the problem situation (disorder), the introduction can be brief. But where the audience may have limited a background, the introduction will have to provide enough information so that they can understand why the study was undertaken.

Statement of objectives and working hypothesis

Once the conditions necessitating the research have been described, the specific goals or objectives of the research project are given. Any hypotheses to be tested in the study should be formally stated in this part of the report.

Description of methodology

The statement of objectives tells the readers what the research is intended to accomplish, and the methodology section describes how it was done. A general description of the secondary sources used may be included in this portion of the report, but its major purpose is to describe the techniques used to obtain primary data. Not only must these techniques be described (briefly), their use should also be defended, e.g., why mail questionnaires were used.

If a sample was involved, the universe from which the sample was drawn should be described along with the methods used to select the sample members and to determine the sample size. How technical should this section be? Enough information should be included to enable readers to evaluate the accuracy and representativeness of any data collected from the sample. In technical reports a great deal of space might be devoted to a description of the sampling method, whereas in a popular report, in-depth information on sampling procedures is not that important. If personal interviews were used, a brief description of how the interviewers were chosen and the training (if any) they received should be included.

Finally, the methodology section should also contain a brief description of the tools used to analyze the collected data—chi-square, correlation, bivariate analysis, etc. An in-depth description of these techniques should be postponed until later portions of the report when the results from these statistical tools are presented.

Acknowledgement of study's limitations

The readers of the report should be made aware of the study's limitations. "These results are based on a survey in Des Moines,

Iowa, and are not necessarily representative of the United States in general." "Only a 15 percent response was received to the mail questionnaire." "The sample was drawn from a list of Ohio manufacturers that is six years old, and thus may not be representative of today's situation."

Statements on the study's limitations are intended to identify certain weaknesses which might affect its results. While researchers should be candid in describing these limitations, they should not go overboard. Too much emphasis on the study's shortcomings tends to raise doubts about its credibility.

If the research report is to be divided into chapters, the "Introduction," "Statement of Objectives," "Description of Methodology," and "Limitations of Study" might all be included in Chapter 1. However, if a lengthy "Methodology" section is necessary, it might be treated as a separate chapter.

Presentation of findings

This section presents the information collected in the study and comprises the majority of the report. It should be emphasized again that in most research projects a lot of information is collected that may not be pertinent; thus this section should include only information related to the study's objectives. If data are not properly culled, the reader will be overwhelmed with a variety of facts and figures and could easily miss the study's key findings.

Depending on the amount and variety of data to be presented, the findings might encompass three or four chapters. For example, the study may have involved gathering data on the effectiveness of new-car warranties as a selling tool. The findings could be divided as follows: one chapter devoted to secondary data on warranties; a chapter devoted to survey results from new-car buyers; a chapter devoted to results of a study among people with cars two to five years old; and a chapter devoted to data collected from personal interviews with new-car distributors.

If the chapters are fairly lengthy (more than eight pages), it helps readers if short summary sections are included. The chapters on findings should not only contain the data collected, they should describe any of the analyses performed on this data and the analytic tools used.

Conclusions and recommendations

This part of the report is usually of most interest to the reader since it pulls together all the key data and specifically relates them to the study's objectives. If hypotheses were established, it is a good idea to restate each one in this section, followed by the evidence for its acceptance or rejection. This may be the only part of the report that some people read. For that reason it really acts as a summary of all the key information presented in the preceding portions of the reports.

Conclusions — These are succinct statements flowing from the analysis and interpretation of the results. They should be an objective interpretation of what the collected data really indicate.

Recommendations — These translate the conclusions into specific actions. The obligations of the researcher to make recommendations is often questioned. The researcher is supposedly an expert in the gathering and analysis of data that can be used in making decisions. But he/she usually lacks the broad company or industry perspective needed to formulate sound recommendations. This is the difference between a consultant and a researcher. A consultant is selling knowledge of a particular procedure or industry. A researcher is selling skills as a data gatherer/analyst. The consultant's forte is recommending actions that should be taken by a person/firm/industry. The researcher's primary job is deriving the information that will enable others to make decisions.

In those cases where the researcher is requested to make recommendations, such recommendations should be viewed as research counsel. The researcher is responsible for providing good counsel, but management still has the responsibility of deciding whether or not to act on this counsel.[1] Additional discussion of the researcher's role in translating research results into specific courses of action for management is found in Chapter 16.

Appendix

An appendix acts as the "catch-all" section of the report. What types of data should it contain? All data germane to the study's findings, but which would disrupt the logical flow of information if presented in the body of the report. Such items would be in-depth descriptions of the sample design; the sample components and the statistical technique used for determining the sample size; lengthy statistical tables; copies of the questionnaires used in the study; and, if personal or telephone interviews were used, the instructions given to the interviewers.

---

[1]Committee Reports, "Preparation and Presentation of the Research Paper." *Journal of Marketing*, Vol. 13, No. 1, pp. 62-72.

Prior to writing, the researcher should deal with two key questions: "Who will read this report?" "What is the purpose of the report?" An illustration frequently used to describe a person who tends to be boring or wordy is "You ask him the time, and he tells you how to build a clock." This illustration also represents the differences between managers (data users) and researchers (data gatherers). Managers want the specific findings of the research (they want the "time"), whereas researchers tend to be more concerned with the process used to obtain the information and methods used to analyze the data (they want to discuss how the clock works). The person preparing the report must recognize this difference in perspective and prepare the report in a manner that best fits the needs of the *user*.

Preparation of written reports

Length of report

A safe rule-of-thumb to follow in preparing reports for business is: the higher the position of the reader, the shorter the report. The nature of the material appropriate for various audiences was touched on in the earlier sections of this chapter when technical and popular reports were discussed.

Too often writers — especially students — are overly concerned with the report's length. They determine what is an acceptable length and write in a manner that ensures meeting that goal. A minimum number of pages (30 or 40) should never be set as a goal since this usually results in including information of little value to the readers.

Use common terminology whenever possible

The following statement taken from a research report illustrates the type of writing that turns readers off. "The use of the analytical techniques of the behavioral sciences will gradually revolutionize the communication arts by predicating their practice upon a body of demonstrably general principles which will be readily available to creative people for increasing their knowledge of consumer responses to advertising communications."[2] This researcher may have felt he was making a profound statement, but the vast majority of people reading this sentence would call it "gobbledygook"!

Remember, the reader, not the writer, dictates the style of language. Strive for simplicity by using language that will be

[2]S. H. Britt, "The Writing of Readable Research Reports," *Journal of Marketing Research*, May 1971, p. 265.

understood by the majority of your audience. This does not mean abandoning all technical terms, but when technical language is used, define these terms so there is no confusion among readers as to their meanings.

Thus words like "random" and "city" should replace "stochastic" and "metropolis." "Now" says the same thing as "this point in time," and "conclude" is much easier to understand than "finalize the termination."

A few years ago the chemical division of an oil company spent large amounts of money reinventing (from scratch) a pesticide that one of its own researchers had discovered five years earlier, but had buried in a tedious, unreadable report.[3]

Have one final writer

When more than one researcher is involved with the project, a great deal of time can be saved if each is assigned specific sections of the report to prepare. Since no two people write in a similar manner, the final report might possibly be in two or three different writing styles. To overcome this problem, one person should be given responsibility for overseeing the entire report, tying it together so that a single writing style emerges.

Develop an outline prior to writing

It is not necessary to postpone the actual writing of the report until all the data have been collected and analyzed and conclusions drawn. Some portions of the report, especially those dealing with secondary data, can be written while the primary data of the report are being gathered. This means that a comprehensive outline of the report must be developed early so that the general nature of the data to be included in each section is identified before any writing is undertaken.

Follow acceptable report format

Use a consistent format for chapter and section headings. Footnoting key sources will also add to the report's clarity. But of equal importance is the fact that such practices enhance the report's appearance and quality in the eyes of the reader. Guidelines on these mechanics are found in books such as Moyer, *The*

---

[3]"Confused, Overstuffed Corporate Writing Often Costs Firms Time and Money," *Wall Street Journal,* August 28, 1980, p. 19.

Research and Report Handbook, or Turabian's *A Manual for Writers of Term Papers, Theses and Dissertations.*[5]

Plan on rewriting

The person preparing the report should realize that a great deal of rewriting will be necessary and should not strive for a "near-perfect" first draft. In fact, knowing that rewriting will occur often enables writers to develop a rough first draft that is usually superior to one in which they "sweat blood" to find words or sentences that are just right. Another advantage of numerous rewrites is that succeeding drafts usually become more concise.

Don't let time constraints lower the quality of the report

The writer needs adequate time to prepare the report, especially if a number of rewrites are needed. Too often, good research is buried in a report that had to be hastily prepared to meet a Monday morning deadline. A common complaint of report writers is, "If only I had more time. . . ."

Student research projects are especially prone to being hampered by time. Students don't realize the amount of time that is needed to compile an effective report and often wind up with only a weekend for its preparation.

Make effective use of graphic materials

Whenever tables, charts, or graphs are included in the report, the writer should make two contradictory assumptions about how the reader will use them. The writer should assume that (1) the reader will not even look at the graphic materials, and (2) the reader will read only the graphic materials and ignore the written portions of the report.

If it is assumed that the reader will *not* look at the graphic material, then the important material contained in these tables, graphs, and charts must be adequately described in the written portion of the report. Such written descriptions should present only key data and not discuss all the information in a table or chart.

If it is also assumed that only the graphic materials will be read, the writer will construct these tables in a manner so that

---

[4]Ruth Moyer, E. Stevens and R. Switzer, *The Research and Report Handbook,* (New York: John Wiley & Sons, 1981). Kate L. Turabian, *A Manual for Writer of Term Paper, Theses, and Dissertation,* 3rd ed. (Chicago: University of Chicago Press, 1971).

they are completely self-explanatory. They will be labeled and organized so that the reader knows what data are being presented, where it was obtained and what it represents without having to refer to the written part of the report.

Suggestions for appropriate use of graphics[5]

1. Be temperate in your use of graphics. Too many graphics tend to overwhelm the report. Fewer graphics usually result in each getting more attention from the reader.
2. Don't convey too much information in one graphic. It is better to use two simple charts than one that is complex to interpret.
3. Tie graphics to the written presentation by placing them adjacent to the section of the report in which they are discussed.
4. Recognize the strengths and drawbacks of the various types of graphics: simple tables, line diagrams, pictographs, pie charts, etc.

It may be necessary to use more than one form of graphic presentation for the same set of data. The unit sales of three products over the past eight years are contained in Table 15-1. The differences in sales growth among the three could be best shown in a line chart, so both forms of data presentation are used (see Table 15-1 and Figure 15-2).

Table 15-1   Unit Sales of Acme Company's Three Typewriters
(1970-1977)

Year	Style A (000s)	Style B (000s)	Style C (000s)
1970	17.3	15.2	12.5
1971	18.2	16.1	12.8
1972	18.2	16.8	13.5
1973	17.7	16.9	11.9
1974	18.4	17.5	12.2
1975	19.5	18.3	13.3
1976	18.4	19.2	13.6
1977	18.9	20.4	13.6

The number of copies to be made of the report will influence the type and quality of graphic materials. Where only a small number of copies are to be made, the use of high-quality graphics may be restricted because of prohibitive costs per copy.

---

[5]R. L. Shorter, *Written Communications in Business*, 3rd ed. (New York: McGraw-Hill, 1971), pp. 403-405.

Arranging tabular data — The writer has to decide what is to be emphasized in the data and then structure the tables so that this emphasis emerges. The following three tables all contain the same basic information but emphasize different points.[6] Each table gives a hypothetical breakdown of sawmills (in terms of production capacity) in six southern states. Table 15-2 contains totals only, with no attempt made to place the information in percentages. While this table is simple in structure, it is difficult to make comparisons on either an interstate or intrastate basis.

Table 15-2

Total Number of Sawmills by Size (Capacity of Production)

State	Small	Medium	Large	Total by State
Alabama	402	266	34	702
Arkansas	158	128	41	327
Georgia	357	142	12	511
Louisiana	78	99	37	214
Mississippi	202	154	40	396
Texas	90	121	25	236
Total	1,287	910	189	2,386

The nature of the comparison differs between Table 15-3 and Table 15-4. Although both present the data in percentage form, each approaches the presentation in a different manner. Table 15-3 emphasizes the location of sawmills according to size whereas Table 15-4 depicts the composition of sawmills within each of the six states. Both of these arrangements of data are accurate and logical, but their real value hinges on the purpose of the research.

Table 15-3

Number of Sawmills by Size and Capacity of Production (In Percentages of Total Mills in Size Groups)

State	Small	Medium	Large
Alabama	31.2	29.2	18.0
Arkansas	12.3	14.0	21.6
Georgia	27.7	15.6	6.3
Louisiana	6.1	10.9	19.6
Mississippi	15.7	16.9	21.2
Texas	7.0	13.4	13.3
Total	100.0	100.0	100.0
Base total	(1,287)	(910)	(189)

[6]These three tables were taken from the textbook by David Luck, Hugh Wales, and Donald Taylor, *Marketing Research*, 2nd ed. (Englewood Cliffs, N.J.: Prentice-Hall, 1961), pp. 286-287.

Figure 15-2

Unit Sales of Acme Company's Three Typewriters
(1970-1977)

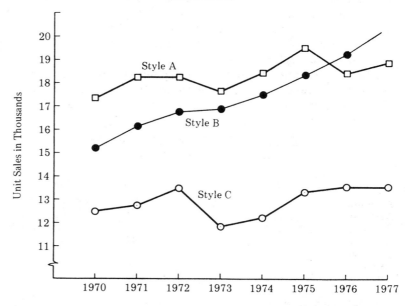

Table 15-4

Number of Sawmills by Size and
Capacity of Production
(In Percentages of Total Mills in Size Groups)

State	Small	Medium	Large	Total
Alabama	57.3	37.9	4.8	100
Arkansas	48.3	39.1	12.6	100
Georgia	69.8	27.8	2.4	100
Louisiana	36.4	46.3	17.3	100
Mississippi	51.0	38.8	10.2	100
Texas	38.1	51.3	10.6	100
Total	53.9	38.1	8.0	100

Computer graphics

In the preceding chapter dealing with the analysis of data, computer graphics were classified as an informal analytic tool. These printouts can also be used as part of the graphic presentations used in the final reports. Their use in the report should be guided by the same suggestions in the preceding section dealing with the "effective use of graphics."

The researcher may be asked to present his/her findings orally to interested parties. Such presentations may be in an informal setting in which the researcher sits face to face with a rather small group, or the researcher may be expected to provide an elaborate presentation to a large audience using visual aids to clarify and strengthen statements.

ORAL PRESEN-TATIONS

The use of oral presentations does not eliminate the need for written reports, and such reports should still be developed and distributed to the audience. Regardless of how spectacular the oral presentation, the audience usually retains only a small portion of what is said and needs the written reports for later reference.

The amount of preparation needed for an oral presentation varies. Informal sit-down presentations are usually "give and take" sessions where the researcher summarizes the study's findings and members of the audience ask questions when elaboration or clarification is desired. It is assumed that the audience will already have read portions or all of the report and merely want to have the highlights reinforced by the researcher.

Informal oral presentation

A formal presentation usually necessitates quite a bit of preparation by the researcher. These steps should precede such presentations: (1) Find out the nature and size of the audience; (2) find out what type of room or facility will be used for the presentation; (3) choose the audio-visual methods (slides, graphs, overlays, etc.) that will most effectively present the data; and (4) decide what portions of the findings should be highlighted.

Formal oral presentation

Don't try to cover everything that is presented in the written report. Limit the oral report to basic background information, the key findings, and the conclusions/recommendations. Keep the oral presentation concise, but lively. Don't overwhelm the audience with numerical data. Incorporate charts, slides, or any other visual aids that will reinforce your presentation.

A written report should be made available to the audience. This report can be handed out just prior to the presentation if reference is going to be made to certain tables within it, or it can be handed out at the conclusion of the report if the researcher wants to keep the full attention of the audience on the oral presentation.

At the beginning of this chapter it was stated that an outstanding research effort can be wasted if a poor report is prepared by the researcher. This is especially true in an oral presentation. Some research firms, recognizing this, follow the practice of having all formal presentations made by specialists adept at oral communication, with the actual researchers available in the audience to handle any sticky questions that might arise.

'Bad News' reports

Howard Cosell gained notoriety as a sportscaster for his willingness to "tell it like it is," regardless of who might be hurt by such information. Should researchers adopt the same philosophy in their final reports when the findings are primarily negative? The client might not be too appreciative of such findings especially when they pertain to a favorite product or new concept.

It is important to present negative findings in a tactful manner. Following are some guidelines for such situations.[7]

1. Don't avoid the negative findings. Remember your role is to aid the client, and you aren't doing this if you mask or play down important negative information.
2. Depersonalize the presentation. Emphasize you are not playing the role of an accuser or judge, you are merely providing your research findings.
3. Whenever possible, work in some positive aspect so the report is not a complete "downer."
4. Emphasize what might be done to counteract some of the negative findings.

SUMMARY ON REPORTS

The weeks and even months of research activities terminate in the preparation and presentation of the study's findings. This final activity can be the most critical part of the entire research undertaking since the report is usually the only tool others have to evaluate the researcher's efforts. Impressions made by the report determine whether the researcher's suggestions are accepted, whether the researcher can establish a reputation in the given subject area, and whether the researcher is rewarded with additional projects.

When preparing a report the key thing to keep in mind are: what are the objectives of the project and who will comprise the audience for this report? Answering these questions will determine whether an elaborate formal presentation is needed or whether a simple written presentation will suffice.

---

[7]Robert W. Joselyn, *Designing the Marketing Research Project* (Mason/Charter Publishers, Inc., 1977), p. 256.

While the contents of the report will vary from project to project, there are certain basic ingredients they all should include such as an "Introduction," "Statement of Objectives," "Description of Methodology," etc. Knowing who the audience is will aid the researcher in deciding how much emphasis should be placed on the various parts of the report and the language used therein. If the audience will be comprised primarily of technicians, more emphasis can be placed on statistical descriptions and methodology. If the audience lacks a technical background, then methodology should be de-emphasized and the findings presented in laymen's language, using very few technical descriptions.

THE RESEARCH PROPOSAL

It probably seems peculiar to the reader that the topic of research proposals is discussed at the *end* of the total research process, when in the normal chain of events it is one of the first research activities. It was felt this subject fits best into this chapter dealing with communications.

Whereas the final report tells what *was done,* the research proposal tells what *will be done* and *why* it should be done. A formal proposal ensures that both parties (researcher and client) understand the purpose of the study and the methods that will be used in its conduct. It also identifies budget and time constraints.

Different types of proposal situations

Research proposals vs. product/services proposals

This discussion of proposal writing deals only with proposals that involve research projects. It does not refer to the type of proposals associated with such situations as when Martin Marietta submits a proposal to NASA for developing some space equipment, or when Ford submits a proposal (bid) to a car rental agency to supply its automobiles for the coming years.

In-house vs. external research

If the research is to be performed as an in-house project (i.e., research department carrying out a test market for one of its own divisions), then the proposal from the researcher may be just a brief set of statements on purpose, procedures to be followed, estimated costs in dollars/man-hours, and expected time of completion.

If the proposal is from an outside research firm, then this proposal is the key factor in determining whether that firm is selected to perform the study. This occurs when private research firms are bidding against other firms for the right to do the research for a business or government agency.

Solicited vs. unsolicited proposals

A solicited proposal takes place when the researcher responds to a request for proposals (RFP) from a firm seeking bids from a number of firms that have the potential to perform such research. The soliciting firm will often provide a written description of its research needs, the time constraints, and in some cases even the financial limits.

An unsolicited proposal occurs when the researcher submits a proposal to Firm A, even though Firm A made no formal request for such a proposal. An important part of any unsolicited proposal is a section aimed at convincing Firm A of its need for the described research.

Government vs. commercial vs. academic research

The format of the proposal will often be determined by the agency for whom the research is being performed. In most situations involving solicited research for government agencies, the proposal format is prescribed in an information booklet accompanying the RFP. In situations where a research proposal is to be submitted to a commercial or nonprofit organization, the research firm has more latitude when choosing the proposal format.

Academic research will be viewed in this text as those situations where the research is being performed to fulfill an academic requirement such as a thesis, professional paper, or dissertation. In some cases the proposal format for academic research may be prescribed by graduate schools, but ususally the student has a great deal of freedom in developing such a proposal.

Basic components of formal proposals

Most proposals should contain the following three components: (1) technical information, (2) management information, and (3) cost information. (Academic research proposals will usually not contain cost information.)

1. Technical information—This portion of the proposal details what you expect to do in your research. The topics generally covered are:

- *Introduction* — Identify the condition(s) necessitating the research and provide an overview of the research effort. Give key information from the literature that defends your position.
- *Presentation of objectives* — State the specific goals of the research project and identify the benefits to be derived from the research.
- *Identification of other issues* — Hypotheses to be tested should be listed, along with additional issues to be considered.
- *Description of methodology* — Specific research techniques to be employed are described along with evidence justifying their use. If samples are to be used, the sampling process should be covered.
- *Description of project's manpower* — Identify the people who will be performing the research, their unique capabilities, and their specific responsibilities on this project.

The above information may be covered in one total section, or may comprise a number of subsections under the heading of technical information. In unsolicited proposals, the most critical aspect is to convince the potential user that the research is really necessary. In a solicited proposal situation, the most critical aspects are your research plan and your firm's research capabilities.

2. *Management information* — This part of the proposal describes in detail how the proposed research will be managed. It should include:

- *Information about the research firm* — Description of the firm's size, structure, past projects (especially those that might be related to the proposal), and facilities or equipment (if crucial to the research).
- *Breakdown of tasks* — Who will perform them, man-hours involved.
- *Work schedule* — Specific listing of the tasks to be performed and the times/dates of their performance.

The management information section must be explicit enough to convince the potential user that the researcher has the capabilities and know-how to perform the described research.

3. *Cost information* — The costs of the proposed project are identified along with a description of the methods used to derive these costs.

- *Pricing summary* — List of all major cost items.
- *Supporting schedules* — A detailed breakdown of each major cost item into its component parts and a description of how these costs were derived.

As stated earlier, while most proposals will contain technical, management, and cost information, the extent to which each is dealt with depends upon the general nature of the proposal (solicited or unsolicited) and the agency for whom the proposal is being prepared. It is not unusual that more time and effort go into the preparation of the proposal than go into the write-up of the project's findings. In fact, some portions of the proposal are often used as introductory sections of the final report.

Evaluating proposals

The persons preparing a proposal can do a more effective job if they are aware of those factors that influence the people who will be evaluating the proposal. Figures 15-3 and 15-4 contain guidelines followed by many evaluators of government proposals. They can also be viewed as guidelines for preparing proposals.[8]

Figure 15-3

Factors Used to Evaluate
Merit of the Technical Approach

- Does the proposal address a problem in the solicitation booklet? If unsolicited, does the proposal deal with a problem of major concern?
- Do the investigators display an in-depth awareness of the extent of the problem? Can it be solved by their approach? Is their approach an efficient and effective means of solving the problem?
- Is there a clear step-by-step description of the work the investigators plan to do?
- Does the technical approach make appropriate use of accepted techniques such as simulations, surveys, models, analogies, comparisons, assessment, iteration, etc.?
- Does the approach have verification? Validation? Course correction capability? Feedback evaluation?
- Is the literature review adequate and timely?

---

[8]The information in Figures 15-3 and 15-4 was condensed from a publication on proposal writing by Harry F. Krueckeberg, *Research Project Proposals — Format and Instructions* (Ft. Collins, Colorado: College of Business, Colorado State University, 1979).

- Will the research make a substantial improvement or advance the state-of-the-art?
- Who will use the results of this research? What will be the overall benefits from the research?
- Are the credentials of the investigators valid for the particular problem that they propose to study?
- Do one or more of the investigators have a past history of research in the problem area? Competence?

Factors Used to Evaluate
Merit of the Management Approach

Figure 15-4

- Are the program plan, work tasks, and work schedule clearly stated and adequate? Does the proposal state objectives? Milestones? End products? Plans for implementation of results?
- Is the work compatible with the budget? Scale of effort? Man-months? Division of labor?
- Does the team have adequate organization? Leadership? Administration? Coordination? Accountability? Control? Incentives?
- Will the management approach assure flow of the results to the user?
- Is the probability of achieving successful results high? Risk versus reward? Cost versus benefit?
- Does the proposal discuss barriers to implementing the results and how will these barriers be overcome?

---

1. "Many fine research undertakings are victims of poor communications." Discuss.

QUESTIONS
AND EXERCISES

2. Under what circumstances might it be necessary to prepare two or three different reports?

3. What is the role of the section "Limitations of Study"?

4. How does a researcher differ from a consultant?

5. What are some key things to keep in mind when developing graphics for the report?

6. What is the difference between unsolicited and solicited research proposals? How does this difference affect the preparation of each type of proposal?

CASES

Case 1

The world is facing an energy crisis. The earth's nonrenewable fossil energy sources such as coal, oil, and natural gas will eventually be depleted if alternative sources of energy are not developed. Solar energy is one alternative that can help alleviate this problem.

There are a number of reasons justifying the interest in solar energy. The use of solar energy as an alternative fuel source can help offset rising utility costs from nonrenewable resources such as natural gas and oil. Solar heating and cooling will be available in the event of fossil fuel curtailment. Solar energy causes the least environmental degradation of all energy sources. And as an ultimate, safe, endless energy supply, solar energy appears to be the most technically feasible.

According to the Solar Energy Industries Association, solar heating and cooling installations for new housing and retrofits are expected to grow from some 2,400 units in place in 1977 to more than 37,000 by 1981. At the end of the ensuing decade (1990), a total energy market in excess of $20 billion annually is forecasted.

Although great things have been predicted for solar energy, thus far its adoption rate for use in commercial buildings or private homes has been very disappointing. The Johnson Corporation is a major manufacturer and distributor of gas furnaces for homes. They are now contemplating becoming involved with the distribution of solar heating systems. Before committing the firm to solar products, however, they first want to learn more about the factors that have caused the unusually slow adoption of solar systems by the public. The Johnson Corporation does not want to tie up its own research staff with this project, so it contacts three commercial research firms and asks them to submit competitive proposals. You are the research director of one of these outside firms. Your task is to prepare a proposal that describes the type of research your firm would perform to shed light on why solar heating systems have had slower than expected adoption by the general public. Describe the methodology you would follow in obtaining these data and give the estimated costs to Johnson for your research efforts.

Case 2

The Boone Brewing Company produces three brands of beer — "Lurk," "BBC," and "Hite." Sales data since 1967 on each brand are contained in the following table. Develop some different graphic methods that will make these data more meaningful than it is in its simple tabular form.

Sales of Three Brands of Boone Beer from 1967 to 1976
(In Millions of Barrels)

Brands	1967	1968	1969	1970	1971	1972	1973	1974	1975	1976
Lurk	102.6	108.9	124.2	118.9	131.7	175.4	182.1	199.1	220.4	236.9
BBC	50.3	62.9	62.4	80.7	115.2	120.1	118.9	138.4	161.2	173.4
Hite	21.2	23.4	29.8	36.3	39.2	37.1	38.4	41.3	42.8	44.4
Totals	174.1	195.2	216.4	235.9	286.1	332.6	339.4	378.8	424.4	454.7

16

Industrial
marketing
research

Dear Sir,

I am returning your Marketing Research Questionnaire unanswered. We do not have a marketing research program of any kind. We never had and we probably never will in the foreseeable future.

We have no new product research going on, no strategy evaluations of any kind, have no idea what our market potential is and we are a successful company. How and why beats me, just lucky I guess. . . .

I, as an individual, am interested in your findings. If the company is able to outlive the present Directors, I will be in a decision-making position and intend to do some modernization. . . . *

The above letter is from an assistant general manager in a medium-sized industrial firm. It is his response to a survey pertaining to his firm's research activities. While this situation does not represent the majority of industrial firms, it does represent a surprising number of companies.

---

*This example was obtained from the following monograph: Lee Adler and Charles Moyer, *Managing the Marketing Research Function*, Monograph Series #5, American Marketing Association, 1977, p. 4.

Most principles of marketing texts recognize that major differences exist between consumer and industrial markets. A separate chapter is usually included to describe the unique characteristics of industrial markets, emphasizing that when developing the marketing mix, different strategies are needed for industrial customers than for final consumers.

CONSUMER VS. INDUSTRIAL MARKETS

In marketing research texts, however, the differences between consumer and industrial markets are seldom acknowledged; the implication being that both markets can be researched in the same manner. In reality, the differences between the two markets significantly affect their respective research activities. The purpose of this chapter is to identify those differences and the changes they require in industrial marketing research.

In Chapter 3 of this text, a procedural model for marketing research was presented. The basic steps of that model apply to marketing research for both consumer and industrial markets. Variations occur, however, in the specific ways these procedures are applied to the two markets. For example, differences exist in the types of data sources used, the sampling procedures employed, the types of survey emphasized, and the analytic techniques applied to the collected data.

Same research procedures used

Before describing the reasons for these variations in research activities, it is necessary first to distinguish an industrial market from a consumer market. Industrial markets are comprised of those firms/agencies that purchase goods and services either to aid in the production of other goods and services or for resale purposes. This includes manufacturing firms, government agencies, public utilities, and educational institutions as well as intermediaries such as retailers and wholesalers.

Industrial market defined

Consumer markets, on the other hand, comprise individuals, families or households who purchase goods and services for their own final consumption.

Although there are a number of major differences between industrial and consumer markets, only those that affect their respective research activities are included in the following list.

Differences between two markets

Consumer markets more numerous – Numerically, consumer markets are much larger than industrial markets. In the United States there are approximately 225 million people and 72.5 million households whereas the industrial market is comprised of only 12-14 million firms/agencies.

Industrial markets bigger dollarwise—The dollar value of industrial market transactions is almost twice the total dollar value of consumer purchases.[1] The reason for this disparity is the complex chain of sale-resale transactions that occur in the industrial market prior to, and following, the production of a product/ service.

Derived demand—The demand for industrial goods is derived from the demand for final consumer goods. If the domestic auto industry has a bad year, the steel industry will also suffer because its sales are closely tied to the demand for automobiles. Because of this relationship, the demand for industrial goods can be very volatile; industrial marketing research must therefore be concerned with general business and economic conditions, levels of inventory, prices of raw materials, etc.

80-20 principle—It is quite common in an industrial market to have a small number of customers account for the vast majority of a firm's sales. The situation is exemplified by the 80-20 principle—80 percent of the business comes from 20 percent of the customers. Such a relationship influences the types of sampling procedures used in industrial markets since a great deal can be learned from surveying only a few larger customers.

Multiple buying influences—When trying to determine which factors influence purchase decisions, the industrial researcher's task is made more difficult by the fact that more than one person is usually involved in making such decisions. A single interview in a firm will usually not uncover key buying influences.

Different buying motives—Quality of service, availability of supplies and consistent quality of materials are critical factors in the purchase decisions made in the industrial market. Industrial buyers are usually more knowledgeable about their own needs and are swayed less by promotional appeals than are consumers.

Other differences—Less frequent purchases are made in the industrial market, but they generally involve greater dollar amounts. Because of these larger dollar outlays, renting and leasing are quite common.

---

[1]Frederick E. Webster, *Industrial Marketing Strategy* (New York: Wiley and Sons, 1979), p. 4.

In addition to the above described differences between industrial and consumer markets, there are some other factors that also affect industrial marketing research activities.

Other factors

Decision makers less accessible — When conducting consumer research, the persons to be surveyed or observed can usually be identified and contacted fairly easily. (This does not imply that a high proportion participate in the research, only that original contacts are reasonably easy to make.)

In industrial markets, not only are the appropriate subjects hard to identify because of multiple buyers, but once identified, these subjects may be difficult to reach directly since many are higher-echelon managers and are shielded by secretaries or assistants from such "intruders" as researchers. In addition, these subjects are less accessible because they travel frequently and have little uncommitted time. The fact that they are being contacted for their business knowledge usually prevents making such contacts in the evening hours or during weekends.

Less emphasis on marketing concept — Most manufacturers of consumer products attempt to follow the marketing concept, i.e., build the firm's offerings around identified customer needs. This concept is not as prevalent among industrial firms, primarily because their research activities are strongly influenced by technically-oriented people who seem to place more emphasis on "distinctive" features and technological breakthroughs.

Less ongoing research — Consumer product firms such as Proctor and Gamble and General Mills can purchase information from Nielson or SAMI that will give them a monthly review of how their products (and their competitors') are doing in terms of unit sales and market share. No similar type of information exists for industrial products from either syndicated firms or the firm's own research staff. There seems to be less interest in continuous monitoring of the sales of industrial products. Part of this is due to the nature of the products themselves (infrequent sales, specially designed, etc.) but also to a difference in philosophy among industrial firms. Many industrial marketers still feel exchanging or gathering information on market positions is a form of industrial espionage.[2]

---

[2]William Hall, "Marketing Research for Industrial Products," *Industrial Marketing Management*, April 1975, p. 209.

Fewer research dollars available—A startling difference between the two markets is the amount each spends on research. This disparity was revealed in a 1978 study of the research activities and expenditures of manufacturers of consumer and industrial goods.[3] The mean expenditure on marketing research by 145 manufacturers of consumer goods (all with formal marketing research departments) was $1.07 million, whereas manufacturers of industrial goods (135 firms in the survey) had mean expenditures of only $257,000.[4] A similar disparity between their research expenditures was found in a 1973 study.

When these marketing research expenditures were broken down on the basis of a firm's annual sales, it was found that the firm's size was not a factor. Consumer goods manufacturers spent more for marketing research in every size category.

While the evidence indicates researchers with industrial firms have fewer research dollars available, the picture isn't totally clear. The old chicken/egg question arises. Do researchers with industrial firms perform less marketing research because they have fewer dollars available, or are fewer dollars spent on industrial marketing research because the researchers initiate fewer studies?

TYPES OF RESEARCH BEING PERFORMED

The major study previously cited also obtained information on the types of consumer and industrial manufacturers research activities. Table 16-1 presents these results, showing the different emphasis placed on each type of research by consumer product firms and industrial product firms.

Table 16-1 contains only 15 different types of research activities, whereas the original study had 32 specific categories. Most of those deleted were those this author felt were less important research categories. Both groups were quite similar in their usage of the deleted categories.

Key findings—The primary finding was that there was a great deal of similarity between the types of research undertaken by consumer product firms and industrial product firms. Areas in which major differences did emerge are now identified.

---

[3]Dik Twedt, *1978 Survey of Marketing Research*, (Chicago: American Marketing Association, 1978).

[4]Ibid, p. 28.

Proportion of Firms Performing Selected Types of Marketing Research*

Table 16-1

	Manufacturers of Industrial Products (n = 199) %	Manufacturers of Consumer Products (n = 186) %
Advertising Research		
Copy Research	37	76
Media Research	43	69
Ad Effectiveness	47	85
Economic and Sales Forecasting		
Short–Range Forecasting	98	90
Long–Range Forecasting	96	87
Business Trends	97	79
Location Studies	84	76
Product Research		
Competitive Product Studies	95	93
Test Existing Products	84	95
Package Research (Design, etc.)	65	83
New Product Acceptance-Potential	93	94
Sales-Market Research		
Market Share Analysis	97	96
Distribution Channel Studies	87	86
Test Markets, Store Audits	43	83
Market Characteristics Studies	97	92

*Research performed either by individual departments or an outside firm.

This information was excerpted from Dik Twedt, *1978 Survey of Marketing Research* (Chicago: American Marketing Association, 1978), pp. 41-43.

— Consumer product firms are significantly more involved with all types of research related to advertising.

— Both groups are heavily involved with economic and sales forecasting, but this type of research is more prevalent among industrial product firms.

— Both groups are heavily involved with most aspects of product research with one exception: industrial product firms are significantly less concerned with research on packaging—its physical characteristics and design.

— Both groups are heavily involved with sales and market analysis, although test markets are dramatically less important to industrial product firms.

DIFFERENCES IN RESEARCH APPLICATIONS The major distinctions between industrial and consumer markets were identified in an earlier section. At that time it was emphasized that in spite of these differences the same general research procedures were appropriate for both types of markets although the specific application of these procedures might differ. In this section these different applications are identified.

Different types of secondary data needed

Many of the secondary data sources listed in Chapter 5 are used by industrial marketing researchers. However, the nature of the information sought usually results in greater reliance on those sources with information about business firms and their activities. Some of the sources most frequently used are listed below.

The *Thomas Register of American Manufacturers,* an annual eight-volume publication of the Thomas Publishing Company of New York, is an excellent source for names of manufacturers in different product categories.

Predicasts and *U.S. Industrial Outlook* are two primary sources of information for researchers assigned sales forecasting responsibilities. Two Department of Commerce publications *Survey of Current Business* and *Business Statistics* provide a variety of information useful to determining past industry sales.

A publication of great value when developing sales potentials is the "Survey of Industrial Purchasing Power," an annual publication of *Sales and Marketing Management.* It is the industrial counterpart of the "Survey of Buying Power," published by the same magazine.

Most states have agencies responsible for bringing industry into their state; they are good sources for information involving location studies. Reports filed with the Securities Exchange Commission provide in-depth information about firms that often can't be obtained from other sources.

Heavy emphasis on SIC data – The market for most industrial products is comprised largely of other manufacturers or middlemen. Information on these firms is usually contained under Standard Industrial Classification (SIC) headings and includes such information as total shipments, number of employees, and size of payroll. Much of this data, provided on a county-wide basis, emanates from state and federal agencies. To make best use of SIC data, the researcher needs to understand the numbering process of the system and should possess a copy of the *Standard Industrial Classification Manual* published irregularly by the Government Printing Office.

Trade association data very important—Most firms belong to one or more trade associations and the publications of these associations are major sources for statistics about a particular industry. These publications also cover a variety of topics relevant to their member firms.

Abstract and indexing services widely used—Because many industrial firms serve unique markets, appropriate secondary data may be difficult to acquire. Thus, they often use the services of such indexing agencies as Chemical Abstracts or Engineering Index to provide information sources on unique topics or groups of customers. These agencies search many data sources (journals, association publications, etc.) to accumulate citations of articles of possible value to their clients.

Firms that have a regular need for secondary data sources might use the services of a retrieval service vendor (RSV). RSVs often provide their clients with in-house terminals and sophisticated software that enable them to continually receive information accumulated from a variety of abstracting and indexing services.[5] Lockheed's DIALOG system is probably the most widely used service along with SDC Search Service and Dow Jones and Co.

Greater emphasis on surveys

Of the three methods available for obtaining primary data, the survey method is most important for industrial researchers. The complexity of the buying process in most industrial markets usually precludes the use of either observations or experiments.[6]

---

[5]James M. Comer and Alok Chakrabarti, "The Information Industry for the Industrial Marketer," *Industrial Marketing Management*, July 1980, p. 67.

[6]Michael Hutt and Thomas Spek, *Industrial Marketing Management* (Chicago: Dryden Press, 1981), p. 378.

And, of the different survey possibilities, personal interviews are used more frequently than either mail or telephone surveys. The reasons for the emphasis on personal interviews are:

— Target population is usually small and geographically concentrated.
— Uniqueness of information sought often requires a personalized questioning process.
— Demonstrations, pictures, or models are often an important element of the interview.
— Greater amounts of information can usually be obtained within the time constraints.

Probability samples not as important

Probability sampling is not used to a great extent among industrial marketing researchers.[7] The reasons are that most markets are fairly small and can be completely surveyed, or the surveys concentrate on the bigger customers in the market. Many industrial researchers ignore sampling; they prefer to obtain information through a series of interviews until satisfied they have obtained an accurate picture of the market.[8]

When sampling is used, the most common method is judgment sampling of knowledgeable persons. Probability sampling is used by those firms involved with mass industrial markets, or where enough customers exist that sample data are needed to estimate market size.

More involvement with planning

Consumer marketing research is intended primarily to provide the data needed to evaluate present and future markets and to identify product potential. While these same tasks are performed by industrial researchers, they also tend to be more involved in

---

[7]L. L. Gordon, "The Methodology of Industrial Market Research," *IMRA Journal*, August 1974, p. 20.

[8]William E. Cox, and Luis Dominguez, "The Key Issues and Procedures of Industrial Marketing Research," *Industrial Marketing Management*, August 1979, pp. 81-93.

providing input to their firm's longer–range marketing plans. Many industrial firms are beginning to realize how much money they have been spending with outside research firms, and are re-evaluating the role they expect their own market research people to play in the firm's planning process.[9] They now use their re-searchers much earlier in the planning process and no longer view them as just "fire fighters," i.e., used only when problems arise.

Less emphasis on sophisticated analysis

Since industrial researchers place less emphasis on sampling in general, and probability samples in particular, it is not surprising that they also use less "sophisticated" methods when analyzing their data. Table 16-2 lists nine analytic techniques and the pro-portion of industrial and consumer firms using each. This infor-mation was obtained from a survey of the persons in charge of marketing research for each of the participating firms.

The study's results strongly suggest a wide difference exists between the two groups in their use of these methods, especially the more sophisticated techniques. Of the nine analytic tech-niques included in the table, only four were frequently used by more than 25 percent of the responding industrial firms.

This finding is not meant to be a criticism of industrial mar-keting research, but rather an acknowledgment that these firms are less enamored of quantitative research and its analysis than are researchers with consumer product firms. Their attitudes are merely an outgrowth of such conditions as fewer firms in their market, emphasis on personal interviews and qualitative data, less emphasis on probability sampling, etc.

Overview of differences

Another view of the differences that exist between consumer and industrial marketing research is provided in Figure 16-1. It re-iterates many of the differences identified in the previous section and provides explanations for these differences.

---

[9]John Roberts, "Marketing Research," *Industrial Marketing,* January 1981, p. 50.

Table 16-2

Use of Analytic Techniques
By Type of Firm
(Percentage Using)

Analytic Tool	Consumer Product Firm (n = 42)	Industrial Product Firm (n = 68)
Regression/Correlation	64	54
Confidence Intervals	76	34
Time Series	67	59
Test of Significance	76	28
Analysis of Variance	41	12
Factor Analysis	36	15
Cluster Analysis	21	9
Multidimensional Analysis	29	6
Discriminant Analysis	31	6

Source: Barnett A. Greenberg et al., "What Techniques Are Used by Marketing Researchers in Business?" *Journal of Marketing,* April 1977, p. 64.

Figure 16-1

Consumer vs. Industrial Marketing Research:
What are the differences?

	Consumer	Industrial
Universe/ population	Large. Dependent on category under investigation but usually unlimited. 72.5 million U.S. households and 215 million persons.	Small. Fairly limited in total population and even more so if within a defined industry or SIC category.
Respondent accessibility	Fairly easy. Can interview at home, on the telephone or using mail techniques.	Difficult. Usually only during working hours at plant, office, or on the road. Respondent is usually preoccupied with other priorities.
Respondent cooperation	Over the years has become more and more difficult, yet millions of consumers have never been interviewed.	A major concern. Due to the small population, the industrial respondent is being over-researched. The purchaser and decision makers in an industrial firm are the buyers of a variety of products and services from office supplies to heavy equipment.

Sample size	Can usually be drawn as large as required for statistical confidence since the population is in the hundreds of millions.	Usually much smaller than consumer sample, yet the statistical confidence is equal due to the relationship of the sample to the total population.
Respondent definitions	Usually fairly simple. Those aware of a category or brand, users of a category or brand, demographic criteria, etc., etc. The ultimate purchaser is also a user for most consumer products and services.	Somewhat more difficult. The user and the purchasing decision maker in most cases are not the same. Factory workers who use heavy equipment, secretaries who use typewriters, etc., are the users and, no doubt, best able to evaluate these products and services. However, they tend not to be the ultimate purchasers and in many cases do not have an influence on the decision making process.
Interviewers	Can usually be easily trained. They are also consumers and tend to be somewhat familiar with the area under investigation for most categories.	Difficult to find good executive interviewers. At least a working knowledge of the product class or subject being surveyed is essential. Preferably more than just a working knowledge.
Study costs	Key dictators of cost are sample size and incidence. Lower incidence usage categories (for example, users of soft-moist dog food, powered breakfast beverages, etc.) or demographic or behavioral screening criteria (attend a movie at least once a month, over 65 years of age, and do not have direct deposit of social security payments, etc.) can up costs considerably.	Relative to consumer research, the critical element resulting in significantly higher per-interview costs are: the lower incidence levels, the difficulties in locating the "right" respondent (that is, the purchase decision maker), and securing cooperation (time and concentration of effort) for the interview itself.

Source: Martin Katz, "Use Same Theory, Skills for Consumer, Industrial Market Research," *The Marketing News*, January 12, 1979, p. 16. Reprinted by permission of American Marketing Association.

Use of outside research firms

A number of industrial product manufacturers use the services of outside research firms in addition to having their own in-house research state. There are four primary reasons for using these outside researchers.[10]

Time — The research may have to be performed quickly and the in-house researchers are tied up or they don't have a large enough staff to complete the research within the time constraints. Also, the outside firm may already have established contacts in the markets to be researched.

Objectivity — Management may want an unbiased study of alternatives and feels the in-house staff might be biased because of previous knowledge or preconceived ideas.

Expertise — The desired research may either require technical skills or equipment not possessed by in-house researchers, or the outside researcher may have extensive experience in the market to be researched.

Anonymity — Management may not wish its firm to be directly associated with the research, and this would be difficult if the staff conducted the research.

Drawbacks of outside researchers

Certain problems can arise when outside researchers are used. One of the most crucial is that the outside research firm may not be familiar with the client firm, its products, or the industry, and may spend a great deal of time obtaining the necessary background (a situation analysis).

Another common problem is the difficulty in establishing effective communications between the client and the outside researcher. Do they agree on the objectives of the research? Is the client willing to provide all of the internal data needed by the researcher? Are key personnel of the client firm willing to spend the time to educate the outside researchers?

A third shortcoming is that outside researchers tend to be more technique oriented and less pragmatic in their research efforts.[11] They are often enamored of sophisticated data gathering and analysis whereas the client usually prefers more practical approaches.

---

[10]Ian MacFarlane and Jim Pepitone, "Outside Consultant for Marketing Research," *Industrial Marketing*, October 1979, pp. 71-73.

[11]Gordon, p. 19.

Key differences exist between industrial and consumer markets that affect their respective research activities. Although both use the same general research procedures, they apply these procedures in different ways.

Industrial marketing research is characterized by smaller budgets and greater reliance on secondary data. It places greater emphasis on surveys (especially personal interviews) and is less concerned about probability sampling and the size of the sample. It emphasizes less sophisticated techniques both in its collection and analysis of data.

SUMMARY

QUESTIONS AND EXERCISES

1. If the same basic research procedures are used for both industrial and consumer markets, why then is it important that researchers understand the differences between the two markets?

2. How does the fact that the demand for many industrial goods is a derived demand affect the marketing research activities of a firm that manufactures automobile steering wheels?

3. a. Table 16-1 indicated that research on packaging is less important to industrial product firms than it is to consumer product firms. Explain this difference.
   b. Why are test markets not an important research tool for industrial marketers?

4. Sudsy Brewery, a regional beer producer (Rocky Mountain area), is contemplating expanding its market into the southwestern United States. What information sources would it use to identify the competitive situation and existing distributors? Would the brewery use the same information sources to develop a consumer profile?

5. A manufacturer of forklifts is conducting a survey among present customers and potential customers to determine what factors are most critical to those firms when deciding which forklifts (brand and style) to purchase. What difficulties do you feel the firm will encounter if it uses a mail survey? A telephone survey? Personal interviews?

17

Organization and ethics

In ancient times, important news was communicated to emperors and other leaders through messages carried long distances by runners. If the message contained unusually bad news, the runner often times was killed on the spot, even though he was merely the bearer of the bad news. There are many users of research who would like to treat researchers in a similar manner, especially when the researchers provide information that differs from the outcome desired by the user.

Excerpted from a June 1981 presentation made by this writer to a research seminar.

The previous chapters concentrated on the mechanics of research, following a consistent "how to" approach. But there are nonprocedural aspects related to research that are also important to the reader, and some of these topics are now presented. Because of the diverse subjects covered, this chapter is really an amalgam of marketing research topics.

At the outset of this text it was emphasized that the role of marketing researchers is to provide data that guide the decisions of others. This implies that researchers have little or no direct involvement in the decision making process. But an astute observation by John Galbraith indicates that researchers have major impacts on decisions even though they may not sit in with top management. "... there must always be questions as to how much the individual is deciding and how much is being decided for him by the group which has provided the relevant information; the danger of confusing ratification with decisions must be emphasized."[1]

Researchers as decision makers

The implication of the previous statement is that in large corporations with multi-management levels, the decisions made by top management are frequently just accepting or rejecting the recommendations of others. This means they are heavily dependent on the type and quality of information that filters up to them.

As firms become involved with more diverse products/services and product life cycles continue to shorten, top management will be forced to make increasingly complex decisions over shorter periods of time. Thus, they will be relying more and more on the conclusions and recommendations of others. This suggests that the researcher's role will expand not only as a data gatherer and analyzer, but also into the decision process.

A study was carried out among both marketing researchers and marketing managers to determine the role each group felt researchers should play in the firm and the role they actually do play.[2] The two key findings were: (1) most researchers are willing to accept responsibility for making decisions; and (2) the majority of researchers who accepted this responsibility experienced higher job satisfaction and higher performance evaluation. These results suggest that the previously held image of researchers as people solely concerned with gathering and analyzing data is not accurate.

---

[1]John K. Galbraith, *The New Industrial State* (Boston: Houghton Mifflin, 1967), p. 83.

[2]R. J. Small and L. J. Rosenberg, "The Marketing Researcher as a Decision Maker: Myth or Reality?" *Journal of Marketing*, Vol. 39, January 1975, pp. 2-7.

Conflicts — Although many researchers may want to become more directly involved in decision making, this view is not necessarily shared by their superiors or other marketing managers. The Krum study indicated many managers want marketing researchers to maintain a staff status and limit themselves to just presenting data in an objective manner. They oppose researchers' infringement into decision making, an area they consider to be solely the manager's domain.[3]

Organization of research function

How should a company organize its own research personnel? There is no one correct place for them in all companies, since each company has to devise an organization that is best suited to its own unique needs. When such an organization is developed, it should frequently be reviewed since markets and product lines are continually changing.

The organization possibilities can be placed on a continuum from complete centralization to complete decentralization. If a firm is active in only one industry (one product or a few related products), one centralized marketing research department is the logical organization. But if a company is a conglomerate with operating units in diverse industries and no staff services are provided by its corporate headquarters, complete decentralization of the research function is needed. The majority of companies fit somewhere between these extremes and thus require some type of hybrid organization.

Complete decentralization — With complete decentralization operating divisions have research departments but there is no research group at corporate headquarters.

Complete decentralization plus corporation research — This category is the same as above except that there is a corporate research group which deals only with *corporate* matters.

Decentralized research units, but under guidance of corporate research director — This guidance may be technical only and of a voluntary nature, or it may be more formal where all major projects are approved and reviewed by the director.

Centralized departments with subunits located in the divisions — These subunits work closely with each division but are professionally accountable to the central research department.

---

[3]James R. Krum, "Perception and Evaluation of the Role of the Corporate Marketing Research Department," *Journal of Marketing Research*, Vol. 6, November 1969, p. 464.

Complete centralization – There are no research departments in the operating units; the central group makes all studies.

Advantages of centralization

- Greater economy and efficiency of operations.
- Greater likelihood of increased stature of research and increased likelihood of obtaining adequate budget.
- More effective use of personnel.
- Broader perspective of company's research needs.
- Can have specialists and higher quality personnel; by grouping them together there is greater opportunity for them to exchange ideas.

Advantages of decentralization

- Researchers closer to actual research situations, thus results are more attuned to the users' needs.
- Research personnel will have skills closely attuned to users' needs.
- Division managers may feel more comfortable with their own researchers.

Using outside research firms

Many firms are too small to have their own research personnel. Other firms may have research departments but their research needs are so extensive or unique that they also require the services of an outside research agency. In either situation, someone in the firm will be faced with the decision of which agency to use.

The number of outside research agencies has grown tremendously in the past decade. A check of the yellow pages in telephone directories of major metropolitan areas will attest to this growth as will a perusal of the annual editions of *Bradford's Directory of Marketing Research Agencies and Management Consultants in the U.S. and the World* (Middleburg, Vt.: Bradford Co.).

Selecting the appropriate research firm[4]

Assuming that the buyer has an idea of what the firm's research needs are, some criteria must be developed for selecting the outside firm to perform that research.

---

[4]Most of the data in this section are taken from the following source: Lee Adler and Charles Moyer, *Managing the Market Research Function* (American Marketing Association, Monograph #5, 1977), pp. 92-97.

Among those criteria are:

- What is the firm's track record? Check out its work with some of its clients (past and present).
- Is the firm a specialist or does it do varied types of research? Some firms may specialize in a category of research (e.g., floral products) or in one type of research method (e.g., group interviews).
- Does the firm have the specific facilities you need? If you are testing consumers' handling of a package, does the firm have a facility in which movies can be used to record consumer actions?
- How large is the firm? What kinds of specialists are on its staff? Can they handle a nationwide survey?
- Who will be assigned to the project? The firm may have certain outstanding people, but if they don't work on your project, their reputations will be of little value to your firm.

There are two rules of thumb to follow:

- Favor the smallest firm consistent with scope of the work and the quality desired.
- Buy quality, but no more than is needed.

Judging proposals

If research proposals are sought from a number of outside research firms, criteria must be established for evaluating these proposals. The key things to consider were covered in Chapter 15 of this text and lists of questions to use in such an evaluation are contained in Figures 15-3 and 15-4 of that chapter.

If the buyer has provided a very precise description of what the research entails, the major factors to evaluate then become the time and cost information of each proposal.

ETHICAL ISSUES   The past decade was a period of tremendous growth in the use and impact of marketing research, but it was also a period in which researchers were forced to scrutinize the ethical aspects of their activities. The rise of consumerism, women's lib, equal rights legislation, etc., made people more assertive of their rights in all areas, especially the marketplace. Increased concern for privacy, a reluctance to be used as "guinea pigs" for new products, increased reluctance to accept the so-called research claims for products in ads are a few examples of changes affecting research activities.

This section will look at ethical issues from three perspectives: (1) researchers' treatment of respondents/subjects, (2) researchers' treatment of buyers/clients, and (3) buyer/client treatment of researchers.

Code of ethics

The American Marketing Association adopted a Marketing Research Code of Ethics in 1962, which was then revised in 1972. As is the case with most codes of ethics, this one merely represents minimum standards and does not prescribe an all encompassing list of "dos and don'ts." The code provides guidelines for research users, practitioners, and field interviewers, with no one area covered to any great extent. Since sociologists and psychologists are also heavily involved with human research, their professional associations have also adopted codes pertaining to their members' research activities. Their codes are much more strict and encompassing than the code for marketing researchers, especially concerning the protection of the subject/respondent.[5]

Treatment of participants/subjects

The AMA code covers two areas involving participants:

- The activity must be research and not have as its real purpose the sale of merchandise to the respondent.
- If so informed, the particpants' anonymity must be protected.

But these two aspects just scratch the surface of possible ethical issues pertaining to participants. Following are five examples used in a survey to obtain ethical perspectives on research activities from two groups—research directors and marketing managers.[6] What are your reactions to each situation? As a client or manager, would you approve or disapprove of these activities? The responses for each group are shown in Table 16-1.

1. *Ultraviolet ink.* "A project director requests permission to use ultraviolet ink in precoding questionnaires on a mail survey. He pointed out that the cover letter referred to it as being an anonymous survey, but he said he needed respondent identifica-

---

[5]Gerald Zaltman and Philip Burger, *Marketing Research: Fundamentals and Dynamics* (Hinsdale, Ill.: Dryden Press, 1975), pp. 615-640.

[6]C. M. Crawford, "Attitudes of Marketing Executives Towards Ethics in Marketing Research," *Journal of Marketing*, Vol. 34, April 1970, pp. 46-52.

tion to permit adequate cross tabulations of the data. The M.R. Director gave his approval."

2. *Hidden tape recorders.* "A study was intended to probe deeply into the buying motivations of a group of wholesale customers by use of semi-structured personal interviews. The M.R. Director authorized the use of special attache cases equipped with hidden tape recorders."

3. *One-way mirrors.* "One product of the X Company is brassieres, and the firm has had difficulty making some decisions on a new line. Information was critically needed concerning the manner in which women put on their brassieres. So the M.R. Director designed a study in which two local stores cooperated in putting one-way mirrors in their women's dressing rooms. Observers behind these mirrors successfuly gathered the necessary information."

4. *Fake long-distance calls.* "Some of X Company's customers are busy executives, hard to reach by normal interviewing methods. Accordingly, the market research department recently conducted a study in which interviewers called 'long-distance' from nearby cities. They were successful in getting through to busy executives in almost every instance."

5. *Fake research firm.* "In a study concerning magazine reading habits, the M.R. Director decided to contact a sample of consumers under the name of Media Research Institute. This fictitious name successfully camouflaged the identity of the sponsor of the study."

There was fairly strong disapproval of the ultraviolet ink, hidden recorders, and one-way mirror situations, but strong approval of the use of fake long-distance calls and fake research firms.

Certainly a couple of the examples were quite extreme, especially the hidden mirror one. Was the respondent's disapproval due to the intimacy of what was being observed, or was it a general disapproval of using one-way mirrors when the participants are unaware? In actuality, the brassiere example is not only unethical, but probably illegal as well.

Other questionable situations

In running tests on product prices, is it ethical to charge certain groups higher prices in an attempt to measure the elasticity of

Responses of 401 Executives to Fictitious
Research Situations

Table 17-1

Examples	Percentage Approving
Ultraviolet Ink	
Research directors	29
Marketing managers	22
Hidden Tape Recorders	
Research directors	33
Marketing managers	36
One-Way Mirrors	
Research directors	20
Marketing managers	18
Fake Long-Distance Calls	
Research directors	88
Marketing managers	84
Fake Research Firms	
Research directors	84
Marketing managers	83

Source: C. M. Crawford, "Attitudes of Marketing Executives Towards Ethics in Marketing Research," *Journal of Marketing,* Vol. 34, April 1970, pp. 46-52.

the demand for the product? In testing TV commercials, is it ethical to tell the paricipants they are merely evaluating the potential of a new show and then use some indirect methods to determine their reactions to the ads in the show?

A $2 rebate is given on a new product, but people have to send in a signed coupon to obtain the rebate. This list of respondents is then sold to another firm which sells a product that complements the one on which a rebate was given. The examples could go on and on.

Right to privacy

Of all the issues involving ethics in marketing research, the "right to privacy" seems to be the most critical one. Consumers can presently request they not be sent "junk mail"; they can have their telephone numbers placed on a list that solicitors cannot call. As people continue to become more concerned with protecting their privacy, there may eventually be a list of households that do not want any unsolicited contact from business or related

Specific rights of subjects

(research) firms by phone, mail or direct visit under penalty of fine.[7]

To prevent the occurrence of such a condition, researchers will have to demonstrate to consumers that the research activities will ultimately benefit them through products and services more attuned to their needs and desires. Even with such positive actions, it would seem that researchers are going to be facing an increasingly reticent population.

Right to choose[8]

Subjects have the freedom to choose whether or not they will participate. This should be made clear to them at the outset. Some subjects mistakenly attribute expert or legal power to researchers and thus assume they *must* participate. In this same vein, the researchers should make enough information available to the subject so that he/she can make an informed choice about such participation. This freedom of choice does not exist in the case of federal census studies, however, since subjects contacted must participate.

Right to safety

This covers protection of subject's anonymity as well as protection from psychological and physical harm. Marketing research rarely results in physical harm, but it can lead to some psychological damage. Research procedures may induce stress that is not ultimately relieved. Discovering that three unmarked cans of beer which he identified as being different were actually all the same brand could lead the subject to doubt his competence as a shopper in other areas as well; or, placed in a somewhat competitive test situation with other subjects, poor performance (e.g., inability to open a package or effectively use a new baking mix) may lead to personal embarrassment that would not have occurred had the subject not participated.

Right to be informed

The subjects should be informed about all aspects of the research as it might affect them. This means information prior to the re-

---

[7]"A Revolt Against Junk Calls," *Business Week,* Feb. 20, 1978, pp. 26-27.

[8]The three following rights are discussed in the article: Alice M. Turbout and Gerald Zaltman, "Ethics in Marketing Research: Their Practical Relevance," *Journal of Marketing Research,* Vol. XI, November 1974, pp. 357-368.

search as well as a "debriefing" after the research to relieve the possible stress the research may have imposed on the subject.

A body of legal constraints on research activities appears to be slowly developing at the national, state, and even local levels.[9]

Government's role

Privacy Act—This act, passed in 1974, emphasizes the individual's right to privacy. The total ramifications of the act are not yet known since various facets are still being interpreted in court cases. It implies that no information can be extracted from an individual without his/her expressed consent. The researcher must also disclose how the information will be used and the persons/firms/organization that will have access to the information.

A subsection of the Privacy Act prohibits federal departments from selling or renting names and addresses of respondents. It also requires that private firms must allow individuals to remove their names from mailing lists if they so desire.

FTC powers—Since 1966, the Federal Trade Commission has initiated a large number of cease and desist orders against firms it felt were misusing marketing research. FTC's prime targets have been firms using marketing research as a ruse or scheme to eventually sell something. Under the Magnuson-Moss Act of 1975, the FTC's powers in regulating research were greatly enhanced, primarily through a more precise definition of what are "unfair and deceptive" practices.

"Junk" phone call legislation—At the time this book was written, no specific federal legislation existed barring "junk" phone calls. However, the increased use of automated telephone calling equipment with prerecorded sales pitches will probably stimulate legislation in this area which could even affect legitimate telephone surveys.

A number of local communities already require that anyone soliciting door-to-door (researchers included) must be licensed by some city agency and this license must be frequently renewed.

The AMA Marketing Research Code of Ethics touches on three areas in which researchers have obligations to their clients.

Treatment of buyers/clients

---

[9]Much of this information is drawn from the following articles. Cynthia Frey and Thomas Kinnear, "Legal Constraints and Marketing Research: Review and Call to Action," *Journal of Marketing Research*, August 1979, pp. 295-302.

- The methods used and the results obtained must be accurately represented.
- The client's identity as well as the information obtained will be held in confidence.
- Research should not be undertaken for competitors if such research will jeopardize the confidential nature of previous client-researcher relationships.

The researchers are obligated to use effective research procedures in obtaining and analyzing data. They are also obligated to counsel clients in situations when they make ill-advised research requests. If a researcher knows of an existing study that fits the needs of a client, he/she should inform the client rather than duplicate what has already been done.

The researcher must inform the client of any critical weaknesses or limitations in the collected data, especially those that could result in major errors if the results are projected to different segments of the population. If field interviews are conducted, the research firm should ensure the quality of this performance and validate (within reason) that the surveys were actually conducted and in the proper manner.

Objectivity

There are situations where the client wants the research findings to prove a point. The client takes a position and then seeks data to confirm that position. In these cases the researcher may be asked to gather data in a biased manner.

Example: A product manager has come up with an idea for a new wine drink that will appeal to college students. To get it into at least regional distribution, the market tests will have to show an acceptance level of 60 percent among the sample. The tests are conducted in such a way that this percentage is almost guaranteed.

Example: A bank is applying to its state commission for approval to open a branch in another part of town. It conducts a survey that shows that the majority of people in that area feel the bank is needed. The way the bank asks the questions guarantees the outcome.

Overt cheating did not occur in either of these examples—just questionable practices. A research firm that will go along with such requests will ultimately hurt itself since other potential clients will question the quality of the firm and may refrain from using it.

Buried reports

Many research reports never leave the clients' files, especially if they dispute the clients' viewpoints. The researcher has no obligation to make the results available to anyone other than the client.

Example: A trade association wanted to show the government that its industry needed restrictions on imports if the home industry was to survive. The association paid to have a study conducted to show the financial problems individual firms within the industry were having. The data collected indicated that these firms were not nearly as bad off as expected. The study's findings were never made public.

Confidentiality

Any actual or prospective client approaching or using a research firm has the right to expect that what is revealed to that firm as part of this relationship is confidential.[10] This rule applies not only to the research firm's key people, but to all personnel involved in the research. There have even been court cases in which researchers have been asked to provide confidential data against their previous clients, and questions were raised as to the propriety of making researchers provide such information.[11] Some researchers feel the relationship between a research firm and its clients is comparable to that of a lawyer-client or doctor-patient.

Treatment of researchers

Discussions of ethics in marketing research tend to emphasize the researchers' obligations to clients and subjects. But there are many cases in which researchers are the victims of questionable practices of others; so the researchers' rights should also be recognized in any discussion of ethical behavior.[12]

---

[10]Sidney Hollander, Jr., "Ethics in Marketing Research," *Handbook of Marketing Research* (New York: McGraw-Hill, 1974), pp. 107-121.

[11]"A Growing Problem for Researchers: Protecting Privacy," *The Chronicle of Higher Education,* Vol. XIV, May 2, 1977, pp. 1ff.

[12]Much of the discussion in this section is taken from the following article: Robert Bezella, Joel Haynes, and Clifford Elliot, "Ethics in Marketing Research," *Business Horizons,* April 1976, pp. 83-86.

Many of the situations in which the research firm is victimized are related to the system of competitive bidding. Researchers submit proposals, and the clients select the most favorable one from among those submitted. Since this solicitation method is widely used by private firms and government agencies, it can lead to many abuses, some of which are now identified.

Picking the researchers' brains

Research firms provide proposals for a project. The client takes the best proposal and turns it over to another firm to carry out at a cheaper price. The client obtains Firm A's ideas and implements them at Firm B's price. In some cases 20 to 30 percent of the total project's cost can be incurred in the proposal development stage. Since Firm B can save all these expenses by merely following Firm A's blueprint, it is understandable how Firm B can perform the research for less money. Another possibility is that the client uses the information obtained from solicited proposals and incorporates them into a project carried out by their own research staff.

Closed bidding situation

A firm's purchasing policy may require that all proposed projects receive at least three bids. The buyer prefers Firm A at the outset and merely goes through the formality of getting bids from other research firms.

Research not formally authorized

Someone solicits proposals before higher management in the firm even authorizes funds for such a project. This does not mean all projects must eventually be carried out. There will always be situations where the research project is legitimately cancelled after proposals are obtained because the research would cost too much or the situation has changed, lessening the need for the research. But it is highly questionable for clients to solicit proposals when there has been no actual authorization for such projects.

Restricted funds

While it makes sense that the client not tell potential bidders exactly how much money the firm has set aside for the research, there is an obligation to give these bidders some idea of any existing budget constraints. A $30,000 maximum expenditure would limit a study to a regional basis, and if the researcher has no indication of this ceiling, the proposal developed could be national in scope and thus way out of line.

Reneging on promises

Once the research is under way, the researchers may find that some things that were promised in the original agreement never come to fruition. Much of this reneging involves the client's unwillingness to give the researcher access to sales and cost data. The client may have stated at the outset that all the company's data would be available to the researcher, but later it restricts the data it will disclose.

This situation occurs most often when a research firm is hired by a trade association to do a study using its members' data. The individual members often times are reluctant to open their records for such a project.

Excessive requests

A contract usually spells out the obligation of the researcher to the client, but the client often times makes unreasonable demands on the researcher. A written final report may have been all that was originally requested, but the client then demands that the researcher also provide additional oral presentations or appearances to explain the findings to a variety of the client's employees, directors, or customers.

Another area of abuse occurs when the client makes "small" additions in what is to be done during the data collection stage or analysis stage. Seemingly, the researcher could handle such requests by charging extra for them, but a client paying $200,000 for research may not understand why these "extras" can't be included at no additional cost.

Summary of ethical aspects

Since ethics deals with the morality of certain actions, it is not possible to develop a precise listing of the dos and don'ts surrounding research activities. The area of ethics is both complex and controversial since each person judges actions from the perspective of his/her own personal value system. So this section has merely identified areas in which potential ethical problems might exist for both researchers and potential clients.

If subjects' rights are continually abused, they will look to others for protection, and this will result in legislation restricting marketing research. If client's rights are violated, they will lose faith in the credibility of research and return to greater reliance on "seat of the pants" decision making.

THE FUTURE   What will be the role of marketing research in the next 10 years? Will it increase in importance? Decrease? Stay about the same? Conditions exist that suggest that any of the three possibilities may occur. No attempt will be made here to predict the future importance of marketing research, since such predictions have a way of coming back to haunt their developer. This final section will merely identify some of the key factors that will influence the role of marketing research in the 1980s.

Product life cycles will continue to shorten, which means decisions about the introduction and withdrawal of products will have to be made more quickly. Competitors will be able to mimic new successful products in shorter periods of time so firms will not have much lead time in the market. With firms having to meet increasingly tough environmental/pollution standards, more money will have to be spent in this area, possibly cutting down on funds available for research and new product development.

Increased shortages of materials (especially oil-related ones) will lead to less emphasis on totally new products and more reliance on smaller cosmetic changes in products. Increased usage of automated checkouts in retail stores will provide an abundance and a wide variety of sales information. Two-way communication between interviewer and interviewee will be possible through the use of cable TV. Questions will be flashed on the screen, and the viewers will respond by pressing buttons on their sets.

Consumers will become increasingly concerned with their right to privacy, and this right will be championed by numerous activist groups. Consumers will seek increasingly more input into decisions involving new products and services. This should make them more amenable to research projects where they know their ideas will be used by firms.

Decision makers in business firms will continue to become more knowledgeable about computers and statistics and thus will expect and be able to handle more sophisticated research.

Increased usage of desk computers (with cathode ray tubes) will make data more accessible to decision makers, even those at middle management levels. Continual improvements in company information systems will lead to concise daily reports individualized to the needs of each decision maker. Computer systems will be linked to information libraries of outside research firms. Requests for information on subjects such as solar hot water systems or sales of vodka in California in 1981 will be easily accessed. The increased amount of secondary data and its accessibility, through computer systems, microfiche files, etc., will make this type of data increasingly important to marketing research.

This is just a sampling of changes that will occur in the next few years. What does it mean in terms of the future role of marketing research? That's not a bad topic for some research project!

QUESTIONS AND EXERCISES

1. What role should the marketing researcher play in a large firm's decision making processes?

2. Write a four- to five-page paper describing what you feel the role of marketing research will be in the next decade.

3. Assume that you are the owner of a small firm manufacturing plastic containers. You have developed a new plastic package that you think has great commercial possibilities. (1) You want to test it among a group of housewives to get their reactions, and (2) you want to obtain information on its sales potential. You have no experience with marketing research so you will have to use a private research firm to provide the desired information. How would you select an appropriate firm?

4. What impact will the public's increasing concern for its "right to privacy" have on marketing research?

5. Should the public's "right to privacy" supersede the researcher's obligation to provide data to clients?

6. Read the Marketing Research Code of Ethics of the American Marketing Association. Does it provide effective guidance to researchers?

18

Guidelines for users of research

We don't replace decision makers, we just make their jobs easier.

*Motto of a Colorado marketing
research firm*

As stated in the Preface, the majority of people using this book will not be full-time researchers. Most users will either be college students or businesspersons wanting to learn more about research procedures for a particular research assignment, or because they are frequent users of the research of others.

Purpose of chapter

This chapter is intended for the latter group—users of research data. These decision makers are the people who receive the blame for a bad decision, even though it was caused by faulty research. Thus, it is important that users of research data understand the research process and the role they can play in enhancing the quality of the research they receive. This chapter will provide guidelines for accomplishing those goals.

The key steps of the research process were identified in Chapter 3, with each step described more fully in Chapters 4 through 15. Most of these same steps will be cited in this chapter, but from the decision makers' perspective. Figure 18-1 lists the general activities decision makers should perform to improve the quality of research they receive. The remainder of this chapter describes specific guidelines to be followed when performing these activities.

Role of the Research User in the Research Process	Figure 18-1

Recognize the need for additional data
Identify the type of investigation required
Select the researcher
Establish the project's direction
Evaluate the secondary data provided
Evaluate the techniques used to obtain primary data
  —If sampling is involved, assess critical sampling procedures
Aid in the selection of methods for analyzing the collected data
Activate the research findings

Recognizing the need for additional data

Managers constantly face decision situations without having adequate prior information. In many of these situations, however, the effect of a wrong decision is not serious enough to warrant its postponement until more information can be obtained. There are, however, a number of situations where the financial impact of a wrong decision can be quite significant, so the decision maker actively seeks more information. In this chapter, it is assumed the decision maker feels there is a need for some additional information and seeks the services of someone to perform the research. For the remainder of this chapter, the decision maker or person seeking the additional research will also be called the client/user.

Identifying the type of investigation required

An initial decision the client/user must make is what type of investigation is necessary. If the information needed is data on competitors' market share or the amount of customer traffic in a mall, then a "fact gathering" investigation is needed. If the decision maker is faced with a more complex problem requiring fairly extensive information, then a "solution oriented" investigation is necessary. Solution oriented research requires the greatest input from the client/user.

The third possible type of investigation – basic research – usually does not involve the client/user to any major extent. Most of the decisions involving basic research are made by the researchers themselves since its primary purpose is new knowledge and is usually not undertaken for the direct benefit of the decision maker.

Selecting the researcher

Once the general type of investigation has been identified, the client/user can decide who will perform the investigation. Simple fact gathering might be performed by the firm's librarian or a subordinate of the client/user. Conversely, since a solution-oriented investigation is usually more complex and requires more formalized research procedures, research professionals are generally used.

In-house vs. outside researcher – If the decision maker's firm has its own research staff, the logical action will be to inform that staff of his/her research needs. After a discussion with the person in charge of research, it might be decided that the research is beyond the firm's capabilities and should be handled by an outside firm. For example, a series of regional test markets may be too large an undertaking for the firm's own staff. Or, unique testing equipment may be needed and only a firm specializing in that type of research has such equipment.

If the firm does not have its own research staff or its staff cannot provide the desired research, then the decision maker will seek an outside researcher. This may involve soliciting proposals from a number of firms, with the decision maker using the proposals to choose the eventual researcher.

Situation analysis — One major drawback of using outside researchers is their lack of knowledge about the decision maker's firm and/or the industry. This necessitates that the researcher perform a situation analysis. The client/user must either personally provide the researcher with the needed background information or make sure it is provided by others in the firm.

Establishing the project's direction

Fact gathering investigation — If the information needs are easily identified, e.g., amount of vacant office space in Des Moines, Iowa, extensive discussion between the user and the researcher about the project's direction may not be necessary. But even in relatively simple research requests, confusion can arise.

- Should the research include office space in the entire city or just the downtown area? What are the boundaries of the downtown area?
- What determines office space — space in formal office buildings, or does it also include space that could be used for a retail store?
- Does it include space in medical buildings and government buildings?

A number of so-called "simple" research projects have resulted in wasted dollars and effort because the information obtained was not what the user really wanted. To ensure this does not happen, the client/user should work closely with the researcher in identifying the direction of the research, and monitor the data gathering to make sure the appropriate data are being obtained.

Solution oriented investigation — The client/user should realize that a researcher's skills include the ability to identify the type of research needed. Thus, it is important that client and researcher cooperate on the actual research needs and the specific direction of the project. This cooperative effort usually results in a different direction for the research than would have emerged if the researcher had just accepted the client's idea of what the research should entail. The example used to introduce Chapter 4 effectively illustrates this point.

Evaluating secondary data

Since a major portion of the information used in decision making is secondary data, it is important that the client/user be able to evaluate the quality of this type of information. Following are some guidelines for such an evaluation.

Identify the time period represented by the data — Is the information current enough to be useful for decision making? A 1976 study of office space in Des Moines, for example, would be of questionable value in determining present demand for office space in that city.

Identify the source of the information — Who initially gathered the data? What was the purpose in gathering the data? What publication(s) did the data appear in? Always be alert for factors that might have biased the data. A Chamber of Commerce's description of a situation (e.g., office space available in Des Moines) may well differ from that of other agencies.

Identify crucial terms — Be sure the information is in correct terms. Data on households are not the same thing as data on family units. The value of statistics on the elderly residents of a city, for example, depends on how the term "elderly" is defined. What age group does it include — all residents over 55 years of age or only those over 65 or 70? Does the term "unit sales" mean gross shipments made by a firm, or does it mean the net sales after returns and allowances?

Identify the techniques used in obtaining the data — Is the information based on a total census of the population under study or is it based on projections made from a sample of that population? If projections are used, how recent were the data on which these projections were based? Were appropriate sampling methods used?

The gist of the above guidelines is that the client/user should not assume all secondary data are of acceptable quality. They should be evaluated for timeliness, accuracy, and potential bias.

Evaluating techniques used to obtain primary data

The client/user should help decide which methods (surveys, observations, or experiments) will be used to obtain the primary data. If surveys are used, the client should have a final say over which specific survey method is used — telephone, mail, or personal interview.

Know the key strengths and weaknesses of the methods for gathering primary data. Since budgets will often significantly influence the method chosen, know the trade offs that may be involved, e.g., mail surveys reaching a large audience vs. personal interviews with a much smaller group. Review all survey questionnaires used. The client/user should have final approval over all questionnaires used in the project to identify possible bias, embarrassing questions, unnecessary questions, etc.

Inquire about all observation methods. Obtain a description of the procedures used, the training given to the observers, environment in which observations will be made, etc.

Evaluate the validity of any experiment. If performed in a lab, are the results applicable to a real world situation (external validity)? If carried out in the field, how were extraneous factors handled (internal validity)? If control groups were used, how similar in composition were they to the test groups?

The above guidelines indicate that the client/user should be closely involved in all decisions associated with obtaining primary data. But in this involvement, it should also be recognized that the researcher is the expert. Thus, while the client/user should keep abreast of what is going on, he/she should not dictate the research activity. You don't want researchers to be merely your "Yes" men.

Assessing sampling procedures

Because sampling involves sophisticated terms such as "95 percent confidence intervals," "standard errors of the mean," and the use of statistical formulas, many client/users leave sampling entirely to the researchers. This writer recognizes that sampling activities can indeed be quite complex, but there are certain elements of the sampling process that the client/user should monitor.

Evaluate the sample frame — How representative is the sample frame? Are the people/firms included in the frame the most appropriate units? For example, are purchasing agents the right people to survey about factors influencing their firm's decisions on purchasing computer supplies, or would information systems' personnel be more appropriate?

Evaluate the procedures used for selecting the specific sample members – The researcher intends to interview people randomly selected in a shopping mall or intends to send mail surveys to every fifth name on a mailing list of members of a Production Control Association. Does the process by which the sample members are selected make sense to you?

Try to understand key sampling terminology – Understand the general meaning of key terms such as sampling error, confidence intervals, probability samples, etc. Remember, confidence intervals pertain only to sampling errors, so if nonsampling errors seem to be quite extensive in the data, confidence intervals can be quite misleading. Recognize how sample size influences the confidence interval, and how large increases in sample size are needed to attain just small increases in "confidence." Is the cost of obtaining a 99 percent confidence interval worth the added expense?

The above suggestions do not imply that the client/user should be *deeply* involved with all sampling activities. What is recommended is that the client/user be knowledgeable about those activities in which he/she should provide some input – selection of sample frame, selection of sample size, desired confidence interval (if probability sample is used).

Involvement with analysis and interpretation

This is the research activity the client/user usually feels most uncomfortable with. Data analysis often involves complicated statistical procedures so most clients prefer leaving these decisions *entirely* to the researcher. The client/user must realize, however, that since he/she will be making key decisions based on the collected data, he/she should assist with the selection of the techniques used to analyze and interpret it.

Inquire about the appropriateness of the analytic tools – The researcher should be required to explain the analytic procedures he/she will use and the reasons for his/her selections. For example, if the researcher intends to use analysis of variance to determine the most effective package design, the client/user should have some understanding as to why this technique is being used and what it will show.

Seek the help of outside experts (statisticians in your firm or academicians) if you don't feel the researcher is adequately explaining the proposed analytic procedures.

Don't attempt to influence the research outcome – In many research situations, the client/user has a preferred outcome, and there is a temptation to attempt to influence the results of the research. For example, the client/user may have strongly advocated the addition of a particular product to the firm's present product line, and the research program involves a market test to show the new product's potential acceptance by customers. There would be a great temptation on the client/user's part to ensure a successful test result.

An analytic technique can usually be found that will enable the research data to fit the outcome desired by the user. Or the data can be interpreted in such a way as to suggest an outcome in line with the user's desires. Don't let this happen.

Involvement with final report

The client/user will often make suggestions for the report's format, but the actual compilation of the report should rest solely with researcher.

Read the entire report – Many managers feel they don't have time to read entire research reports, so they read only the summary or "highlights" section. Such a practice may be appropriate for those managers only slightly involved with the research topic, but any decision maker who is going to rely heavily on the research findings should read the entire report.

A person using the findings from a research project should feel comfortable with the data; he/she must, therefore, know how the data were gathered, sample size involved, limitations of the research, etc. Reading just the "highlights" section will not provide this information.

Set up "post research" meetings with researchers – The researcher usually provides the research findings in a formal presentation to the client/user and other interested parties. At this time the written reports will usually be distributed. While questions about the findings will certainly arise at this time, additional questions will also occur once the report is thoroughly read. Therefore, the client/user should plan to meet with the researcher at a future time to clarify any of these questions.

Make sure the research findings reach the proper people — If the firm has an effective information system, the research findings should be included in that system so others within the firm will have access to them. Too often research conducted for one department never circulates to other areas. Whether the people in these other areas actually read the report is not the responsibility of the original client/user, but those people should at least be afforded the opportunity. There are numerous examples of research being duplicated by different divisions of the same company.

React to the research — Numerous research reports gather dust in files or on shelves. In some cases, this occurs because the situation that originally necessitated the research has changed, e.g., a location study for a proposed warehouse is not needed now because the whole idea was abandoned by the president of the company.

In many cases the research findings are in opposition to some manager's desired outcome, so the report is buried. A newspaper undertook a major study intending to show that the majority of its readers were people under the age of 30. The research indicated the readers were primarily households headed by people over 35 years of age, so the report was "buried."

But burying the report is preferable to a more common situation of just ignoring it. The client/user fails to implement the report's recommendations or to use the findings in his/her decision making.

Overview

This chapter contains guidelines that will enable client/users to enhance the value of the research performed for them. The central theme throughout was that the client/user should *participate*. Research should not be viewed as a "we" and "they" type of activity. Rather it should be viewed as an "us" situation where the client/user works closely with the researcher throughout most phases of the research.

Repeating a point made at the outset of the chapter — it is the decision maker who will be held responsible for the success or failure of the decision, not the researcher. Thus, it behooves the decision maker to do everything possible to ensure the quality of the research being used.

QUESTIONS AND EXERCISES

1. "I'm being paid to make decisions and the researcher is being paid to do research. Each of us is supposedly an expert in his

own area. Why then should we consult with one another during a project?" What is your reaction to this manager's point of view?

2. "I need to know the number of people shopping at the Acme Mall during a typical weekday evening." While this appears to be a fairly straightforward request to a researcher, there are some potential areas of confusion. What are these areas, and what additional questions should the researcher ask to ensure he/she is obtaining the right information?

3. What are major problems the researcher often encounters when performing a situation analysis?

4. From the user's point of view, why is a 95 percent confidence interval often preferable to a 99 percent confidence interval? Why might a 90 percent confidence interval be the most desirable of the three?

5. Evaluate each of the items of secondary data from the perspective of a data user. What questions would you ask about each set of data before you would use it to make an important decision?

   a. Information on job opportunities, expected growth in population, etc. for the city of Fort Collins, Colorado, published in a brochure prepared by the "Fort Collins Committee for Growth."

   b. Sixty percent of the elderly have incomes below the poverty level.

   c. Station KHAK has the largest audience of young people of any radio station in northeast Kentucky.

   d. Acme Corp. has 60 percent of the fiberboard market in the state of Missouri.

6. You are the marketing director for Top-Flite Gym Company. You requested an outside firm to conduct a survey among hotels and motels to determine the potential demand for a special padded chair, equipped with overhead pulleys and a bicycle pedaling device. It would enable guests to work out in the privacy of their own rooms and would sell for around $500. When the research report is given to you, it indicates there was little interest among the hotels/motels for the product. You disagee with these research findings because you have a "gut feeling" this product holds great potential. What are your obligations in terms of this research report? Should you make it available to others or bury it?

Appendix

Selected Statistical Tables

Proportion of the Area under the Normal Curve with Values as Extreme as the Observed Values of Z

Z	.00	.01	.02	.03	.04	.05	.06	.07	.08	.09
.0	.5000	.4960	.4920	.4880	.4840	.4801	.4761	.4721	.4681	.4641
.1	.4602	4562	.4522	.4483	.4443	.4404	.4364	.4325	.4286	.4247
.2	.4207	.4168	.4129	.4090	.4052	.4013	.3974	.3936	.3897	.3859
.3	.3821	.3873	.3745	.3707	.3669	.3632	.3594	.3557	.3520	.3483
.4	.3446	.3409	.3372	.3336	.3300	.3264	.3228	.3192	.3156	.3121
.5	.3085	.3050	.3015	.2981	.2946	.2912	.2877	.2843	.2810	.2776
.6	.2743	.2709	.2676	.2643	.2611	.2578	.2546	.2514	.2483	.2451
.7	.2420	.2389	.2358	.2327	.2296	.2266	.2236	.2206	.2177	.2148
.8	.2119	.2090	.2061	.2033	.2005	.1977	.1949	.1922	.1894	.1867
.9	.1841	.1814	.1788	.1762	.1736	.1711	.1685	.1660	.1635	.1611
1.0	.1587	.1562	.1539	.1515	.1492	.1469	.1446	.1423	.1401	.1379
1.1	.1357	.1335	.1314	.1292	.1271	.1251	.1230	.1210	.1190	.1170
1.2	.1151	.1131	.1112	.1093	.1075	.1056	.1038	.1020	.1003	.0985
1.3	.0968	.0951	.0934	.0918	.0901	.0885	.0869	.0853	.0838	.0823
1.4	.0808	.0793	.0778	.0764	.0749	.0735	.0721	.0708	.0694	.0681
1.5	.0668	.0655	.0643	.0630	.0618	.0606	.0594	.0582	.0571	.0559
1.6	.0548	.0537	.0526	.0516	.0505	.0495	.0485	.0475	.0465	.0455
1.7	.0446	.0436	.0427	.0418	.0409	.0401	.0392	.0384	.0375	.0367
1.8	.0359	.0351	.0344	.0336	.0329	.0322	.0314	.0307	.0301	.0294
1.9	.0287	.0281	.0274	.0268	.0262	.0256	.0250	.0244	.0239	.0233
2.0	.0228	.0222	.0217	.0212	.0207	.0202	.0197	.0192	.0188	.0183
2.1	.0179	0174	.0170	.0166	.0162	.0158	.0154	.0150	.0146	.0143
2.2	.0139	.0136	.0132	.0129	.0125	.0122	.0119	.0116	.0113	.0110
2.3	.0107	.0104	.0102	.0099	.0096	.0094	.0091	.0089	.0087	.0084
2.4	.0082	.0080	.0078	.0075	.0073	.0071	.0069	.0068	.0066	.0064
2.5	.0062	.0060	.0059	.0057	.0055	.0054	.0052	.0051	.0049	.0048
2.6	.0047	.0045	.0044	.0043	.0041	.0040	.0039	.0038	.0037	.0036
2.7	.0035	.0034	.0033	.0032	.0031	.0030	.0029	.0028	.0027	.0026
2.8	.0026	.0025	.0024	.0023	.0023	.0022	.0021	.0021	.0020	.0019
2.9	.0019	.0018	.0018	.0017	.0016	.0016	.0015	.0015	.0014	.0014
3.0	.0013	.0013	.0013	.0012	.0012	.0011	.0011	.0011	.0010	.0010
3.1	.0010	.0009	.0009	.0009	.0008	.0008	.0008	.0008	.0007	.0007
3.2	.0007									
3.3	.0005									
3.4	.0003									
3.5	.00023									
3.6	.00016									
3.7	.00011									
3.8	.00007									
3.9	.00005									
4.0	.00003									

Tables A-1, A-2, and A-3 are taken from Tables III and IV of Fisher and Yates: *Statistical Tables for Biological, Agricultural and Medical Research*, published by Longman Group Ltd., London (previously published by Oliver and Boyd, Edinburgh), and by permission of the authors and publishers.

Table A-2

Table of Critical Values of t

df	Level of Significance for One-Tailed Test					
	.10	.05	.025	.01	.005	.0005
	Level of Significance for Two-Tailed Test					
	.20	.10	.05	.02	.01	.001
1	3.078	6.314	12.706	31.821	63.657	636.619
2	1.886	2.920	4.303	6.965	9.925	31.598
3	1.638	2.353	3.182	4.541	5.841	12.941
4	1.533	2.132	2.776	3.747	4.604	8.610
5	1.476	2.015	2.571	3.365	4.032	6.859
6	1.440	1.943	2.447	3.143	3.707	5.959
7	1.415	1.895	2.365	2.998	3.499	5.405
8	1.397	1.860	2.306	2.896	3.355	5.041
9	1.383	1.833	2.262	2.821	3.250	4.781
10	1.372	1.812	2.228	2.764	3.169	4.587
11	1.363	1.796	2.201	2.718	3.106	4.437
12	1.356	1.782	2.179	2.681	3.055	4.318
13	1.350	1.771	2.160	2.650	3.012	4.221
14	1.345	1.761	2.145	2.624	2.977	4.140
15	1.341	1.753	2.131	2.602	2.947	4.073
16	1.337	1.746	2.120	2.583	2.921	4.015
17	1.333	1.740	2.110	2.567	2.898	3.965
18	1.330	1.734	2.101	2.552	2.878	3.922
19	1.328	1.729	2.093	2.539	2.861	3.883
20	1.325	1.725	2.086	2.528	2.845	3.850
21	1.323	1.721	2.080	2.518	2.831	3.819
22	1.321	1.717	2.074	2.508	2.819	3.792
23	1.319	1.714	2.069	2.500	2.807	3.767
24	1.318	1.711	2.064	2.492	2.797	3.745
25	1.316	1.708	2.060	2.485	2.787	3.725
26	1.315	1.706	2.056	2.479	2.779	3.707
27	1.314	1.703	2.052	2.473	2.771	3.690
28	1.313	1.701	2.048	2.467	2.763	3.674
29	1.311	1.699	2.045	2.462	2.756	3.659
30	1.310	1.697	2.042	2.457	2.750	3.646
40	1.303	1.684	2.021	2.423	2.704	3.551
60	1.296	1.671	2.000	2.390	2.660	3.460
120	1.289	1.658	1.980	2.358	2.617	3.373
∞	1.282	1.645	1.960	2.326	2.576	3.291

Table A-3

Critical Values of Chi-Square (X^2)

Probability under H_o that $x^2 > $ Chi-Square

	.99	.98	.95	.90	.80	.70	.50	.30	.20	.10	.05	.02	.01	.001
1	.00016	.00063	.0039	.016	.064	.15	.46	1.07	1.64	2.71	3.84	5.41	6.64	10.83
2	.02	.04	.10	.21	.45	.71	1.39	2.41	3.22	4.60	5.99	7.82	9.21	13.82
3	.12	.18	.35	.58	1.00	1.42	2.37	3.66	4.64	6.25	7.82	9.84	11.34	16.27
4	.30	.43	.71	1.06	1.65	2.20	3.36	4.88	5.99	7.78	9.49	11.67	13.28	18.46
5	.55	.75	1.14	1.61	2.34	3.00	4.35	6.06	7.29	9.24	11.07	13.39	15.09	20.52
6	.87	1.13	1.64	2.20	3.07	3.83	5.35	7.23	8.56	10.64	12.59	15.03	16.81	22.46
7	1.24	1.56	2.17	2.83	3.82	4.67	6.35	8.38	9.80	12.02	14.07	16.62	18.48	24.32
8	1.65	2.03	2.73	3.49	4.59	5.53	7.34	9.52	11.03	13.36	15.51	18.17	20.09	26.12
9	2.09	2.53	3.32	4.17	5.38	6.39	8.34	10.66	12.24	14.68	16.92	19.68	21.67	27.88
10	2.56	3.06	3.94	4.86	6.18	7.27	9.34	11.78	13.44	15.99	18.31	21.16	23.21	29.59
11	3.05	3.61	4.58	5.58	6.99	8.15	10.34	12.90	14.63	17.28	19.68	22.62	24.72	31.26
12	3.57	4.18	5.23	6.30	7.81	9.03	11.34	14.01	15.81	18.55	21.03	24.05	26.22	32.91
13	4.11	4.76	5.89	7.04	8.63	9.93	12.34	15.12	16.98	19.81	22.36	25.47	27.69	34.53
14	4.66	5.37	6.57	7.79	9.47	10.82	13.34	16.22	18.15	21.06	23.68	26.87	29.14	36.12
15	5.23	5.98	7.26	8.55	10.31	11.72	14.34	17.32	19.31	22.31	25.00	28.26	30.58	37.70
16	5.81	6.61	7.96	9.31	11.15	12.62	15.34	18.42	20.46	23.54	26.30	29.63	32.00	39.29
17	6.41	7.26	8.67	10.08	12.00	13.53	16.34	19.51	21.62	24.77	27.59	31.00	33.41	40.75
18	7.02	7.91	9.39	10.86	12.86	14.44	17.34	20.60	22.76	25.99	28.87	32.35	34.80	42.31
19	7.63	8.57	10.12	11.65	13.72	15.35	18.34	21.69	23.90	27.20	30.14	33.69	36.19	43.82
20	8.26	9.24	10.85	12.44	14.58	16.27	19.34	22.78	25.04	28.41	31.41	35.02	37.57	45.32
21	8.90	9.92	11.59	13.24	15.44	17.18	20.34	23.86	26.17	29.62	32.67	36.34	38.93	46.80
22	9.54	10.60	12.34	14.04	16.31	18.10	21.24	24.94	27.30	30.81	33.92	37.66	40.29	48.27
23	10.20	11.29	13.09	14.85	17.19	19.02	22.34	26.02	28.43	32.01	35.17	38.97	41.64	49.73
24	10.86	11.99	13.85	15.66	18.06	19.94	23.34	27.10	29.55	33.20	36.42	40.27	42.98	51.18
25	11.52	12.70	14.61	16.47	18.94	20.87	24.34	28.17	30.68	34.38	37.65	41.57	44.31	52.62
26	12.20	13.41	15.38	17.29	19.82	21.79	25.34	29.25	31.80	35.56	38.88	42.86	45.64	54.05
27	12.88	14.12	16.15	18.11	20.70	22.72	26.34	30.32	32.91	36.74	40.11	44.14	46.96	55.48
28	13.56	14.85	16.93	18.94	21.59	23.65	27.34	31.39	34.03	37.92	41.34	45.42	48.28	56.89
29	14.26	15.57	17.71	19.77	22.48	24.58	28.34	32.46	35.14	39.09	42.56	46.69	49.59	58.30
30	14.95	16.31	18.49	20.60	23.36	25.51	29.34	33.53	36.25	40.26	43.77	47.96	50.89	59.70

Table A-4

F Distribution (Upper 5% points)

n\m	1	2	3	4	5	6	7	8	9	10	12	15	20	24	30	40	60	120	∞
1	161.4	199.5	215.7	224.6	230.2	234.0	236.8	238.9	240.5	241.9	243.9	245.9	248.0	249.1	250.1	251.1	252.3	253.3	254.3
2	18.51	19.00	19.16	19.25	19.30	19.33	19.35	19.37	19.38	19.40	19.41	19.43	19.45	19.45	19.46	19.47	19.48	19.49	19.50
3	10.13	9.55	9.28	9.12	9.01	8.94	8.89	8.85	8.81	8.79	8.74	8.70	8.66	8.64	8.62	8.59	8.57	8.55	8.53
4	7.71	6.94	6.59	6.39	6.26	6.16	6.09	6.04	6.00	5.96	5.91	5.86	5.80	5.77	5.75	5.72	5.69	5.66	5.63
5	6.61	5.79	5.41	5.19	5.05	4.95	4.88	4.82	4.77	4.74	4.68	4.62	4.56	4.53	4.50	4.46	4.43	4.40	4.36
6	5.99	5.14	4.76	4.53	4.39	4.28	4.21	4.15	4.10	4.06	4.00	3.94	3.87	3.84	3.81	3.77	3.74	3.70	3.67
7	5.59	4.74	4.35	4.12	3.97	3.87	3.79	3.73	3.68	3.64	3.57	3.51	3.44	3.41	3.38	3.34	3.30	3.27	3.23
8	5.32	4.46	4.07	3.84	3.69	3.58	3.50	3.44	3.39	3.35	3.28	3.22	3.15	3.12	3.08	3.04	3.01	2.97	2.93
9	5.12	4.26	3.86	3.63	3.48	3.37	3.29	3.23	3.18	3.14	3.07	3.01	2.94	2.90	2.86	2.83	2.79	2.75	2.71
10	4.96	4.10	3.71	3.48	3.33	3.22	3.14	3.07	3.02	2.98	2.91	2.85	2.77	2.74	2.70	2.66	2.62	2.58	2.54
11	4.84	3.98	3.59	3.36	3.20	3.09	3.01	2.95	2.90	2.85	2.79	2.72	2.65	2.61	2.57	2.53	2.49	2.45	2.40
12	4.75	3.89	3.49	3.26	3.11	3.00	2.91	2.85	2.80	2.75	2.69	2.62	2.54	2.51	2.47	2.43	2.38	2.34	2.30
13	4.67	3.81	3.41	3.18	3.03	2.92	2.83	2.77	2.71	2.67	2.60	2.53	2.46	2.42	2.38	2.34	2.30	2.25	2.21
14	4.60	3.74	3.34	3.11	2.96	2.85	2.76	2.70	2.65	2.60	2.53	2.46	2.39	2.35	2.31	2.27	2.22	2.18	2.13
15	4.54	3.68	3.29	3.06	2.90	2.79	2.71	2.64	2.59	2.54	2.48	2.40	2.33	2.29	2.25	2.20	2.16	2.11	2.07
16	4.49	3.63	3.24	3.01	2.85	2.74	2.66	2.59	2.54	2.49	2.42	2.35	2.28	2.24	2.19	2.15	2.11	2.06	2.01
17	4.45	3.59	3.20	2.96	2.81	2.70	2.61	2.55	2.49	2.45	2.38	2.31	2.23	2.19	2.15	2.10	2.06	2.01	1.96
18	4.41	3.55	3.16	2.93	2.77	2.66	2.58	2.51	2.46	2.41	2.34	2.27	2.19	2.15	2.11	2.06	2.02	1.97	1.92
19	4.38	3.52	3.13	2.90	2.74	2.63	2.54	2.48	2.42	2.38	2.31	2.23	2.16	2.11	2.07	2.03	1.98	1.93	1.88
20	4.35	3.49	3.10	2.87	2.71	2.60	2.51	2.45	2.39	2.35	2.28	2.20	2.12	2.08	2.04	1.99	1.95	1.90	1.84
21	4.32	3.47	3.07	2.84	2.68	2.57	2.49	2.42	2.37	2.32	2.25	2.18	2.10	2.05	2.01	1.96	1.92	1.87	1.81
22	4.30	3.44	3.05	2.82	2.66	2.55	2.46	2.40	2.34	2.30	2.23	2.15	2.07	2.03	1.98	1.94	1.89	1.84	1.78
23	4.28	3.42	3.03	2.80	2.64	2.53	2.44	2.37	2.32	2.27	2.20	2.13	2.05	2.01	1.96	1.91	1.86	1.81	1.76
24	4.26	3.40	3.01	2.78	2.62	2.51	2.42	2.36	2.30	2.25	2.18	2.11	2.03	1.98	1.94	1.89	1.84	1.79	1.73
25	4.24	3.39	2.99	2.76	2.60	2.49	2.40	2.34	2.28	2.24	2.16	2.09	2.01	1.96	1.92	1.87	1.82	1.77	1.71
26	4.23	3.37	2.98	2.74	2.59	2.47	2.39	2.32	2.27	2.22	2.15	2.07	1.99	1.95	1.90	1.85	1.80	1.75	1.69
27	4.21	3.35	2.96	2.73	2.57	2.46	2.37	2.31	2.25	2.20	2.13	2.06	1.97	1.93	1.88	1.84	1.79	1.73	1.67
28	4.20	3.34	2.95	2.71	2.56	2.45	2.36	2.29	2.24	2.19	2.12	2.04	1.96	1.91	1.87	1.82	1.77	1.71	1.65
29	4.18	3.33	2.93	2.70	2.55	2.43	2.35	2.28	2.22	2.18	2.10	2.03	1.94	1.90	1.85	1.81	1.75	1.70	1.64
30	4.17	3.32	2.92	2.69	2.53	2.42	2.33	2.27	2.21	2.16	2.09	2.01	1.93	1.89	1.84	1.79	1.74	1.68	1.62
40	4.08	3.23	2.84	2.61	2.45	2.34	2.25	2.18	2.12	2.08	2.00	1.92	1.84	1.79	1.74	1.69	1.64	1.58	1.51
60	4.00	3.15	2.76	2.53	2.37	2.25	2.17	2.10	2.04	1.99	1.92	1.84	1.75	1.70	1.65	1.59	1.53	1.47	1.39
120	3.92	3.07	2.68	2.45	2.29	2.17	2.09	2.02	1.96	1.91	1.83	1.75	1.66	1.61	1.55	1.50	1.43	1.35	1.25
∞	3.84	3.00	2.60	2.37	2.21	2.10	2.01	1.94	1.88	1.83	1.75	1.67	1.57	1.52	1.46	1.39	1.32	1.22	1.00

m = degrees of freedom for numeration and n = degrees of freedom for denominator.

Table A-5

F Distribution (Upper 1% points)

n\m	1	2	3	4	5	6	7	8	9	10	12	15	20	24	30	40	60	120	∞
1	4052	4999.5	5403	5625	5764	5859	5928	5982	6022	6056	6106	6157	6209	6235	6261	6287	6313	6339	6366
2	98.50	99.00	99.17	99.25	99.30	99.33	99.36	99.37	99.39	99.40	99.42	99.43	99.45	99.46	99.47	99.47	99.48	99.49	99.50
3	34.12	30.82	29.46	28.71	28.24	27.91	27.67	27.49	27.35	27.23	27.05	26.87	26.69	26.60	26.50	26.41	26.32	26.22	26.13
4	21.20	18.00	16.69	15.98	15.52	15.21	14.98	14.80	14.66	14.55	14.37	14.20	14.02	13.93	13.84	13.75	13.65	13.56	13.46
5	16.26	13.27	12.06	11.39	10.97	10.67	10.46	10.29	10.16	10.05	9.89	9.72	9.55	9.47	9.38	9.29	9.20	9.11	9.02
6	13.75	10.92	9.78	9.15	8.75	8.47	8.26	8.10	7.98	7.87	7.72	7.56	7.40	7.31	7.23	7.14	7.06	6.97	6.88
7	12.25	9.55	8.45	7.85	7.46	7.19	6.99	6.84	6.72	6.62	6.47	6.31	6.16	6.07	5.99	5.91	5.82	5.74	5.65
8	11.26	8.65	7.59	7.01	6.63	6.37	6.18	6.03	5.91	5.81	5.67	5.52	5.36	5.28	5.20	5.12	5.03	4.95	4.86
9	10.56	8.02	6.99	6.42	6.06	5.80	5.61	5.47	5.35	5.26	5.11	4.96	4.81	4.73	4.65	4.57	4.48	4.40	4.31
10	10.04	7.56	6.55	5.99	5.64	5.39	5.20	5.06	4.94	4.85	4.71	4.56	4.41	4.33	4.25	4.17	4.08	4.00	3.91
11	9.65	7.21	6.22	5.67	5.32	5.07	4.89	4.74	4.63	4.54	4.40	4.25	4.10	4.02	3.94	3.86	3.78	3.69	3.60
12	9.33	6.93	5.95	5.41	5.06	4.82	4.64	4.50	4.39	4.30	4.16	4.01	3.86	3.78	3.70	3.62	3.54	3.45	3.36
13	9.07	6.70	5.74	5.21	4.86	4.62	4.44	4.30	4.19	4.10	3.96	3.82	3.66	3.59	3.51	3.43	3.34	3.25	3.17
14	8.86	6.51	5.56	5.04	4.69	4.46	4.28	4.14	4.03	3.94	3.80	3.66	3.51	3.43	3.35	3.27	3.18	3.09	3.00
15	8.68	6.36	5.42	4.89	4.56	4.32	4.14	4.00	3.89	3.80	3.67	3.52	3.37	3.29	3.21	3.13	3.05	2.96	2.87
16	8.53	6.23	5.29	4.77	4.44	4.20	4.03	3.89	3.78	3.69	3.55	3.41	3.26	3.18	3.10	3.02	2.93	2.84	2.75
17	8.40	6.11	5.18	4.67	4.34	4.10	3.93	3.79	3.68	3.59	3.46	3.31	3.16	3.08	3.00	2.92	2.83	2.75	2.65
18	8.29	6.01	5.09	4.58	4.25	4.01	3.84	3.71	3.60	3.51	3.37	3.23	3.08	3.00	2.92	2.84	2.75	2.66	2.57
19	8.18	5.93	5.01	4.50	4.17	3.94	3.77	3.63	3.52	3.43	3.30	3.15	3.00	2.92	2.84	2.76	2.67	2.58	2.49
20	8.10	5.85	4.94	4.43	4.10	3.87	3.70	3.56	3.46	3.37	3.23	3.09	2.94	2.86	2.78	2.69	2.61	2.52	2.42
21	8.02	5.78	4.87	4.37	4.04	3.81	3.64	3.51	3.40	3.31	3.17	3.03	2.88	2.80	2.72	2.64	2.55	2.46	2.36
22	7.95	5.72	4.82	4.31	3.99	3.76	3.59	3.45	3.35	3.26	3.12	2.98	2.83	2.75	2.67	2.58	2.50	2.40	2.31
23	7.88	5.66	4.76	4.26	3.94	3.71	3.54	3.41	3.30	3.21	3.07	2.93	2.78	2.70	2.62	2.54	2.45	2.35	2.26
24	7.82	5.61	4.72	4.22	3.90	3.67	3.50	3.36	3.26	3.17	3.03	2.89	2.74	2.66	2.58	2.49	2.40	2.31	2.21
25	7.77	5.57	4.68	4.18	3.85	3.63	3.46	3.32	3.22	3.13	2.99	2.85	2.70	2.62	2.54	2.45	2.36	2.27	2.17
26	7.72	5.53	4.64	4.14	3.82	3.59	3.42	3.29	3.18	3.09	2.96	2.81	2.66	2.58	2.50	2.42	2.33	2.23	2.13
27	7.68	5.49	4.60	4.11	3.78	3.56	3.39	3.26	3.15	3.06	2.93	2.78	2.63	2.55	2.47	2.38	2.29	2.20	2.10
28	7.64	5.45	4.57	4.07	3.75	3.53	3.36	3.23	3.12	3.03	2.90	2.75	2.60	2.52	2.44	2.35	2.26	2.17	2.06
29	7.60	5.42	4.54	4.04	3.73	3.50	3.33	3.20	3.09	3.00	2.87	2.73	2.57	2.49	2.41	2.33	2.23	2.14	2.03
30	7.56	5.39	4.51	4.02	3.70	3.47	3.30	3.17	3.07	2.98	2.84	2.70	2.55	2.47	2.39	2.30	2.21	2.11	2.01
40	7.31	5.18	4.31	3.83	3.51	3.29	3.12	2.99	2.89	2.80	2.66	2.52	2.37	2.29	2.20	2.11	2.02	1.92	1.80
60	7.08	4.98	4.13	3.65	3.34	3.12	2.95	2.82	2.72	2.63	2.50	2.35	2.20	2.12	2.03	1.94	1.84	1.73	1.60
120	6.85	4.79	3.95	3.48	3.17	2.96	2.79	2.66	2.56	2.47	2.34	2.19	2.03	1.95	1.86	1.76	1.66	1.53	1.38
∞	6.63	4.61	3.78	3.32	3.02	2.80	2.64	2.51	2.41	2.32	2.18	2.04	1.88	1.79	1.70	1.59	1.47	1.32	1.00

Index